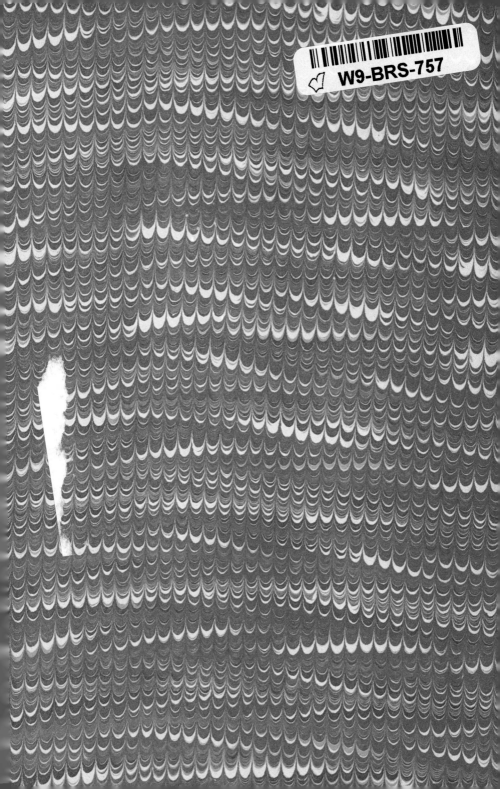

Reprinted 1982 from the 1896 first edition.
Cover design © 1981 Time-Life Books Inc.
Library of Congress CIP data following page 511.

This volume is bound in leather.

A MOSBY SCOUT IN SIGHT OF THE ENEMY.

# MOSBY'S RANGERS:

## A RECORD OF THE OPERATIONS

OF THE

# FORTY-THIRD BATTALION VIRGINIA CAVALRY,

FROM ITS

## ORGANIZATION TO THE SURRENDER,

FROM THE

DIARY OF A PRIVATE, SUPPLEMENTED AND VERIFIED WITH OFFICIAL
REPORTS OF FEDERAL OFFICERS AND ALSO OF MOSBY;

WITH

PERSONAL REMINISCENCES, SKETCHES OF SKIRMISHES, BATTLES AND
BIVOUACS, DASHING RAIDS AND DARING ADVENTURES,
SCENES AND INCIDENTS IN THE

## HISTORY OF MOSBY'S COMMAND.

CONTAINING

OVER 200 ILLUSTRATIONS, INCLUDING PORTRAITS OF MANY OF MOSBY'S
MEN AND OF FEDERAL OFFICERS WITH WHOM THEY CAME IN
CONTACT, VIEWS, ENGAGEMENTS, ETC.; MAPS OF
"MOSBY'S CONFEDERACY" AND LOCALITIES
IN WHICH HE OPERATED;

MUSTER ROLLS, OCCUPATION AND PRESENT WHEREABOUTS OF SUR-
VIVING MEMBERS.

BY

## JAMES J. WILLIAMSON,

OF COMPANY A.

NEW YORK:
RALPH B. KENYON, PUBLISHER.
1896.

The Polhemus Press,
New York.

# PREFACE.

The object of this work is to put in durable form a record of the exciting scenes and events in the career of Mosby's Rangers, in most of which I was an humble actor, and to preserve the memory of the gallant deeds of Colonel Mosby and of his brave companions who shed their blood, and of our heroic dead who gave up their lives, in the cause for which we fought.

It is unnecessary at this late day to vindicate the military career of Mosby, or to justify his taking up arms in obedience to the call of his State. The falsehoods so industriously circulated concerning Mosby's Men during the excitement of the war by partisan newsmongers, who are often too ready to pander to popular sentiment, without regard to truth, have been forever set at rest by the many complimentary letters and notices regarding Mosby from Generals Lee, Stuart, Grant and others—Federal and Confederate.

The main events of the war have long since passed into history, and will now be judged by unprejudiced minds, that will award to all their just measure of commendation or censure.

I have worked with an honest purpose. While I have presented the facts, and have given the best versions I could of matters from my standpoint, I have also deemed it only fair to give the other side of the story, when obtainable, as it is my desire to do justice to all, whether friend or foe.

This book is really the result of the habit of keeping a diary. During my imprisonment in the spring of 1863, in the Old Capitol prison in Washington, I kept a diary as a means of whiling away the tedious hours of prison life. After being exchanged, I joined Mosby in April, 1863, two months before the organization of Company A, his first company, and was with him until the surrender. The habit acquired while in prison still clung to me when I entered upon the active life of a ranger. It then became a pleasure to jot down the events that came under my observation or that I heard related by my comrades or others. I soon began to feel that my work was not completed until I had noted down briefly what had happened during the day. In this way my diary was kept—sometimes written by the wayside, sometimes by the camp-fire, sometimes in the quiet of the fireside. As time went on, my interest in the record increased, though it was kept simply as a matter of habit and amusement—not with any idea of publication.

In after years, realizing that I was growing old, and that my old comrades were dropping off one after another, it occurred to me that the surviving members of the command might be interested in this little diary, if written up and put in suitable form. My first idea, when preparing the manuscript, was to publish it as a magazine article, under the title of "Leaves from the Diary of one of Mosby's Men." Then I set about collecting portraits of officers and members of the command, in which I succeeded far beyond my expectations. I also procured from the records of the War Department, Official Federal Reports relating to many matters, in order to give the Federal version The work grew on my hands.

Meeting my old friend, Ralph B. Kenyon, the publisher, about this time, and telling him what I contemplated, he said that my record supplied too important a chapter of war history to be hidden under such a title and published in such a way, and an arrangement was soon made to print it as a history of Mosby's Rangers.

Once in hand, no pains or expense have been spared to make the work as complete as possible in all its details, so that it might be not only an accurate and authentic record of the doings of Mosby's Men, but that for the surviving members it might be a souvenir of the old days. Whether this has been accomplished or not, the book must speak for itself.

I am glad of this opportunity to make grateful acknowledgment to many friends and comrades whose names and portraits appear in these pages, who have assisted me, both in collecting pictures, and in furnishing details where my record was imperfect or fragmentary. Among these I am particularly under obligations to Mr. George S. Ayre, Lieut. W. Ben Palmer, Charles H. Dear, Capt. Walter E. Frankland, John H. Foster, Joseph W. Owen, Lieut. Channing Smith, John N. Ballard, Lieut. Joseph H. Nelson and Zach. F. Jones. I have also drawn heavily on the pictorial collections of James E. Taylor and Charles Hall, who were both in the ranks of the Federal army, but who have since proved my warm friends and earnest helpers—" Enemies in war; in peace, friends."

Ties of friendship were formed with companions in arms which death alone can sever. It is with mingled emotions of sadness and pleasure that we cast a fond, lingering look back through the misty past, and re-enjoy in some measure many happy hours, which, amid all the hardships and disappointments of those exciting times, appear in the retrospect like green spots in the journey of life.

If this work will refresh the memory of my comrades and thus enable them to live over again some of the old scenes, and at the same time be the means of convincing our Northern brothers that " Mosby's Men " were not quite so bad as they have been represented to be, the hope of the author will be realized.

J. J. W.

Jersey City, N. J.,
    February, 1896.

# LIST OF ILLUSTRATIONS.

# MOSBY'S RANGERS.

## CHAPTER I.

Why I Joined Mosby—Imprisoned in the Old Capitol at Washington—Sent to the Parole Camp near Petersburg and Exchanged—I set out to find Mosby—My First Sight of Him—Brief Sketch of his Life—Mosby a Prisoner—Promoted to a Captaincy in the C. S. A. —Mosby's First Detail—Who "Mosby's Men" Were—How they Lived and How they Fought—Regulars *vs.* Partisans—Guerrillas and Bushwhackers—Jessie Scouts—Tributes to Mosby and his Men—General Grant's Opinion of Mosby—Mosby's Tactics.

Early in the spring of 1863, after an imprisonment of some months in the Old Capitol, at Washington, which had been converted into a political prison, the writer was sent, together with a number of others, via Fortress Monroe and City Point, to the Parole Camp at Model Farm Barracks, near Petersburg, where we were detained about two weeks until exchanged.

Among the acquaintances I had made in prison were six young men who, like myself, being denied the privilege of returning to their homes, had determined to unite their fortunes with Captain Mosby, who was then making a reputation by his dashing and successful exploits. The injustice of my imprisonment and the arbitrary and partisan oath offered me as a condition of release, alienated or rather hardened my feelings, so that I readily joined this party, and together we started in search of the daring ranger.

Journeying from Petersburg to Gordonsville by railroad, we proceeded thence on foot through the country to that portion of Virginia occupied by Mosby.

When we reached the little town of Upperville, in Fauquier County, we learned there was to be a meeting of " Mosby's Men " at that place on the following day. So after a night's rest and breakfast in the morning, we walked out through the town and saw them coming in from various directions.[1]

Soon I beheld Mosby himself. From the accounts which I had heard and read of him, I expected to see a man such as novelists picture when describing some terrible brigand chief. I was therefore somewhat surprised when one of my companions pointed to a rather slender, but

CAPTAIN JOHN S. MOSBY.
From a Photograph taken in Richmond, Va., in January, 1863, when starting on his Partisan career. He wore this uniform the night he captured General Stoughton, March 8, 1863.

wiry looking young man of medium height, with light hair, keen eyes and pleasant expression, who was restlessly walking up and down the street, and said :

" There is Mosby."

[1] My companions were: John H. Barnes, Frank Fox, Philip Lee, Thomas Lee, Charles Ratcliffe and Albert Wrenn.

I could scarcely believe that the slight frame before me could be that of the man who had won such military fame by his daring.

John Singleton Mosby was born at Edgemont, Powhatan County, Virginia, December 6, 1833. His father was Alfred D. Mosby, of Amherst County, and his mother, Virginia I., daughter of Rev. Mr. McLaurin, an Episcopal minister. He graduated at the University of Virginia, and began the study of law. After completing his studies he settled in Bristol, a small town on the boundary line of Virginia and Tennessee, where he successfully practiced his profession. He married Miss Pauline Clarke, daughter of Hon. Beverly J. Clarke, of Kentucky, formerly United States Minister to Central America, and at one time a Member of Congress.

At the commencement of the war Mosby was engaged in the practice of law. He entered the army as a private in a cavalry company, the Washington Mounted Rifles, commanded by Capt. William E. Jones (afterwards General Jones). This company was incorporated in the First Regiment Virginia Cavalry, Captain Jones being promoted to the command, and Mosby was appointed Adjutant of the regiment. By the reorganization of the regiment Colonel Jones was thrown out, and consequently his adjutant relieved of duty. Mosby was then chosen by Gen. J. E. B. Stuart as an independent scout.

GENERAL WM. E. JONES, C. S. A.
From a War-time photograph.

He was the first to make the circuit of the Federal Army while in front of Richmond, thereby enabling General Stuart to make his celebrated raid around the entire army of General McClellan, on which occasion Mosby went as guide.

Feeling that there was a wide field for the successful

career as a partisan which he had mapped out for himself, Mosby urged General Stuart to give him a small detail of men with which to operate until he could enlist a command. While he met with a refusal of this request, he was given a letter recommending him to General Jackson, then in the vicinity of Gordonsville.

It happened that Gen. Rufus King, who was in command of the Federal forces at Fredericksburg at this time, was ordered by General Pope to send out a raiding party for the purpose of destroying as much as possible the Virginia Central Railroad, and so interrupt communication between Richmond and the Valley. Mosby encountered this party near Beaver Dam, was captured by the Second New York Cavalry, "Harris Light," Col. J. Mansfield Davies, and sent as a prisoner to Washington.

After his release from the Old Capitol, and while on the prison transport awaiting exchange, Mosby saw the trans-

OLD CAPITOL PRISON AT WASHINGTON.

ports bringing Burnside's forces from the South, and learned from conversations on board the prison boat that the troops were destined for Fredericksburg to unite with Pope, then on the Rapidan, and not to reinforce McClellan. As soon as the exchange was effected, Mosby hastened to Richmond and imparted this information to General Lee, who immediately dispatched a courier to General Jackson. The result was the battle of Cedar Mountain.

How well Mosby performed his duty as a scout is shown by the following :

*" Special Order No. 82.*

" His Excellency the President has pleased to show his appreciation of the good services and many daring exploits of the gallant John S. Mosby by promoting the latter to a captaincy in the Provisional Army of the Confederate States.

" The General commanding is confident that this manifestation of the approbation of his superiors will but serve to incite Captain Mosby to still greater efforts to advance the good of the cause in which we are engaged. He will at once proceed to organize his command as indicated in the letter of instructions this day furnished to him from this Headquarters.

" By command of General R. E. Lee :

" W. W. TAYLOR, A. A. G."

The winter of 1863, about the time Mosby was budding into notoriety, was a season of remarkable activity for the Confederate cavalry. Their bold and successful raids and daring attacks and surprises had filled the breasts of the young cavaliers with most romantic visions and ardent desires to enter upon this life of wild adventure. Stuart's brilliant achievements, General Imboden's forays in the Shenandoah Valley, Fitzhugh Lee on the Rappahannock, Gen. William E. Jones' attack and rout of Milroy's Cavalry in the Valley, the daring raids of Major E. V. White and his Loudoun Rangers along the Potomac, and the dashes of Captain Randolph, with his famous Black Horse Cavalry, furnished material for stories which read like the deeds of heroes of romance, and charmed the little groups around the firesides of cabin and hall.

At first a few men from the First Regiment Virginia Cavalry[2] were detailed to act with Mosby, but he soon succeeded in obtaining a sufficient number of volunteers, and the detailed men were then, with a few exceptions, sent back to their commands.

" Mosby's Men," when not on duty, were mostly scattered through the counties of Loudoun and Fauquier[3].  There

LIEUT.-COL. ELIJAH V. WHITE.
35th Battalion Virginia Cavalry.
"White's Battalion."

were few indeed, even among the poorest mountaineers, who would refuse shelter and food to Mosby's Rangers.

Having no camps, they made their homes at the farm houses, especially those along the Blue Ridge and Bull Run Mountains.  Certain places would be designated at which to meet, but if no time or place had been named at a former meeting, or if necessary to have the command together before a time appointed, couriers were despatched through the country and the men thus notified.

Scouts were out at all times in Fairfax, or along the Potomac, or in the Shenandoah

[2] Mosby's first detail was composed of 15 men from the First Virginia Cavalry : Fountain Beattie, Charles Buchanan, —— Gaul, William L. Hunter, Edward Hurst, Jasper Jones, William Jones, —— Keys, —— Morgan, —— Seibert, George M. Slater, Daniel L. Thomas, Thomas Turner, Charles Wheatley and John Wild.

[3] *Loudoun County* was originally a portion of Fairfax, and was named in honor of the Earl of Loudoun, Commander of the Military Affairs in America during the latter part of the French and Indian war.  The middle of the county, southwest of Waterford and west of Leesburg, was settled mostly by emigrants from the Middle States, many of them being Friends or Quakers, and that section was generally spoken of as the " Quaker Settlement."  That part northwest of Waterford was originally settled by Germans.

*Fauquier County* was formed in 1759 from Prince William, and took its name from Francis Fauquier, Governor of Virginia from 1758 to 1767.

Valley. Whenever an opening was seen for successful operations, couriers were sent from headquarters and in a few hours a number of well-mounted and equipped men were at a prescribed rendezvous ready to surprise a picket, capture a train or attack a camp or body of cavalry. After a raid the men scattered, and to the Federal cavalry in pursuit it was like chasing a Will-o'-the-Wisp.

The command was composed chiefly of young men from Fairfax and the adjoining counties, with some Marylanders, many of whom had been arrested and imprisoned or had suffered injuries and injustice at the hands of the Federal government or the invading army. It was the custom of many Federal officers to retaliate upon defenseless citizens for injuries inflicted upon them by Confederate soldiers, and can any one feel surprised at "Mosby's Men" taking up arms to protect themselves or to avenge their wrongs?

A large number lived in that portion of Virginia and Maryland where Mosby was operating, and naturally preferred serving with him, as they were kept nearer home and could enjoy the privilege of seeing their families.

There was always a little jealousy existing between the cavalry and infantry, many of whom lost no opportunity of having a thrust at their rivals. Illustrative of this ran the old joke of the day which will be remembered by the survivors of the war:

An old straggling infantryman, trudging wearily on the road, was overtaken by a cavalryman riding briskly along, who called out:

"Hurry up there, old web-foot; the Yankees are coming."

"Did you see 'em, Mister?" queried the infantryman.

"Yes; they are coming on right behind us," replied the trooper.

"Say, Mister, wus your hoss lame, or wus your spurs broke?" retorted the web-foot.

So also the regular cavalry, viewing the comparative freedom of the life of the Partisan Ranger in contrast with the dull routine and more rigid discipline of camp life, sometimes gave vent to their feelings, and half in jest and half in earnest would banter the Rangers, calling them

"Carpet Knights" or "Feather-bed Soldiers"—but when a sacrifice was required, the "Carpet Knights" shed their blood and gave up their lives as freely as did the Knights of old in the palmiest days of chivalry.[4]

BRIG.-GEN. THOMAS L. ROSSER, C. S. A.

[4] The attention of the Confederate authorities was finally called to this matter.

General Thomas L. Rosser, writing to General Lee regarding the efficiency and usefulness of the Partisan Rangers, January 11, 1864, says : "The effect on the service is bad and should be corrected, because :

"First. It keeps men out of the service whose bayonet or sabre should be counted on the field of battle when the life or death of our country is the issue.

"Second. They cause great dissatisfaction in the ranks from the fact that these irregular troops are allowed so much latitude, so many privileges. They sleep in houses and turn out in the cold only when it is announced by their chief that they are to go upon a plundering expedition.

"Third. It renders other troops dissatisfied ; hence encourages desertion."

General Rosser suggested as a remedy " placing all men on the same footing who are of the same rank. If it is necessary for troops to operate within the lines of the enemy, then require the commanding officer to keep them in an organized condition, to rendezvous within our lines, and move upon the enemy when opportunity is offered."

With all due respect to General Rosser, it is a certainty that had his remedy been applied to " Mosby's Men " it would have accomplished, in an incredibly short space of time, what the Federals, with all the resources at their command, after the most persistent efforts failed to accomplish—the destruction of Mosby's command. As Mosby expressed it :

" My men had no camps. If they had gone into camp they would soon have all been captured. They would scatter for safety and gather at my call like the Children of the Mist."

General Rosser's letter was forwarded with the following indorsement by General Stuart :

" Major Mosby's command is the only efficient band of rangers I know of,

The sabre was no favorite with Mosby's men—they looked upon it as an obsolete weapon—and very few carried carbines. In the stillness of the night the clanking of the sabres and the rattle of the carbines striking against the saddles could be heard for a great distance, and would often betray us when moving cautiously in the vicinity of the Federal camps. We sometimes passed between camps but a few hundred yards apart. We would then leave the hard roads where the noise of the horses' hoofs would attract attention and, marching through the grassy fields, take down bars or fences and pass quietly through. The carbine was for long range shooting. With us the fighting was mostly at close quarters and the revolver was then used with deadly effect.

I well remember on one occasion, when falling back before the Federal advance on the Little River Turnpike, alternately halting and retreating, the monotony varied only by an occasional long range shot, brave, bluff Lieut. Harry Hatcher impatiently exclaimed to a superior officer: " If you are going to fight, fight; and if you are going to run, run; but quit this d——n nonsense."

Regarding the custom of our Northern brethren, when speaking of " Mosby's Men," to use the terms " guerrillas,"

and he usually operates with only one-fourth of his nominal strength. Such organizations, as a rule, are detrimental to the best interests of the army at large."

On the 21st of January, 1864, General Lee writes Hon. James A. Seddon, Secretary of War, recommending Mosby's promotion to be lieutenant-colonel, and adds :

" I do this in order to show him that his services have been appreciated, and to encourage him to still greater activity and zeal."

General Lee, in a letter to General Cooper, April 1, 1864, after enumerating the organizations of Partisan Rangers, says :

" Lieutenant-Colonel Mosby has done excellent service, and from the reports of citizens and others I am inclined to believe that he is strict in discipline and a protection to the country in which he operates. . . . With the single exception mentioned [Mosby], I hope the order will be issued at once disbanding the companies and battalions [partisan rangers] serving in this department."

Secretary of War Seddon's indorsement on these papers reads :

" Mosby's and McNeill's commands I prefer to have retained as partisan rangers. In respect to the others Major Melton's suggestions are approved."

" bushwhackers,"[5] "freebooters," and the like, I will only say that Mosby's command was regularly organized and mustered into the Confederate service on the same footing with other troops, except that being organized under the Partizan Ranger Law, an act passed by the Confederate Congress, they were allowed the benefit of the law applying to Maritime prizes. All cattle and mules were turned over to the Confederate Government, but horses captured were distributed among the men making the capture. When it is borne in mind that the men had to arm, equip and support themselves, this did not leave a very heavy surplus, as we received but little aid from the government. The "Greenback Raid" was the only one that brought in any great

"TOBE" FARR, Co. B.
From photograph taken soon after the War.

[5] In the Official Records of the War, published by order of Congress, Vol. XLIII, Part I, page 929, will be found this order from John S. Schultze, Major and Assistant Adjutant-General to Capt. Samuel Walker, dated Chambersburg, Pa., August 26, 1864 :

"The commanding general requests that you get your company together, and with axes and rifles proceed to defend the roads through the gap between Fannettsburg and Burnt Cabins. . . . Have the roads above mentioned made inaccessible by felling trees and other obstructions, and thus *defend the same by bushwacking*, etc.

Also, the following :

" CIRCULAR.]        HEADQUARTERS DEPARTMENT OF THE SUSQUEHANNA,
                    " *Pittsburg, Pa., August 4, 1864.*
" *To the People of the Southern Tier of Counties of Pennsylvania :*

"Your situation is such that a raid by the enemy is not impossible at any time during the summer and coming fall. I therefore call upon you to put your rifles and shotguns in good order, also supplying yourselves with plenty of ammunition. Your corn-fields, mountains, forests, thickets, buildings, &c., furnish favorable places for cover, and at the same time enable you to kill the marauders, recollecting if they come it is to plunder, destroy and burn your property.                        " D. N. COUCH,
                    " *Major-General Commanding Department.*"

Was bushwhacking legitimate warfare in Pennsylvania and not in Virginia? or is it a case where the old darkey's logic applies : "It makes a big diffrens' whose hogs are in de co'nfield and whose co'n dey are eatin'?"

return, and there were only about eighty men who reaped the benefit of it, as the proceeds of a capture went directly to the men making it. The acquisition of arms and accoutrements, or even horses, did not make the men wealthy. Wagons and supplies were destroyed, though of course the men were allowed to appropriate anything they chose before destroying the captured stores.

Mosby was acting under direct orders of General Stuart up to the time of his death, and then under General Lee, and was independent only in the sense that both Lee and Stuart had such confidence in him that they permitted him to act on his own discretion. In fact it would have been folly to hamper him with orders or place him under restrictions when he was so far separated from the main army, and at times so situated that he could with difficulty communicate with his superiors.

It has been charged that " Mosby's Men " went in the disguise of Federal soldiers. Such was not the case. They never masqueraded in the uniforms of Federals, except that through force of circumstances men at times wore blue overcoats captured by them from Federal cavalry. This was done because they could get no others. The Confederate government did not, or could not at all times provide proper clothing, and our soldiers were compelled to wear these to protect themselves from the cold. Rubber blankets were common to both armies and when one was worn it completely hid the uniform.

The " Jessie Scouts " of the Federal army, however, will be well remembered by the soldiers of both armies. They dressed in the regular Confederate uniform, which they wore for the purpose of deceiving our men.[6]

---

[6] Colonel Lazelle, of Sixteenth New York Cavalry, replying to a request from Sheridan concerning information sent headquarters, says it "was obtained from Elkton from several citizens who talked freely to our men, under the impression that they were rebels, *as they were disguised.*"

And Lieutenant Shuttleworth in his report to Lieutenant-Colonel Thompson, commanding the Sixth West Virginia Cavalry, says : " I adopted the following order of march : First, F. A. Warthen, Company D, of your regiment, *dressed in full Confederate uniform*, as scout, followed by an advance of eight men familiar with the country." [See Appendix, XXVI.]

Dr. Monteiro, in his very entertaining volume of reminiscences of Mosby's command,[7] says :

"Every man knew that the slightest suspicion of dishonesty or cowardice would consign him at once to the disgrace of expulsion ; and although there must have been the usual modicum of human meanness always found in a given number of human beings, I am enabled to say after three years of active field service in the regular army that I have never witnessed, amongst eight hundred men and officers more true courage and chivalry, or a higher sense of honor blended with less vice, selfishness and meanness than I found during my official intercourse with the Partisan Battalion."

To this I will add a tribute, which will certainly be regarded as unprejudiced. In the Life of Gen. Sheridan[8], on page 314, in speaking of old rosters, the author says :

"But one of the most remarkable of Confederate cavalrymen is never named in these rosters. Yet he held, having won it fairly, the comission of Colonel. John S. Mosby, the partisan leader of Northern Virginia, deserves a place in any reference to the doings and deeds of the Confederate troopers. He deserves it because he is a man of character enough to win the respect of his foe, and since the war closed to have induced General Grant to write of him as follows, after having appointed him Consul to Kong Kong : 'Since the close of the war I have come to know Mosby personally and somewhat intimately. He is a different man entirely from what I supposed. He is slender, not tall, wiry, and looks as if he could endure any amount of physical exercise. He is able and thoroughly honest and truthful. There were probably but few men in the South who could have commanded successfully a separate detachment in the rear of an opposing army, and so near the borders of hostilities as long as he did without losing his entire command.' (Grant's Memoirs, Vol. II, p. 142.)

"Perhaps nothing will illustrate Mosby's intelligence as a soldier and the amount he accomplished better than his own statement of the theory upon which he acted as a partisan leader, and the recognition of his services in that capacity

---

[7] War Reminiscences by the Surgeon of Mosby's Command. A. Monteiro, M. D., Richmond, 1890.

[8] The Life of Gen. Philip H. Sheridan. Its Romance and Reality. By Frank A. Burr, of the Second Michigan Cavalry and Richard J. Hinton, of the U. S. Colored Troops. J. A. & R. A. Reid, publishers. Providence, R. I., 1888.

From a recent photograph.

which he received from his superiors.  Of the first, Colonel Mosby says that he was never a spy[9], and that his warfare was always such as the laws of war allow.  He epitomizes his theory of action as follows : 'As a line is only as strong as its weakest point, it was necessary for it to be stronger than I was at every point in order to resist my attacks.'

.  .  .  To destroy supply trains, to break up the means of conveying intelligence and thus isolating an army from its base, as well as its different corps from each other, to confuse plans by capturing dispatches, are the objects of partisan warfare.  .  .  .  The military value of a partisan s work is not measured by the amount of property destroyed, or the number of men killed or captured, but by the number he keeps watching.  Every soldier withdrawn from the front to guard the rear of an army is so much taken from its fighting strength."

After Mosby had attracted attention by his daring achievements, men came from all parts of the country to join him. Officers resigned positions in the regular army and came to Mosby to serve as privates ; even the famed armies of the the Old World were not without representatives in his ranks.  Although a dangerous service, there was a fascination in the life of a Ranger ; the changing scenes, the wild adventure, and even the dangers themselves exerted a seductive influence which attracted many to the side of the dashing partisan chief.

An Austrian General speaking of Napoleon I., said indignantly :

" This beardless youth ought to have been beaten over and over again ; for who ever saw such tactics ?  The blockhead knows nothing of the rules of war.  To-day he is in our rear, to-morrow in our flank and the next day in our front.  Such gross violations of the established principles of war are insufferable."

But Napoleon was generally successful.  Mosby, disregarding established rules, fought upon a principle which his enemies could neither discover nor guard against.  He was in their front, in their rear, on their flank—at one place to-day, and to-morrow in their camps at a point far distant. By his enemies he was thought to be almost ubiquitous.

---

[9] The words " scout " and " spy " are incorrectly used by some writers as synonymous terms.

What he lacked in numbers he compensated for by the celerity of his movements and the boldness of his attacks. He generally fought against odds—often great odds; seldom waited to receive a charge, but nearly always sought to make the attack.

A Federal officer whom we captured when Meade's army followed Lee into Virginia after the battle of Gettysburg, said: " Yesterday I heard our cavalry were chasing you in our front, and who would expect to find you this morning in the very midst of our army ?"

" BOOTS AND SADDLES."

# CHAPTER II.

Mosby's growing fame was greatly increased by the capture of Brigadier-General Stoughton, at Fairfax Court-House, on the night of March 8, 1863. This bold enterprise was effected by Mosby, who penetrated the Federal lines with 29 men and succeeded in bringing off his captures without loss or injury.

The raid on Fairfax Court-House and capture of General Stoughton was accomplished a short time previous to my joining Mosby, but being one of the most important events in the history of our command, I make it a prominent feature.

Capt. Walter E. Frankland has given me the following very interesting narrative, embracing reminiscences of his first days with Mosby, the desertion of Sergeant Ames ("Big Yankee") and the particulars of his visit to the camp of the Fifth New York Cavalry in company with Ames, which occurred just one week prior to and suggested the capture of General Stoughton :

## *Captain Walter E. Frankland's Narrative.*

Having served as private in the "Warrenton Rifles," Co. K, Seventeenth Virginia Infantry, from Sunday, April 21st, 1861, until late in 1862, when I was honorably discharged at Richmond, where I had been on detached duty in the Provost Marshal's Office several months, I started with a friend, George Whitescarver, to join Col. E. V. White's Cavalry, then in Loudoun. After spending several weeks among his relatives in Upper Fauquier, Whitescarver and I, about February 10, 1863, were joined at Salem (now Marshall) by Joseph H. Nelson, and at sundown that evening we three drew up at the hospitable home of James H. Hathaway. A

28

little later in the evening a lone horseman, Frank Williams, rode up, and was also welcomed to its cordial entertainment. I little dreamed that the life-ties born at that supper table, where most of us first met, were destined to bind us through scenes of blood and years of strife and peace.

We four—Nelson and Williams mounted, Whitescarver and myself afoot—resolved to go together to Loudoun and fulfill my original purpose, when, for the first time, we were told by Mr. Hathaway of a private scout named Mosby, who had made several successful attacks on the Federal pickets with a detail of fifteen men of Stuart's Cavalry; and they were to meet the next day at Rector's X Roads to make another raid. At Mr. Hathaway's earnest suggestion we concluded to see Mosby the next day before joining White's command.

We set out after an early breakfast and reached the rendezvous in time to see Mosby, who was then but a private in rank with a dozen men (part of his detail having been captured), but who was destined to prove the most remarkable, indomitable and successful warrior in that line developed by the great Civil War, or known in American history. I was made spokesman, and soon we arranged to join him as his "own men," being his "first four."

Frank Williams and Joseph Nelson, having horses of their own, accompanied Mosby on that raid, and as Mosby was to mount Whitescarver and myself from his captures, we secured quarters at the very retired little cottage of a poor widow named Rutter. There we awaited Mosby's return, but to be disappointed by his failure to bring us horses, so Whitescarver borrowed one and went on the next—the Ox Road—raid, leaving me on February 25th.

Just before they rode off, a Yankee deserter, Sergeant James F. Ames, of the Fifth New York Cavalry (afterwards known as "Big Yankee"), came walking up and wanted to join Mosby. No one gave any credence to his story, but I took him with me to the old widow's house, where we slept and ate together several days and nights. He impressed me as a true man, assuring me he had deserted on account of the Emancipation Proclamation, which, he said, showed that "the war had become a war for the Negro instead of a war for the Union."

Mosby's raid proved futile as to mounting me, for the captures were divided among the participants. Ames had so far gained my confidence that I had arranged with him, and we had prepared our arms to make a trip to his late camp at Germantown to supply ourselves with horses.

LIEUT. GEO. H. WHITESCARVER,
CO. A.

Killed at Seneca, Md., June 10th, 1863. Reproduced from an old photograph.

LIEUT. JOSEPH H. NELSON,
CO. A.

From a photograph.

CAPT. WALTER E. FRANKLAND,
CO. F.

From a photograph taken in Winchester, Va., in April, 1865, when arranging with General Hancock for a suspension of hostilities until we could communicate with the Confederate authorities.

LIEUT. FRANKLIN WILLIAMS.
CO. B.

From a photograph taken two days after the fall of Richmond.

MOSBY'S "FIRST FOUR."

The day after Mosby's return we two started from the old widow's house, near Rector's X Roads, February 28th, 1863, for a thirty miles walk to the camp of the Fifth New York Cavalry, at Germanton, about two miles from Fairfax Court House. Before we reached Middleburg a heavy rain was falling and when we turned into the Old Braddock road below Aldie, which we took for privacy, the mud was deep and slippery, like putty. We pushed on, making slow progress, our boots heavy with mud and clothing saturated, and when Saturday night came only half our journey was accomplished, the darkness intense and the rain pouring down. We begged quarters for the night on the roadside several miles from Cub Run, and from there resumed our trip after an early hot breakfast, before day on Sunday morning, March 1st.

Leaving the Old Braddock road we crossed the field and entered the woods in which we soon came to Cub Run on a boom. Every crossing log was gone, so we improvised a raft of fence rails, which the whirling torrent drove to pieces just as it struck the other bank. But it had served our purpose and we were safe and at liberty to pursue our mission. We then took our way leisurely, as we had all day in which to make twelve or fifteen miles, as we wanted twilight to cover our near approach to the camp and caution was necessary lest the Federal scouts or trespassing parties might detect us and defeat our purpose.

We learned from citizens that a raid to capture Mosby was about to be made, and by 7 p. m. when we reached the little pine cliff at the rear of the Fifth New York Camp at Germantown, we found the regiment all astir with preparation. It was Sunday night, March 1st, and we watched their movements from our admirable position. When "taps" sounded all quieted down. The clouds were gone, the moon shone brightly and we could see the sentinel pacing to and fro guarding the officers' horses, our object, but the camp was restless and every now and then others, besides the "guard," could be seen moving about, so we waited for the "dead hour" to come. At midnight the bugle sounded, and the horses were "saddled up," including the two we had come after.

About two hundred men from the Fifth New York and Eighteenth Pennsylvania Cavalry formed on the Little River turnpike and marched off, commanded by Major Joseph Gilmer of the latter regiment. We waited until the sounds of the cavalry horses died away and then deliberately walked to the middle of the camp and talked freely to the "guard," who never suspected us, even when we walked into two of the stalls he was guarding, bridled two of the horses, mounted them in his presence, and rode away in a walk.

We hoped to reached Mosby before the raiding party, but stiff mud roads were too much for us, and before we succeeded in rejoining him, Mosby with a few men had surprised the First Vermont in Aldie (after they, the Vermonters, had scared Major Gilmer and his two hundred men into a most disgraceful retreat of ten miles) capturing Captain Huntoon, 19 men and 23 horses.[1]

---

[1] *Mosby's Report to Stuart.*

*Near Upperville, March 3, 1863.*

GENERAL: Yesterday a Yankee cavalry force of about 400 men came up to Middleburg. As soon as I heard of it I hastily collected together 17 of my men and started in pursuit, having in the meantime ascertained that they had gone back. At Aldie I overtook their rear squadron of 59 men, which I charged and routed, capturing 2 captains and 17 men, together with their arms ; also, 23 horses and accoutrements. Two of my men were slightly wounded. I have sent all the prisoners but 2 on to Culpeper C. H. A wounded captain was paroled.

---

*Lieut.-Col. Robt. Johnstone, Commanding Cavalry Brigade, to C. H. Potter, A. A. G. (Federal Report.)*

*Fairfax C. H., March 2, 1863.*

SIR : Fifty men of the First Vermont Cavalry, from Companies H and M, under Captains Huntoon and Woodward, were surprised in Aldie while feeding their horses by about 70 of the enemy. Both captains captured and about 15 men. They saw no enemy but the attacking party.

Major Gilmer has returned with the scouting party that left last night. They were to Middleburg and saw but one rebel. I have anticipated the report of Lieutenant-Colonel Krepps, now in command, which will be forwarded in probably one hour.

HEADQUARTERS CAVALRY BRIGADE,

*Fairfax C. H., March 3, 1863.*

SIR : By order of Col. R. B. Price I directed on the night of the 1st inst. a reconnoissance to go in the direction of Aldie. The officer who commanded this reconnoissance was Major Joseph Gilmer, of the Eighteenth Pennsylvania Cavalry. He had 200 men. The orders to him were to proceed carefully and send back couriers through the night with information whether they saw any enemy or not. This last order was disobeyed. They were not to cross Cub Run until daylight, and then try and gain all information possible by flankers and small detached scouting parties.

Major Gilmer went to Middleburg, and while returning the vedettes of the First Vermont Cavalry noticed a part of his advance and prepared to skirmish. The advance fell back toward Aldie. Major Gilmer, instead of throwing out a party to reconnoitre, turned off with nearly the whole of his command in the

Thus, after vainly waiting about two weeks for Mosby to mount me—the captured horses each time being only sufficient for the men who were on the raids—I had, accompanied and guided by Ames, penetrated the Federal lines to the camp of the Fifth New York Cavalry at Germantown, within two miles of Fairfax Court House, walking thirty miles to accomplish it, in order to mount myself. The success of this enterprise demonstrated the feasibility of passing in between their camps, evading their pickets and far within their lines quietly executing a purpose without causing an alarm.

Mosby's quick perception turned this to good account by arranging at once to strike deep for some great achievement, and just one week after my success of Sunday, March 1st, Mosby, with twenty-nine of us, on Sunday, March 8th, undertook and successfully executed an enterprise which made him and his command renowned, and brought to his standard hundreds of brave spirits who possessed the very metal he needed to build with, and who were in every way worthy of their illustrious leader. It was the capture of General Stoughton.

---

direction of Groveton to gain Centreville. The horses returned exhausted from being run at full speed for miles. A few of Major Gilmer's men left his command and went along the Little River turnpike toward the Vermont detachment. They reported that the men seen were a part of a scouting party under Major Gilmer, and that no enemy were in Aldie. Captain Huntoon then entered the town and halted to have the horses fed near a mill. Immediately beyond was a rising ground which hid the guerrillas. While the horses were unbridled and feeding the surprise occurred. As both the officers have been captured, and as the detachment was not under my command, and is not attached to this brigade, I have no means of receiving any official or exact report from them, nor is there any one belonging to that detachment here. All men belonging to this detachment seem to have fought well ; the enemy did not pursue them ; they fell back in good order.

Major Gilmer, when he returned, was unable to make a report to Lieut. Col. [John S.] Krepps, who, during the time I was confined from sickness, had charge of the camp.

I ordered Major Gilmer under arrest early this morning, and have sent to Col. R. B. Price charges of which the annexed is a copy.

Major Gilmer lost but one man belonging to the Fifth New York Cavalry, who was mortally wounded by the enemy and afterwards robbed. He was away from the command and on this side of Aldie, his horse having given out. The enemy seem to have been concealed along the line of march and murdered this man when returning, without provocation.

I have the honor to be, very respectfully, your obedient servant,

ROBERT JOHNSTONE, *Lieut.-Col. Commanding Cavalry Brigade.*

The best account of the raid and capture of General Stoughton obtainable is the following article, from the abie pen of Mosby himself, as published in the Belford Magazine in 1892 :

*One of My War Adventures.*

About February 1st, 1863, I began operating on the outposts of the troops belonging to the defense of Washington that were stationed in Fairfax and Loudon counties, Virginia. I had with me a detachment of fifteen men from the First Virginia Cavalry, which Stuart had allowed to go with me while his cavalry corps was in winter quarters. As I had camped several months in Fairfax the year before, and done picket duty along the Potomac, I had acquired considerable local knowledge of the country. By questioning the prisoners I took, separately and apart from each other, I had learned the location of the camps and the headquarters of the principal officers. I had been meditating a raid on Fairfax Court House, where I knew there were many rich prizes, when fortunately Ames, a deserter from the Fifth New York Cavalry, came to my command and supplied all the missing links in the chain of evidence. Whenever we made any captures the prisoners were sent under guard to Culpeper Court House, where Fitz Lee was stationed with a brigade of cavalry. Stuart was then in the vicinity of Fredericksburg. I have heretofore related the affair with Major Gilmer and the First Vermont Cavalry, which occurred on March 2d. As it was necessary to make a detail from the men serving with me to guard the prisoners that were sent to Culpeper, I had to wait several days for them to return before undertaking another enterprise. Gilmer's expedition into our territory had been so disastrous that the Union cavalry seemed to be content to stay in camp and let us alone. On the afternoon of March 8th, the anniversary of the day that my regiment (First Virginia Cavalry) had the year before crossed Bull Run as the rear guard covering the retirement of Johnston's army to Richmond, twenty-nine men met me at Aldie, in Loudon county, the appointed rendezvous. My recollection of events is refreshed by my report to Stuart, written three days afterwards, which is printed in the official records by the Government. I did not communicate my purpose of making a raid on the headquarters of the commanding general at Fairfax Court House to any of the men except Ames, and not to him until we started.

The men thought we were simply going down to make
an attack on a picket post. It was late in the afternoon
when we left Aldie. There was a melting snow on the
ground with a drizzling rain. All this favored my plan.
The darkness concealed us, and the horses treading on the
soft snow made very little noise. We started down the
Little River turnpike which runs by Fairfax Court House
to Alexandria. From Fairfax Court House another turnpike runs easterly by Centreville, seven miles distant to
Warrenton. At Centreville there was a brigade of infantry
with artillery and cavalry. This was the extreme out post.
From Centreville there was a chain of outposts extending in
one direction, by Fryingpan, to the Potomac; and to
Union Mills and Fairfax Station in the other. Near the
junction of the two turnpikes, a mile east of Fairfax Court
House, there was a brigade of cavalry in camp; the railroad from Union Mills to Alexandria was strongly guarded.

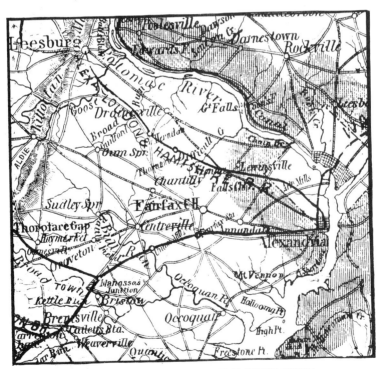

MAP OF THE VICINITY OF FAIRFAX COURT HOUSE.
Taken from an old War Map.

At Chantilly, on the Little River pike, there was also a strong cavalry out-post. The two turnpikes that connected near Fairfax Court House and the picket line from Centreville to Fryingpan thus formed a triangle. I found out where there was a gap in the picket line between the two turnpikes and determined to penetrate it. I knew that if we succeeded in passing the outer line without alarming the pickets we might reach the generals' headquarters at the court house in comparative safety, as we would be mistaken for their own troops even if the enemy discovered us. The headquarters were so thoroughly girdled with troops that no one dreamed of the possibility of an enemy approaching them. In justice to Stoughton, the commanding general, I must say that he had called the attention of the out-post commander to the weak point in his picket line. But no attention was paid to it. He did not conceive that any one had the audacity to pass his pickets and ride into his camps. The commander of the Union cavalry at that time was Colonel Percy Wyndham, an English adventurer, who, it was said, had served with Garibaldi. He had been greatly exasperated by my midnight forays on his out-posts and mortified at his own unsuccessful attempts at reprisal. In consequence he had sent me many insulting messages. I thought I would put a stop to his talk by gobbling him up in bed and sending him off to Richmond. Ashby had captured him in the Shenandoah Valley the year before. When we got to within three miles of Chantilly we turned off to the right from the turnpike, and passed unobserved through the picket line about midway between that place and Centreville and reached the Warrenton turnpike about halfway between Centreville and the court house. I was riding by the side of one of my men named Hunter, and at this point I told him where we were going. He realized, as I did, the difficulties and dangers that surrounded us. I told him our safety was in the audacity of the enterprise. We were then four miles inside the enemy's line and within a mile or two of the cavalry companies. We could no doubt have marched straight into them, or challenge and brought off a lot of men and horses. But I was hunting that night for bigger game, and knew that Wyndham did not sleep in the cavalry camp, but at the court house a mile beyond. I also knew that General Stoughton's headquarters were there. To a man uninitiated into the mysteries of war our situation, environed on all sides by hostile troops, would have appeared desperate. To me it did not seem at all so, as my experience enabled me to measure the danger.

Proceeding a short distance on the pike towards the court house, we turned off to the right, flanked the corps directly in front of us, and came into the town unmolested at two o'clock in the morning. It had been my intention to get there about midnight, but our column got broken in two at one time in the darkness; the rear portion remained standing still for some time, thinking the whole column had halted. We had gone a considerable distance before it was discovered. So I had to turn back in search of the missing. The rear, after standing still some time, moved on, but could not find our trail. They were on the point of going back when by accident we came upon them wandering in the dark like Iris in search of the lost Osiris. This involved considerable delay. With the exception of a few drowsy sentinels all the troops in the town were asleep. Nothing of the kind had ever been attempted before during the war, and no preparations had been made to guard against it. It is only practicable to guard against what is probable, and in war, as everything else, a great deal must be left to chance. Once inside the enemy's lines everything we discovered as easy as falling off a log.

SAMUEL WACGAMAN, CO. A.

From a photograph taken in 1888.

There was not the slightest show of resistance. As the night was pitch dark it was impossible to tell from our appearance to which side we belonged, although all of us were dressed in Confederate gray.

The names of all the cavalry regiments stationed there were familiar to us; so whenever a sentinel halted us the answer was: "Fifth New York Cavalry," and it was all right. Of course we took the sentinel with us. All of my men except Hunter and Ames were as much surprised as the enemies were when they found them-

selves in a town filled with Union troops and stores. As I
had never led them into a place from which I was not
able to take them out, there was not a faint heart among
them. All seemed to have a blind confidence in my destiny.
Hunter was at the time a sergeant in the company to which
he belonged. I explained the situation to him as we were
riding along, as I looked to him more than to any of the men
to aid me in accomplishing my design. He showed great
coolness and courage, and fully merited the promotion he
soon afterwards received. He is now a citizen of California.

I had only twenty-nine men—we were surrounded by hostile thousands. Ames, who also knew to what point he was
piloting us, rode by my side. Without being able to give
any satisfactory reason
for it, I felt an instinc-
tive trust in his fidel-
ity, which he never
betrayed. When we
reached the court-
house square, which
was appointed as a
rendezvous, the men
were detailed in
squads; some were
sent to the stables to
collect the fine horses
that I knew were there,
others to the different
headquarters, where
the officers were quar-
tered. We were more
anxious to capture
Wyndham than any
other.

There was a hospital
on the main street in
a building which had
been a hotel. In front
of it a sentry was
walking. The first
thing I did was to send

COL. PERCY WYNDHAM, U. S. A.
From a War-time photograph.

Ames and Frankland to relieve him from duty and to prevent any of the occupants from giving the alarm. Ames
whispered gently into his ear to keep quiet—that he was a
prisoner. A six-shooter has great persuasive powers. I
went directly with the larger portion of the command to the

house of a citizen named Murray, which I had been told was
Wyndham's headquarters. This was not so. He told us
that they were at Judge Thomas' house, which we had passed
in the other end of the town. So we quickly returned to
the court-house square. Ames was sent with a party to
Wyndham's headquarters. Two of his staff were found
there asleep, but the bird we were trying to catch had
flown—Wyndham had gone down to Washington that
evening by the railroad. My men indemnified themselves to
some extent for the loss by appropriating his fine wardrobe
and several splendid horses that they found in the stables.

The irony of fortune made Ames the captor of his own
captain. He was Captain Barker, Fifth New York Cavalry,
detailed as Assistant Adjutant General. Ames treated his
former commander with the greatest civility, and seemed to
feel his great pride in introducing him to me. Joe Nelson
saw a tent in the courtyard; he went in and took the telegraph operator who was sleeping there We had already
cut the wires before we came into the town to prevent communication with Centreville. Joe had also caught a soldier
who told him that he was one of the guard at General
Stoughton's headquarters. This was the reason I did not go
with Ames after Wyndham. I took five or six men with me
to go after Stoughton. I remember the names of Joe Nelson, Hunter, Whitescarver, Welt Hatcher and Frank Williams. Stoughton was occupying a brick house on the
outskirts of the village belonging to Dr. Gunnell.

When we reached it all dismounted and I gave a loud
knock on the front door. A head bobbed out from an upper
window and inquired who was there. My answer was,
"Fifth New York Cavalry with a dispatch for General
Stoughton." Footsteps were soon heard tripping down
stairs and the door opened. A man stood before me with
nothing on but his shirt and drawers. I immediately seized
hold of his shirt-collar, and whispered in his ear who I was,
and ordered him to lead me to the general's room. He was
Lieutenant Prentiss of the staff. We went straight up stairs
where Stoughton was, leaving Welt Hatcher and George
Whitescarver behind to guard the horses. When a light
was struck we saw lying on the bed before us the man of
war. He was buried in deep sleep, and seemed to be dreaming in all the fancied security of the Turk on the night when
Marco Bozzarris with his band burst on his camp from the
forest shades :

> " In dreams, through court and camp, he bore
> The trophies of a conqueror."

There were signs in the room of having been revelry in the house that night. Some uncorked champagne bottles furnished an explanation of the general's deep sleep. He had been entertaining a number of ladies from Washington in a style becoming a commanding general. The revelers had retired to rest just before our arrival with no suspicion of the danger that was hovering over them. The ladies had gone to spend the night at a citizen's house; loud and long I have been told were the lamentations next morning when they heard of the mishap that had befallen the gallant young general. He had been caught asleep, ingloriously in bed,

BRIG.-GEN. EDWIN H. STOUGHTON, U. S. A.
From a photograph.

and spirited off without even bidding them good bye. As the general was not awakened by the noise we made in entering the room, I walked up to his bed and pulled off the covering. But even this did not arouse him. He was turned over on his side snoring like one of the seven sleepers. With such environments I could not afford to await his convenience or to stand on ceremony. So I just pulled up his shirt and gave him a spank. Its effect was electric. The brigadier rose from his pillow and in an authoritative tone inquired the meaning of this rude intrusion, He had not realized that we were not some of his staff. I leaned over and said to him: "General, did you ever hear of Mosby?" "Yes," he quickly answered, "have you caught him?" "No," I said, "I am Mosby—he has caught you." In order to deprive him of all hope I told him that Stuart's Cavalry held the town and that General Jackson was at Centreville.

With a look of agony and despair he asked if Fitz Lee was there. I told him "Yes." "Then," he said, "take me to him—we were classmates at West Point." "Certainly," I said, "but I am in a hurry—dress quick." He had the reputation of being a gallant soldier, but a fop, and dressed as carefully before a looking-glass as Sardanapalus did when he

went to war.   When we got to the front door Frank Williams handed him his watch, which he had left in the hurry
of departure.   Whitescarver and Welt Hatcher, who had
been left to guard the horses, had not been idle while we
were in the house.   They had surrounded some tents, and
captured seven headquarters couriers, besides several fine
horses which we found bridled and saddled.   I was determined to bring off the general, even if we had to abandon
all our other captures.   So I would not let Stoughton hold
his bridle-reins, but told Hunter to ride by his side and hold
them at all hazards.   I knew that Hunter would stick to him
closer than a brother.   Lieutenant Prentiss also started
with us a prisoner, but as I let him hold his bridle-reins he
left us in the dark, and never even said good-night.   When
we returned to the court-house square all the squads had
collected there and duly done their work.   There were
twenty-nine men with me and we had about one hundred
prisoners and horses to guard.   It was so dark that the
prisoners did not know my men from their own.   In the
town there were several hundred soldiers, but there was no
concert of action among them.   All was panic and confusion.   Each man was in search of a safe hiding-place.   Just
as we were moving out of the town a ludicrous accident
occured.   As we passed by a house an upper window was
lifted and a voice called out in a peremptory tone and asked
what cavalry that was.   It sounded so funny that the men
broke out in a loud laugh.   I knew that it must be an officer
of rank; so the column was halted, and Joe Nelson and Welt
Hatcher were ordered to search the house.   Lieutenant-
Colonel Johnstone, of the Fifth New York Cavalry, was
spending the night there with his wife.   For some
reason he suspected something wrong when he heard my
men laugh, and immediately took flight in his shirt tail out
of the back door.   Nelson and Hatcher broke through the
front door, but his wife met them like a lioness in the hall,
and obstructed them all she could in order to give time for
her husband to make his escape.   The officer could not be
found; but my men took some consolation for the loss by
bringing his clothes away with them.   He had run out
through the back-yard into the garden and crawled for shelter in a place it is not necessary to describe.   He lay there
concealed and shivering with cold and fear until after daylight.   He did not know for some time that we had gone,
and he was afraid to come out of his hole to find out.   His
wife didn't know where he was.   In squeezing himself under shelter he had torn off his shirt, and when he appeared

before his wife next morning, as naked as when he was born
and smelling a great deal worse, it is reported that she refused to embrace him before he had taken a bath.   After he
had been scrubbed down with a horse-brush and curry-comb
he started in pursuit of us, but went in the opposite direction from which we had gone.   I started with my prisoners
and booty towards Fairfax Station just to deceive the enemy
as to the route we were going to retreat.   After going back
half a mile we wheeled around at right angles, and made for
the pike that leads from the court-house to Centreville.
Our safety depended on getting beyond the lines before
daylight.   We struck the
pike about half way between
Centreville and the court-
house.   Stoughton re-
marked to me as we were
riding along : " Captain,
you have done a bold thing,
but you are sure to be
caught."   He was certain
every moment of hearing
the hoof-strokes of his
cavalry coming in hot pursuit.   The fact was that
everybody at the court-
house seemed to have lost
his head ; no one seemed to

FAIRFAX COURT HOUSE.

have the presence of mind to try to rally the troops to the
defense of the place.   We had spent an hour there, raiding
all the stables and headquarters and came away loaded
down with prisoners and spoils without even firing a shot or
having one fired at us.   I knew though that they would collect their senses after they found out we were gone and
would come after us.   After reaching the Centreville pike
the principal danger was in front.   Although we were
rapidly getting away from the danger behind us we were
still approaching another, and had to pass by Centreville
before we would be safe.   Before going out on the pike I
halted the column and told Hunter to close it up.   Some of my
men were riding in the rear and some on the flank to keep
the prisoners from running away.   It was so dark
however that we lost a considerable number.   I rode out
some distance in advance to reconnoitre along the road.
Wyndham's cavalry corps were then a mile behind us.   No
sound disturbed the deep stillness of the night.   No hostile
form was there to intercept us. I called to Hunter to come on.

We were then about four miles from Centreville. I ordered Hunter to go forward at a fast trot; with Joe Nelson I staid some distance in the rear. Hunter was ordered, no matter what happened, to hold on to the general.

No doubt Stoughton thoroughly appreciated the interest I felt in him. Nelson and I frequently stopped to listen— nothing but the hooting of owls could be heard. Every moment my heart beat higher with hope. I am sure that Cæsar was not more oppressed with anxiety, nor felt higher aspirations on the eventful morning when he gave the order to the legions that changed the history of the world. My fate was then trembling in the balance If we should get caught it would end my career as a partisan; everybody would say that I had tried to do what I ought to have known to be impossible. The camp-fires on the heights around Centreville soon became visible through the darkness. I had begun to feel pretty safe from pursuit, but the chief peril lay in flanking the troops at Centreville without running into hostile camps not far away on either side of it. It was as difficult a problem to solve as steering between Scylla and Charybdis. Yet I was cheered by the knowledge that if I succeeded an adventure so full of romance would strike a deeper impression on the imagination of men than a battle. Nelson and I rode up at a gallop to overtake the column when we saw that it had halted. When we caught up with it we could see a smouldering fire by the pike about a hundred yards ahead of us. It was evidently a picket post. I rode forward alone to reconnoitre. No one was about the fire; the post had just been deserted. I called to Hunter to move on. We were then about a half mile from Centreville, and the gray dawn was just beginning to appear. We passed the picket post and then turned off to the right to go over the forts at Centreville. It had been the habit to establish a picket there every night and withdraw it early in the morning. The officer in charge concluding that there was no danger in the air, had returned to camp and gone to sleep just before we got there. The camps were all quiet; no sign of alarm; we could see the cannon bristling through the embrasures of the redoubts not more than two or three hundred yards away, and heard the sentinel on the parapet call us to halt. But no attention was paid to it. I was riding down a short distance ahead of the column when I heard a shot. Turning around to see what it meant I saw Captain Barker dashing toward a redoubt.

One of my men, a Hungarian named Jake, who had fired the shot, was just about giving him another when Barker and his horse tumbled in a ditch, which spared Jake the necessity of shooting again. He was soon extricated and mounted, and we marched on. I asked Barker if he was hurt. He replied, "No." All this happened in full view of the enemy's camp, which was in gun-shot of us. As there were more prisoners with me than I had men, no doubt the sentinels mistook us, as we came right from the direction of the cavalry camp, for a body of their own cavalry going out on a scout.

Nothing so far as they knew had occurred during the night to break the monotony of the cry—"All quiet along the Potomac to-night." We were not long in getting around Centreville. Soon after we passed outside the enemy's lines we got to Cub Run, where a new danger confronted us. The stream was swift and so swollen from the melting snow and rain that we either had to run the risk of swimming it, or turn back. But in full view behind were the white tents of the enemy at Centreville, and the cannon pointing at us. I did not deliberate a moment, but plunged into the raging torrent and swam to the other shore. The current was strong, but so was my horse. Stoughton followed next to me. As he emerged shivering from his morning bath he said: "Well, Captain, this is the first outrage that I have to complain of." It was a miracle that not a man or a horse was drowned, although many were swept down in the stream. When all were over I knew that we were comparatively safe, and that no cavalry would attempt to swim after us. As we had to make a circle to get back onto the Warrenton pike, which passes through Centreville, there was danger of a cavalry force being sent from there to intercept us. So again putting Hunter in command of the column, in company with George Slater I galloped on to see what was ahead. We passed Sudley and came on the pike at Groveton. This was the very spot where Fitz John Porter had met such a bloody repulse from Stonewall Jackson the year before. We rode off on a high hill from which we could see the road all the way back to Centreville. No enemy was in pursuit, and in a few minutes Hunter appeared in sight. We were safe. Just then there was a glorious sunburst. In the rapture of the moment I said to Slater: "George, that shines as glorious to me as the sun of Austerlitz." I felt that I had drawn a prize in the lottery of life, for

"Who can contemplate Fame through clouds unfold
The star which rises o'er her steep, nor climb?"

When Stoughton saw the Union camp seven miles away

on the heights around Centreville, he lost all hope of being recaptured. He was young, a professional soldier and ambitious; having been captured in a way that would subject him to ridicule, his pride was deeply touched. It is reported that Mr. Lincoln, when he heard of it, remarked with cynical humor that he didn't care so much about the general, as he could make another in five minutes, but that he hated to lose the horses. Stoughton's mortification deeply excited my sympathy. When he cast a despairing look at the Union camp behind him it recalled to my mind the pathetic story of Boabdil when he turned to look back on the towers of Granada and breathed "The last sigh of the Moor." At Warrenton men, women and children came out to give us an ovation. I was as proud of it as a Roman general when the Senate had decreed him a triumph. Stoughton had been there before. At West Point he had been a classmate of a young man named Beckham, whose home was there, and he had spent a vacation with him. We stopped at his house a short time, and he was kindly received by the family. Early the next morning I reached Culpeper Court House with my captures: one general, two captains, thirty privates and fifty-eight horses. I remember Fitz Lee's look of surprise when I introduced his old classmate to him. During the day Stuart arrived from Fredericksburg. He came to attend a court-martial. I met him at the train and shall never forget the delight with which he heard my story. Only two months before we had parted at his tent when I started off to seek for adventures. He announced in flattering terms in a general order my exploit to the cavalry. Praise from Stuart was all the reward I wanted. Stoughton's reputation as a soldier was blasted; he was soon exchanged, but never returned to the army. Wyndham was relieved; his successor had no more success in suppressing my depredations than Wyndham, and soon had to relinquish his command. Colonel John-

HENRY N. BRAWNER, CO. A.
From a photograph.

stone did not survive the ridicule he incurred by his
selection of a hiding-place and appearing stark naked
at headquarters.   Major Gilmer, whom he had put under
arrest a few days before for making a fool of himself when
he came after me, now had the laugh on him.   He too made
his exit from the stage.   I was never able to duplicate this
adventure; it was one of those things a man can do only
once in a lifetime.   The Northern cavalry got too smart to
allow the repetition.   My calculation of success was based
on the theory that to all appearances it was an impossibility.
It was charged at the time that citizens of the place were in
collusion with me, and had given the information on which
I had acted.   It was not true; I had had no communication
with any one there.   Several men, and also a young lady at
whose house Stoughton's guests had slept that night, were
arrested and sent to prison in Washington.   They were all
as innocent of the charge of complicity in the act as Mr.
Lincoln.   The young lady got her revenge by marrying the
provost-marshal.[2]                                JOHN S. MOSBY.

---

[2] The Provost Marshal at Fairfax Court House made the following report :

PROVOST-MARSHAL'S OFFICE,
*Fairfax Court House, Va., March 10, 1863.*

COLONEL WYNDHAM,

*Commanding Cavalry Brigade and Post:*

SIR :

On the night of the 8th instant, say about two or half-past two a. m., Captain Mosby, with his command, entered this village by an easterly direction,
then advanced upon my outer vedette, when he challenged (no countersign out).
The rebel picket or scout advanced, presenting at the same time two revolvers
to his head and threatening to blow his brains out if he said a word, demanding his arms, &c., when the force came up and captured every man on patrol,
with horses, equipments, &c., until reaching the Provost-Marshal's stables,
when they halted and entered the stables, taking every horse available
with them.   They then proceeded to Colonel Stoughton's stables, captured
his guard, took his horses and those of his aids.   They then proceeded
to Colonel Wyndham's headquarters and took all the horses and movable
property with them.   In the meantime others (of Captain Mosby's command)
were despatched to all quarters where officers were lodged, taking them
out of their beds, together with the telegraph operator, assistant, &c., &c.
They searched the Provost-Marshal's office, and, finding him absent, went to
the post hospital and there made diligent search for him, offering a reward for
him.   The Provost-Marshal had just left the street, say ten minutes before they
entered, and went across some vacant lots to ascertain from one of his vedettes
if he had caught any horses or horse thieves.   Another party, ten in number,
proceeded to Colonel Stoughton's headquarters, taking him and one of his aids,
named Prentiss, who afterwards made his escape, prisoners.   They then proceeded to Colonel Wyndham's headquarters and took Captain Barker, of the

This achievement elicited the following complimentary notice from Gen. J. E. B. Stuart:

"*General Order No. —.*

"Captain John S. Mosby has for a long time attracted the attention of his Generals by his boldness, skill and success, so signally displayed in his numerous forays upon the invaders of his native State.

"None knew his daring enterprise and dashing heroism better than those foul invaders though strangers themselves to such noble traits.

"His late brilliant exploit—the capture of Brigadier-General Stoughton, U. S. A., 2 captains, 30 other prisoners, together with their arms, equipments and 58 horses—justifies this recognition in General orders. This feat, almost unparalleled in the war, was performed in the midst of the enemy's troops at Fairfax Court House, without loss or injury.

"The gallant band of Captain Mosby share the glory, as they did the danger of this enterprise and are worthy of such a leader.

"J. E. B. STUART,
"*Major-General Commanding.*"

Mosby was then promoted to the rank of Major, with authority to organize a battalion.

---

Fifth New York Cavalry, and also Baron Vardner, who was stopping at the Colonel's. In the meantime another party of them entered the residence of Colonel Johnston and searched the house for him. He had, previous to their entering the town, heard of their movements, and, believing them to be the patrol, went out to halt them, but soon found out his mistake. He then entered the house again—he being in a nude state—and got out backwards, they in hot pursuit of him. He, however, evaded them by getting under a barn, and had scarcely concealed himself when a guard of three men were placed upon it.

It is supposed that they entered our lines between Frying Pan and Herndon Station, taking a diagonal course to come in at the lower end of the village. On leaving they went out by way of Colonel Wyndham's stables (southwest) and proceeded towards Centreville, cutting telegraph wires as they went along. I am told by parties who had seen them that they were some three hundred strong.     I have the honor to remain,

Respectfully your obedient servant,
LIEUT. D. L. O'CONNOR,
*Provost-Marshal.*

# CHAPTER III.

A very important aid to Mosby in his successful attacks and surprises was the selection of skilful and intelligent guides and scouts--men familiar with the section of country in which he operated—knowing all the little roads and cow-paths; who could creep through the dense undergrowth or dark ravines like foxes, unobserved, and if discovered easily elude pursuit. Prominent among these were the Underwood brothers, John[1], Samuel and Bushrod, in Fairfax; John S. Russell, in the Shenandoah Valley, and Walter Bowie, in Maryland.

On Tuesday, the 17th of March, Captain Mosby attacked the reserve picket post of the First Vermont Cavalry at Herndon Station, in Fairfax. Gaining their rear, he advanced on the post. The sentinel, seeing them coming from the direction of the Federal camp , supposed them to be a patrol and allowed them to approach within a short distance before challenging. The pickets being surprised made but little resistance and the majority were captured, among them 1 major, 1 captain, 2 lieutenants and 21 privates, together with 26 horses and equipments. One of the Federals was wounded and left on the field. Some of the enemy who escaped gave the alarm, and a force was started in pursuit,

---

[1] John Underwood, after a few months' service, was killed by a deserter from the Confederate army

but coming up with Mosby's rear guard and receiving a check, abandoned the pursuit.[2]

Mosby announced his success to General Stuart in the following report :

*Near Piedmont, Va., March 18, 1863.*

GENERAL: Yesterday I attacked a body of the enemy's cavalry at Herndon Station, in Fairfax county, completely routing them. I brought off 25 prisoners, a Major Wells, 1 captain, 2 lieutenants and 21 men, all their arms, 26 horses and equipments. One severely wounded was left on the ground. The enemy pursued me in force but were checked by my rear guard, and gave up the pursuit. My loss was nothing. The enemy have moved their cavalry from Germantown back of Fairfax Court House on the Alexandria pike.

In this affair my officers and men behaved splendidly.

JNO. S. MOSBY, *Captain Commanding.*

[Indorsements.]

H'DQ'RS LEE'S CAVALRY BRIGADE, }
*March 20, 1863.* }

Respectfully forwarded. Such performances need no comment. The soldiers were paroled. The officers will be sent to Richmond.

FITZ LEE, *Brigadier General.*

Respectfully forwarded and attention called to this latest achievement of Captain Mosby.

In the absence of General Stuart, and by command,

R. CHANNING PRICE, *Asst. Ad'jt Gen.*

Respectfully forwarded for the information of the department and as an evidence of the merit and continued success of Captain Mosby.

R. E. LEE, *General.*

---

[2] *Report of Major Chas. F. Taggart, Second Pennsylvania Cavalry.*

*Dranesville, March 24, 1863.*

To Col. R. BUTLER PRICE,, *Comdg. Cav. Brigade :*

COLONEL : I have the honor to report that on the 17th inst., at 1 p. m., the reserve picket post at Herndon Station, consisting of 25 men, under command of Second Lieut. Alexander G. Watson, Company L, First Vermont Cavalry, was surprised by Captain Mosby, with a force of 42 men, and 21 of our men, together with Major William Wells, Captain Robert Scofield, Company F, Second Lieut. Alexander G. Watson, Company L, and Perley C. J. Cheney, Company C (Second Lieut.), captured, all of the First Vermont Cavalry ; the first 3 were visiting the post.

The surprise was so complete that the men made but little or no resistance. The enemy were led on by citizens and entered on foot by a bridle path in the

While scouting in Fairfax with John Underwood to ascertain the position and strength of the Federal forces, Mosby determined to attempt the surprise of outposts at Chantilly and Frying Pan—there being about 100 cavalry at each of these places.

Starting from Rector's X Roads on the 23d of March, 1863, he proceeded down the turnpike until within about six

LAFAYETTE BROWNING, CO. B.
From a photograph.

miles of Chantilly, when he left the road, though still keeping the same direction. Coming out from a piece of woods within a mile of the Chantilly mansion, he moved towards the picket posted on a little run on the Little River Turn pike. Seeing the vedettes, some of our men left the ranks and dashed off in pursuit. They suddenly came upon a picket of 10 men which had been thrown out on the turnpike. One was killed and 5 or 6 surrendered and were taken back to Mosby.

The alarm being given, the reserves were called out, and Mosby finding the force quite a large one, fell back up the turnpike, the Federals following.

Halting at a place where there was a barricade of fallen trees, Mosby formed his men behind this obstruction and awaited their coming. On they came, but in the pursuit they were strung out along the road, and on receiving

rear of the post, capturing the vedette stationed out on the road before he was able to give the alarm. Every effort was made by me on receipt of the intelligence to capture the party, but without avail. Had Second Lieut. Edwin H. Higley, Company K, First Vermont Cavalry, who had started with the relief for the post, consisting of 40 men, together with 10 of the old guard who joined him, performed his duty, the whole party could and would have been taken. I cannot too strongly urge that orders may be given that all citizens near outposts must remove beyond the lines. Such occurrences are exceedingly discreditable, but sometimes unavoidable, not only calculated to embolden the enemy but dispirit the men.

Mosby's fire, wavered. A charge was now ordered; the Rangers rushed forward with a yell and the fight became a chase. The Federals were driven back and could not be rallied.

The chase was continued for about three miles, back to the place where it commenced. Here the Federals were re-inforced by the reserve from Frying Pan Church, and Mosby was compelled to halt and then retreat. The enemy did not pursue very far, as night was coming on, and they were afraid of being led into a trap.

Mosby sustained no loss. The Federals lost 5 killed, several were wounded, and 35 prisoners were taken[3]. [See Mosby's Report, Appendix, II.]

In response to his despatch, General Stuart sent the following to Mosby :

HEADQUARTERS, CAVALRY DIVISION, }
*Army of Northern Virginia, March 27, 1868.* }

CAPTAIN : Your telegram, announcing your brilliant achievements near Chantilly, was duly received and forwarded to General Lee. He exclaimed upon reading it, "Hurrah for Mosby! I wish I had a hundred like him!"

Heartily wishing you continued success, I remain

Your obedient servant,

J. E. B. STUART,

*Major-General Commanding.*

On Tuesday, the 31st of March, Mosby, with his detail and such volunteers as he had been able to muster, numbering in all less than 70 men, moved off towards Dranesville;

---

[3] *Report of Lieut.-Col. Robert Johnstone, Fifth New York Cavalry.*

*Fairfax C. H., March 23, 1863.*

SIR : At 5 p. m. our picket in front of Chantilly was attacked. The vedettes were on the alert and gave the alarm. The reserve of about 70 men were immediately under arms and charged the enemy, who fled for two miles along the Little River turnpike. Between Saunders' Toll-gate and Cub Run there is a strip of woods about half a mile wide, through which the road runs. Within the woods and about a quarter of a mile apart are two barricades of fallen trees ; our troops pursued the enemy between these barricades. Behind the latter some of the enemy were concealed. The head of the column was here stopped by a fire of carbines and pistols, and also by a fire upon the flank from the woods. The column broke, and was pursued by the enemy one and a half miles. It was then rallied by the exertions of Majors Bacon and White. Captains McGuinn and Hasbrouck, when they heard of the alarm, proceeded thence up the Leesburg turnpike and camped for the night at Miskel's farm, on the north side of the road and about half a mile from the Potomac River.

Miskel's was selected as a camping ground for the reason that it was the only place for miles around where forage could be procured. Some of the men slept on the floor in the house where there was a good fire, but the majority took up their quarters in the barn where there was a plentiful supply of hay. The horses were hitched to the high fence surrounding the barnyard. This fence had a gate opening into a field through which a road ran leading to the turnpike. The presence of Mosby in the neighborhood was communicated by a Union citizen to the officer in command of the First Vermont Cavalry, camped on Difficult Run, and Captain Flint, with two squadrons of selected volunteers, started out to surprise and capture the Partisans.

Dick Moran, one of "Mosby's Men," had stopped for the night with an old acquaintance named Green, who lived on the road between Dranesville and Miskel's, and Captain Flint, in passing, stopped at Green's house. Moran hid until the Federals had passed, and then, mounting his horse, took a short cut across the fields to warn Mosby of their approach.

About sunrise next morning one of the men came into the house and said he noticed the enemy in the Federal camps on the opposite side of the river were making signals. Mosby went out into the yard to look at them, when he spied Dick Moran riding towards him at breakneck speed waving his hat and shouting, " Mount your horses ! The Yankees are coming ! " ·

Mosby rushed to the barnyard on foot to rally his men

---

on a gallop from Frying Pan, and joining Major White's command, pursued the enemy for eight miles. Night coming on, and the enemy being more numerous than we were, and our horses exhausted, the column halted and returned to Chantilly. The line of pickets is now re-established.

Our loss is : Killed, Corporal (Charles) Gilleo, Company H, Fifth New York Cavalry ; James Doyle, Company C ; John Harris, Company K. Mortally wounded, Sergeant (William) Leahey, Company C. Lieut. Merritt taken prisoner.

I have ordered returns to be sent in at once, but as the line of picket is very extensive, I will not be able to give you the list of prisoners and missing for some hours.

THE FIGHT AT MISKEL'S (BROAD RUN)

and found Flint's first squadron marching through the gate into the field and they soon opened a brisk fire on the Rangers engaged in bridling and saddling their horses. The fire was returned, however, and Captain Flint fell, mortally wounded, pierced by six bullets.

Harry Hatcher, seeing his leader on foot, dismounted and gave his horse to Mosby who, once in the saddle, led his men in the charge and Harry was soon mounted on a captured horse and into the thickest of the fight.

In their efforts to escape from the furious onslaught of the Rangers, the terror-stricken Federals became wedged in the narrow passage through the gateway, and thus hemmed in, they suffered terribly from the murderous fire poured into them, until, bursting through, they rushed frantically out to the woods and turnpike, pursued by the Rangers who fiercely hung upon their rear.

Mosby lost one man killed—Davis, of Kentucky, and three wounded—Edward Hurst, of Fauquier, Keys of the First Virginia Cavalry, and R. A. Hart, of the Black Horse Cavalry. (See Mosby's Report, Appendix, II.).

The Federals lost 10 killed, 15 wounded, 83 prisoners; and 95 horses were captured.[4]

---

[4] *Report of Gen. R. E. Lee, Army of Northern Virginia.*

*Hdqs. Camp Fed's, April 4, 1863.*

MR. PRESIDENT: Major John S. Mosby reports that he was attacked early on the morning of the 2d (1st) instant, near Dranesville, by about 200 Vermont cavalry. He promptly repulsed them, leaving on the field 25 killed and wounded, including three officers, and brought off 82 prisoners, with their horses, arms and equipments. His force consisted of 65 men and his loss was four wounded. The enemy has evacuated Dranesville.

I had the pleasure to send by return courier to Major Mosby his commission of Major of Partisan Rangers, for which I am obliged to Your Excellency.

I am, with great respect, your obedient servant,

R. E. LEE, *General.*

His Excellency JEFFERSON DAVIS,

*President Confederate States of America.*

---

*Report of Major-General Julius Stahel, U. S. A. Commanding Cavalry Division, Department of Virginia.*

HEADQUARTERS STAHEL'S CAVALRY DIVISION,

*Fairfax C. H., April 2, 1863.*

GENERAL: I have the honor to submit the following report, which is, how ever, made up from verbal information received from Col. Price, Lieut. Col.

In Colonel Mosby's " Reminiscences " he relates an incident which our artist has shown in the picture of the " Miskel Fight " :

" There was with me that day a young artillery officer— Samuel F. Chapman—who at the first call of his State to arms had quit the study of divinity and became, like Stonewall Jackson, a sort of military Calvin, singing the psalms of David as he went into battle. I must confess that his character as a soldier was more on the model of the Hebrew prophets than the apostles or the Baptist in whom he was so devout a believer. Before he got to the gate Sam had already exhausted every barrel of his two pistols and drawn his sabre. As the fiei y Covenanter rode on his predestined course the enemy's ranks withered wherever he went. He was just in front of me—he was generally in front of everybody in a fight—at the gate. It was no fault of the Union cavalry that they did not get through any faster than they did, but Sam seemed to think that it was. Even at that supreme moment in my life, when I had just stood on the brink of ruin and had barely escaped, I could not restrain a propensity to laugh. Sam, to give more vigor to his

CAPT. HENRY C. FLINT,
First Vermont Cavalry.
From a photograph taken during the War.
Killed at Miskel's (Broad Run)
April 1, 1863.

Johnstone and Major Taggart. I will forward the written report as soon as it is received, and shall take all possible means to ascertain the true state of the case.

It appears that on the evening of the 31st ultimo, Major Taggart, at Union Church, two miles above Peach Grove, received information that Mosby, with about 65 men, was near Dranesville. He immediately despatched Capt. Flint, with 150 men of the First Vermont, to rout or capture Mosby and his force.

Captain Flint followed the Leesburg and Alexandria road to the road which branches off to the right just this side of Broad Run. Turning to the right they followed up the Broad Run toward the Potomac to the place marked " J. Mesed." Here at a house they came onto Mosby, who was completely surprised and wholly unprepared for an attack from our forces. Had a proper disposition been made of our troops, Mosby could not, by any possible means, have escaped. It seems that around this house was a high board fence and ordinary farm gate. Captain Flint took his men through the gate, and at a distance from the house fired a volley at Mosby and his men, who were assembled about the house, doing but slight damage to them. He then ordered a sabre charge, which was also ineffectual, on account of the fence which intervened. Mosby waited until the men were checked by the fence, and then

blows, was standing straight up in his stirrups dealing them right and left with all the the theological fervor of Burly of Balfour.   I doubt whether he prayed that day for the souls of those he sent over the Stygian river.   I made him a captain for it."

While General Stahel's Division of Cavalry was picketing the line of the Orange and Alexandria Railroad, Mosby, with 98 men, bivouacked on the night of May 2d about two miles from Warrenton, and early on the morning of the 3d moved off towards Warrenton Junction, where a force of the enemy was reported.

Here he found the First Virginia (Federal) Cavalry who had just been relieved from duty and were resting in fancied security.   Some were under the shade of the trees, others in the block buildings, their horses unsaddled, unbridled, and many turned out in a field to graze.

---

opened his fire upon them, killing and wounding several.   The men here became panic-stricken, and fled precipitately toward this gate, through which to make their escape.   The opening was small and they got wedged together, and a fearful state of confusion followed, while Mosby's men followed them up and poured into the crowd a severe fire.   Here, while endeavoring to rally his men, Captain Flint was killed and Lieutenant Grout, of the same company, mortally wounded (will probably die to-day).

[Captain Flint and Lieut. Charles A. Woodbury were the officers killed. Lieut. Josiah Grout, Jr., was discharged (as captain) October 1, 1863.]

Mosby's men followed in pursuit and sabred several of our men on the road.   Mosby, during his pursuit, is supposed to have received a sabre wound across the face which unhorsed him.   The rebels took some prisoners and a number of horses, and fell back in great haste.   In comparison to the number engaged, our loss was very heavy.

Since Major Taggart received the report he sent Major Hall in pursuit of Mosby and to bring in our killed and wounded.   Upon receiving the first intelligence I immediately sent out Colonel Price with a detachment of the Sixth and Seventh Michigan and First Virginia, who searched in every direction, but no trace could be found of Mosby or his men, as information reached me too late.

I regret to be obliged to inform the Commanding General that the forces sent out by Major Taggart missed so good an opportunity of capturing this rebel guerrilla.   It is only to be ascribed to the bad management on the part of the officers and the cowardice of the men.   I have ordered Colonel Price to make a thorough investigation of this matter, and shall recommend those officers who are guilty to be stricken from the roll.

The list of killed and wounded will be forwarded as soon as received.

I have the honor to remain, your obedient servant,

JUL. STAHEL, *Major-General.*

Maj.-Gen. S. P. HEINTZELMAN, *Commanding, &c.*

They took but little notice of " Mosby's Men " at first, mistaking them for a party of their own men who had been sent out on a scout, but they were soon undeceived when Mosby ordered a charge. Many of those scattered around surrendered immediately, but about one hundred took refuge in the largest building and prepared to defend themselves. Then the fight commenced in earnest. Those inside poured out a galling fire on their assailants, while " Mosby's Men " rode up to the windows and discharged their weapons at those within.

After the fight had gone on in this manner for about half an hour, and the Federals still refused to surrender, Mosby ordered Alfred Glasscock to set fire to a pile of hay near by and burn the house. In the meantime Samuel Chapman, John DeButts, Harry Sweeting and a few others, dismounted, burst in the door and entering the building opened fire on those inside, at the same time demanding their surrender. The officer upstairs, deeming it useless to resist further, hung out a white flag.

MAJOR-GENERAL JULIUS STAHEL, U. S. A.
From a War-time photograph.

Gathering up the prisoners, horses, and captured spoils, the Rangers were preparing to retire, when the First Vermont and Fifth New York Cavalry, attracted by the firing, came up from near Cedar Run Bridge, where they had been bivouacked, and fiercely attacked Mosby. His men now being thoroughly disorganized, were forced to retreat.

leaving most of their prisoners, horses and other captures behind.

Templeton, one of Stonewall Jackson's best scouts, was killed, and about 20 men wounded—among them, Capt. Ducheane, T. W. T. Richards, T. M. Grigsby, Sam. Underwood and Dick Moran.

General Stahel in his despatch to General Heintzelman, admits a loss of 2 killed and 15 wounded. Major Steele, of the First Virginia (Federal), Cavalry was mortally wounded. [5]

Mosby brought out 7 prisoners and a few horses.

-----

[5] *Report of Gen. Julius Stahel.*

*Fairfax C. H., May 5, 1863.*

CAPTAIN : I have the honor to report that on the 31 of May, between 8 and 9 a. m., Mosby, with his band of guerrillas, together with a portion of the Black Horse Cavalry and a portion of a North Carolina regiment, came suddenly through the woods upon 50 of our men of the First (West) Virginia Cavalry, who were in camp feeding their horses, just having returned from a scout, the remainder of that regiment being out in a different direction to scout the country on the right of the Warrenton and Alexandria railroad and toward the Rappahannock.

Our men being surprised and completely surrounded, rallied in a house close at hand and where a sharp fight ensued. Our men defended themselves as long as their ammunition lasted, notwithstanding the rebels built a large fire about the house, of hay and straw and brushwood. The flames reaching the house and their ammunition being entirely expended they were obliged to surrender. At this juncture a portion of the Fifth Regiment New York Cavalry which was posted in the rear some distance from the First Virginia Cavalry came to their rescue, making a very brilliant charge, which resulted in the complete annihilation of Mosby's command and recaptured our men and property. Our men pursued the rebels in every direction, killing and wounding a large number, and had our horses been in better condition and not tired out by the severe service of the last few days, Mosby nor a single one of his men would not have escaped.

The rebel loss was very heavy, their killed being strewn along the road from Warrenton Junction to Warrenton, and besides these many were immediately removed from the fields and woods by the citizens in that vicinity.

The citizens report having seen a great many of Mosby's men who were wounded in the beginning of the engagement crawling through the woods seeking shelter and hiding places.

We have thus far captured only 30 prisoners and 40 horses ; 16 of the prisoners were badly wounded and were sent with the rest to the provost-marshal at Alexandria.

Among the killed of the rebels is Templeton, the notorious spy, and among

While the prisoners were sitting on the green at Upperville, after the return from the raid, talking with the men
around them, the subject of their conversation being the
fighting qualities of the different regiments, one of our men
said:

"Every one thinks his own regiment the best, but I have
a very poor opinion of the First Virginia Cavalry."

Mosby, overhearing the remark, said:

"What do you want to talk that way to prisoners for?"

Then, turning to the prisoners, he added:

"You all fight as well as we want to have you fight."

---

the wounded and captured is Dick Moran, Mosby's leading man, Capt. S. P.
Dushane and Lieut. (T. M.) Grigsby, and Samuel (L.) Underwood.

The loss on our side in killed is 2 privates; in wounded 5 officers and 10
privates, a list of which is enclosed.

I take the liberty of recommending to your notice the officers and men who
so gallantly repulsed and totally destroyed this rebel force, and particularly I
would mention Col. De Forest, Major Hammond, Capt. Krom, Capt. Penfield,
Capt. McMaster, and Lieuts. Munson and McBride, of the Fifth New York
Cavalry; Major Steele, Capt. Harris and Capt. McCoy, of the First (West)
Virginia Cavalry, and Capt. Bean, of the First Vermont Cavalry.

---

*Report of Brigadier General John J. Abercrombie, U. S. A.*

HEADQUARTERS ABERCROMBIE'S DIVISION,

*Centreville, May 4, 1863.*

CAPTAIN: The following information obtained from Colonel Blunt, Twelfth
Vermont, commanding infantry on the line of the Orange and Alexandria Railroad is respectfully submitted for the information of the Major-General commanding:

Between the hours of 9 and 10 o'clock on the morning of the 3d inst. an
outpost of the First Virginia (Union) Cavalry, at Warrenton Junction, numbering about 100 men, under Lieut. Col. Krepps' command, were surprised and
attacked by Major Mosby, with his force of about 125 men. The men of the
First (West) Virginia, were scattered about the station, their horses being for
the most part unsaddled in order to be groomed and fed. Mosby's force
came in upon them from the direction of Warrenton, which place they left at
daylight. Their front rank was dressed in the uniform of U. S. soldiers, and
they were supposed to be a force of Union cavalry until within a short distance
when they charged and surrounded the house, in and about which the First
(West) Virginia lay. After a short fight in which several of the rebels were
killed and wounded the men of the First (West) Virginia, for the most part, had

Raiding parties of Federals, both cavalry and infantry, were constantly scouring the country in all directions in search of Mosby. On their way, these raiders gathered up all the horses and cattle they could find, killed the farmers' stock and poultry, and plundered and destroyed private property. Inoffensive citizens, sometimes old and feeble men, were taken off, exhibited as "Mosby's Men," guerrillas, or bushwhackers, imprisoned for months, and finally released, without knowing why they were taken. In consequence of these practices, as soon as a raiding party commenced its march through the country, everything was in a state of excitement. The men and boys hurried off to the mountains, or to secluded spots with the horses and cattle, notifying their neighbors of the approach of the enemy. Within doors all was bustle. Everything of value was hidden away in places most likely to escape the scrutiny of a search. Meanwhile the soldiers, who were the least troubled on such occasions, mounted their horses and were secure in the mountains, or they combined for defense or attack, as opportunity might offer.

---

surrendered, and about 40 were being taken towards Warrenton by their captors, when a detachment of 70 men of the Fifth New York Cavalry, which was camped near by, under command of Major Hammond, came up, charged upon the rebels, and a running fight ensued, which was continued for five miles, in course of which all the prisoners taken by Mosby were recaptured, with the exception of two. Three rebels were killed on the spot, among them one shown by passes found on his person to be Templeton, a notorious scout and spy. Seventeen rebels were wounded and taken prisoners, among them 2 captains, 1 lieutenant, and Dick Moran, rebel spy. Six were taken uninjured, making 23 prisoners. Moran and several others were mortally wounded. Our loss was— of the First (West) Virginia, Major Steele, mortally wounded ; Captain McCoy, slightly wounded ; 1 private killed and 9 men wounded. Of the Fifth New York, Captain Krom, badly, and Lieutenant McBride and Munson, slightly wounded. Mosby is reported wounded in the shoulder. His force was pursued through Warrenton, scattered with the exception of about 20 men, and a number now are supposed to have been wounded who escaped capture.

About 30 of Mosby's horses were taken. Three men of the Twelfth Vermont were captured near their camp, but escaped. A party of the First Vermont Cavalry, Major Hall, commanding, joined in the pursuit but were not engaged in the skirmish. The prisoners were sent in by railroad at 6 p. m.

Very respectfully, your obedient servant,

J. J. ABERCROMBIE, *Brig. Gen. Commanding.*

Persons misled by a false alarm, or some even in a spirit of mischief, would at times send out the warning cry of " The Yankees are coming ! " when there were no grounds for such reports.   On these occasions, however, there would

A FEDERAL RAIDING PARTY.

be the same activity displayed and the same confusion existing as in cases of real danger.

On the 6th of May, 1863, Major Mosby, Edwin Rowzee and myself were at the house of Mr. George S. Ayre, near Upperville. Dinner was just over and we remained sitting around when our host came into the room and said, " Major, the Yankees are coming ! "   Mosby picked up his hat and pistols, mounted his horse, which stood saddled at the stile, and rode off. Row-zee and I started for the stable to get our horses, but before we reached it heard firing in the woods at Blakeley's Grove, about a mile from the house. We halted and in a few moments saw a blue-coat skirmish line on the crest of a hill opposite, and soon a body of infantry came in view. We concealed ourselves behind a stone fence and crept along, watching them as they moved towards Upperville. A farm bell which was used to call the hands from the fields to the house was sounded at this time, and the Federal infantry, evidently thinking it a signal, halted and drew up in line.

Rowzee and I hastened back to the house, where we were told there had been a fight in the woods and a number of wounded men were there. We threw off our coats and and jumped into an ox-cart which stood by, and with an negro driver hurried off to the scene of the fight. As we neared the place a Federal cavalryman rode up and said: " Are there any rebels in the neighborhood? " "I don't know," said I. He said they had been attacked by about 150 rebels. In the woods we found 5 wounded, and in the road 1 man and 2 horses killed. The main body had gone towards Upperville, while a few had been left to look after the wounded, who were taken temporarily to the school-house at the grove. One of the Federals was very communicative. He told me they had 2 killed and 6 wounded ; that among the wounded were Lieutenants Boyd and Wyckoff of the First New York Cavalry, and Lieutenant Hawkins of the Sixth Maryland.

From conversation with the Federal soldiers and the account given me by our own men who were in the fight, I learned that at this time the First New York Cavalry, the Sixth Maryland and Sixty-seventh Pennsylvania Infantry were camped at Berryville. That on the night of the 5th of May, the Sixty-seventh Pennsylvania, about 400 men, under Colonel Staunton, set a trap to catch Mosby.

They had captured a few skiffs at Front Royal, which they had brought down the Shenandoah River to Castleman's Ferry for the purpose of ferrying the infantry across. They were accompanied by about 20 cavalry under Lieutenants

Boyd and Wyckoff, who rode a little in advance with orders that in the event of their meeting "Mosby's Men," a trooper was to gallop back and notify the infantry, who were to conceal themselves ; the cavalry, after skirmishing, were to retreat and draw Mosby into the ambuscade.

Leaving a small force as guard at the Ferry, they marched through Snicker's Gap. Near Blakeley's Grove, between Bloomfield and Upper-ville, the cavalry were charged by 15 of "Mosby's Men," and running back to the infantry were received by a volley of musketry. The infantry were so excited they did not wait for the Confederates to come up, but fired on their own men.

Only one of "Mosby's Men" (Robert Gray) was slightly wounded, for discovering the "trap" in time, they wheeled their horses and were soon out of range.

The Federals made but a short stay in Upperville, and returning to the scene of the

F. F. BOWEN, CO. B.
From a photograph taken in 1864.

recent conflict, gathered up their wounded and recrossed the river.

The Orange and Alexandria Railroad was at this time closely guarded, the army on the Rappahannock receiving all its supplies from Washington by that route. Pickets were stationed at all the principal bridges and exposed places, patrols were sent from post to post, and each train was in charge of a guard. Yet in spite of all this vigilance Mosby never lost sight of the purpose for which he was de-tailed, and neglected no opportunity to harass and annoy the enemy.

On Friday, May 29th, there was a meeting of the com-mand at Patterson's. A small howitzer which General Stuart had sent Mosby at his request, was brought out, and the men selected for this branch of the service were put through a drill by Lieut. Samuel F. Chapman, who had been an officer in the Dixie Battery. Mosby then proceeded to Greenwich, where a halt was made for supper, after which he moved a few miles further on and camped for the night.

Early on the morning of the 30th a hurried march was made in the direction of the railroad, coming out at a point near Catlett's Station. After cutting the telegraph wire, a rail was unfastened and a wire attached to it, extended some distance from the road where the patrols would not observe it, while a man concealed behind a tree stood ready to draw

CATLETT'S STATION.

the rail out of place as soon as the engine approached, throwing it off the track.

Soon the train came steaming along, but it halted suddenly on reaching the treacherous rail. The little howitzer had been placed in position by Lieutenant Chapman and a shot was fired into the engine, while a charge was made upon the infantry guarding the train. The guard fired a volley, and then, jumping from the cars, fled to the woods, leaving the train of eleven cars heavily loaded with supplies in possession of the Rangers, who took such articles as they fancied and then set fire to the train.

As there were cavalry camps within a mile on either side, the Rangers knew they could spend but little time in plundering, yet when mounted to return they were well laden with spoil, some with boxes of oranges or lemons, others with sides of leather, or mail bags, or boxes of dainties, hastily picked up, either by chance or from choice.

Colonel Mann, of the Seventh Michigan Cavalry, who was in command of that portion of Stahel's Cavalry at Bristoe, hearing the firing, started the Fifth New York, under Captain Hasbrouck, across the country to intercept Mosby, while he followed the railroad towards the burning train, with the First Vermont and Seventh Michigan Cavalry.

Mosby had marched but a few miles when he observed the Fifth New York Cavalry in his front. Chapman sent a shell into their ranks which checked their advance, and the command was again started. Thus the pursuit was continued for some time, until Mosby, finding his pursuers increasing in numbers (Colonel Mann, with the Seventh Michigan, and Colonel Preston, with the First Vermont, having come up), determined to make a stand and sell his gun dearly.

JOHN H. CORE,
CO. D.
From a photograph.

Chapman took up a position near Grapewood Farm, about two miles from Greenwich, at the head of a short, narrow lane, with a high fence on either side. The Federals coming up, charged in column of fours, and at a little over fifty yards received a fire of grape which killed 3 and wounded 7. Mosby now made a dashing charge, which drove the enemy in confusion. Twice they rallied and each time were driven back. Our men fought bravely, but the odds were too great. At last when the ammunition was exhausted, the gun had to be abandoned, but only after a desperate hand-to-hand fight.

The Federals admitted a loss of 4 killed and 15 wounded. After the fight they made no attempt to pursue us.[6]

---

[6] *May 30, 1863.—Skirmish near Greenwich, Va.*

General STAHEL to TAYLOR :                    *Fairfax C. H., June 3, 1863.*

I am just in receipt of an official report from Colonel Mann, of the recent engagement near Greenwich. He informs me that at 9 a. m. on the 30th ult.

Mosby lost 5 men killed and about 20 wounded and prisoners. Captain Bradford Smith Hoskins, an Englishman, formerly a captain in the Forty-fourth Royal Infantry in the Crimean War, was with Mosby, and was mortally wounded. He lingered two days and died at the residence of Mr. Charles Green, near the scene of the conflict. He was a brave soldier, and had made many friends while with the command.

---

he heard from his camp artillery firing in the direction of Warrenton Junction. The train for Bealeton had just passed up, and believing it to have been attacked he immediately went with a detachment of the Fifth New York, under command of Captain A. H. Hasbrouck, a detachment of the First Vermont, under command of Lieutenant-Colonel Preston, and a small detachment of the Seventh Michigan. The detachment of the Fifth New York was sent directly across the country in order to intercept the rebels, while the balance of the command went directly to the scene of action. The advance of the Fifth New York, led by Lieut. Elmer Barker, came up with the enemy first, and found them with a howitzer posted on a hill, with the cavalry drawn up in line in the rear to support it. Lieutenant Barker, with his small detachment of about 25 men, dashed up the hill, and when within about 50 yards of the gun, received a charge of grape and canister, which killed 3 and wounded 7 of our men and several horses. The enemy then charged upon us, but were met with stubborn resistance by the Lieutenant and his men, although the Lieutenant had received two grape shot in his thigh. We were, however, overpowered and driven back a short distance. Just then Colonel Preston, of the First Vermont (Lieutenant Hazleton, with Companies H and C, being in advance), came up at a full charge upon their flank and were again received with a discharge from the howitzer of grape and canister. Our men pressed on, however, until they came to a hand-to-hand conflict, when the enemy gradually fell back. We took their howitzer and they fled in every direction.

Colonel Mann pursued the rebels until his horses were completely tired out, he having been obliged to ride at full speed before overtaking them, and then, after collecting his dead and wounded, returned to camp.

Our loss was 4 killed and 15 wounded, the names of which please find enclosed. We lost also 11 horses killed and several wounded. None of our men are missing. The force engaged on our side was 170. The rebels had, as nearly as can be ascertained, 200 men, besides his gun.

Capt. B. S. Haskins, of the rebel army, formerly of the British army, and Lieutenant Chapman, formerly of the U. S. Regulars, who was in command of the howitzer, were so badly wounded that they could not be removed. They were consequently paroled. Captain Haskins has since died.

The loss of the enemy was 6 killed and 20 wounded, besides many others severely wounded, who escaped in the woods.

We have 10 prisoners and many carbines and pistols; the number Colonel Mann did not state.

I desire again to recommend to the favorable consideration of the Major-

Lieut. Samuel F. Chapman, who was in charge of the gun, was so badly wounded that he could not be removed, and was paroled on the field. Beattie and Montjoy stood by the gun until surrounded and captured.

Mosby came out of the fight hatless, and his horse ran against a tree with him, bruising his face.

General commanding the officers and men engaged in this fight, in which they all displayed such great valor.

The dead and wounded have all been brought in to this place, and the wounded are doing well in the hospitals attached to their respective brigades.

Colonel Mann reports that had the guards on the train offered the slightest resistance the train might have been saved. They could have detained the enemy until our cavalry came up and also reinforcements from the battalion of infantry which was at Catlett's Station.

*Report of Colonel Mann, Seventh Michigan Cavalry.*

NEAR GREENWICH, 2 p. m.,
*Via Union Mills, May 30, 1863.*

MANN to STAHEL:

SIR : Mosby, with 200 men and one howitzer, attacked our train near Catlett's ; guard fled ; Mosby burned train. Heard firing in camp and went in search with First Vermont, Fifth New York and a detachment of Seventh Michigan. Came up with Mosby in strong position two miles southwest of Greenwich and charged him. He gave us grape ; boys never faltered ; took his gun. Captain Haskins mortally wounded, and Lieutenant Chapman severely wounded, and also several privates. Our loss, 4 killed, and 1 officer, Lieutenant Barker, and 7 enlisted men wounded. Several horses killed.

The rebels scattered in the thickets and in the mountains. We shall return to camp as soon as the wounded and dead are cared for.

Engine is not much damaged ; train destroyed. A strong patrol from my command had passed the very spot but one hour before and were but three miles distant at the time and came promptly up. No other news. Full report by mail.

*Bristoe Station, May 31, 1863.*

Colonel MANN to Major BALDWIN : Returned at dark, bringing in our cannon and all our dead and wounded. The wounded number 15 on our side. It was an extremely hot affair for a small one; many of the wounds very severe. Our captures of the day are 10 prisoners, including Captain Haskins, an English officer of 7 years' service, now in the Confederate service, and Lieutenan Chapman, who had charge of the artillery. Both these officers so severely wounded could not be removed and were paroled. I sent in prisoners by train to-day.

The enemy lost heavy in wounded, as they received a terrific fire from revolvers at close range, followed by a determined sabre charge. Many were severely cut with sabre, but clung to their horses and fell back into the thicket.

George Turberville made his appearance with a bunch of fresh fish, which he had brought from the captured train and carried safely through the desperate fight.

---

Our horses were completely blown when we had overtaken the enemy, so rapid had been our pursuit, and after thoroughly scattering them to all points, in that thick country I found it impossible to follow up with the hope of catching them. Lieutenant Barker has two grape shot through thigh, but is quite comfortable. He crossed sabres with them and fought desperately after this wound.

# CHAPTER IV.

On the morning of the 10th of June, 1863, at a meeting held at Rector's X Roads, on the turnpike, four miles west of Middleburg, the command was for the first time regularly organized, and as Company A, Forty-third Battalion Partisan Rangers, elected James William Foster, Captain ; Thomas Turner, of Maryland, First Lieutenant ; W. L. Hunter, Second Lieutenant, and George H. Whitescarver, Third Lieutenant.

After the election, joined by Captain Brawner's Company, Prince William Cavalry, Mosby moved off in the direction of the Potomac. He struck the river early on the morning of the 11th, at a ford one mile below Seneca. Joseph H. Nelson, Alfred Glasscock and William Trunnel were first sent across and captured the picket, after which the command crossed the river to attack a camp of the Sixth Michigan Cavalry at Seneca Mills. Mosby dashed up the tow path, while the Federals fell back and took up their position behind the bridge near the Mill, and along the creek, which was bordered by trees and underbrush. We charged over the bridge, the enemy giving way, but in a deep cut in the road a sharp hand to hand fight took place. Captain Brawner and Lieutenant Whitescarver were killed, and Alfred Glasscock and William Hibbs wounded. John Ballard, seeing Captain Brawner fall, rode up to the Federal soldier who killed him, and cutting him over the head with his sabre, knocked him from his horse.

After routing the Federals, Mosby returned to Seneca, destroyed the camp, and recrossed the river, bringing off 17 prisoners, 23 horses and 5 mules.

The Sixth Michigan lost 4 killed and a number wounded. [1]

CAPT. JAMES W. FOSTER, CO. A.
Familiarly known as Captain "WILLIE" FOSTER.
From a photograph taken after the war.

[1] *Report of Major John S. Mosby, Virginia Partisan Rangers.*

*Middleburg, June 10 (11th), 1863.*

GENERAL : I left our point of rendezvous yesterday for the purpose of making a night attack on two cavalry companies of the enemy on the Maryland shore. Had I succeeded in crossing the river at night, as I expected, I would have had no difficulty in capturing them; but unfortunately, my guide mistook the road, and, instead of crossing about 11 o'clock at night, I did not get over until after daylight.

The enemy (between 80 and 100 strong), being apprised of my movement, were formed to receive me. A charge was ordered, the shock of which the enemy could not resist, and they were driven several miles in confusion, with the loss of 7 killed, a considerable number wounded and 17 prisoners ; also, 20-odd horses or more. We burned their tents, stores, camp equipage, etc.

I regret the loss of two brave officers killed, Captain Brawner and Lieut. [Geo. H.] Whitescarver. I also had one man wounded.

Respectfully, your obedient servant,

JNO. S. MOSBY, *Major Partisan Rangers.*

[Indorsement.]

HEADQUARTERS CAVALRY DIVISION, }
*June 16, 1863.* }

Respectfully forwarded. In consideration of his brilliant services, I hope the President will promote Major Mosby.

J. E. B. STUART, *Major-General.*

*Report of Col. Albert B. Jewett, Tenth Vermont Infantry, Commanding Brigade.*

*Camp Heintzelman, June 20, 1863.*

I have the honor to report that on the 10th (11th) instant about 250 of the enemy's cavalry crossed the Potomac River, Muddy Branch, at daybreak.

The enemy dashed rapidly up the canal, driving in the patrols and attacked

On the night of Thursday, June 18th, while Hooker's army was in motion, Mosby, accompanied by Joseph H. Nelson, Norman Smith, and Charles L. Hall, penetrated the Federal lines, and at Birch's house on the pike below Aldie, captured two Federal officers and an orderly[2]. One of the

Captain Dean's Company, I, Sixth Michigan Cavalry, on duty at Seneca Locks.

Captain Dean fell back toward Poolesville, forming line three times, and only retreating when nearly surrounded.

The enemy followed to within three miles of Poolesville, when he rapidly retired, destroying the camp of Captain Dean and recrossing the river at the point where he had crossed.

Our loss was 4 men killed, 1 man wounded and 16 men missing. The men above reported "missing" are men who were absent from Captain Dean's camp doing patrol duty along the canal, along a line extending to Muddy Branch, more than 13 miles from my headquarters, and were not reported by me in my telegraphic despatches because they were not then considered to be properly "missing," in the absence of any information to that effect. The enemy left killed on the field their commanding officers, Capt. [W. G.] Brawner and his second lieutenant.

HEADQUARTERS FIFTH NEW YORK CAVALRY,<br>
Kettle Run, June 13, 1863.

Colonel DE FOREST, Fairfax C. H. :

COLONEL : Returned last night at 11 p. m. with one captain and six men of Mosby's command and ten horses.

Mosby returned from raid in Maryland about 2 p. m. on the 11th. He brought 17 prisoners of the Sixth Michigan and dispersed his men at Middleburg four hours before the telegram was written ordering us in pursuit of him. He is reported to have had 110 men, but no artillery.

The prisoners will be sent in by first train.

J. HAMMOND, Major Commanding Detachment.

[2] Federal Report.<br>
HEADQUARTERS PICKET RESERVE,<br>
June 18, 1863.

Lieut. JOHN M. CLARK, <i>Acting Assist. A. G.:</i>

In accordance with directions from the Commanding Officer of the brigade I report the facts in regard to the capture of Major [William R.] Sterling and Captain Fisher, as related to me by the people of the house where they were taken. Major Sterling and Captain Fisher were on their way to communicate with General Pleasonton when they halted at the residence of Mr. [Almond] Birch for supper and to inquire how far it was to Aldie. Having finished their supper they started for their horses which were left with their orderly at the yard gate. The horses and orderly had been removed, and before Major Sterling and Captain Fisher had reached the gate 10 or 12 cavalrymen seized them and hurriedly mounted them and bore them off. This took place last evening at 10 o'clock, about 400 yards from the picket outpost at the house of Mr. Birch

officers was Captain Fisher, a signal officer, and the other, Major Sterling, who was the bearer of important despatches from Hooker to Pleasonton, at Aldie, giving information •as to his (Hooker's) plans, with his letter of instructions to Pleasonton. These Mosby placed in the hands of Norman Smith, and by daylight on the morning of the 19th, Smith had delivered them to General Stuart, who made the following mention in his report :

"Major Mosby,with his usual daring, penetrated the enemy's lines and caught a staff officer of General Hooker, bearer of despatches to General Pleasonton, commanding U.S.Cavalry near Aldie. These dispatches disclosed the fact that Hooker was looking to Aldie with solicitude; that Pleasonton with infantry and cavalry occupied the place, and that a reconnoissance in force, of cavalry, was meditated toward Warrenton and Culpeper."

MAJOR-GENERAL JOSEPH HOOKER, U. S. A.
From a photograph taken during the war.

on the Little River turnpike. Mr. Birch and family are from Clifton Park, Saratoga County, New York. They are Union people, known to some of the officers of our regiment. I am satisfied that these people had no complicity with this affair, and had no knowledge of the enemy's being anywhere near their house. The capture of these officers appears to have been as unexpected to the enemy as it was to the officers captured, since the enemy was unaware of our forces being so near.

I also report that I have re-established the picket line in some respects since coming upon duty this morning, so as among other points to include the house of Mr. Birch. All is quiet upon the line.

I am, most respectfully, your obedient servant,

JAMES C. RICE, *Colonel Commanding Outposts.*

Sending Nelson and Hall off with the prisoners, Mosby proceeded alone to within a short distance of the Potomac, gathered all the information he could concerning the location, strength and movements of Hooker's forces, and started on his return.

He stopped at a farm house (Mr. John Coleman's), for the purpose of making some inquiries, when hearing a noise in his rear, he turned and perceived two Federal cavalrymen picking cherries from a tree. Riding to where the two men were standing, he asked, " What regiment do you belong to?" The waterproof which Mosby had thrown over his shoulders to protect him from the drizzling rain, hid his gray uniform, and the cavalrymen, not suspecting who he was, answered that they were from the Fifth New York. He told them who he was and demanded their surrender. As they were unarmed and had only straggled from their camp near by, there was no alternative and they yielded.

Coming in sight of the pike he discovered a long train of wagons passing, guarded by Federal cavalry. Turning to his prisoners, he told them he was in a tight place and meant to get out; that if either showed the slightest sign of an intention to betray him he would instantly shoot him. Having thus cautioned them, he tied their horses' heads together to prevent their parting, and trotting along at a brisk gait, passed through the train and made his way safely to General Stuart's headquarters. The train guards no doubt mistook Mosby for one of their own officers and the prisoners for his orderlies or escort. The boldness of his action threw them completely off their guard.

While Hooker was in front of Washington, awaiting the advance of Lee, the latter was moving his forces north by way of Culpeper, thence across the Blue Ridge and down the Valley to Maryland and Pennsylvania. Milroy was driven out of Winchester, and the greatest excitement existed along the border. The President of the United States issued a proclamation calling for 100,000 men from the states of Maryland, Pennsylvania, Ohio and West Virginia to repel the invasion.

The Army of Northern Virginia, under General Lee, had been reorganized into three Army Corps; the First Corps under Lieutenant-General Longstreet, the Second Corps under Ewell, and the Third Corps under A. P. Hill.

The Second Corps, under General Ewell, the first to move, crossed the Shenandoah River, near Front Royal, on the 12th of June, 1863, and was followed by Gen. A. P. Hill, with his three divisions, composing the Third Corps.

MAJOR-GENERAL J. E. B. STUART, C. S. A.
From a photograph taken during the war.

General Longstreet, with his Corps (the First), marched by Ashby's and Snicker's Gaps into the Valley, on the 17th of June.

General Stuart with his cavalry covered these movements and guarded the approaches to the Gaps.

For several days there was sharp skirmishing between Stuart's cavalry and the Federal forces under Pleasonton, who were endeavoring to penetrate the mystery which surrounded the movements of the Confederate Army. Baffled in his efforts, Pleasonton, being heavily reinforced, attacked Stuart with his entire force on Sunday, June 21st.

The morning of the 21st was cloudy and threatening. Booming of cannon in the direction of Middleburg warned us that a fight was going on. As the sounds approached nearer, mingled with the rattle of small arms, we knew that our cavalry was falling back towards Upperville, where the hardest of the fighting took place. The battle, in which the whole of Pleasonton's cavalry was engaged, lasted until night, when Stuart fell back to Ashby's Gap.

During the excitement of a battle one does not so fully realize the terrible effects as when going over the field afterwards. On the morning after the fight (Monday, 22d) white men and negroes were engaged in burying the dead. One poor fellow lay in a fence corner, his brains spattered over the rails, while another had one-half of his head carried away by a shell. Another looked as if calmly sleeping, death had come to him so quickly. In one field, in front of the house at Ayreshire (the residence of Mr. Geo. S. Ayre), where Stuart made a desperate charge to save his train of wagons and ambulances, I counted 31 dead horses. The ground in many places was torn up in great holes and furrows by shot and shell. Roads through the fields in all directions, and big

MAJOR-GEN. PLEASONTON, U. S. A.

gaps in the stone fences, showed where the cavalry and artillery had ploughed through. The country around presented a scene of desolation; wheat fields trodden down and cornfields in many places looking as though they had never been planted. A poor horse that had one of its hind legs shot away, had grazed around in a circle. I thought it an act of mercy to put a ball through the head of the suffering creature.

A little darkey, looking over the fence into a clover field, saw a fine cavalry boot among the clover and ran to get it, saying in great glee, " Oh, see what a nice boot I've found ! " But when he attempted to pick it up and discovered that there was a foot and part of a leg in the boot, he was paralyzed with fright for a few seconds ; but he soon recovered the use of his legs and scampered off in a hurry.

GATHERING UP THE DEAD AND WOUNDED.

At this time Mosby crossed the Bull Run Mountains with a part of the command, and fell into an ambuscade which had been prepared for him near Ewell's Chapel.[3]  Mr. J. N. Ballard, who was severely wounded on that occasion, furnished me with the following account of the affair :

" On the evening of June 21st, while Stuart was fighting Pleasonton and gradually falling back to Ashby's Gap, Mosby, with a portion of his command, left a point on General Stuart's right, not far from Five Points, and passing close to the enemy's left, reached the Bull Run Mountains near Landmark.  The gaps in the mountains were in possession of and well guarded by the Federal troops, and Mosby was compelled to cross by a little mountain path.

---

[3] General Meade sent his *regrets* to General Howard in the following letter :

HEADQUARTERS FIFTH CORPS,

*June 22, 1863.*

Gen. O. O. HOWARD :

I came near catching our friend Mosby this morning.  I had reliable intelligence of his expected passing a place about four miles from here at sunrise.  I sent 40 mounted men (all I had) and 100 infantry, who succeeded in posting themselves in ambush at the designated spot.  Sure enough, Mr. Mosby, together with 30 of his followers, made their appearance about sunrise ; but I regret to say, their exit also, from what I can learn, through the fault of both foot and horse.  It appears Mosby saw the cavalry, and immediately charged them.  They ran—that is, my horses—toward the infantry posted behind a fence.  The infantry, instead of rising and deliberately delivering their fire, fired lying on the ground, and did not hit the rebels, who immediate y scattered and dispersed.  Thus the prettiest chance in the world to dispose of Mr. Mosby was lost.                    Truly yours,

GEO. MEADE, *Major-General.*

---

*Report of Capt. Harvey Brown, Fourteenth U. S. Infantry.*

*Camp Near Alaie, June 22, 1863.*

I have the honor to report in obedience to the instructions I received this morning from you to take a sufficient force for the purpose of capturing a certain guerrilla party which was supposed to frequent the house of Dr. Ewell, in this vicinity, that I left the camp for that object at 1 a. m. with 100 men and 3 officers (Captain Ilges, Lieuts. P. Collins and Douney) and 30 cavalry and 3 officers of the Seventeenth Pennsylvania Volunteers, and proceeded by the Aldie and Thoroughfare Gap road to a small church near the head waters of Bull Run, or about 4 miles from this camp.

My object was to reach the point before daylight, but the difficulties I encountered in passing our picket lines, in addition to the heavy roads, prevented me from accomplishing my purpose until broad daylight.  The country being very open I had but little choice in selecting a favorable position.  I placed

The road was rugged and the night very dark, and by some mishap a good number of our men lost their way and had to return, so that there were only about twenty-five men left with Mosby, who halted on top of the mountain and slept till morning. In the valley the enemy's camp fires were seen in every direction.

" Early next morning we descended the eastern slope of the mountain and passed through the farm of Dr. Ewell. At a small house we captured two Federal cavalrymen, who told us there was only a small force of cavalry at the church near by. Coming in sight we charged them. There was a fence and a gate between us, and just as we got through the gate a body of infantry who were lying in ambush inside of and around the church gave us volley after volley. We did not see the infantry until we got quite near the church. Montjoy had a finger shot off; Charles Hall received a ball in his

---

about half my cavalry and a portion of the infantry in the rear of the church, and at the head of a lane leading to Dr. Ewell's house, which place it was supposed the said party would pass. The balance of my force I stationed on the left of the above-mentioned lane and facing toward the house. But a short time had elapsed after I had made this disposition of my forces until I was informed by one of my men whom I had placed in a tree that there was a body of mounted men rapidly approaching. I permitted them to advance within pistol shot, when we commenced to exchange firing, but almost immediately they fell back at full speed, and in consequence of the rolling ground on our front, they were for a short time hidden from our view. To make a successful charge under the circumstances was impossible, although we pursued the enemy for about a mile, until they found refuge in the mountains beyond. Nothing was then left me but to return.

I regret to state that the efficiency of the cavalry did not in all respects answer my expectations. I was also much mortified to find that nearly one-half of the guns of the infantry were useless in consequence of defective ammunition, or for the reason that they had been damp before having been loaded, caused, no doubt, by a shower we had in the evening.

Casualties : One sergeant killed, Seventeenth Pennsylvania Volunteer Cavalry.

[Indorsement.]

Respectfully forwarded for the information of the Commanding General. This expedition was sent out by my order on information given by a colored man, who stated Mosby had passed this place the morning previous and had been overheard to tell Dr. Ewell that he would return at sunrise the next day. The result greatly disappointed my expectations, and a court of inquiry called at the request of the officer commanding the infantry detachment will investigate the facts of the case.

GEO. G. MEADE, *Major-General.*

shoulder, and I (Ballard) was shot in the leg. My horse had an eye shot out and became unmanageable. The Federals had one man killed and several wounded. We then galloped back to the mountains and the Federals did not attempt to pursue us."

Young Ballard's leg was crushed by the ball, and the rough riding back to the mountains made the fracture worse. He was taken to Mr. Robert Whitacre's, near the top of the mountain, where his leg was amputated, and he was kindly nursed and taken care of until he could be moved to Ben Venue, the home of Mr. William Ayre. The following winter he was again in the saddle and with the command, but had his artificial leg crushed in a charge with Capt. A. E. Richards, on a Federal camp near Halltown. He afterwards came in possession of the leg of Col. Ulric Dahlgren[4], with which he was enabled to continue in active service to the end.

JOHN N. BALLARD, CO. A.
From a photograph taken in the early part of the war.

On the 27th of June Hooker was relieved from the command of the Army of the Potomac, and Meade was appointed his successor.

*Sunday, June 28th.*—The command met at Glasscock's Burnt House, 4 miles from Upperville, and about noon Mosby, with about 50 men, started for the Valley. We crossed the Blue Ridge at Snicker's Gap and thence to the Potomac River, near Hancock, where we crossed on the morning of July 1st, passing through Maryland into Franklin county, Pennsylvania.

It was Mosby's intention to join General Lee in Pennsyl-

---

[4] Colonel Ulric Dahlgren, son of Admiral Dahlgren, U. S. N., was killed March 3, 1864, in his raid on Richmond, with the Federal cavalry under Kilpatrick.

vania, but when we reached Mercersburg, where we expected to find a portion of the army, it had moved. Our number being so small, and as we were ignorant of the country as well as of the position of our army, Mosby determined to return to Virginia, which he did, but not until he had gathered up 218 head of cattle, 15 horses and 12 negroes. Returning through Washington county, Maryland, we recrossed the Potomac without interruption.

On this trip to Pennsylvania I rode with Ames ("Big Yankee"). As we crossed the line into Pennsylvania he said: "Well, I am going with you, but I will not fire a shot. When the Emancipation Proclamation was issued and I saw the war was for the negro and not for the Union, I joined the South, and am willing to fight to repel the invasion of her soil, and am willing to give my life in her defense, but I will not fight on Northern soil."

As we were driving the cattle along towards the Maryland line, an old lady said to Ames, in a voice whose tones expressed more forcibly than words the bitterness of her heart:

"Well, now, you've got them, but my earnest prayer is that you may not get across the river with them."

"Old lady," said Ames, "did you ever hear of Mosby?"

"Yes," she replied.

"Well, these are Mosby's men."

The old lady's faith in the efficacy of prayer seemed somewhat shaken at this announcement, for she abruptly turned away, saying:

"Oh, then, you'll get off safe enough, I'll be bound!"

About the middle of July Lee's Army fell back from Maryland after the battle of Gettysburg, and was followed by Meade, who crossed the Potomac and advanced through Loudoun County.

The result of the battle of Gettysburg proved a great disappointment to the hopes of the Southern people, who had thought to transfer the field of warlike operations from the South to Northern territory, and the failure, together with the disasters at Vicksburg and Port Hudson, cast a shadow over the Confederacy.

After passing the night in the woods at Hathaways,

Mosby and ten men were joined by as many more on the morning of July 20th, and with this force we started for Five Points, near Rectortown, knowing we would pick up more men as we moved on. At the Five Points we halted and grazed our horses, while the Major and two men rode out towards Rector's Cross Roads, where the advance of the Federal cavalry had camped the night before, to see if they were preparing to move. Very soon the two men came galloping in, calling out:

"Mount your horses; they are coming!"

In a few moments Mosby came in sight, riding slowly, looking back, with his pistol in his hand. A few shots were fired at him and he waved his hand for us to move on.

At Rectortown, as the last of our men were leaving, the Federal cavalry was coming in at the other end of town. Between Rectortown and Salem the chase was quite lively. At one time we were running almost neck and neck—we in one field and the Federals in an adjoining one. Near Salem they gave up the pursuit. We then moved back under cover of the Bull Run Mountains to the rear of the advancing corps, halted for the night near Mountville, and as the bands of music were playing in the camps, the sweet strains borne on the night air lulled us to repose.

A Colonel, Major, Sergeant and one private were captured at Benton's Ford on Goose Creek and brought in by Bush. and Samuel Underwood and David Hixon.[5]

Lieut. Norman Smith went to a house which had been occupied as a headquarters by General Howard. One of his aids was still there, sitting at a table, writing a note.

"Good evening, Major," said Smith.

---

[5] *Extracts from Gen. O. O. Howard's Report, Sept. 9, 1863.*

"July 20: The corps marched under orders to Mountville via Mount Gilead, making about 16 miles. During this march the enemy's guerrillas and bushwhackers annoyed us considerably, captured a few stragglers.

"During the 21st the corps remained stationary, sending out scouting parties in different directions, one of which (from General Schurtz) met a detachment of Mosby's guerillas and after a little skirmish recaptured those taken the day before.

"On the 22d a forage train having started before its guard was ready, lost 9 wagons, 8 of which were retaken, but without the animals."

"You have the advantage of me, sir," said the Major, looking up from his writing.

"Yes," said Smith, "I have, for you are my prisoner."

"What command do you belong to?" asked the Major.

"Major Mosby's."

"Why didn't you take the General? You might have done so. He has left but a few moments."

GENERAL O. O. HOWARD, U. S. A.
From a War-time photograph.

The Major did not relish the idea of being taken prisoner, and for a time was rather surly, but he soon found he had companions in misfortune and was disposed to make the best of his situation.

During the night 12 or 15 more men joined us. Early in the morning 3 sutlers' wagons loaded with good things:

14 horses, 1 mule and 47 prisoners were captured near Mount Gilead.

Leaving the prisoners and wagons in a hollow, under guard, Mosby started back to get more. Seeing a few cavalry in a field, our men galloped forward with a yell to attack them, and they fled towards a piece of woods. William Hibbs (usually called " Major " Hibbs), who was in advance, saw a force of infantry in the woods and wheeling his horse, called to our men to come back, but a volley was fired before they had time to obey. A young man named Flynn was shot and fell from his horse, which came out with us sprinkled with its master's blood ; and William Hibbs, Jr., had his horse killed. One of the prisoners, who was within range, was killed, and another fell from his horse and broke his neck as we were moving off.

Orders were given to push on with the prisoners and horses, and the captured wagons were set on fire. We had to move very cautiously, being completely surrounded. Often finding our way blocked by Federal troops, we had to retrace our steps and seek other outlets. When we reached the Snikersville pike a brigade of cavalry was passing, and we had to fall back and lie close until they passed. We succeeded, however, in getting our captures safely to the Bull Run Mountains, and the next morning the prisoners were sent off under guard, in charge of Thomas Lake, to Culpeper Court House.

There was now no time for rest, in the midst of Meade's army on those hot July days—the sun glaring down with intense fierceness, the air filled with dust raised by the steady tramp of the thousands of cavalry and infantry, and the long trains of wagons and batteries of artillery that lumbered along the roads. Our little band was darting in here and out there—at one time making a dash into a wagon train before the guards were aware of our presence, and before they could recover from their surprise dashing off under cover of the woods ; at another time gobbling up some luckless sutler and refreshing ourselves from his stores. Men were covered with dust, through which the perspiration trickled down their faces, making them look more like painted or tattoed savage warriors than civilized beings. The horses were covered with sweat and dust, panting—many with their tongues hanging out, or, like those of their masters, glued to their mouths. Some of the poor animals dropped from exhaustion and the riders were compelled to take to captured horses, and in some straits even to mount captured mules.

Although our presence in the army was known and felt, as we were constantly changing our position—scurrying off from one point to another—it was impossible to locate us. We made a dash at General Sedgwick's headquarters and carried off some fine horses and mules.

J. WM. DEAR, CO. D.

Captured in Loudoun Co. and sent to Fort McHenry by Gen. Sheridan, not to be exchanged until after the war.

From a photograph taken after the war.

On the 24th we captured a few prisoners and 33 mules within one hundred yards of General Howard's headquarters. Thomas Burke's horse gave out and he mounted a captured mule. The poor brute was soon shot from under him, and we are of the favored few who can answer affirmatively that well known query: "Who ever saw a dead mule?"

It was now impossible to send the prisoners South, and Major Mosby could not spare the men to send them off in small squads as they were being brought in, so a temporary camp had to be established on the Bull Run Mountains, a short distance north of Hopewell Gap. The prisoners pitched their little shelter tents on the mountain side and we compelled them to cut off small branches of trees and spread over them so as to hide them from the view of the army passing along in sight of the camp. At times they would sing and make as much noise as possible to attract the attention of the Federal soldiers, but no attempt was made to release or recapture them, although threats were made that a force would be sent to scour the mountains and drive us out.  The prisoners, seeing parties of our men constantly coming in with other prisoners during the few days the army was passing, were afraid to risk an attempt to escape.  One of them said to me, while speaking of the small force guarding them :

" You could keep us here almost without a guard, for we know nothing about the roads, and would not be able to find our way out ; and if we did, your men are scattered in all directions, so that we would either be shot or recaptured."

Nearly 200 horses and mules were captured.

As soon as the Federal army had passed, 153 prisoners, including a number of officers, were sent South under a guard of 17 men, and all reached their destination safely.[6]

On the evening of July 30th, at Fairfax Court-House and in its vicinity, Mosby, with about 30 men, captured sutlers' wagons and other property, together with a number of prisoners.  Collecting together 29 wagons filled with rich stores, Mosby attempted to bring them off.  He had suc-

---

[6] *Report of Major John S. Mosby to General Stuart.*

*Fauquier Co., Va., July 28, 1863.*

" I sent you in charge of Sergeant [F.] Beattie, 141 prisoners which we captured from the enemy during their march through this county.  I also sent off 45 several days ago ; included in the number, 1 major, a captain, and 2 lieutenants.  I also captured 123 horses and mules, 12 wagons (only 3 of which I was able to destroy), 50 sets of fine harness, arms, etc."

[Indorsements.]

HDQRS. CAVALRY DIVISION, ARMY NORTHERN VA., *July    , 1863.*

Respectfully referred to the War Department for its information. Mosby has richly won another grade and I hope it will be conferred.

J. E. B. STUART, *Major Gen.*

HEADQUARTERS, *Culpeper, July 31, 1863.*

Respectfully forwarded for the information of the department, and as evidence of the merit and activity of Major Mosby and his command.

R. E. LEE, *General.*

ceeded in bringing them up the Little River Turnpike as
far as Mt. Zion Church, when he was overtaken by Colonel
Lowell with a detachment of the Second Massachusetts
Cavalry, which had started out from Centreville in pursuit,
and Mosby was compelled to relinquish his captures and retreat, with a loss of one man wounded and one prisoner.[7]
[See Mosby's Report, Note 8.]

---

[7] *Report of Col. Chas. R. Lowell, Jr., Second Massachusetts Cavalry.*

*Centreville, July 31, 1863.*

I have the honor to report that immediately upon receiving from you the
information that Mosby had been seen upon the Little River pike I ordered
Captain Manning, with 30 men, to proceed by Old Road to Aldie, and picket
quietly the approaches from the east ; I at the same time made the desired
detail (Lieutenant Stone and 20 men) to go with the ambulances to Davis' hospital. At 8.30 p. m. started with 150 men along Old Road toward Aldie.
Arriving at Gum Springs road, sent Lieutenant Manning, with 20 men, to pass
through Gum Springs and picket the road from there to Little River pike, thus
hoping to stop all escape by the north, if Mosby attempted to return. Reached
Aldie myself about one a. m.; communicated with Captain Manning and
Lieutenant Stone, and went into bivouac in the woods one mile east of town.

At daybreak was aroused by firing to the eastward. Moved out upon the
road in time to meet my pickets, with some of Lieutenant Manning's detachment pursued by about 20 or 25 rebels. Started after the rebels immediately.
They scattered, 4 or 5 going down the road, the rest taking to the fields. Sent
a party after the latter and followed down the road at a smart pace. After 3
miles ride came up to the wagon train where the first firing had occurred.

Mosby, however, had made off when we appeared on the top of the most
distant hill. Followed 3 miles farther, taking road to the south and then sent
a detachment but couldn't overtake him, though he was embarrassed by
prisoners.

It seems that Mosby, with about 75 men and a sutler's train captured at
Fairfax, moving west along the Little River pike, reached the junction with the
Gum Springs road 4 miles from Aldie just as Lieutenant Manning arrived from
the north. Lieutenant Manning at once attacked, and with only 6 or 8 men
charged Mosby's advance guard in upon the wagons, and charged through to
the rear of the train, losing 2 killed, 2 wounded and 2 prisoners. Mosby's
advance, on recovering from their surprise, and seeing the small force, attacked
the rest of Lieutenant Manning's men and followed them till met by the other
force advancing as above.

After getting the ambulances and sutlers' train started for Centreville under
a guard, I took the turnpike westward, and then the Old Carolina road southward till I struck Mosby's trail running up into Bull Run mountains. Followed
it over the ridge and came upon all the prisoners (2 privates from my squadron
and 7 non-commissioned officers from Pennsylvania Cavalry regiment taken at
Fairfax Court House) ; also took about 20 of Mosby's horses, some of them

I was one of the men detailed to go South as guard with the prisoners captured while Meade's army was marching through Loudoun, and on my return learned that Mosby had continued his active operations in Fairfax, as may be seen by the accompanying reports of captures on the 3d and 11th of August.[8]

On the 24th of August, Mosby with 35 men came upon a detachment of the Second Massachusetts Cavalry, who were taking a drove of horses to the Federal Army. They had halted to water the horses at Billy Gooding's Tavern on the Little River Turnpike, 10 miles from Alexandria. Mosby decided to attack them and make a large capture if possible, or at least stampede their horses and disarrange their plans. He divided his force, sending Lieutenant Turner to attack

saddled, but was much disappointed not to capture a single rebel—[not] one of his men. They took to the woods which are very thick in the mountains.

I have to report 2 killed, 2 wounded not severely, and 1 man missing (he was taken prisoner but escaped into the woods himself and has not reappeared). Of the rebels we are sure of 5 wounded. The sutlers report some killed, but I didn't see them.

CHAS. R. LOWELL, JR.,
*Colonel Second Massachusetts Cavalry.*

ZACH. F. JONES, CO. D.

[8] *Mosby's Report to Stuart.*

*Fauquier Co., Va., Aug. 4, 1863.*

I send over in charge of Sergeant Beattie about 30 prisoners captured on an expedition into Fairfax, from which I have just returned. Most of them were taken at Padgett's, near Alexandria. I also captured about 30 wagons brought off about 70 horses and mules, having only ten men with me. We lost a great many on the way back, as we were compelled to travel narrow, unfrequented paths. Among the captures were three sutlers' wagons.

At Fairfax Court House a few nights ago I captured 29 loaded sutlers' wagons, about 100 prisoners and 140 horses. I had brought all off safely near Aldie, where I fell in with a large force of the enemy's cavalry, who recaptured

them in front, while he fell on their rear. The combined charge routed the guards, with the exception of a few who took shelter in the tavern and fired from the windows until their ammunition was exhausted, when they surrendered. We lost 2 killed—Lieutenant Norman Smith and Charles E. Shriver.

Lieutenant Norman Smith, of the Black Horse Cavalry, was a son of Blackwell Smith, of Fauquier County; he was

---

them. The enemy had several hundred. I had only 27 men. We killed and captured several. My loss: one wounded and captured.

Respectfully, your obedient servant,

JNO. S. MOSBY, *Major Commanding.*

[Indorsement.]

HEADQUARTERS ARMY NORTHERN VIRGINIA, *August 17, 1863.*

Respectfully forwarded for the information of the War Department.
This bold Partisan leader deserves promotion.

J. E. B. STUART, *Major-General.*

HEADQUARTERS, *August 18, 1863.*

Respectfully forwarded for the information of the War Department.
I greatly commend Major Mosby for his boldness and good management. I fear he exercises but little control over his men. He has latterly carried but too few on his expeditions apparently, and his attention has been more attracted toward the capture of wagons than military damage to the enemy. His attention has been called to this. R. E. LEE, *General.*

Col. A. H. GRIMSHAW to Brigadier-General KING, August 3, 1863: "The following just received: 'Fairfax Court House has been surrounded all day by Mosby's guerrillas. Every team going down and returning has been captured. They are 200 strong. They are trying to get to the mountains with their booty.'
" MOSES SWEETER."

PLEASONTON to HUMPHREYS, August 2, 1863: " General Custer also states that he has sent a party of 300 picked men under an excellent officer to hunt up Mosby. He has strong hopes they will either capture Mosby or drive him out of the country. No bushwhackers have appeared on our left."

*Centreville, August 4, 1863.*

SIR: The cavalry sent out yesterday to look after the guerrillas said to be at or near Fairfax Court House, have returned to camp. One party moved by Fairfax Station to Burke's Station, and thence to the pike and Court House; the second party proceeded by way of Fox Mills to the Court House, and the third went directly along the pike, all three rendezvousing at the Court House about 11 a. m. None of them saw more than two or three guerrillas. The

a splendid scout and had distinguished himself by his bravery under General Ewell. In his report of this affair Mosby says:

"Among the killed was Norman Smith, who thus early terminating a career of great usefulness and of brilliant promise, has left the memory of a name that will not be forgotten till honor, virtue, courage, all, shall cease to claim the homage of the heart."

Charles Eltinge Shriver was only 17 years of age, but had proved himself a gallant young soldier. He was a son of Charles Shriver, of Frederick City, Maryland, and was a nephew of General Edward Shriver, who served in the Federal Army during the war.

MAJOR-GEN. GEO. G. MEADE, U. S. A.

Mosby was shot through the side and thigh. He was carried to the woods and attended by Dr. Dunn, our surgeon. Joseph Calvert was shot in the ankle, and two or three others received trifling wounds.

---

second party heard that a band of 30 or 40, with some 20 mules in their possession, had passed Fox Mills up toward Frying Pan. Our cavalry pursued them vigorously to Frying Pan, but could not overtake them. Major Forbes, who commanded our forces, is confident that the entire marauding party will not exceed 40 or 50 men, and had not more than 20 or 30 mules.

RUFUS KING.

*Report of Major John S. Mosby, C. S. A.*

*Culpeper, August 20, 1863.*

On Tuesday, August 11, I captured a train of 19 wagons near Annandale, in Fairfax County. We secured the teams and a considerable portion of the most valuable stores, consisting of saddles, bridles, harness, &c. We took about 25 prisoners.

Respectfully, your obedient servant,

JNO. S. MOSBY, *Major.*

*Report of Colonel Lowell (Federal).*

*August 12, 1863.*

"Mosby's and White's men, together about 140 strong, came down the Little River turnpike the day before yesterday and passed the night near Gum

The Federals lost 3 killed, 3 wounded, and 12 prisoners. Over 100 horses were captured, but only 85 were brought out.  (See Mosby's Report, Appendix, IV.)

Lieutenant Turner, with the greater portion of the command, pushed on with the prisoners and horses, while a few trusty followers remained with Mosby, who could travel but slowly, owing to the painful nature of his wounds.

Colonel Lowell started from Centreville with a force of cavalry in pursuit.  On their approach, Mosby was carried into the pines, where he lay concealed until his pursuers passed by endeavoring to overtake Turner with the prisoners and captured horses.  After the Federal cavalry had passed out of sight, Mosby was taken up in their rear and removed South.

---

Springs.  Moved down yesterday forenoon through Ox Road Junction toward Flint Hill.  Hearing that our pickets were there, turned to the north again and passing through Vienna by Mills' Cross Roads to the Little River pike near Gooding's Tavern ; captured one sutlers' train there between 3 and 4 p. m., and another about a mile further east.  An hour later half plundered some of the wagons, took all the horses and mules, and started back in a hurry through Vienna toward Hunter's Mill.  About one mile south of the mill they divided, half going toward Dranesville, the other by Hunter's Mill, nearly down to Chantilly, then turned to the right, and, I presume, passed through Gum Springs early this a. m."

# CHAPTER V.

In the absence of Major Mosby, Lieutenant Turner, of Company A, was in command, Captain Foster having been captured by a raiding party a day or two after his election.

Turner was an active and efficient officer and proved himself fully capable of fulfilling the duties of his position.

*Saturday, September 5th.*—Turner, with 40 men, set out to attack a picket post at Gaskins' Mill, on Carter's Run, near Waterloo.[1]

We proceeded leisurely along, not wishing to reach the vicinity of the federal camps until after night had set in. We then moved along quietly, and arrived at our destination about midnight. Turner went forward with the guide

---

[1] *Skirmish at Carter's Run—Federal Reports.*

September 6th, 1863.

I forward herewith a report of casualties that resulted from an attack of the enemy on the pickets of the First Brigade at Carter's Run at 1 o'clock this a. m.

At about dark last night an attack was made on the pickets of the Second Brigade, on the right of the line on Aestham river ; the attack was repulsed without loss.

D. McM. GREGG.

In the attack at Carter's Run one officer and one corporal killed and 5 men captured ; 20 horses and 3 mules captured. The officer was Lieutenant Lyon, First Pennsylvania Cavalry.

The cause of this surprise was due to the sentinel leaving his post without firing his piece or giving any alarm ; he is in confinement and charges are preterred against him.

I have directed Colonel McIntosh to go after the rebels at Middleburg and Upperville.

A. PLEASANTON.

to observe the position of the enemy and arrange his plans
for the attack. Getting between the camp and the reserve
picket, we charged upon them, killing 3, wounding a number, and bringing out 7 prisoners, 25 horses and 3 mules.

There were two regiments of cavalry camped a short distance from the post, and after the alarm was given we could
hear the officers giving orders to the men to "Fall in."
Turner had no one injured, but lost one man, C. A. Fox,
who wandered off in the darkness and was captured.

On the night of September 16th Lieutenant Turner captured 4 sutlers' wagons, 12 horses and 2 mules. There was

a great quantity of sutlers'
goods of every description,
and the men loaded them-
selves with as much as they
could carry off, and then set
fire to the wagons and the remainder of the goods. The
capture took place at Fayetteville, five miles from Warrenton.

About this time Mosby re-
turned to the command, having nearly recovered from the
effects of his wounds.

**C. A. FOX, CO. A.**
From a photograph taken in 1878.

On the 21st of September
Mosby was again in the sad-
dle, and we started for a raid on the Orange and Alexandria
Railroad. We halted at night near Warrenton Junction,
got some hay for our horses, and lay in the woods until daylight on the morning of the 22d, when we mounted and
moved on to within about two miles of Bealeton Station,
where we again halted in the pines, while Mosby, Wm. R.
Smith, John Edmonds and Walter Whaley went out to reconnoitre. They observed a long train of pontoons moving
in the direction of the Rappahannock, each truck drawn by
eight mules, and all so heavily guarded that we could not
attack. We could hear the drums beating, the bugles
sounding, and the rumbling of the trains along the railroad.

Knowing these pontoons were going to Meade's army, and that they indicated the intention of the Federals to attempt the crossing of the river, Mosby immediately despatched Sergeant Horace Johnson to General Lee with the information, and we marched off to Auburn.

While sitting on our horses in front of a saw-mill, a squad of 7 Federal cavalrymen came in sight from towards Catlett Station. Lieutenant Turner and a few of the men immediately started in pursuit. The Federals drew their sabres and used the flat sides to belabor their horses, while they vigorously plied the spurs and succeeded in making their escape.

Finding the railroad too heavily guarded for us to attempt any demonstration, Mosby determined to abandon that line and strike out through Fairfax. At Buckland, Mosby sent Lieutenant Turner back to Fauquier with the greater portion of the command, while he detailed 20 men to go with him to Fairfax. Our march led us over the old battlefield of Manassas. Here we met a party of thirty-odd Federal cavalrymen returning to their camp at Centreville, we judged from a plundering expedition, as they were leading some 12 or 15 horses. We concealed ourselves behind a little hill until they drew sufficiently near, and then charged them with a yell. They made no resistance—their only thought appeared to be how they should get away. We succeeded, however, in capturing 9 prisoners and 12 horses. The horses were newly branded, and all the equipments were new. In the pursuit the men got separated—some who were leading captured horses being left behind, and Mosby continued his march with only 15 men.

Near Burke's Station we saw a number of mules grazing in a field near an infantry camp. The guard was captured and 8 mules driven off in sight of the infantry, who stood looking on in amazement without making the slightest effort to recapture them.

On the night of September 28th, 1863, Mosby with 5 or 6 men proceeded down Fairfax with the intention of capturing Governor Pierpont. Arriving at his house near Alexandria he learned that the Governor had gone to Washington that

evening. Not wishing to return without accomplishing
something, he went to the residence of Colonel Dulany, aide
to Governor Pierpont, and taking that gentleman prisoner,
sent him to Richmond. French Dulany, a son of Colonel
Dulany, was a member of Mosby's command and was present and aided in the capture of his father. A bridge over
Four Mile Run was burned on the homeward route. [See
Mosby's Report, Appendix, IV.]

A meeting of the command was held at Scuffleburg[2] on the
1st of October, 1863. Up to this time Company A comprised the Battalion, but Mosby now thought there were
men enough for two companies. The men were drawn up
in line and 60 selected to go into an election for officers of
Company B. William R. Smith, of Fauquier, a lieutenant
in the Black Horse Cavalry, was chosen as captain; Franklin Williams, of Fairfax, First Lieutenant; Albert Wrenn, of
Fairfax, Second Lieutenant, and Robert Gray, of Loudoun,
Third Lieutenant.

In Company A Joseph H. Nelson was elected Third
Lieutenant, to fill the vacancy occasioned by the death of
Lieutenant George Whitescarver, who was killed at Seneca,
Maryland.

*Friday, October 9th.*—Mosby started from Rector's X
Roads with 40 men, and marching in the direction of Fairfax, bivouacked at night in the pines near Frying Pan. After
lying concealed in the pine forest all day, fearing the enemy
might become aware of our presence, we moved off after
nightfall to a point near Guilford, where we halted, fed our
horses, and a little before day on Sunday morning, the 11th,
rode out near the turnpike about 5 or 6 miles from Alexandria. While the command was concealed in the thick pines
a few hundred yards from the turnpike, Mosby and Walter
Whaley hid in some bushes by the roadside where they
could observe what was passing, and Captain Smith, with
John Munson, took a like position further up the road. Soon
a body of about 250 cavalry passed, which proved to be the

---

[2] Scuffleburg was situated in a hollow of the Blue Ridge, between Paris and
Markham, and the *burg* consisted of a blacksmith shop, with residence, and a
wheelwright shop.

escort of a long train of wagons that came lumbering along in their rear.

At this point there was an ugly hole in the road which the teams had difficulty in passing, and the third wagon from the rear stalled and blocked the way so that the other two could not pass.

As the column moved on without waiting for the stalled team, Mosby and Whaley rode out and ordered the wagons driven into the woods. Captain Smith also captured a stray wagon which came on at some distance behind the train. The prize was a rich one to the hungry Rangers, who had been kept waiting so long in the pine forest. The wagons were loaded with clothing, coffee, tea, sugar, cheese; cans of meat, oysters, sardines, fruits; boxes of cakes and crackers, tobacco, segars, stationery, and a general variety of goods such as were usually found among the sutlers' stores. Each man helped himself to what pleased him best, and it was amusing to see the men pick up one thing and then throw it away to take something

CAPT. WILLIAM R. SMITH, CO. B.
Killed in an attack on Cole's Camp, Loudoun Heights, January 10, 1864.

else which took their fancy. We could not take all, and it was hard to decide what was most necessary or profitable. There was but one article that all felt a common interest in, and that was a lot of one hundred and thirty pairs of boots.

While this was going on, our picket gave the alarm and a solitary Jersey wagon coming along was overhauled and brought in. In it was a Mr. Dunham and wife, returning

from an unsuccessful trip to Alexandria, where they had
gone to purchase groceries, but had been refused permission by the authorities.  We not only gave them our sympathy—something that is freely given by most persons to
their fellow creatures in want—but we also gave a more
substantial expression of feeling which was more gratifying
to this couple.  We loaded up their wagon free of cost and
sent them on their way rejoicing.  We then returned to
Fauquier.

Mosby was a brave man, and as a scout he was unsurpassed.  He was generally taciturn, particularly towards
strangers.  At times he was quite talkative and very agreeable, while at others he would scarcely answer a question put to him.  In conversation his voice was low, his utterances usually slow and distinct, but when conversing on a subject in which he took more than an ordinary interest he became quite a rapid talker.  He spoke plainly and to the point, and there was no mistaking the meaning of his words.  He had a pleasant face, white and reg-

HARRY BROCK, CO. D.
From a picture taken after the war.

ular teeth, and keen, restless eyes, which seemed an index to
the mind.   I have often watched him as he would stand in-
tently gazing at a man—staring as though he were reading
him through with those eyes, like a book, and then only
removing his gaze as he walked off apparently satisfied with

the result of his conclusion or decision as to the man's worth or character. His reasoning was good and the conclusions arrived at were generally correct, yet he was very set in his opinions, and when he had once made up his mind it was hard to change. In his manner he was plain and unassuming. Cool in danger, quick to think and practical in carrying out his ideas—these were qualities which aided materially in his success.

There was a rich vein of humor running through his nature so close to the surface that it required but little digging to reach it, and no schoolboy ever enjoyed a bit of fun with keener relish than Mosby. Sometimes, when on the march, we would turn into the woods and stop to rest the tired horses. On such occasions Mosby would often call on John Sinclair to describe the capture of a sutler's train. Sinclair was a clever actor and could not only suit the action to the word, but possessed sufficient power of mimicry to show off the little peculiarities of the different sutlers in their fright and their vain attempts to escape. Mosby would walk up to Sinclair with a smile and say : " How was it, John? Let's have it about those sutlers." Then Sinclair would proceed, throwing his arms wildly about and illustrating the alarm and excitement of the sutlers ; would tell how a big wagon would stop in the road while a little two-horse wagon came rushing down ; then the war of words: " Drive on! What are you stopping up the road for ?" " What in the hell are you about ?" " There now, you've broke my tongue!" " Don't run into my wagon!" " Don't *you* run your mules into *my* wagon!" " You've run your mules through mine!" " Now, we're all tangled up!" One old fellow comes along spurring and lashing up his horses—" There they come! 'Taint no use to run! They've got us all!" He would picture the scene so naturally that Mosby and all around would roar with laughter, making the old woods ring.

Mosby was greatly annoyed by men in the regular service wishing to join him. They would send applications requesting him to procure transfers for them, or seeking to know if he would receive them in the event of their resigning positions. At meetings letters would be handed him, which he would open and on seeing from their beginning that they were of this character, often, without reading further, he would tear them up, saying he did not wish to be bothered with them ; that if the writers were anxious to join his command they could come and see him and he could then tell better what he would do.

At one of the meetings a young man walked up to Mosby and extending his hand, said :

" How are you, Major?"

" How are you?" said Mosby, looking up, thrusting his hands into his pockets, and surveying him from head to foot.

" I came here to join you, Major."

" Where are you from?"

" I belonged to McNeil."

" What are you doing here?" said Mosby.

" Want to join your command." At the same time the young man mentioned something about a transfer or furlough.

" Where's your paper?" said Mosby ; " let me see it."

It was handed him, and looking at the date he raised his eyes, saying :

" Where have you been all this time? "

He said he had been getting horses, and that he had several.

" I don't want you," said Mosby. " Go back to your command, and don't tell people you are one of ' Mosby's Men'—that you belong to my command. I heard you robbed a Yankee deserter of $2.50. I don't want you with me."

" I never did such a thing," said the man.

" Don't you live at Smith's?"

" Yes."

" Then you are the man ; I don't want you," and tearing up the paper, Mosby turned his back and walked away.

*Friday, October 16.*—Mosby went on a raid down in Fairfax County. Leaving Company B camped in the woods near Frying Pan, he took Company A, and at Stuarts, near

Chantilly, on the turnpike above Fairfax Court House, captured about 40 prisoners and 64 horses and mules. A Federal lieutenant was killed by Edward Hurst, but no other casualities occurred on either side.[3]

Sending the prisoners and horses out with Company A, Mosby remained behind with Company B, capturing a picket post of 9 men and horses on the turnpike at the crossing of the old Ox Road.

As Mosby was riding along the road he saw a Federal colonel a short distance ahead. Thinking he had a prize, Mosby dashed up and found himself within about twenty yards of a regiment of infantry. Wheeling his horse, he came off in a hurry. The infantry fired at him, without effect.

The Federal army now falling back towards Alexandria, Mosby found himself surrounded on all sides. A complete chain of camps was around him, with a line of vedettes, one at every two hundred yards, through which he must pass to get out. The enemy were aware of his being inside their lines, and endeavored to trap him.

---

[3] *Fairfax Court House, Va., October 17, 1863.*

General MEADE, *Headquarters :*

I sent out the two companies of cavalry at this post, on the different roads, to warn me of the approach of any enemy; and just learn that 15 men were captured about 5 miles from here, on the Chantilly road, by about 75 cavalry under Mosby. Three have escaped and arrived here. I am sending out 4 companies of infantry. I have no cavalry. I have sent word to Colonel Lowell.                    MICHAEL CORCORAN,
                                                            *Brigadier-General.*

The following received from Colonel Lowell, at Vienna :
                                                            *October 18.*

We have taken one of Mosby's men this morning, who says that Mosby, with 275 men, is prowling around below here to take supply trains. It will be well to delay all wagon trains without heavy escort till something more definite is learned about Mosby's movements. If you could post strong infantry pickets at points between here and Fairfax, Mosby might be ambushed on his way back.                    C. R. LOWELL, JR.

I will communicate the above to General Buford, commanding cavalry, and General Griffin, commanding corps now stationed here. I have just learned that a company of our cavalry has been attacked about 3 miles from here toward Alexandria, and the Captain captured.

                                            MICHAEL CORCORAN,
                                            *Brigadier-General Commanding.*

Going to Lieutenant Williams, who was in command of Co. B, in the absence of Captain Smith, Mosby told him he must lead the company out while he drew the attention of the enemy in another direction. Mosby then rode out in view of the enemy and started at a gallop down the turnpike towards Alexandria, the Federal cavalry in pursuit.

Lieutenant Williams led the company along to Gantts Hill, where he suddenly came out on the vedette, saying:

" Is all quiet?"

" Yes," said the soldier, looking at him, thrown completely off his guard by the suddenness of his appearance and also by his question. Before he could recover from his surprise Williams was at his side with a pistol at his head. He was taken from his post, and the command came through safely, bringing out 27 prisoners and 18 horses. Mosby also came out, after a close race.

*Thursday, October 22.* — Lieut. Frank Williams, with Charles Mason, Dr. Ed. Stratton, John H. Barnes and Robert Harrover, were scouting inside the enemy's lines in

JOHN H. BARNES, CO. D.
From a photograph taken after the war.

Fairfax, when they discovered a number of United States horses grazing in a field near a Federal camp. They attempted to drive them off, when they were seen by a citizen, who reported their presence to the officers at the camp, and a detachment of about 40 men of the California Battalion and Baker's Rangers were sent to capture them. The Federals approached through a thick woods and were within fifty yards of the Partisans before they were observed. Lieutenant Williams and his party attempted to escape, but their horses being tired out by a march of 40 miles, as well as by several lively races from pickets during the night, they were soon run down by the Federals with their horses fresh from the camp. Charles Mason was killed, and Dr. Stratton, Barnes and Harrover were taken prisoners.[4] Lieutenant Williams alone escaped, but lost his horse. Finding himself so closely pressed, he rode up to a high fence, sprang from his horse, leaped over the fence and made his way off on foot, sheltered from the shots of the enemy by the heavy timber.

Robert M. Harrover was taken to Washington and tried by a Military Commission "for leaving Washington City after he had been enrolled, and attaching himself to a band of guerrillas." He played his part in the farce of a trial which followed and was sentenced to be shot. This sentence was afterwards commuted to imprisonment in the Albany Penitentiary for ten years. He had been confined for eight months in the Carroll Prison and two months in the Old Capitol, and

ROBERT M. HARROVER, CO. D.

as the time approached for his removal to the Albany Penitentiary he determined to make an effort to escape. He and a fellow prisoner named Harrison, a Mississippian belonging to the Jeff Davis Legion, made a rope of their bed clothes, and on the night of August 19th, 1864, lowered themselves from an upper window to the pavement,

---

[4] *Report of Col. Lafayette C. Baker, First District of Columbia Cavalry.*

*Near Annandale, Oct. 22, 1863.*

This morning about 10 o'clock a detachment of my battalion, under command of Major E. J. Conger, and a detachment of the California Battalion under command of Captain Eigenbrodt, encountered a squad of Mosby's men some three miles this side of Fairfax Court House, and near the Little River turnpike. One of Mosby's men (named Charles Mason) was shot and instantly killed. The celebrated guerrilla Jack Barnes, Ed. Stratton and Bill Harrover, were captured and forwarded to the Old Capitol Prison. These men state that they were looking for government horses and sutlers' wagons. None of our force were injured.

when the sentinel's back was towards them in pacing his beat, and escaped in the darkness.  As they touched the ground and ran off in opposite directions the guard turned and snapped his gun at them.  Harrover sought the house of a friend, where he was furnished with civilian's clothes and passed out through Georgetown.  Near Rockville he overtook a party of young Marylanders on their way South. He joined them, and being provided with firearms, they captured a picket post, mounted the horses, and crossing the Potomac, were soon safe in " Dixie land."[5]

*Tuesday, October 27th.*—Mosby left Salem (now called Marshall) at 6 P. M., with about 50 men, and two miles below Warrenton discovered a large train of wagons, guarded by two regiments of infantry, which were in the front and rear of the train.  He divided his men into three parties, and coming out on the side of the train, those in front, under Captain William H. Chapman, stopped the wagons, while others set to work unhitching the mules and horses.  This operation occupied but a few moments, and before the guards were fully aware of the cause of the stoppage, Mosby was on his homeward journey.[6]  The teamsters

---

[5] After the close of the war Harrover applied for pardon and his application was at first rejected, but afterwards being favorably considered, he received the following notice of his pardon and that he would be paroled on the same footing with other Confederate soldiers :

<table>
<tr><td>GENERAL COURT MARTIAL } <br> ORDERS, No. 71. }</td><td>WAR DEPARTMENT, } <br> ADJUTANT GENERAL'S OFFICE, } <br> *Washington, March 10, 1866.* }</td></tr>
</table>

In the case of Robert M. Harrover, citizen, sentenced by a Military Commission " To be shot to death by musketry, at such time and place as the Secretary of War may direct ; " two-thirds of the Commission concurring therein, which sentence was commuted " To confinement at hard labor in the penitentiary for ten years," as promulgated in General Court Martial Orders, No. 314, War Department, Adjutant General's Office, October 3, 1864, the sentence is hereby remitted, and he will be paroled, as recommended by Lieutenant-General Grant, upon taking the oath of allegiance.

By order of the President of the United States.

E. D. TOWNSEND,
*Assistant Adjutant General.*

---

[6] *Report of Major John S. Mosby.*

*Fauquier, Oct. 27, 1863.*

Last night I attacked a long wagon train of the enemy hauling stores for the army at Warrenton, from their depot of supplies at Gainesville.  The point of

made signals to give the alarm, and a regiment of cavalry was afterwards sent in pursuit and came into Salem next morning, but too late to overtake Mosby, who had carried off nearly 200 mules and 40 horses, with their harness. A

A STRAGGLER FROM THE YANKEE CAMP.

great many of the mules and horses were lost in driving them out, but some were picked up several days afterwards. One hundred and twenty mules, 27 horses, 17 white and 16 negro prisoners were secured, however, together with a large quantity of harness. Not a shot was fired. The cap-

attack was about the center of the train (which had a heavy guard of cavalry, artillery and infantry both in front and rear), on the pike about 2 miles from New Baltimore and Warrenton where there are large Yankee camps.

After unhitching the teams of from 40 to 50 wagons I started them off under charge of Lieutenant Turner, remaining behind myself with a few men with the intention of burning the wagons. A force of Federal cavalry appearing prevented the accomplishment of my purpose. We succeeded in bringing off 145 horses and mules and upward of 30 negroes and Yankees (among them 1 captured horses were divided among the men, and the mules, prisoners and negroes sent to General Stuart's headquarters. When they were brought in Stuart was much pleased, and said :

" Hurrah for Mosby ! This is a good haul. Mules ! and fat, too ! "

Late Saturday night, Oct. 31, two correspondents of the New York *Herald*, L. A. Hendricks and George A. Hart, were captured at the house of Mr. McCormick, in Auburn. Mosby gave them permission to write letters home. In Appendix, XXXIII., will be found one of those letters as published in the *Herald*. This gives a full account of the capture, etc., and being written by one of the correspondents, will be of greater interest than any other account I can furnish.

---

tain) to a place of safety. Many of the captured animals were lost in the night march, but I have sent out a party which I am in hopes will succeed in recovering some of them. I sent to you yesterday 6 cavalrymen whom I captured near Manassas. In the affair of the wagons I had 50 men.

Respectfully, etc.,

JNO. S. MOSBY, *Major*.

[Indorsements.]

Respectfully forwarded for the information of the commanding general.

This is but another instance of Major Mosby's skill and daring in addition to those forwarded almost daily.

J. E. B. STUART.

*Nov. 3, 1863.*

Noted with admiration at the fearlessness and skill of this gallant partisan.

J. A. SEDDON, *Secretary*,

General MEADE to HALLECK : " Last night a supply train coming from the depot at Gainesville was attacked between New Baltimore and Warrenton, and some 100 animals taken from it. The train had an escort, which was in front and rear, but was unable to reach the center of the train before the guerrillas had made off with the animals. The wagons were left untouched."

# CHAPTER VI.

November and December, 1863.—Certificates of Membership Issued—Deserters and Horse Thieves—The Rangers enter Wagon Camp near Warrentown—Unhitch Mules but couldn't get them out—Turner and the Sutler—Capture Five Wagons loaded with Medical Stores near Bealeton Station—Federal Cavalry in pursuit—They surround a house where some of "Mosby's Men" stop, and Richards fights his way out—The "Charley Binns Raid"—Good Haul of Mules at Brandy Station—Capture of Picket on Hazel River—Company C organized—Close of the year 1863.

*Monday, November 2, 1863.*—There was a meeting of the command at Rectortown. We were drawn up in line and letters from Generals Lee and Stuart, complimentary to Mosby and his command, were read by Capt. Wm. H. Chapman. The men were furnished with printed certificates of membership signed by Mosby. This was now a necessity, because men wearing Confederate uniforms, many of them deserters or absent from their commands without leave, were roaming about the country representing themselves as belonging to Mosby's command. The Major told us to arrest all horse thieves and deserters found and bring them to him.

The region of country in which Mosby operated being disputed territory outside of the lines, was left entirely unprotected during the war by the civil and military authorities on both sides, and but for the presence of "Mosby's Men" the defenseless people would have been at the mercy of the roving bands of deserters left in the tracks of both armies as they passed back and forth over the country, from Washington to Richmond and Fredericksburg. The mountains were infested with horse thieves and desperadoes, who were ready to prey upon the inhabitants, regardless as to whether their sympathies were with the North or South. "Mosby's Men" performed the duties of police as well as soldiers, and were the sole guardians of the territory; while Mosby, acting as military ruler and also as judge, not only kept the lawless element in check, but also settled differences between individuals, without the tedious process of litigation, and without fear or favor.

On the night of November 6th, Mosby with 40 men made a descent on a wagon camp near Warrenton. There was a heavy infantry guard at the camp and sentinels were pacing around on all sides: it was necessary to remove one in order to permit the passage of a party to unfasten the mules and horses from the wagons. This was readily accomplished by Montjoy, and about 200 mules and horses were unhitched in a very short time, but after they were loosed it was found impossible to lead or drive them. Coming to a little ditch they refused to cross and ran about

**Headquarters Mosby's Battalion,**

**Partizan Rangers,** *Nov. 2* 186*3*

**This is to Certify,** *That James J. Williamson,*

*is a Member of this Command.*

*Jno. S. Mosby*

*Major Commanding Partizan Rangers.*

THE AUTHOR'S CERTIFICATE OF MEMBERSHIP.

in great confusion, braying and neighing. This aroused the camp. The startled guards thus waked from their slumbers grasped their arms and fired a volley into the crowd of men and mules, inflicting no injury, however, on the men.

The attempt to bring off all the captured animals had to be abandoned, and only 12 mules and 6 horses were brought away.

*Saturday, November 14.*—Lieutenant Turner, with 5 men, scouting in Fairfax, lay in the woods watching the road between Vienna and Fairfax Court House. In order to prevent anyone from notifying the Federals of their presence, they stopped all persons coming along the road and carried them into the woods.

Among the wagons thus taken in was one sutler's team. His goods were emptied in a pile—gloves, calico, buttons, cakes, crackers, canned goods—a variety store, indeed. One wagon brought in carried a supply of milk and this was seized to wash down the sutler's cakes and pies. Cans of oysters and turkey were broken open with stones and the Rangers regaled themselves, while the sutler, looking on with a melancholy air, said : "Now, you've taken everything, what are you going to do with me? You are not going to take me to Richmond?" "Yes," said one, "you'll have to go." He drew up his face as if in pain and limped around, saying "Oh, I'm sick. I know I'll never live to get there. Gentlemen, I'm really sick." After a while he saw that they were only amusing themselves at his expense and that they did not think him of sufficient importance to burden themselves with the task of taking him to Richmond. He then soon recovered his health.

When leaving, each man put on a pair of new buckskin gloves taken from the stock and extended his hand to bid the sutler good-by. He took the men's hands, but his eyes wandered from the gloved hands to the scattered remnant of his stock lying around and he could find no words to express his feelings, even though he was a sutler.

His little boy hesitated for a moment and then said :

"Well, I suppose I must bid you good-by, but I hope I will never see you again. I always heard the rebels were ragged and dirty, but I suppose since you've got to robbing sutlers you can dress as well as our men."

"Good-by, son ;" said John Sanders, as he trotted off, singing :

> " When I can shoot my rifle clear,
> At Yankees on the roads,
> I'll bid farewell to rags and tags
> And live on Sutlers' loads."

*Friday, November 20th.*—About sunset, Mosby, with Captain Stringfellow, one of General Stuart's scouts, for a guide, started from The Plains with 75 men, passing between New Baltimore and Warrenton, and lay in the pines until daylight. Gregg's Division of Federal Cavalry were then camped in the neighborhood of Warrenton.

At early dawn on the 21st we moved off and halted in the woods, out of sight of the road, near Bealeton Station,

Walter Whaley and John Munson, who were on picket, captured and brought in a courier going from one camp to another with mail and despatches; he also had in his custody, when captured, a prisoner who was condemned to death, and who was therefore greatly rejoiced to fall into our hands.

On one side of us was a cavalry camp and on the other an infantry camp. The rain was falling in torrents and the air was cold and raw, consequently our position was anything but comfortable, as we lay for hours in the woods waiting for a train.

About noon a patrol of 12 men passed along the road. They were suffered to pass unmolested, and in about half an hour 5 wagons were seen coming along, guarded by about 30 cavalry.

Mosby ordered Captain Smith, with Company B, to charge in front of the escort, while Lieutenant Turner, with Company A, was to take them in the rear. Owing to a mistake of the guide, or too great impatience to get at the wagons, both companies came out at nearly the same point, and most of the guard escaped by running down the road, leaving the wagons standing. They were followed until they ran into an infantry picket, who were busily preparing their dinners, and we here gave up the chase. It was too far to attempt to bring out the infantry prisoners, as we would be inside the Federal lines until we passed Warrenton, so they were left behind.

Dr. W. L. DUNN,
(Our Doctor.)
From a War-time photograph.

The wagons were filled with valuable medical stores, and had it been possible we would have brought them off and sent them to General Lee. As it was, a few articles were secured by some of the more thoughtful men and turned over to Dr. Dunn, our surgeon. Twelve prisoners, 10 horses and 17 mules were captured and sent off under guard to Oak Hill, while Company A was detailed to follow on as rear guard.

Captain Stringfellow, A. E. Richards, then a private in Company B, and Ludwell Knapp, of Company A, stopped at the house of Mr. James K. Skinker, about six miles from Warrenton, intending to pass the night, while most of the men crossed the Bull Run Mountains into Fauquier. Detachments of Federal Cavalry were sent in pursuit of us. One of the pursuing parties surrounded Skinker's house, thinking some of our men were there, and fired a number of shots through the doors and windows; then they searched the house from top to bottom.[1]

---

[1] *Report of Brig.-Gen. John C. Robinson, U. S. A., Commanding Second Division, First Army Corps.*

*November 21, 1863.*

ROBINSON to KINGSBURY : " A body of rebel cavalry, variously estimated at from 50 to 100 men, attacked a train of 3 wagons and 2 ambulances on the way to the cavalry camp near Fayetteville about noon to-day. The escort was driven into the picket line of my camp at Liberty, where the pursuing party was arrested. One sergeant was wounded slightly, and one private on an advanced picket post captured. Some 2 or 3 others were captured, but escaped. The Sixteenth Maine Volunteers was immediately sent out, and word sent to General Gregg, who ordered out a squadron of cavalry. The rebel force was dressed in our uniform, and are supposed to belong to Mosby's gang. The animals attached to the wagons were taken off, but they had no time to rifle the wagons. The men on picket behaved well. A fuller report will be sent as soon as possible."

*November 22, 1863*

General GREGG to Col. C. ROSS SMITH : " I have the honor to report that the party sent out yesterday afternoon in pursuit of the guerrillas who made the attack on the wagons going to Fayetteville hotly chased the party to within a mile of Thoroughfare Gap. At about 8 p. m., and when about to be overtaken, the guerrillas scattered to houses. A house in which it was supposed some had taken refuge was surrounded, the door was broken down (admission having been refused) and 3 guerrillas were found. Of these 2 were captured and the other escaped by a back door. One of the captured guerrillas was badly wounded. Seven horses and 2 mules and some U. S. saddles and clothing were recovered. The party that was thus pursued was commanded by a Captain Turner. Mosby is off in the direction of Manassas with the greater portion of his command.

" I have to-day a regiment off toward Salem, where it is reported there is a nest of guerrillas. This regiment has for a guide one of Mosby's men captured two days ago. The guerrilla Lucas, captured last night, has a certificate of

At the first alarm Stringfellow and Knapp ran upstairs, and hiding in the garret, were covered with some loose flooring by a faithful colored servant; but Richards, less fortunate, fell on the stairs.  Being thus left behind, he determined to fight his way out.  With pistols in hand he jumped into the yard, drove off a couple of soldiers who attempted to bar his passage, and escaped on foot in the darkness.  He succeeded in getting a horse from a friend, when he fell in with the same party near Salem, and exchanged shots, but again escaped, with a slight wound in the arm.

*Sunday, November 22.*—A body of cavalry, composed of detachments from the Second Massachusetts and Sixteenth New York, under Colonel Lowell, came last night to the neighborhood of Middleburg, where they were joined by another detachment from the Second Massachusetts Cavalry, the whole force numbering about 300 men.  They were piloted by " Yankee " Davis and Charles Binns.[2]  Binns had been a member of Mosby's command.  While on a drunken frolic he committed some acts of rascality for which

---

membership in the Partisan Rangers signed by Major Mosby.  I hope Lucas will be brought before a military commission and be made an example of.

" In the attack made by Mosby on our pickets at Warrenton 4 days ago, he had 5 men wounded.

" The loss in the escort to the wagons yesterday was 3 men captured."

---

[2] Colonel Lowell, in his report dated Vienna, November 17, says : " The man Binns arrived safely and gives information which leads me to hope that an expedition to start to-morrow will be successful in taking some prisoners."

*Vienna, Nov. 26, 1863.*

LOWELL to TAYLOR : " I have the honor to report that in accordance with your instructions Captain Rumery, with 25 mounted and 75 dismounted men of the Second Massachusetts Cavalry, was on the 18th inst. sent out toward the Blue Ridge to endeavor to capture guerrillas.  He had orders to march chiefly by night, to show only his mounted men by day and keep the presence of the dismounted party an entire secret.  He took as guides Yankee Davis and the deserter Binns.

" The party passed near Frying Pan and Gum Springs, crossed the Negro mountain and Goose Creek to Mountville, thence up the north side of Goose Creek to Rectors Cross Roads.  On Sunday morning at daybreak I joined them by agreement at a point between Middleburg and Rectors Cross Roads, with 100 mounted men, Second Massachusetts Cavalry, and 50 of the Sixteenth New York Cavalry.  Having learned exactly what information Captain Rumery had obtained, Lieutenant Sim, Second Massachusetts Cavalry, with 40 mounted

Mosby ordered his arrest.  In order to escape the punish-
ment he knew he deserved and which he feared Mosby
would inflict, he deserted and fled to the Federal camp in
Fairfax.  Being familiar with the country in the vicinity of
Middleburg, he carried the Federal cavalry around to
places where he knew they were likely to find Confederate
soldiers, particularly those houses where Mosby's men made
their homes.  Some 12 or 15 were captured, most of them
being taken from their beds.

*Thursday, November 26th.*—It being reported that the Federal forces camped at Warrenton had crossed the Rappahannock, and that the whole of Meade's Army was in motion,
Mosby ordered the command to assemble at Rectortown.
One hundred and twenty-five men answered the summons
and marched to Coon's Mill, while Mosby, with Montjoy,
Walter Whaley and Guy Broadwater, went forward to
reconnoitre.  At Brandy Station was a heavy wagon train
with an infantry guard.  Mosby determined to attack the
camp at night.  He ordered Montjoy with one party to fire
the wagons; Captains Smith and William H. Chapman, each
in command of a party, were to drive off the mules.  In the
meantime Lieutenant Turner was to hold the remainder of
the command in reserve, to be in readiness in case of attack.

---

men, was sent northward through Philomont ; Captain Rumery, with another
40, southward through White Plains, across Manassas Gap railroad and back
across Bull Run mountain by Hopewell Gap ; Lieutenant Manning, Second
Massachusetts, with 50 dismounted men, crossed the mountain a few miles
south of Aldie, where Mosby was said to have a rendezvous ; the remainder of
the force to move down the pike and wait for these parties at Mount Zion
Church, near Aldie.  The last party reached the church about midnight and all
returned to camp on Monday night without the loss of a man.

" There were captured (chiefly by Captain Rumery's dismounted party) 18
uniformed soldiers, who claimed to be Mosby's men and were provided with his
passes, though in some cases belonging to regular regiments, 7 notorious smug-
glers and horse thieves, besides one of Mosby's men killed and one prisoner
who escaped, and 35 horses, 13 sets of horse equipments, 25 revolvers of various patterns and 30 army blankets.

"Captain Rumery managed his part of the expedition with great judgment
The deserter Binns proved of great assistance.  As I wish to employ him
again on similar work, and as he shows no unwillingness to expose himself, I
recommend that he be allowed the same pay as other Government scouts while
in my employ."

The wagons were standing around, while beside them the mules were fastened and stood lazily dozing. Some of the teamsters were sleeping, rolled up in their blankets, while others were sitting around the fires, chatting and smoking. The sentinels were quietly taken from their posts, and every precaution used to avoid giving an alarm. As Mosby rode along among the wagons a quartermaster, mistaking him for one of his own men, asked ; " Have they gone ?" " No," said Mosby, "just going." He rode off without the quartermaster discovering his error.

A group of negroes were sitting around one of the fires enjoying the warmth as only negroes can, when Captain Chapman, drawing his revolver, told them he would shoot the first one who made any noise. With trembling voices they begged him not to shoot. In the meantime the men busied themselves in unhitching the mules from the wagons.

One old negro, poking his head out from under his blanket, looking like a huge turtle peering from his shell, said :

" Look heah ! Go 'long 'way frum dem mules. You jes' want to steal one."

Another, observing the gray uniforms by the flickering light of a camp-fire, said in a low voice :

" Hush, Bill ; dem's rebs—dem's Moseley's Men ! "

At length a shot was fired by some one and then ensued a scene of confusion baffling description. Negroes and whites ran wildly about in their alarm. The negroes particularly appeared to be unable to decide on what was to be done—

" Please, Massa, don't shoot ! Which way mus' I run ? "

" Unhitch them mules ! "

" Yes, massa."

Then they would set to work with trembling hands, all the while looking anxiously and fearfully around. Occasionally an order would be heard given to one of them : " Jump on that mule ! " And now and then would be heard a heavy thump as some mischievous mule would land an unfortunate darkey upon the ground and run off, kicking up its heels and braying vehemently.

" Please, massa, don't let me git on dat mule any mo'; he never bin rode befo'."

An Irishman, running up to one of our men, said hurriedly :

" Indade, sur, I niver fired a gun agin yees in my life."

" What the devil are you doing here, then ? "

" I'm a tamester, sur; I'm partly engaged in dhrivin' cattle."

He jumped up behind one of our men and rode off to lend a helping hand in gathering up the scattered mules.

After taking the mules we set fire to the wagons. Amid the confusion one very ugly old negro, awakened by the bustle, put his head out of the wagon, where he had been enjoying a comfortable nap, and seeing his wagon on fire, exclaimed :

" 'Fore God, who dun sot my wagon afire ? " and jumped to the ground.

An individual in the garb of a civilian, with a valise or satchel in his hand, was seen walking off, in the light of the fires. Charley Tyler, thinking he might be a paymaster or a sutler making off with his money or valuables, spurred his horse after him, and,

E. F. WAYMAN, CO. C.
From a photograph taken after the war.

with pistol levelled at his head, called out, "Halt! Halt!" But the man paid no attention to the call and kept on his way, looking neither to the left nor right. Tyler followed for some distance, threatening to shoot if he did not halt and surrender, but at last reined up his horse and returned. One of our men, who had witnessed the affair, said to him as he came up:

"Why didn't you shoot him, Charley?"

With a look of disgust, Tyler answered:

"Do you think I'd shoot such a d—d fool?"

The infantry guarding the train were grouped around their fires when the alarm was given. They seized their arms, and their officers were soon forming them as best they could. Our men were so scattered about the camp in every direction that the firing upon them by the infantry did very little damage. One man received a ball in his thigh, and Mosby's horse was shot in the breast.

FRENCH FRISTOE, CO. B.
From a photograph.

After the command had moved off a short distance from the camp, the whole scene was lighted up by the burning wagons, presenting a picture of war well worthy of an artist's pencil.

We captured 160 mules and 7 horses, with a large quantity of harness; also a number of prisoners, mostly teamsters. Thirty head of cattle were taken, but we were compelled to leave them behind. The large number of wagons and great quantity of supplies burned was a very serious loss to the enemy.

*Friday, November 27.*—A body of Federal cavalry having pitched their camp in the vicinity of the Hazel River, Mosby sent Lieut. Thomas Turner, with Montjoy, Henry S. Ashby and three others, to reconnoitre their position and see what the chances were for a successful foray. Crossing the river,

Turner concealed his men in a thicket while he rode out in view of the camp. A cavalryman, coming out to see who he was, found himself a prisoner, and another following shared the same fate. With his two prisoners in front, Turner now advanced on a picket of 10 men posted a short distance from the camp. As our men drew near they were ordered to halt, but seeing their own men in front, the pickets allowed them to approach until they suddenly found themselves covered by the pistols of Turner and his men, who compelled them to surrender. They then recrossed the river, bringing over the 12 prisoners, with their horses and equipments. The Federals sent out a party of cavalry in pursuit, but they soon gave up the chase and returned to their camp.

HENRY S. ASHBY, CO. B.
From a photograph taken during the war.

*Tuesday, December 15.*—Company C was organized at Rectortown. William H. Chapman, of Page, was elected Captain; Adolphus E. Richards, of Loudoun, First Lieutenant; Frank Fox, of Fairfax, Second Lieutenant, and Frank Yeager, of Page, Third Lieutenant.

Scott, in his "Partisan Life with Col. John S. Mosby," says:

"Capt. William H. Chapman was 21 years of age the very day that the Ordinance of Secession was passed at Richmond. He was at that time a student at the University of Virginia, and belonged to a company of students which was ordered to Harper's Ferry for active duty, but was soon disbanded by Governor Letcher for the sufficient reason that those who belonged to it might return to their homes, and there recruit, drill and officer troops for the Southern army. Chapman was elected lieutenant in the Dixie Battery, which went from Page, his native county, and was afterward promoted to the captaincy, a position which he filled with great credit until the consolidation of batteries in January, 1863, by which act so many meritorious officers lost their commands. Still holding his artillery commission, he was assigned to duty as enrolling officer for Fauquier County, but his official duties were often interrupted by the incursions of the enemy. This, however, afforded him an opportunity for mingling in more congenial scenes, and he often volunteered to go with Mosby on his raids."

Lieut. Adolphus E. Richards, from Loudoun County, near Upperville, served in the Shenandoah Valley under Gen. Turner Ashby, and was afterwards on the staff of Gen. William E. Jones, who succeeded Ashby, but resigned his commission and joined Mosby as a private in Company B.

On Christmas Day, 1863, a detachment of the Thirteenth New York Cavalry, piloted by Charley Binns, came up from Vienna to the neighborhood of Leesburg, searching houses, but doing no great damage. They picked up a few men, mostly citizens. As they marched at night, their movements attracted but little attention.[3]

During the dead of winter there was but little to be done. The armies had all gone into winter quarters, and the cavalry were recruiting horses preparatory to the opening of the spring campaign. Scouts who were sent out in all directions, and parties " going on raids," generally returned unsuccessful. The camps were too strong to be attacked by Mosby with his small force, and, dispensing with pickets, few of them had more than a camp guard. For a season quiet reigned, broken only by an occasional raiding

---

[3] *Vienna, Dec. 27, 1863.*

LOWELL to TAYLOR: "I have the honor to report that the party of 10 mounted and 40 dismounted men of the Thirteenth New York Cavalry under Major Coles, with Binns as guide, sent out night before last, scouted the country as far as Leesburg and carefully this side of Broad Run. They searched houses and brought in 8 prisoners, among whom was Pettingall (a notorious scout), Joe White, Bridges (one of Mosby's men), and Beavers, with other suspicious citizens pointed out by Binns.

"They found no large force. Mosby had been at Guilford Station with 80 men the day before. A few shots were exchanged with a small mounted party who scattered through the woods. Another party of 30 men sent out at the same time have not returned."

party, hunting for Mosby. Many of our officers and men procured furloughs to spend the holiday season at their homes or with friends at a distance. The thoughts of others were with the little ones at home, who would miss papa's usual presence at Christmastide.

The severity of the wintry weather, the scarcity of all the necessaries of life, the high prices, and the reverses which the Confederates had experienced in the last campaign, combined with the sadness felt for the loss of relatives and friends, shed a deep gloom over this usually festive season.

WHY DON'T PAPA COME HOME?

# CHAPTER VII.

*Friday, January 1, 1864.*—A detachment of Cole's Second Battalion Maryland Cavalry, composed of a detail of 20 men from each company, numbering in all 80 men, under command of Capt. A. N. Hunter, came from Harper's Ferry on a scout and in search of Mosby. In passing through Upperville one of their number was killed. They proceeded on to Rectortown, where they remained some time. A meeting of " Mosby's Men " had been ordered at this place, but the men on coming to the town, finding it occupied by the enemy, rode around and were seen on every little hill and knoll, watching their movements.

Mosby collected about 10 or 15 men. It was difficult to get the men together, as many would not approach large parties through fear of their being enemies. Captain Smith of Company B, with 32 men, went into town as soon as Cole's men had left, and getting on their trail, followed them out on the Salem road. Cole's party turned off, crossing the fields, in the direction of Middleburg. Captain Smith cut across the country to come out on their flank near Five Points. Soon shots were heard in front, as Montjoy, Henry Ashby and John Edmonds, who were riding in advance came upon their rear. Our men drew their pistols, and with Smith at their head, charged with a yell. At the first fire Captain Hunter's horse was shot and he was made prisoner. The Federals seemed more determined on flight than fight, and hurried on towards Middleburg. Captain Smith followed, but had to send a great portion of his force back with prisoners and horses.

Mosby, seeing Smith's command in the town, thought it still occupied by the enemy and manœuvred around cautiously, but when they moved off he rode into town. Learning that they were a portion of his own command and had gone in pursuit of the Federals, he dashed off and soon, too, was on the track of the raiders, who had scattered and were now fleeing in every direction, closely pursued by our men. It was a regular Gilpin chase. Cole's men threw away bags of corn, sabres, carbines, pistols and everything they could well rid themselves of, and some, as though thinking their horses not fleet enough, jumped down, and leaving them in the road, ran through the woods on foot.

COL. HENRY A. COLE,
First Maryland Potomac Home Brigade
(Cole's Battalion).
From a photograph taken during the war.

In this affair but two of " Mosby's Men " were wounded—John Gulick severely. Four of the Federals were killed, 10 or 12 wounded and 41 captured. Over 50 horses fell into our hands.

Three of Cole's men, with their horses, were picked up near Waterford and one near Salem on the day after the fight, and one between Middleburg and Rectortown on the 3d of January. The men had wandered off and escaped for the time, but not knowing where to go, were afterwards captured.

In the following report sent in by Mosby about this time will be found mention of this affair:

*Report of Major John S. Mosby.*

Major H. B. McCLELLAN, *January 4, 1864.*
    *Assistant Adjutant-General.*

MAJOR: I have the honor to report that during the month of December there were captured by this command over 100 horses and mules and about 100 prisoners.   A considerable number of the enemy have also been killed and wounded.   It would be too tedious to mention the various occasions on which we have met the enemy, but there is one which justice to a brave officer demands to be noticed. On the morning of January 1, I received information that a body of the enemy's cavalry were in Upperville.   It being the day on which my command was to assemble, I directed Capt. William R. Smith to take command of the men while I went toward Upperville to ascertain the movements of the enemy.   In the meantime the enemy had gone on toward Rectortown, and I pursued, but came up just as Capt. Smith with about 35 men had attacked and routed them (78 strong), killing, wounding and capturing 57.

Respectfully, your obedient servant,

JNO. S. MOSBY,
*Major Commanding.*

[First Indorsement.]

HDQRS. CAVALRY CORPS, *February 13, 1864.*

Respectfully forwarded.

A subsequent report of subsequent operations has been already sent in, this having been mislaid.   Major Mosby continues his distinguished services in the enemy's rear, relieving our people of the depredations of the enemy in a great measure.        J. E. B. STUART, *Major-General.*

[Second Indorsement.]

*February 15, 1864.*

A characteristic report from Colonel Mosby, who has become so familiar with brave deeds as to consider them too tedious to treat unless when necessary to reflect glory on his gallant comrades.   Captain Smith's was a brilliant and most successful affair.        J. A. S. (SEDDON.)

An article published in one of the papers north of the Potomac a short time after the fight stated that this party was " attacked by 700 of Rosser's Brigade, and of the 75 or 80 Federals engaged, but 18 escaped, many of whom were badly frozen." [1]

---

[1] The following is the Federal list of prisoners and missing :

*Company A*. (Captain Vernon.)—Joseph Betson, F. Kline, J. A. Crome. Jas. Edwards, D. C. Grams, E. V. Harris, C. Horine, D. Jones, J. A. Kelly,

*Wednesday, January 6th.*—Lieutenant Turner left Salem about sunset with 32 men, and keeping along the west side of Watery Mountain crossed the pike near Warrenton. It was a bitter cold night, with the thermometer registering below zero and the ground covered with snow. There was a picket post on Lee's Ridge, and the command was left at a house to warm themselves, while Lieutenant Turner with 4 or 5 men went forward to find out something about the the post. Soon they came upon two men who had been placed on picket, but had gone into a little hollow to shelter themselves from the cold wind. Gregg's Division of Cavalry was camped around in the neighborhood, but Turner did not know the exact situation of the camps, though we could see the camp-fires blazing.

As soon as the pickets saw Turner they mounted their horses, and one of them immediately galloped off to camp. Signalling for the men to get between the remaining picket and the fires, Turner advanced on the man, who leveled his carbine and called out:

" Halt! Who goes there?"

" Friends," said Turner.

"Advance, one."

Turner put his hand under his cape, drew his pistol, and riding up to the picket suddenly pointed it at his head and commanded him to surrender. The carbine was instantly dropped with the exclamation:

" I knew you were ' Mosby's men.' "

This occurred about 9 p. m. The prisoner was taken

E. W. Moore, J. H. Shaefer, J. H. Slott, A. J. Slottlemeyer, C. Sweeney, C. S. Wachter, J. W. Watson, Geo. Young.

*Company B.* (Captain W. Fiery.)—Sergt. P. M. Bell, Wm. H. Butts, R. P. Deihl, G. W. Heilmer, D. R. Holland, W. S. Myers, J. Newcomer, J. Sniffer-cool, A. Turner, W. Wentz, J. Wiley.

*Company C.* (Captain A. M. Hunter.)—Sergt. J. E. Wilson, Corpl. G. W. Shriver, Bugler M. J. Coble, A. M. Fritchez, T. Fites, J. Hertzell, J. Sponceler, E. Wenschof, W. J. Waddle, W. B. Wenk, J. McCullough.

*Company D.* (Captain F. Gallagher.)—Sergt. J. S. Sakers, Corpl. D. C. Nicewoner, R. B. Beal, Wm. Carr, F. Delivan, Thomas Hawk, Wm. Millholland, D. McGuigan, J. E. McCabe, J. Moore, Wm. Reindollar, G. E. Steele, Wm. Turner, C. B. Bennett.

back to where the command had been left. Turner, as he was leaving, turned towards the reserve picket, where the fires were burning brightly, and said:

"I will come back directly and play the mischief with those fellows."

After the prisoner was taken out Turner said to him:

"I want you now to tell me truth, and nothing else; if you do not, it will be worse for you."

"You needn't fear," said the prisoner, "I'll tell you all about the post, and go with you, too."

This he did, and sat on his horse while we charged the picket. There was a reserve post of 40 men; 8 men were usually on post on the ridge, but on this night all had been drawn in but two.

WALTER W. GOSDEN, CO. E.
From a War-time photograph.

About 4 o'clock in the morning Turner led his men to the rear of the post and then along the pike. The sound of the wind whistling through the trees drowned the clatter of the horses' feet on the frozen pike. Soon we came in sight of the blazing watchfires on the roadside. Lieutenant Turner said:

"Go along quietly—make no unnecessary noise, and when the head of the column reaches the last fire the rear will be at the first. Then, when the command is given to charge, wheel your horses and fire. They will think we are their own men until we get close enough to charge."

The main body was encamped but a short distance from the post.

When opposite the fires Turner gave the word—

"Charge!" and the men wheeled their horses and dashed in among the surprised and affrighted party, firing as they went. A few of them dropped around the fires, and the rest threw up their arms, exclaiming :

" For God's sake, don't shoot ! We surrender."

The captain in command, Gillmore, was shot. One of the prisoners said :

" Indade, I'm glad yees came, and if yees had rode up and surrounded us, yees might have taken us all without firing a shot, for we wor all so cold; and we would rather go to Richmond, no matter how hard we wor treated, than to stand picket on that bleak mountain."

They were a portion of the Third Pennsylvania Cavalry. They stated that the picket who first escaped came into camp and said the Rebs had captured his comrade, and that he saw 4 or 5. When the pickets were relieved, the relief seeing no signs of Confederates about, came to the conclusion that we had gone. They were standing or sitting around the fires, as one of the prisoners told us, talking over the matter and joking one another on the probability of Mosby dashing in and taking them to Richmond, when, said he—" You charged in and tuk the hull of us."

Eight or ten Federals were killed and wounded, 20 prisoners and 46 horses captured. [See Mosby's Report, Appendix, VIII.]

A picket who was stationed on the pike, sat on his horse while the firing was going on, and as our men rode up on their return he took off his belt and gave up his arms.

Wm. B. Walston lost several toes by frost, John W. Corbin had hands and feet frozen, and several others were more or less frostbitten, but with these exceptions none of our men was injured.[2]

---

[2] HEADQUARTERS THIRD PENNSYLVANIA CAVALRY,

*January 7, 1864.*

WALSH to WRIGHT : " I have just received a report from Captain Gillmore, who is picketing in my front, that the rebels charged on his reserve, coming from the Warrenton side, capturing all his horses, the greater portion of his men and wounding a great many. The captain reports himself wounded. He wishes two ambulances to be sent out to bring in the wounded. I will have the

About this time Captain Stringfellow suggested to Major Mosby that he co-operate with him in the capture of Cole's Camp on Loudoun Heights.

Stringfellow entered the army at the beginning of the war and had so distinguished himself by his skill and daring as

REV. FRANK STRINGFELLOW,
Formerly "Capt. Frank Stringfellow, the Scout."
From a photograph taken after the war.

to attract the attention of General Stuart, who was always quick to observe and as ready to reward true merit. Having a thorough knowledge of all the stretch of country from the Blue Ridge to Washington, Stringfellow was selected as a scout and given a detail of 10 men to operate with. He enjoyed the confidence of both Generals Lee and Stuart, and many of their most important movements were made from information acquired by him. The incidents in his dashing career—his daring exploits, his perilous journeys, his hairbreadth escapes and his brilliant forays, would of themselves fill a volume.

As Stringfellow had reconnoitred the camp and made himself familiar with its details, Mosby readily agreed with

picket lines established in as quick time as possible. He reports the rebels having left in quick meter after collecting up the horses and men."

CAMP OF THIRD PENNSYLVANIA CAVALRY,
*January 8, 1864.*

Major J. W. WALSH :

SIR : I have the honor to report that on the 5th day of January, 1864, Captain Gillmore relieved a detachment of the First Brigade, First Division, Cavalry Corps, on the Sulphur Springs road, taking up the line as established under the supervision of the brigade officer of the day.

Everything remained quiet on the line until the morning of the 7th, when the corporal of the fifth relief started from camp to relieve the pickets. On reaching No. 3 post he discovered 10 or 12 men drawn up in line at the post. He immediately reported the fact to Captain Gillmore, who sent me with 10

him that the place could be surprised and captured with no great effort. Accordingly on the afternoon of Saturday, January 9th, Mosby started from Upperville with 106 men. About 8 o'clock we halted at Woodgrove, Loudoun County,

---

men to his support. In the meantime they had made good their retreat without firing a shot. I scouted around the whole line, finding No. 3 post vacant, but no other indications of the presence of an enemy. The pickets received additional instructions as to vigilance, and nothing further occurred until between the hours of 4 and 5, when the second relief started from camp. They had been gone but a short time when a party of 35 or 40 men charged upon the camp from our rear, taking us totally by surprise. Their movements were hidden by a ridge, and the darkness and high wind which prevailed aided their attack. Captain Gillmore sprang to his feet, and in attempting to rally his men, many of whom were asleep, was shot down and surrounded by a dozen mounted men. At the same time 6 men were wounded and 18 captured. As we were weakened by the absence of two reliefs, the command was totally overpowered and at the mercy of the enemy. It is my opinion that they entered the line between Captain Gillmore's extreme left post and the right of the First Pennsylvania pickets, considerable distance intervening. This opinion is strengthened from the fact that there was not a shot fired on the line, and in the morning I examined the ground, finding a trail through the snow at the point designated.

They retreated out the Sulphur Springs road, carrying with them 18 prisoners and 43 horses with their equipments, leaving 8 wounded, including Captain Gillmore, which comprised the whole command, with the exception of 3 or 4 who escaped.

I am, sir, very respectfully, your obedient servant,

G. S. LUTTRELL WARD,
*Second Lieutenant Third Pennsylvania Cavalry.*

---

HDQRS. FIRST BRIG., SECOND DIV., CAVALRY CORPS, }
*Warrenton, Va., January 7, 1864.* }

Capt. H. C. WEIR, *A. A. G., Second Division, Cavalry Corps.*

CAPTAIN : I have the honor to report that, in compliance with orders from Second Division headquarters, 100 men from First New Jersey Cavalry, under command of Lieut. J. Hobensack, of same regiment, were ordered out to pursue the enemy, who had attacked the reserve of the Third Pennsylvania. Lieutenant Hobensack reports that he took the Warrenton and Waterloo pike ; found the track of the enemy; thence to the Salem and Waterloo road ; followed its course to within 3 miles of Salem, where it changed its course, taking the Orleans road. The lieutenant reports the enemy at this point three hours in advance of him ; his horses much fatigued and gave up pursuit, returning by the Salem and Waterloo road. He captured 2 of Mosby's men, who he delivered to the division provost-marshal.

Most respectfully, your obedient servant,

J. P. TAYLOR,
*Comdg. First Brigade, Second Division, Cavalry Corps.*

at the residence of Mr. Heaton, where we warmed ourselves and partook of refreshments, which were supplied without stint. At 10 o'clock we resumed our march. Within two miles of the camp we were joined by Stringfellow with his 10 men. They reported favorably, and the command pushed on. The night was clear, the stars shone brightly ; and the cold was sharp and biting. Many of the men would dismount at times and run or walk beside their horses to keep their feet from freezing. No sound broke the stillness of the night except the dull, heavy tramp of the horses as they trod the snowy path. Fields, roads, trees and shrubs were alike clothed in the white robes of winter, and it seemed almost a sacrilege against the beauty and holy stillness of the scene to stain those pure garments with the life blood of man, be he friend or foe.

Marching on, we soon came in sight of camp fires on the opposite side of the river. These were passed and many of the men thought the post had been found too strong to be attacked. As the whistle of an engine fell upon their ears at this time, some were under the impression that an attack would be made on the train. The command moved up along the mountain side in single file, strung out for some distance on the narrow path. Suddenly "crack!" went the report of a pistol; then " bang-bang-bang," went the carbines from the camp in front, accompanied by loud shouts from Cole's camp. Above the din rang out the clear voices of Smith and Turner—" Charge them, boys! Charge them! " The first row of tents was captured when Stringfellow's men, who had charged into the rear of the camp contrary to orders, came on yelling and shooting. Our men, supposing them to be Federals, fired upon them, killing and wounding several. Taking advantage of the confusion which ensued, Captain Vernon, of Cole's Battalion, rallied his men and opened on us a withering fire. Some sheltered themselves in an old log house, firing on us from the door, windows and through the chinks. Turner was advancing towards the tents when a ball struck him ; he threw up his hands exclaiming " I am shot! " Two of the men caught him and holding him on his horse, led him off. Paxson fell from his horse, calling out as he fell: "You are not going to leave me here on the field?" Captain Smith was advancing to assist him, when a shot from one of the tents a short distance ahead put an end to the career of this brave soldier. Cap_ tain Chapman caught him and disengaging his feet from the stirrups, laid him on the ground. Robinson fell from his horse, dead. Colston, a brave young Baltimorean, was shot down while endeavoring to encourage and rally our men. Owens was also killed. Still the fight went on.

Montjoy, with a squad of men, was sent down to a bridge to take a picket and guard the bridge. When he reached the bridge the picket had fled and he kept it undisturbed.

Lieut. F. Beattie had his horse shot and he himself received a ball in his thigh.

The dead and dying lay around. From the tents came forth moans of pain and shrieks of agony. Some of the combatants stood almost in reach of one another, firing into each other's faces, crying out:

LIEUT.-COL. GEO. W. F. VERNON,
First Maryland Potomac Home Brigade
(Cole's Battalion).

"Surrender!"

"No, I won't! You surrender!"

Many of the Federals, driven from their tents, sought refuge among the thick bushes higher up the mountain side and from this vantage ground poured a galling fire into our ranks. The balls striking the ground, threw up the frozen earth in our faces.

Hearing the signal gun at Harper's Ferry, where several thousand troops were quartered, in readiness to march upon us at a moment's notice, and seeing that nothing could be gained by prolonging the fight, Mosby gathered up his shattered forces and retired from this disastrous attack in the direction of Hillsborough, taking 7 prisoners and 35 horses. The Federals did not attempt to follow, though they continued firing as long as the command was within sight or hearing.

Five of our men were left dead in the camp: Captain William R. Smith, of Company B; William E. Colston, Captain Robinson, Owens and Yates. Lieut. Thomas Turner, of Company A; Charles Paxson and William H. Turner of Baltimore, were mortally wounded and all died shortly after. Lieut. Fountain Beattie, Henry Edmonds, Boyd Smith and others were wounded. One man, Leonard Brown, was taken prisoner; he had gone off to secure some horses, and after doing so, returned, leading two horses. He was greatly surprised to fine his comrades gone, and there was no alternative for him but to surrender.

Lieut. Thomas Turner was taken to the house of Mr. Levi Waters, about a mile distant from the camp, where he died the following Saturday. [See Mosby's Report, Appendix, VIII.]

There were from 175 to 200 men at the camp attacked. They lost 4 killed and 17 wounded, some mortally. [3]

---

[3] *Cumberland, Md., Jan. 10, 1864.*

Brigadier-General CULLUM, *Chief of Staff:*

SIR: The following dispatch is just received:

I cheerfully comply with the request of General Sullivan in calling the attention of the General-in-Chief to the gallant conduct of Major Cole and his brave comrades. His repulse of the murderous attack made by an overwhelming force at 4 o'clock on a dark, cold morning evinced a discipline, a watchfulness and a bravery most commendable.    B. F. KELLY, *Brigadier-General.*

---

HDQRS. BATT. P. H. B. CAVALRY, MARYLAND VOLS.,
*Loudoun Heights, Va., January 10, 1864.*

Capt. WILLIAM M. BOONE, *Assistant Adjutant-General:*

SIR: I have the honor of addressing you for the purpose of reporting the facts of an attempt by Major Mosby's battalion of guerrila cavalry to surprise and capture my camp between the hours of 3 and 4 a. m. of this day.

They studiously avoided my pickets; divided themselves into small bodies, which were speedily consolidated in sight of my camp. They then made an impetuous charge with a yell on the right of the same. In consequence of the

The march homeward was indeed a gloomy one. A sad and sullen silence pervaded our ranks and found expression in every countenance. All that we could have gained would not compensate for the loss we sustained: Captain Smith dead and Lieutenant Turner mortally wounded, besides losing many other brave companions in arms. Even the Major, though he usually appeared cold and unyielding, could not conceal his disappointment and keen regret at the result of this enterprise. He knew and felt that he had suffered a loss which could not well be repaired.

Capt. William R. Smith, of Company B and Lieutenant Turner, of Company A, were without doubt at the time of their deaths the two most efficient officers in the Battalion. The first to go into a fight, they were always the last to leave. They always led the charges in their respective companies. Not only for their bravery and soldierly traits were they admired and beloved, but also on account of the many noble qualities of head and heart with which they were endowed. Both men were universal favorities, not only in their own companies but also with the whole Battalion, and their loss was regretted by all.

---

suddenness of the same this company could offer but feeble resistance. In the meantime Company A, the second in the line, was speedily rallied by its commanding officer, Captain Vernon, who contested their further advance in such a sanguinary manner that [they] formed a rallying point for the balance of the command, who were now thoroughly aroused of the danger that threatened them, and one and all, from the officer to the private, entered into the contest with such a determined zest as led to the utter rout and discomfiture of the enemy and the signal failure of their base attempt.

They experienced a loss of 1 captain, 2 lieutenants and 2 privates killed, and 2 privates mortally wounded, and 1 prisoner. It was also very evident that they removed a large portion of their wounded with them in their precipitate flight, as a detachment of the command, subsequently sent in pursuit, found evidence of blood all along the line of retreat. I experienced a loss of 4 enlisted men killed and 16 wounded. Captain Vernon experienced a serious wound in the head, but it is the opinion of Batt. Surg. W. R. Way that it will not prove fatal. I am deeply indebted to the officers and men of my command for the daring displayed by them on this occasion, and earnestly commend them to the division commander for his favorable consideration.

I have the honor to remain, very respectfully, your obedient servant,

HENRY A. COLE,
*Major Commanding.*

The " Souvenir of the Maryland Line " has the following sketch of Colston:

William E. Colston was born in Washington, March 24th, 1839, but his early years were spent in Virginia, the home of his ancestors. He came to Baltimore about 1857, and was among the first to go to Virginia when the war broke out.

On June 1st, 1861, he enlisted as a private in Company B, Maryland Guard, attached to the 21st Virginia Infantry, but when the First Maryland Regiment was formed was transferred to Company H, Capt. Wm. H. Murray, June 18th, 1861. In this company he served in all the campaigns and battles of the year, and at the battle of Cross Keys, June 8th, 1862, in Jackson's Valley Campaign he was desperately wounded, being shot through the body. He was permanently injured by this wound and disabled for a long time, but as soon as able to ride he was appointed Volunteer Aid to Major-General Trimble. General Trimble being wounded and left at Gettysburg, Colston then volunteered into Mosby's command, and was killed in the night attack on Harper's Ferry, January 10th, 1864. He is buried in the Confederate lot at Loudoun Park with his old comrades of Company H, First Maryland Infantry.

WILLIAM E. COLSTON, CO. A.

Killed in the attack on Cole's Camp, Loudoun Heights, January 10, 1864.

A Memorial Room to him has been furnished in the Confederate Home at Pikesville, Md., by his brother, Capt. Frederick M. Colston.

I met Major Mosby on the road a few days after the fight,

and in course of conversation he remarked that he was sorry he had made the attack on Cole's camp, "although," said he, "if my plans had been carried out, the expedition would have been a success." He said Stringfellow was to have gone on ahead with his men to the house occupied by Major Cole as headquarters. This they were quietly to surround, and after securing the Major and whoever else might be with him, proceed on to the camp and unite with him in the attack. Instead of doing this, they dashed on and into the camp. Mosby rode down the line in search of Captain Smith to order him to dismount his company and charge with them on foot into the camp to prevent the enemy firing from their tents and to secure the horses. Company A, under Lieutenant Turner, were to remain mounted and attack the camp. The men were straggling along the road, totally unprepared for a charge. Before he could find Cap-

tain Smith or issue any orders whatever, he heard Stringfellow's men yelling and shooting in our front. The camp being aroused, there was no alternative but to charge and hazard the chance of an engagement, as he was disappointed in making it a surprise.

In the "Life of Sheridan," already alluded to, is a very interesting sketch of this affair, entitled "A Battle in the Snow," which concludes with the following neatly written little episode:

There were a thousand thrilling incidents connected with this barefooted fight on the mountains, in the snow, worth relating, and the conspicuous instances of almost unexampled bravery would include almost every man in the

CHARLES PAXSON, CO. A.
Killed at Loudoun Heights in attack on Cole's Camp.

command. But there is one touching incident necessary to join the woof and warp of this narration.

When daylight broke upon the scene there was a young

Confederate soldier lying upon the field with a fatal wound in the neck, near the jugular vein.  He was not more than twenty years of age, and a boy in appearance as well as in years.  The officer who appears at the cross-roads in the beginning of this story found him.  He raised up the dying lad and asked him his name.

"My name is Paxson," replied the boy in broken tones.

"My God! are you Mr. Paxson's son who lives at the cross-roads towards Waterford?" eagerly inquired the officer.

"I am," was the simple response.

The humane act of his father in 1862 was recalled, and, full of emotion, the officer picked the lad up, carried him to the hospital, laid him upon an easy couch and summoned the doctor, who replied petulantly:

"We can't care for those men until we look after our own wounded."

"But this boy must be cared for," said the officer, and in as few words as possible he told the story of 1862, when five of their men belonging to Cole's Cavalry lay wounded upon Paxson's farm at the cross-roads.

There was no more parleying, and the boy was at once carefully attended to, but he was beyond human aid.  All that could be done for him to ease his last moments was done.  All the command felt, terribly as they themselves had suffered and were suffering, that this boy was entitled to every attention that could be shown him.

"I do this," said Mr. Paxson in 1862, when he assisted in taking the wounded men (Federals) toward the river, "because I would want others to do the same by my boy, who is in the Confederate Army, if he should be wounded."

The same officer and the same men who heard these words and received that favor, dealt the death-blow to that son.  Yet his dying moments were made easier by them for the favor his father had done.

# CHAPTER VIII.

On the 5th of February, Capt. William H. Chapman, while on a scout in the Valley with 14 men, came upon a party of 15 Federal cavalry between Millwood and Berry-ville. He attacked them on sight, killed 3, captured 3 prisoners and 4 horses; the balance made their escape.

In order to guard against raiding parties of Federal cavalry which were continually scouring the country, often capturing some of our men, pickets were detailed from the different companies for duty each night on the main roads leading to our section. To Company A was assigned the turnpike below Middleburg; to Company B, the roads between Bloomfield and Upperville; and to Company C, the road from Salem to the Plains.[1]

---

[1] Lieut. W. Ben Palmer, of Richmond, furnished me, from an old memorandum book in his possession, the following list of details from Company A for picket duty on the turnpike below Middleburg when he was Sergeant of Company A :

Sergeant Palmer—Mosby (W. H.), Rudd, Brawner, Lake (L.), Lake (T.W.), Lake (J. R.), Cocke, Glasscock.

Sergeant Rowzee—Rutter, Burke, Barton, Coiner (J. E.), Coiner (J. W.), Ellis, Smallwood. Rowzee (G. A.)

Sergeant Thomas—Betts, Bishop, Bowie, Castleman, Walston, Fletcher, Williamson, Ayre.

Sergeant Rector—Hatcher (W.), Walls, Wilson, Symons, Robey, McDaniel, Wilson, Simpson.

Corporal Davis—Underwood (B.), Underwood (S.), Richards (D.), Trammell, Smallwood, Rogers, Minor, Shaw.

Corporal Skinner—Dulaney, De Butts, Darden, Donahue, Reed, Crosen, Adrian, Beavers.

Corporal Whaley—Crowley, Berryman, Hammond, Heflein (J. W.), Heflein (W. A.), Oden, Robinson, Williams, Waggaman, Mohler.

Corporal Gulick—Cromwell, Woolf, Gulick (G. M.), Knapp, Hibbs, Hutchinson, Flannery, Fox (C. A.)

On the night of February 17th I slept at the house of my old friend Redmond F. Brawner, in the upper edge of Fauquier.   Mr. Brawner and his family were refugees from Prince William County, being driven from their farm, which was located on the battle ground of Manassas.  My companions in the room were Charles Tyler, John Kirwin, William A. and Henry N. Brawner.

I was awakened on the morning of the 18th by a noise in the room and, looking up, saw the boys hastily putting on their clothes.   First one and then another would go to the window, where a large gray blanket had been nailed up to keep out the cold, and cautiously peeping out, would say in

suppressed tones: "They are Yankees."   "They are going along the road, past the house."   "Oh, gee! what a crowd of them."   "They are looking up this way."

Charley Tyler, who had not left his bed, would send out from beneath the blankets a sepulchral voice in reply to these exclamations: "Come away from the window." "Well, if they are Yankees, can't you let 'em go by?"   "D—— you, come away from that window."   It was alternately an entreaty and a curse.

WILLIAM A. BRAWNER,
CO. A.

I sprang out of bed and putting my eye to the peephole in the blanket, saw a body of Federal cavalry passing along the road towards Paris.   They were sitting bolt upright on their horses, like so many statues, muffled up in their overcoats and seemed to look neither to right nor left.

As soon as I slipped on my clothes I went downstairs and out the back door, picked up my saddle and bridle, and keeping the house between myself and the cavalry in the road, ran as fast as I could through the orchard to where I expected to find my horse.   The horses, to protect themselves from the biting wind, had sought the shelter of a little knoll which completely hid them from the view of those passing on the road. Seeing no horses, and the house being a small one, with no barn or stable in sight, the Federal cavalry were not attracted to it, and the morning being intensely cold, they appeared anxious to push on and not loiter on the way. Calling my horse, I was soon in the saddle and dashing over the mountain in hopes to come on the road ahead of the raiders and give warning of their approach.

I came out on the road in front of Ben. Triplett's house. The old man was sitting at the stile as I rode up, wildly clapping his hands. "The Yankees have been here and ransacked the house," said he, "and have taken all the horses."

"Did they get any of the boys?" I asked.

"No," said he; "the boys ran out with what clothes they could pick up and are now hiding somewhere about the mountain. Jim Wrenn jumped out of the window with only what he had on in bed, and I think he and Ab. Wrenn are up on Mount Ida. The Yankees have been to Gibson's and there they captured Sergeant Corbin, Walston and some more of the boys."

"Which way did they go?" I inquired.

"There they are now!" said Triplett, pointing over towards Simper's. As I looked in that direction I saw the road filled with blue-coats, and a warning shot and the sound of a bullet whizzing by my ear told its own story.

While sitting on my horse looking towards them, I observed a commotion in their ranks, while the sharp cracking of pistols, and the wild yell which sounded so familiar to my ear told me that "Mosby's Men" were hanging on their trail and had made a dash at them. I then put spurs to my horse and crossed the fields to join my comrades.

Captain William Chapman and Montjoy had collected about 25 men. Seeing the two parties of Federal Cavalry unite and gallop into Paris, leaving pickets outside, we moved on towards town, while Chapman and Montjoy went forward to reconnoitre. We saw the enemy's sharpshooters creeping along to cut them off and called to them to come back. This they started to do, but not until Montjoy's horse was wounded. The Federals now dismounted sharpshooters who, sheltered behind stone fences, opened fire on us with their carbines.

Charles Tyler was sent off to hunt up more men, but ran into another body of Federals coming along the mountain road from Markham to Paris. He quickly wheeled his horse and made his escape. We saw them winding along a narrow lane and charged in their rear, but they were too strong for us, and soon the three parties were united at Paris. Captain Chapman said our force was too small to accomplish anything, and dismissed us with orders to gather up what men we could and meet at Piedmont about two or three o'clock in the afternoon, to endeavor to cut off and recapture prisoners. The Federals stopped a short time at Paris and then started down the pike, closely followed by Lieutenant Hunter with about 30 men, who harassed them as they moved along. We had one man wounded, Aquilla Glasscock.

The raiding party consisted of detachments of the First New Jersey, First Pennsylvania, Third Pennsylvania and First Massachusetts Cavalry—about 400 in all—and were guided by a man named John Cornwell. Cornwell had been sent by Capt. Walter E. Frankland, then our Quartermaster, to Charlottesville with a wagon to bring us some ammunition, and on his return presented a bill of expenses which Frankland would not allow. He then appealed to Mosby, who sustained Frankland. Cornwell then went to Warrenton, where Gregg's Cavalry Division was in camp, and volunteered to pilot the Federals through "Mosby's Confederacy" and capture the whole command,

They started from Warrenton about half-past ten o'clock on the night of Wednesday, February 17th, reached Salem about midnight, and from this place they commenced searching houses for "Mosby's Men." At Rectortown they divided, one party going to Middleburg and thence to Upperville, while others marched by way of Piedmont, Oak Hill, Markham and Paris. Some even scouted along the little mountain road from Markham to Paris. At the house of Mr. Jamieson Ashby, where Captain Frankland lodged, the Federals surrounded and searched the house, threatening

the servants to compel them to tell where they would find
Captain Frankland, Hamner and Henry Ashby ; but the
faithful negroes would not disclose their hiding places, and
they remained concealed until the enemy had left.

In the afternoon we met at Piedmont and were joined by
Mosby, who had just returned to the command, being promoted to the rank of Lieutenant-Colonel. With 60 men we
followed the trail of the raiders to within six miles of Warrenton, where we gave up the pursuit.

In the Federal reports the officers claimed to have captured 28 of our men, but in this they included a number of
citizens who were not members of our command.[2]

*Saturday, February 20th*—Cole's Second Battalion Maryland Cavalry, about 250 men, made a raid through Loudoun
and Fauquier Counties, capturing several of our men. Mc-
Cobb, of Baltimore, was surprised at Bartenstein's, near
Upperville, and was killed in attempting to escape. John
and Bartlett Bolling were captured at their father's resi-

---

[2] *Federal Reports of the Cornwell Raid.*

HEADQUARTERS CAVALRY CORPS, ARMY OF THE POTOMAC,
*February 17, 1864.*

Brig.-Gen. GREGG, *Commanding Second Cavalry Division :*

GENERAL : The Commanding General directs that you send a sufficient force
of your command at once for the purpose of capturing Mosby and his party,
who are to be at Markham to-night.

The prisoner, Cornwell, will give you information as to where Mosby will
be found. The officer in charge of the party will take with him the prisoner,
and if he should lead your party into a trap he will be shot. It is believed that
the prisoner's statement is reliable, and you are directed to question him.
After the party returns Cornwell will at once be sent to these headquarters.

The General directs that you will send the party as soon as possible, in
order that they may arrive at Markham during the night. Please report by
telegraph as soon as the party returns.

I am, very respectfully, your obedient servant,
                                        E. B. PARSONS,
                            *Captain and Acting Assistant Adjutant-General.*

---

HEADQUARTERS SECOND CAVALRY DIVISION,
*February 18, 1864.*

Lieut.-Col. J. W. KESTER, *Commanding First New Jersey :*

COLONEL : The General commanding directs that with 300 men placed under
your command, you will proceed to-night at 10 o'clock to Markham and Paris

dence, and William A. Brawner and J. W. Coiner rode into
a party of Cole's men, near Upperville, mistaking them for
our own men, and were taken prisoners.

After going as far as Piedmont, on the Virginia Midland
Road, Cole started to return.  Mosby, with John Edmonds,
John Munson and J. Lavender, got on their track.  He
gathered up others as he went along, at the same time
annoying the raiders as they marched.  When near Upper-

---

and vicinity, where it is reported bands of guerrillas have their headquarters.
Every effort will be made to capture or destroy the leaders and men composing
these bands.  The guide who will accompany you is familiar with the country
and reported to be worthy of confidence.  In searching houses supposed to con-
tain guerrillas, all injury to property will be avoided.  In making your dispositions suggestions of the guide will be valuable.  It is expected that your
command will return to camp to-morrow evening.

Very respectfully, your obedient servant,          D. McM. GREGG,
*Brigadier-General of Volunteers, Commanding Second Division.*

---

HEADQUARTERS FIRST NEW JERSEY CAVALRY,
*February 19, 1864.*

Capt. HENRY C. WEIR,
*Assistant Adjutant-General, Second Cavalry Division :*

CAPTAIN : I have the honor to report that in obedience to instructions I
started from Warrenton with 350 men comprising the following commands : 150
First New Jersey, 100 First Pennsylvania, 50 Third Pennsylvania and 50 First
Massachusetts.  It being very cold I marched rapidly, and at Salem I sent
Lieutenant Bradbury, Third Pennsylvania, with 50 men of the First Massa-
chusetts, to pass through Upperville and meet the rest of the command at
Paris, in Ashby's Gap.  I took the main column on to Piedmont ; at that point
I sent Captain Hart with 150 men of the First New Jersey Cavalry to pass
through Piedmont Valley, and stop at Paris until I arrived.  With 100 men of
the First Pennsylvania, under Captain McGregor, and 50 men of the Third
Pennsylvania, under Captain Wetherill, I marched to Markham Station in
Manassas Gap.  From that point I crossed the mountains by a by-path and
joined the other parties at Paris at 12 o'clock on the day of the 18th.  The
column under Lieutenant Bradbury lost their way and came into Paris without
passing through Upperville, and captured some horses and arms without seeing
any of the enemy.  The column under Captain Hart passed through Piedmont
Valley, and surprised and captured 15 of Mosby's guerrillas and furloughed
soldiers, and a quantity of arms, equipments and horses.  The other column
with myself passed into Manassas Gap to Markham, and from there to Paris,
capturing 13 of Mosby's guerrillas and furloughed soldiers, and a quantity of
arms, equipments, horses and some medical stores ; the latter we destroyed.
As we came near Paris about 40 guerrillas charged on my rear guard.  I sent
a squadron and charged, scattering them.  No casualties on our side.  I stopped
one hour at Paris, and started to return at one o'clock.  By this time the guer-

GEN. DAVID McM. GREGG AND STAFF.
From a War-time Photograph.

ville, where Cole halted to feed and rest his horses, Mosby
had collected about 50 men, and with these he charged the
rear of the Federal column and threw them into some confusion.  Capt. Wm. L. Morgan, of Cole's Command, was
killed by Montjoy.  At Blakeley's Grove School House,
Cole made a stand, and taking a position behind the stone
fence at the Cross Roads, sought to give us check, but
Mosby, throwing his men on their flank, drove them from
their shelter and forced them to retreat.  We followed them
as far as Bloomfield, and there gave up the chase.[3]

The Federals lost 7 killed, including Captain Morgan, and
8 prisoners, with their horses and equipments.  They carried
off most of their wounded — one, shot through the head,
lingered some time at the school house at Blakeley's Grove,
but died and was buried in the fence corner.  We found 2

rillas had collected together in a body numbering nearly 100 men, who made
repeated attempts to capture my rear guard, which they paid dearly for.  At
one time one man was shot from his horse ; at another two were knocked over,
and another an officer was dismounted and wounded, and was rescued by his
comrades, but his horse and trappings fell into our hands.

The casualties on our side were : Captain Hart, First New Jersey, slightly
wounded, and 2 horses killed.  The guide you furnished me was of great
assistance.

Very respectfully, your obedient servant,

JOHN W. KESTER,
*Lieutenant-Colonel Commanding.*

HEADQUARTERS ARMY OF THE POTOMAC,
*February 18, 1864.*

Major-General HALLECK : General Pleasonton, chief of cavalry, reports that
a scouting party sent from General Gregg's command at Warrenton, captured to-day at Piedmont 28 of " Mosby's men."

GEO. G. MEADE,
*Major-General Commanding.*

[3] *Abstract from Record of Events on Return of Cavalry Brigade, Department of
West Virginia, for February, 1864.*

February 20.—Three parties were sent out of 200 men by way of Loudoun,
under command of Major Cole, who met Mosby's troops at or near Upperville,
and after a severe skirmish lost 1 captain and 1 private killed and several
missing ; eaptured 18 rebels.  Another party under command of Colonel Taylor went to Front Royal ; drove the rebels from there, who took to the mountains.  We captured 8 prisoners.  The third party went to Strasburg without
meeting the enemy.  Captain W. L. Morgan, Co. A., First N. Y. Veteran
Cavalry, was killed in action near Upperville.

of their dead near Bloomfield a week after the fight, half eaten up by hogs.

In our command Lieutenant Fox, Starke and Spinkx were wounded. Montjoy and Geo. H. Ayre had their horses shot.[4]

---

[4] *Report of Lieut.-Col. John S. Mosby, Forty-third Battalion Virginia Cavalry.*

*February 21, 1864.*

Major H. B. McCLELLAN, *Asst. Adjutant-General Cavalry Corps.*

MAJOR : I have the honor to report that about 8 o'clock yesterday morning, on being informed that a large body of the enemy's cavalry were in Upperville, I took immediate steps to be prepared to meet them. The enemy proceeded some distance along the pike toward Piedmont, when they started back. I did all in my power to retard them by annoying them with a few sharpshooters in order to give my men time to collect. After getting between 50 and 60 together I attacked them about 2 miles beyond Upperville. A sharp skirmish ensued, in which we repulsed them in three distinct charges and drove their sharpshooters from a very strong position behind a stone wall. They fled in the direction of Harper's Ferry. We pursued them about 2 miles. They were enabled to cover their retreat by means of their numerous carbineers posted behind stone fences. As my men had nothing but pistols, with only a few exceptions, I was compelled to make flank movements in order to dislodge them, which, of course, checked a vigorous pursuit. Citizens who counted the enemy inform me that they numbered 250 men, under command of Major Cole. They left 6 of their dead on the field, among them 1 captain, 1 lieutenant, and 7 men prisoners ; also, horses, army equipments, etc. The road over which they retreated was strewn with abandoned hats, haversacks, etc. They impressed wagons to carry off their wounded.

While all acted well, with but few exceptions, it is a source of great pride to bring to your notice the names of some whose conspicuous gallantry renders their mention both a duty and a pleasure. They are Captain and Lieutenant Chapman, Lieutenants Fox and Richards, Sergeants Palmer, Lavender, and Privates Munson, Edmonds, Montjoy, Starke and Cunningham. My loss was 2 wounded. Respectfully, your obedient servant,

JNO. S. MOSBY,
*Lieutenant-Colonel Commanding.*

[First Indorsement.]

HEADQUARTERS CAVALRY CORPS, ⎫
*February 28, 1864.* ⎭

Respectfully forwarded.

Colonel Mosby's gallantry and skill highly commended, and attention called to the officers and men specially mentioned.

J. E. B. STUART, *Major-General.*

[Second Indorsement.]

HEADQUARTERS, *March 8, 1864.*

Respectfully forwarded, concurring in the commendation of General Stuart bestowed upon Colonel Mosby, the officers and men of his command.

R. E. LEE, *General.*

*Sunday, February 21st.*—The command was ordered to meet at Piedmont to attend the funeral of McCobb, who was killed by Cole's men. While assembling, a report was brought in that a scouting party composed of 150 of the Second Massachusetts Cavalry [5] and a platoon of the Sixteenth New York Cavalry, under command of Capt. J. Sewell Read, of the Second Massachusetts Cavalry, a major by promotion, were at Rector's X Roads. We moved on to that place, but they left before our arrival, going in the direction of Mountville. Sam Underwood was sent with one man to follow their trail and report to Mosby, while we

GEO. L. REVERCOMB,
Corporal, Co. E.[6]

marched towards Dranesville, with the intention of intercepting them on their return to camp at Vienna. They camped at night at the farm of Mr. Kephart, on the road to Dranesville, where they were joined by a body of cavalry under Major Frazar. We halted near Dranesville, tied our horses in the thick pines, built fires and lay down to rest.

We had less than 175 men. Mosby appeared in excellent humor; said he had been running his parallels all day, but had headed them; that they would come down the Leesburg pike and he would attack them in the morning.

*Monday, February 22d.*—Early in the morning the command was moved out to the pike and halted near Anker's shop, about two miles below Dranesville, to await the coming of the enemy. A short distance in our rear the road

---

[5] *Second Massachusetts Cavalry.*—Companies A, E, F, L and M of this regiment were organized at San Francisco, Cal.; Company H, at Boston; Companies B, C, D and I, at Readville, Mass., from December 10, 1862, to June 20, 1863, to serve three years. It was mustered out of service July 20, 1865, in accordance with orders from War Department.—*Official Record.*

We usually spoke of this command as the " California Battalion."

[6] George L. Revercomb, a veteran of two wars—the Mexican and the Civil War—enlisted in 1861 in Company C., Fourth Virginia Cavalry; was honorably discharged on account of wounds received in battle, and afterwards enlisted under the banner of Colonel Mosby.

forked, and as it was uncertain whether the Federals would follow the pike or take the county road, Walter Whaley was sent to watch their movements. He soon came in with the intelligence that the Second Massachusetts was coming along the pike, and that Major Frazar's party, which had camped with them at night, had left them and gone by the other road.

Company A, with part of Company B, under Lieut. Frank Williams, were now placed along the edge of a thick pine woods, in columns of fours, to charge in their front; Company C, with balance of Company B, under Capt. William Chapman, were to charge in their rear; while 15 dismounted men with carbines, under Montjoy, were posted in the pines along the road about the center of the position.

J. PENDLETON CHAPPALEAR,
Co. B.
Killed in fight with Second Massachusetts Cavalry, near Dranesville, February, 1864.

After all arrangements had been made, Mosby said: " Men, the Yankees are coming and it is very likely we will have a hard fight. When you are ordered to charge, I want you to go right through them. Reserve your fire until you get close enough to see clearly what you are shooting at, and then let every shot tell."

Very soon the Federal cavalry was seen moving slowly down the pike, two vedettes riding about two hundred yards ahead of all, then the advance of about 20 men, and lastly the main body. The vedettes had passed by without noticing us, and coming upon our pickets, who had been placed on a hill in full view of the turnpike, one of them raised his carbine and fired; then, turning around and seeing our men formed along the edge of the pines, he waved his hand to his men, calling to them to charge. At this moment Mosby blew a whistle—that shrill whistle! The impression fixed on my mind at that time is just as strong now as when we sat motionless on our horses, holding our breaths, with heads thrown forward and ears strained, watching and waiting in anxious expectation for the approach of the enemy and the signal for the attack. There was an unnatural, an unearthly stillness around us at that moment—a stillness which seemed to creep over our flesh like a chill, and to be seen and felt ; when suddenly out of this ghostly silence there came that shrill, warning signal, like the fierce, wild shriek of the wind rushing through the trees of the forest, giving warning of the coming storm. Then came the rattling fire of the carbineers as they poured a volley into the advancing column, which immediately halted and hurriedly formed to await the onset.

With Mosby at the head, Company A and part of Company B now charged, sweeping down the pike, scattering the advance and coming upon the main body, who stood firm until we were in their midst. Company C and the other portion of Company B now came out on their flank and rear. At first the Federals made a hot fight, but, unable to withstand the impetuosity of our charge, they broke and fled in every direction, some down the pike, others over the fences and across the fields. Their officers were unable to rally them. The pike and fields around were strewn with dead and wounded men and horses; arms, clothing, etc., were scattered around.

The Federals lost 12 or 15 killed and about 25 wounded, 72 prisoners and 90 horses were captured. Captain Read, who was in command, was killed.[7] Captain Manning, 3 lieutenants and several non-commissioned officers were among the prisoners.

---

[7]Among the killed belonging to the Second Mass. Cavalry were Capt. J. Sewell Read, of San Francisco ; Geo. W. Ferrier, California ; Byron H. Grover, California ; Wm. Downey, Boston ; James B. Hayden, Boston ; James Miles, Brookline, Mass ; Richard Powers, Roxbury ; Stephen Spooner, Ashland ; Abraham Waters, Medford ; Henry H. Dexter, Barton, Vt. ; James McCammon, Warren, Ill.

We had only one man killed, J. Pendleton Chappalear, of Fauquier. Among our wounded was Baron Von Massow, a Prussian. He had been seven years in the Prussian army without seeing any active service, and for the purpose of gratifying his curiosity in this respect he had come to this country. His first introduction was in the attack on the guards of a wagon train at Bealeton station. He was a brave soldier. He received a painful wound from a pistol in the hands of Captain Read, and Captain Chapman, seeing the Baron fall, killed Read by a well-directed shot.

B. H. SWEETING, CO. A.
(Harry Sweeting.)[8]

Harry (B. H.) Sweeting, of Baltimore, John Munson, Thos. Burke and John Edmonds were severely wounded, and several others slightly. We procured a carriage and brought out Edmonds and Munson. Young Chappalear's body was also brought off. In the engagement Mosby's horse was twice shot.

This raiding party was piloted through our territory by Charles Binns, a deserter from our command. Every effort was made to capture him, but

---

[8] B. H. Sweeting, more familiarly known in the command as "Harry" Sweeting. I received his picture in the same letter which informed me of his death. The Baltimore *Sun* contained the following notice of his death :

AN OLD SOLDIER'S DEATH.—*Dr. B. H. Sweeting was the hero of a thrilling war incident.*—Dr. B. H. Sweeting, an inmate of the Confederate Home at Pikesville, died yesterday morning (January 6, 1896,) at the City Hospital from injuries received by falling through the Philadelphia, Wilmington and Baltimore Railroad Bridge at Havre de Grace on Tuesday of last week.

He had been visiting friends in Hartford County, and started to walk across the bridge. After he had gone a few steps he slipped and fell through, injuring his right hip and receiving internal injuries. His fall was caused by his defective eyesight. He was brought to Baltimore and sent to the City Hospital, where it was at first thought he would recover.

Dr. Sweeting entered the service of the Confederacy in the First Maryland

mounted on a fleet horse he made off at the beginning of the
fray and escaped.[9]

---

Regiment, but afterward joined Mosby's battalion.  At Mountville, Va., his
horse was killed under him and he fought single-handed a scouting party,
killing and wounding several of its members.  His eyesight was almost destroyed in that fight and he was left for dead on the field, covered with sabre
cuts and stab wounds.

---

[9] *Report of Lieut. Col. John S. Mosby, Forty-third Va. Cavalry.*

*February 23, 1864.*

Major H. B. McCLELLAN, *Assistant Adjutant General, Cavalry Corps.*

MAJOR:  I have the honor to report that about 11 o'clock on the 21st instant, having learned that a body of 180 of the enemy's cavalry were on a raiding expedition in the vicinity of Middleburg, I started in pursuit with about
160 men.  On reaching Middleburg I found they had gone toward Leesburg via
Mountville, and that they had come from Vienna, in Fairfax.  Directing Captain Chapman, whom I left in command, to move down Goose Creek near to
Ball's Mill, I went with a small squad to reconnoitre in person.  On reaching
Leesburg I discovered they had taken the Dranesville pike.  After going about
6 miles in this direction they went into camp about 2 o'clock at night.

In the meantime I had ordered my command to Guilford Station, in order to
keep pace with their movements and to be in a position to intercept them.
After having ascertained where they had encamped, I moved my command out
to the pike about 2 miles from Dranesville, at a point offering fine natural
advantages for surprising an enemy.  Distributing the different companies in
positions where I could attack their front, flank and rear simultaneously, we
awaited the approach of the enemy.  Soon the concerted signal—a volley from
the carbineers under Montjoy—announced the time for attack.  With a terrific
yell, Chapman, Hunter and Williams, with their brave commands, dashed on
the unsuspecting Yankees.  Surprised and confounded, with no time to form,
they made but feeble resistance, and were perfectly overwhelmed by the shock
of the charge.  They fled in every direction in the wildest confusion, leaving on
the field at least 15 killed and a considerable number wounded, besides 70
prisoners in our hands, with all their horses, arms and equipments.  Among
their killed was the captain commanding.  A captain and 2 lieutenants are
among the prisoners who belong to the California Battalion.  Many of them
were also driven into the Potomac.  The gallantry of both my officers and men
was unsurpassed.

My loss was 1 man killed and 4 wounded ; none dangerously.

My thanks are due Captain Chapman and Lieutenants Williams and Hunter and Adjutant Chapman for their fidelity in executing every order.

Respectfully, your obedient servant,        JNO. S. MOSBY,

*Lieut. Col. Commanding.*

[First Indorsement.]

HEADQUARTERS CAVALRY CORPS,

*February 28, 1864.*

Respectfully forwarded.

This is another of the many brilliant exploits of this gallant leader.  His
boldness and skill are highly commended, as evidenced by the complete rout of

the enemy with so small loss.   Attention is invited to the special mention made of certain officers and men.                         J. E. B. STUART, *Major-Gen.*

[Second Indorsement.]

Respectfully forwarded, uniting in the commendation bestowed by General Stuart.                                                        R. E. LEE, *General.*

*Report of Brig.-Gen. Robert O. Tyler, U. S. Army.*

HEADQUARTERS TYLER'S DIVISION,
*Fairfax Court House, Va., February 23, 1864.*

TYLER to TAYLOR :   " I have the honor to report that a detachment of 125 men of the Second Massachusetts Cavalry, and 25 men of the Sixteenth New York Cavalry, under command of Capt. J. S. Read, Second Massachusetts Cavalry, encountered, on the 21st inst., in the vicinity of Circleville Post-office, 70 of Mosby's men, whom they defeated with severe loss to them.   On their return, within 2 miles of Dranesville, on the Leesburg turnpike, they were ambuscaded by a force of between 200 and 300 men, under command of Mosby.   Captain Read's command fought well, but were finally driven toward the Potomac, in the vicinity of Muddy Branch.   On receipt of the intelligence, a large force went immediately in pursuit, without, however, overtaking the enemy, who had ten hours the start, and the pursuit beyond Goose Creek was abandoned.   Our loss was 10 killed and 7 wounded.   Among the former, I regret to say, was Captain Read, a brave and noble soldier.   About 60 of the

BARON VON MASSOW.

detachment are yet unaccounted for.   A report will be sent by mail to-morrow."

*Fairfax Court House, February 23, 1864.*

TYLER to TAYLOR :   " The cavalry sent out last night have returned.   They followed the route of the rebel cavalry as far as Goose Creek.   Mosby had about 15 hours' start, and was moving rapidly toward Snicker's Gap.   Seven wounded men and the bodies of 8 killed have been brought in.   About 70 men are still unaccounted for.   I will telegraph more fully to-night."

# CHAPTER IX.

The Spring Campaign of 1864 opened with the prospect of being a very eventful one. In February, President Lincoln issued a call for 200,000 men to recruit the armies in the field, in March for 200,000 more, and in July followed a call for 500,000. In March, General Grant was appointed Lieutenant General and made his headquarters with the Army of the Potomac. General Meade was its immediate commander, but the movements were directed by General Grant.

As soon as the weather and the condition of the roads permitted, the armies were pushed forward, and again "On to Richmond!" was the war cry.

The vast bodies of troops moving around in all directions gave us plenty of work, and large and small parties of our men, either with Mosby himself, or under command of some of our officers or trusty men, were constantly engaged in scouting for the purpose of gathering information or cutting off communication and destroying supplies in the rear of the advancing armies, thus annoying and crippling them in their movements and compelling them to send back men from the front to protect their rear. As soon as we discovered a weak point, advantage was taken of it, and as a consequence the line would be strengthened. If this was done by weakening another place, we soon ascertained that fact and would swoop down on it like a hawk on a chicken yard. When the Federal armies were pushing on to Richmond, as their lines became more extended, greater numbers were required to guard them from our attacks, and in this way Mosby with his few men kept thousands of Federal soldiers from active duty in the front, to say nothing of the damage inflicted by these constant assaults.[1]

While the enemy were compelled to guard their lines, Mosby had none. When a body of troops was sent in search of him it was a very easy matter to keep out of their way if in heavy force, or cut off and attack any detachments from the main body and harass them on their march ; or, by ignoring their presence altogether, compel them to return to protect their own camps. It would have been folly for our little band to have met and fought every force sent against us. The enemy's resources being so much greater than ours, the contest would have been too unequal and it would have simply been a question of time as to when we would be utterly destroyed or driven out of the country.

The section chosen by Mosby as his base was well adapted for his purpose, having the Potomac river on the north, the

---

[1] *375 Men Sent Out to Capture 6.*

*Alexandria, February 29, 1864.*

Colonel TAYLOR, *Chief of Staff.*

COLONEL : It is reported that Mosby and 5 men are inside the lines beyond Falls Church. Two companies of cavalry from Vienna are in pursuit, and all my men are out to intercept him if possible.     H. H. WELLS,
*Lieut.-Colonel and Provost-Marshal-General.*

HEADQUARTERS DIVISION,  }
*February 29, 1864.*  }

Lieut.-Col. J. H. TAYLOR,
*Assistant Adjutant-General, Department of Washington.*

I have the honor to report all quiet. A party of 5 of "Mosby's men" were seen this morning near Chichester Mills. A scouting party, consisting of 200 men, under command of Major Nicholson, Sixteenth New York Cavalry, was sent out at 2 p. m. to-day to scour the country from Annandale to the Occoquan, by Wolf Run Shoals ; thence, between Bull Run battlefield and Centreville, to Gum Spring, Frying Pan, and around Dranesville. It is supposed from information received that a considerable force of the enemy's cavalry is in our vicinity. Three parties of dismounted men, two of 50 and one of 75 men, will go out to-night to operate by ambuscade in the region through which it is believed the enemy will be compelled to pass.

A. H. GRIMSHAW,
*Colonel, Commanding Division.*

line of railroad from Washington to Fredericksburg and Richmond on the east, and the line of advance from Harper's Ferry up the Shenandoah Valley on the west—all within easy striking distance ; and having once occupied this territory he was never driven out.

*Tuesday, March 8.*—The heavy rain of last night changed to snow this morning, and then again to rain, but towards noon the rain ceased, and the cheery sunshine peeping through the scattering clouds made it pleasant overhead, though the roads were in bad condition for traveling. Lieutenant Hunter came to Upperville and said to those of our men he found in town :

MAJOR JERRY A. SULLIVAN,
First New York Veteran Cavalry.
Killed in a skirmish at Kabletown, March
10, 1864.
From a Photograph.

"Colonel Mosby wants 40 good men to whip 60 Yankees, as he wants a few extra horses after dividing the captures."

Rectortown was designated as the rendezvous. Mosby accordingly started from that place, marching to a point on the road from Bristoe Station to Greenwich, where we kept close in the pines, awaiting the approach of the patrol which was sent daily along the road for the protection of the Orange and Alexandria railroad. When the patrol passed by we charged in their rear. They did not tarry to receive the charge, but fled at the first alarm, scattering through the woods. We captured only 9 men and 10 horses. None of our party was injured, though a few of the Federals were wounded. [See Mosby's Report, Appendix, VIII.]

*Wednesday, March 9.*—Company C met to-day at Paris. Lieut. A. E. Richards, with between 40 and 50 men, crossed the Shenandoah river in the evening, and halted about midnight a few miles beyond Kabletown. John Chew had advised Richards of the situation of a picket post near his father's house, on the road to Charlestown, and now acted as guide. Lieutenant Bryandt of the First New York Veterans, was in command of the picket. Just as day was breaking, Richards entered the camp from the direction of Charlestown. The few who were awake were under the impression that our men were the relief picket and no resistance was offered. One of the Federals was killed, however, by a shot fired by one of our men as we rushed into the camp.

As soon as the Federals became aware of the capture of the picket, a party of 25 cavalry under Major Jerry A. Sullivan was sent from Charlestown in pursuit of Richards. At Kabletown they overtook 6 of our men, Robert S. Walker, Fountain Beattie, Dr. J. R. Sowers, B. S. Edmonds, John Hearn and Rucker, who had loitered in the rear. Although far behind their comrades, they did not hesitate, and without waiting for their pursuers to come up, charged upon them, killing Major Sullivan and two or three others and wounding several. The Federals, seeing their leader fall and so many with him, became panic stricken and fell back in confusion. Our men then pushed forward and rejoined the command. William Martin had been captured by Major Sullivan before the fight, and as soon as our men charged he disarmed his guard, and seizing his carbine, took part in the melee[2].

Altogether 20 prisoners, including Lieutenant Bryandt, and 30 horses with arms and equipments, were brought off by Richards. [See Mosby's Report, Appendix, VIII.]

---

[2] *Report of Col. R. F. Taylor, Commanding Brigade.*

HEADQUARTERS CAVALRY BRIGADE, }
*Halltown, Va., March 11, 1864.* }

TAYLOR to BOONE : " I have the honor to report that our pickets were attacked between Charlestown, Va., and the river, at the crossing of the Keys' Ferry and Kabletown roads, yesterday morning at 6 o'clock by what is supposed to be a portion of Mosby's command, numbering from 40 to 80 men. The force passed to the left of the vedette on the Kabletown road, seen by them, but sup. posed to be a reserve from Charlestown, they being dressed in our uniform. The mistake was not discovered until the rebels had obtained a position and fired a volley into the reserve at less than 10 rods distant, completely surprising

Mosby was very active in searching for and breaking up distilleries. He would send details of men to destroy the stills and empty out the liquor. They were also sent to places where liquor was kept for sale, with orders to pour out all liquor found on the premises. This was done not only on account of the demoralizing influence the traffic would have upon his men, but also on account of the scarcity of grain, all of which was needed to supply food for man and beast.

Downey's still-house in Loudoun, near the Potomac river, will be remembered as a notorious place, being quite a resort for the Federal soldiers stationed along the river. A party of " Mosby's Men " sent there on one occasion destroyed the still and emptied the liquor into the creek. The Downeys, in revenge for this, concealed a number of Federal soldiers in the house, and shortly afterwards, when our Quartermaster, Captain James, John Bolling and Major Hibbs, who were pressing corn and bacon in Loudoun, went to the house to collect their quota, they were seized by the enemy and carried prisoners across the Potomac to Berlin. [See Chapter XXVII.]

them. The loss at the reserve post is 1 killed and 4 wounded, and 2 lieutenants and 11 privates missing.

"After the attack they retreated with great rapidity by the way of Kabletown, recrossing at Sampson's Ford, about 3 miles this side of Snicker's Ferry, except small parties, which went to the right below Kabletown, crossing near and at Snicker's Ferry. Major Sullivan, commanding picket, pursued the enemy with 9 men, overtaking them at Kabletown ; found them concealed behind an old building, from which they fired a volley, killing Major Sullivan and 2 privates, and severely wounding Lieutenant Baker, all of the First New York Veteran Cavalry. The balance of the reserve, under Lieutenant Conway, numbering about 50 men, came up a few moments after, but failed to overtake the enemy. The firing was distinctly heard at this place, and the entire force ordered out. Lieutenant Wyckoff, with 15 men, got to the ford just as they had succeeded in crossing. Anticipating an attack, I sent Lieutenant Wyckoff to Charlestown on the evening of March 9, informing Major Sullivan of the probability of an attack, ordering him to strengthen his pickets and order them to keep on the alert, which I learn he did. I also informed him that I had 150 men in readiness to re-enforce him at any moment. I learn that there were a number of shots fired by the vedette at the post attacked between the hour of 3 and the time of the attack.

" I forbear to express an opinion as to where the blame should attach until I can further investigate the matter."

One day a detail was sent to a certain house with the usual instructions to pour out all liquor found on the premises. They were met by an old lady who told them she was very poor; that she had no other means of gaining a living, and it was hard to lose her stock in trade. The boys relented, but the Colonel's orders were plain and imperative. At last one said:

"Old woman, have you a big wash tub?"

"Yes," she answered.

"Bring it here, then."

It was accordingly brought and the liquor poured into it.

"The Colonel said we must pour out the liquor, but he didn't say where we should pour it."

Filling a canteen for themselves, they went on their way, not only rejoicing themselves, but leaving the old lady to rejoice also.

*Friday, March 25* —As Mosby, with 6 men, was returning from a scout in the Valley, with 4 prisoners and horses, he stopped at a house a few miles below Paris, leaving Sergeant Wrenn in charge of the prisoners while he went into the house. Among the prisoners were Sergeant Weatherbee, of Company B, and

DR. J. R. SOWERS, CO. D.

Corporal Simpson, of Company H, Griswold Light Cavalry, Twenty-first New York. Corporal Simpson, who had been watching his opportunity, pretended to fasten his horse to the stile, but really put his foot in the stirrup, suddenly sprang upon the horse belonging to Mosby, drew a pistol from the holster, fired at Sergeant Wrenn and galloped off. Weatherbee made his escape at the same time on another horse. They were followed to Paris, but it was snowing so heavily at the time that it was impossible to see fifty yards ahead, and once fairly started the prisoners were safe from capture. Mosby regretted the loss of his noble gray horse, which was a fine animal and a great favorite, more than he did the loss of the prisoners.

*Monday, March 28.*—At a meeting held at Paris, Company D was organized. R. P. Montjoy was chosen Captain; Alfred Glascock, First Lieutenant; Charles E. Grogan, Second Lieutenant, and William Trunnell, Third Lieutenant.

Capt. R. P. Montjoy was a Mississippian and entered the army as a private in an infantry regiment from his native State, but he afterwards obtained a transfer to Mosby's command.

Lieut. Alfred Glascock, of Fauquier, first entered the army as a private, but was promoted to a lieutenancy in Capt. (afterwards General) Turner Ashby's Cavalry Company. After the death of Ashby he joined Mosby, where by his gallant conduct he soon attracted the attention of his superiors as well as of his comrades.

CAPT. ALFRED GLASCOCK, CO. D.
From a Photograph taken whon he was a Lieutenant under Gen. Turner Ashby.

Lieut. Charles E. Grogan was born in Clarke County, Virginia, but made his home in Maryland. In July, 1861, he crossed the Potomac into Virginia and enlisted in Capt. William H. Murray's Company, First Maryland Regiment, under Colonel, afterwards Gen. George H. Stewart; was first under fire at the Battle of Bull Run; afterwards acted as aid to Gen. I. R. Trimble, and received his first wound at Chancellorsville, where he was officially commended for conspicuous service by Gen. R. E. Colston, who in that battle commanded General Trimble's Division, Trimble at the time being disabled from a wound received at the second battle of Manassas. In the battle of Gettysburg, Grogan was twice wounded while acting as aid to General Trimble.

When Lee fell back he was left wounded in hospital near Gettysburg, and after some weeks was sent with Trimble and other prisoners, first to Fort McHenry and thence to Johnson's Island on Lake Erie, from which place he made his escape, and after a long and tedious journey succeeded in reaching Virginia, where he joined Mosby.

Lieut. William Trunnell was a Marylander, a brave soldier, who had by his daring exploits won the esteem of the command and of his commander.

In Company A, Harry Hatcher, formerly of the Seventh Virginia Cavalry, was elected Third Lieutenant to succeed Nelson, who had been promoted to the position filled by Lieutenant Hunter, who had in turn succeeded to the vacancy occasioned by the death of Lieutenant Turner.

LIEUT. CHARLES E. GROCAN, CO. D.
From a Photograph taken during the War.

On the day previous to the election in Company D, Lieutenant Trunnell went over into the Shenandoah Valley on a scout with John S. Russell, John Castleman and a man named Coyle, of the Twelfth Virginia Cavalry. On the night of March 27th, near Bunker Hill, they were fired upon by a party of Federal soldiers in ambush, and Coyle and Trunnell were killed, but Russell and Castleman escaped. The fact of Trunnell's death was not known until after the election, and then David S. Briscoe, of Baltimore, was chosen to fill the office.

*Wednesday, April 13.*—A young man named M. W. Flannery, belonging to Company A, was killed to-day near Catlett's Station. He had already been twice in the Federal camp, and was approaching a picket with the intention of capturing him when the picket ordered him to halt. While parleying with the soldier a sudden gust of wind blew open his overcoat, exposing his gray uniform, and the soldier fired at him, the ball entering his breast. Flannery thrust his handkerchief into his bosom to staunch the flow of blood, and drawing his pistol, fired twice at the picket, and raised the weapon to fire a third time, but fell to the ground before he could pull the trigger. He was a determined man and a brave soldier.

*Tuesday, April 19.*—It was now rumored that the Federal forces camped around Warrenton were contemplating a raid through " Mosby's Confederacy," and with the Cornwell and Binn's raids fresh in their memory, our men were determined to give them a warm reception. Mosby ordered the command to assemble at Somerset Mills, on the road from Piedmont to Paris. Soon after dark we moved, with 180 men, to the woods near Mrs. Shacklett's, about a mile from Piedmont, where we lay concealed, awaiting the approach of the raiders. Pickets were placed to warn us of their coming ; wire was stretched across the road to drag them from their horses, as they were expected to dash

LIEUT. DAVID S. BRISCOE, CO. D.
From a Photograph.

along the road. Every description of old firearms—shot guns and muskets, were brought out and heavily loaded with shot and slugs. In many cases it was, no doubt, as fortunate for our own men as for the enemy that these guns were not discharged. Each man then had his revolvers to finish up the work of destruction. We waited until daylight, when we were dismissed, with instructions to meet again at night (April 20th). This we did, and with 220 men went through the same performance, which was also repeated on the night following (April 21st). But the enemy failed to materialize. Whether they had friends among us who gave them warning, or whether they were content to rest on their laurels rather than risk their lives by attempting another such raid we knew not—we only knew that they did not come.

*Friday, April 22.*—Mosby, with 30 men, attacked a picket post near Hunter's Mill, in Fairfax. Mosby dismounted his men, leaving a few in charge of the horses, and charged on foot, killing 1 and capturing 5 prisoners and 18 horses. Most of the Federals escaped in the darkness.

After the capture Lieutenant Hunter was ordered to take the command back to Fauquier, while Mosby went on a scout with Bush. Underwood.

In the meantime, some of the fugitive pickets had notified the Federal cavalry at Vienna of the attack on the post, and Colonel Lowell started a detachment of the California Battalion in pursuit of the Rangers, who were overtaken near Aldie, on the Little River turnpike.

As soon as the Federals came in sight, Hunter sent forward the prisoners and horses under guard, and with Lieutenant Nelson halted his command and boldly charged upon the enemy. The contest was a sharp one, but the forces being too unequal in point of numbers, the Rangers were defeated. Lieutenant Hunter of Company A, was riding a fine-looking gray horse, which had been captured at the picket post. In the fight the horse fell and Hunter endeavored to make his escape on foot, but was taken prisoner. Nelson, in attempting to save Hunter, was shot in the hip, but made his way out, and was taken to Sam Craig's, in the Bull Run mountains. Welt Hatcher was also wounded slightly. All the prisoners and horses were brought out.[3] [See Mosby's Report, Appendix, VIII.]

---

[3] HEADQUARTERS CAVALRY BRIGADE, <br> *Vienna, Va., April 23, 1864.*

LOWELL to LA MOTTE : " I have the honor to report all quiet in this vicinity. The pickets near Hunter's Mills were attacked about 4 A. M. to-day by a dismounted party, with a loss of 9 horses and 3 men captured and 1 man wounded. No resistance was made by the pickets, only 3 shots being fired. A party started out about reveille this morning, as soon as the news of the attack reached camp, and, after finding the trail, started after the party in rapid pursuit, came

In April Lieut. A. E. Richards was promoted to the command of Company B, as appears by the following order:

SPECIAL ORDER, }  HEADQUARTERS 43D BATTALION,
   NO. —.   }        PARTIZAN RANGERS.
*April 26, 1864.*

First Lieutenant Adolphus E. Richards, Company C, having been promoted by his Excellency, the President, to the Captaincy of Company B for gallantry and skill displayed in action, will be respected and obeyed accordingly.
JOHN S. MOSBY,
*Lieut.-Colonel Commanding.*

*Friday, April 29.*—A detail of our men being down in Loudoun on a foraging expedition, Colonel Lowell started from Vienna with a brigade of cavalry, supported by General Tyler's brigade of infantry from Fairfax C. H., to drive them out and "gobble up" Mosby. A body of the Federal cavalry came up to Leesburg and moved on to Middleburg, where they were joined by the larger force, and together they scoured the country around for three or four days. Being so vastly superior to us in numbers, we could not risk an open field fight, but by hovering around their camps, making sudden dashes and firing on them, we kept them from straggling and doing more damage. Some sharp skirmishes took place at times, in which quite a number were lost on both sides.

MAJOR ADOLPHUS E. RICHARDS, Forty-third Battalion, Virginia Cavalry. From a Photograph taken when Captain of Company B.

---

in sight of them about 10 miles of Aldie, and chased them up the pike through the town, the rebels scattering in all directions.

"Lieut. W. L. Hunter, of Co. A, Mosby's Battalion, was taken prisoner during the chase and brought to this camp. Two horses were re-taken and 1 shot. One man was wounded slightly. The party consisted of 50 men, under the command of Mosby himself. They came down to the vicinity of the picket and crossed the creek mounted, where a portion of them dismounted and advanced on foot to the attack."

When the Federal cavalry entered Leesburg tnere were about a dozen of " Mosby's Men " in town. A number were in and around the hotel, with their horses standing in the street. The Federals were within two hundred yards of the hotel when their approach was first noticed by a group on the veranda. Ewell Atwell and —— Flack rushed to their horses, mounted and dashed off, with the enemy in hot pursuit. Flack was shot on the edge of town. Atwell, finding his pursuers gaining on him, abandoned his horse and jumping through an Osage orange hedge, made his escape. Will. Devine and —— King ran through the hotel and out into the back yard, the former taking refuge in the house of a friend of Union sympathies and the latter in the Episco. pal church ; both escaped. All who were in the bar-room were captured except John P. DeButts of Company A. He had stopped in Leesburg to have his horse shod and being cut off from the black-smith's shop, attempted to fight his way to his horse, but was shot through the breast and captured. He

JOHN P. DeBUTTS, CO. A.
From a Photograph taken in 1868.

was taken to Fort Delaware, where he was kept a prisoner for eleven months.

DeButts joined Mosby soon after he started out as a Partisan and some months before his first company was or-ganized. He was one of the 29 who raided Fairfax Court House and captured General Stoughton. In the early part of the war DeButts served in the First Virginia Cavalry, under Col. R. Welby Carter. He was one of 35 men of Company H of that regiment who made the famous charge near the Henry House at the first battle of Manassas, in which 8 men were killed and the majority of the company wounded; he having his pistol shot out of his hand and a finger taken with it.

Flack was a member of Company D. His remains were taken to his home in Baltimore by his brother a few days after his death.

The Federal Cavalry marched through Bloomfield, by Wernels, Quaker Lane and Trapp road to Upperville, cap-

COL. CHARLES RUSSELL LOWELL, Jr.,
Second Massachusetts Cavalry.
Killed at Battle of Cedar Creek, Oct. 19, 1864, while
commanding Reserve Cavalry Brigade of
Sheridan's Army.

turing on their way Edwin Rowzee, George H. Ayre, Champ Fitzhugh and others. Captain Richards followed in their rear with about 40 men and charged them near Loughborough's, killing one and wounding several, and capturing one man with his horse and equipments.

The Federals then went to Holland's Factory, where they destroyed and carried off a quantity of wool, and afterwards came back to Upperville, camping at night near Hatcher's Mills, a short distance below town.

One of our men named Ware was shot in the hip while running up the mountain above Upperville.

*Saturday, April 30.*—Mosby returned to-day from Fairfax, where he had been scouting with Walter Whaley, bringing with him 2 prisoners, a lieutenant and a private, with their horses and accoutrements. Lieutenant Glasscock came in from the Valley with three prisoners and their horses.

Giving no heed to the presence of the enemy, Mosby, taking a few men with him, went over into the Shenandoah Valley on a scout.

Our men still hung around the Federals, watching their manœuvres and occasionally exchanging shots. Edward Smith, of Company B, was killed near Melton's.

The Federals on their route seized a wagon loaded with bacon, the property of Mr. George Calvert, an old resident of Upperville. When in the vicinity of that town the negro teamster turned the horses loose and they were driven home by his dog.[4]

---

[4] *Federal Reports.*

*Fairfax Court-House, May 1, 1864.*

TYLER to TAYLOR : "The cavalry, Colonel Lowell, have returned to Vienna, after visiting Leesburg, Upperville, Rectortown, &c. They bring 23 of 'Mosby's Men' prisoners, 3 blockade runners, 20 to 25 horses, some wool, tobacco and other contraband goods. Colonel Lowell lost one sergeant and 2 privates killed, 2 wounded and 4 prisoners. Mosby lost 2 killed and 4 wounded (2 prisoners). The body buried at Upperville was brought to Vienna, where it is subject to order."

HEADQUARTERS CAVALRY BRIGADE, }
*Vienna, Va., May 1, 1864.* }

LOWELL to LA MOTTE : " I have the honor to report return of the cavalry scout sent out on Thursday after visiting Leesburg, Upperville, Paris, Bloomfield, Union and Rectortown. No force but Mosby was found there. We searched most of the houses designated by General Auger, and have brought in quite a number of arms and contraband goods ; also 21 of 'Mosby's Men' and 2 blockade runners (besides 1 of 'Mosby's Men' and 1 blockade runner turned over by Colonel McMahon), and from 20 to 25 horses. A report in full from the Provost Marshal will be forwarded to-morrow. We brought off a portion of the wool indicated in the letter to General Auger, and supplied the command pretty well with tobacco. It was impossible to get teams to haul the remainder of the wool. The houses where the bulk of the tobacco must have been stored we did not visit, as the direction of some was given erroneously in the letter, and a good deal of time thus lost. Those below Salem must be left for another visit.

" We lost 1 sergeant killed, 1 prisoner and 2 wounded of Second Massachusetts Cavalry, 2 privates killed and 3 prisoners Sixteenth New York Cavalry ; 1 of the killed and all of these prisoners were straggling away from the command improperly. We killed 1 of Mosby's Battalion and 1 of Sixth Virginia Cavalry, serving with Mosby; wounded 2, besides 2 wounded brought in."

## CHAPTER X.

The Federal Army under General Grant was now moving
towards Fredericksburg, their cavalry had all left the neighborhood of Warrenton, and the terrible struggle in the
Wilderness had already commenced.

The command assembled at Rectortown on Saturday, May
7th, and bivouacked, awaiting the return of Mosby, who
was on a scout near Brandy Station. He returned before
noon on the 8th and issued his orders to the command.
Lieutenant Hatcher was sent down Fairfax with a small
party, but accomplished nothing worth noting. Captains
Richards and Chapman, with 15 to 20 men each, were instructed to operate in the Shenandoah Valley. *Major* Hibbs,
with a detail, was sent down to Loudoun to press corn for
the use of the Battalion, while Mosby, with about 50 of
the best mounted men, started towards the Rappahannock
and the rear of Grant's army.

Mosby left Salem about 5 P. M., halting at Warrenton for
supper. Near Rappahannock Station[1] we came upon a deserted camp. The old roads were blockaded with felled
trees, new roads had been cut, and owing to the darkness we
had some difficulty in getting through the barricades. At
last we halted in a thick body of pines, and haltering our
horses to the trees, lay down beside them until morning.
At times, when there were no convenient places to fasten
our horses, we would throw the bridles over the horses'
heads, and putting one hand through the bridle, fold our
arms and stretch ourselves on the ground, sometimes finding
our tired animals sleeping by our sides when we awoke.

---

[1] Now called Remington.

At daylight on the morning of the 9th we were again on our road, passing through an old camp which a sign-board informed us had been honored with the name of "Liberty." The logs and stone chimneys of the roofless huts remained standing, and scattered around were coffee pots, tin cups and cans, old clothing, etc., left by the late occupants. The old guard-house and the officers' quarters could be easily distinguished among the ruins. We halted in the pine woods about a mile and a half from the railroad, while Mosby and Sergeant Johnson went along the line of the road to reconnoitre. In the evening he returned, and taking 35 men proceeded towards Fredericksburg.

The remainder of the men, under Sergeant Johnson, were ordered to burn two bridges near Bealeton Station, and on the night of the 9th started to perform that task. Going through an abandoned camp, each man in obedience to orders dismounted and picked up an empty box, numbers of which were lying around, to be used in firing the bridges. The night was dark, and after riding two or three miles, the guide

SERGT. HORACE JOHNSON, CO. B.

said: "Put down your boxes and go back." He had lost his way.

Reaching a piece of woods, the party lay by their horses to await the coming of day to see where they were, and in the morning found themselves within half a mile of the starting place of the previous night. The guide said that though born and reared within three miles of the place, the whole face of the country was so changed that he could not recognize it.

Mosby with his party was more fortunate. Detaching about a dozen of his men to destroy some bridges in the direction of Culpeper Court House, he moved on, intending to strike Grant's line of communication between Fredericksburg and the Potomac river. Near Belle Plain he discovered a wagon train moving towards the Potomac. He divided his command, directing Grogan to take one-half to the rear of the train and counting off ten wagons, to tell the

CULPEPER COURT HOUSE IN WAR TIMES.

driver of the tenth wagon to turn off to the left—that he was on the wrong road. This would cause the wagons behind to follow, while those in front went ahead without the loss being noticed. The ruse worked well and the wagons wheeled off out of the road. W. Ben Palmer was then ordered to go to the front with 10 men, stop the train and take the remainder of the wagons. Just as Palmer started on his mission, a Federal officer rode back from the front of the train and said roughly:

"Who in the hell has stopped these wagons and turned them off the road?"

"Colonel Mosby," answered Palmer, covering him with his pistol.

The officer gave utterance to a feeble grunt and was turned over to Mosby.

Palmer then went on. The train meanwhile had come to a halt, the rear wagons having been missed and the captured officer being on his way back to learn the cause of the stoppage. Mosby had instructed Palmer not to fire a shot if he could avoid it, but some of the drivers resisted and a number of shots were exchanged. It was soon over, however, and all the teams were unhitched from the wagons. The night was dark, with a drizzling rain, and as Palmer moved off with his captures to rejoin Mosby, he found himself in the vicinity of a Federal camp. The camp-fires were burning and the voices of the soldiers could be plainly heard. He quickly took the back track and soon heard some one call him in a low tone. It was Mosby, who said:

"I heard the shooting and thought you had run into some Yankee cavalry. I went to Grogan to get his men to help you out."

While Mosby was on this errand, Palmer had passed by and was on the road to the camp,

Twenty-five prisoners, 45 horses and 15 mules were captured on this raid, without the loss or injury of a man.

Mosby was so well pleased with his success that on his return to Fauquier he immediately called his command together and with 50 fresh men and horses moved down for another attack, but found the line of communication so heavily guarded with cavalry and infantry that it was useless to make any demonstration.

We will now return to Captains Richards and Chapman, who had been detailed to operate in the Shenandoah Valley in the rear of Sigel's forces, now moving up the Valley.

Crossing the Shenandoah at Berry's Ferry, Richards, with 16 men, on the morning of the 9th of May, pushed on towards Newtown, where he lay in the woods all day, occasionally picking up a few stragglers. About noon 3 Federal cavalrymen were observed riding along the pike and Richards, with Charles H. Dear, Boyd Smith and Charles L. Hall galloped out and followed them into the village. Spurring their horses, they were soon beside the trio and escorted them off to the woods, whence they were sent with the other prisoners under a guard of 4 men to Fauquier.

Towards night Richards moved off in the direction of Winchester, with 12 men, telling them to keep quiet; that

if they met any Yankees he would do the talking, and if only a small detachment, the Rangers should ride up beside them and capture them. It was raining and darkness soon set in. After riding about three miles, the tramp of horses was heard on the pike and in a few moments came an order to halt, with the query:

"Who comes there?"

"First New York Cavalry," replied Richards.

"All right, First New York," said the Federal officer, "we are the Twenty-first New York; come on. We are the advance guard of a wagon train." (24 men.)

MAJOR-GENERAL FRANZ SIGEL, U. S. A.

Richards then learned that the train, with a heavy guard of cavalry, was only a few hundred yards behind. Continuing the conversation, Richards said his party was on its way to Martinsburg to telegraph to Washington that Sigel had whipped the Rebs and had gone on to Staunton. The Federals replied with a cheer. Richards said he had no time to stop, and rode by with his men in single file. As his twelfth man reached the head of the column, they wheeled and covering the Federals with their revolvers, demanded a surrender. The Rangers were proceeding to disarm them quietly, when a pistol shot was fired and the fight became general. Reinforcements from the main body charged up and Richards was compelled to retreat. The Rangers escaped by taking to the woods. Charles H. Dear was wounded, receiving a ball in his side. A number of the Federals were killed and wounded. (See Mosby's Report, Appendix, X.)

Chapman, with his party, proceeded to the vicinity of the Winchester turnpike, hoping to encounter one of the scouting parties of Federals in their daily excursions. He overtook a detachment of the First New York Cavalry, and after a sharp skirmish captured 6 prisoners and 7 horses, but was compelled to retire on the approach of the regiment, bringing off his captures safely. Lieut. Chapman and Dr. Sowers had their horses shot, but none of the men were injured.

CHARLES H. DEAR, CO. E.
From a Photograph taken during the War.

*Monday, May 16.* — Learning that a portion of Keyes' command (the Loudoun Rangers) had crossed the Potomac and were then in Loudoun County, Captain A. E. Richards started from Bloomfield with 30 men, hoping to have a brush with them. We reached Hillsborough about 10 o'clock at night and getting on their trail, followed on to Waterford, near which place we halted. Shortly after daylight on the morning of the 17th we approached the town, keeping out of sight behind a hill, while Richards with two men went into town to draw the enemy out. He was soon observed and fired upon, and 6 of Keyes' men gave chase, following nearly to where we were concealed. As Richards came in sight he waved his hat and away we went, firing into the advancing party. Of the 6 men but one returned —3 were wounded and 2 captured. We dashed through the town and saw the enemy forming in a field some distance beyond. We charged them with a yell and they broke and ran. We kept up the chase for about three miles, running them into the Kittoctan Hills, where many jumped from their horses, leaving them standing while they hid in the bushes. Two were killed, 4 wounded; five prisoners and 15 horses with their equipments were brought off. One of the prisoners told us they had 45 men. We did not have a man injured.[2]

*Saturday, May 21.*—Command met yesterday, but the Shenandoah River could not be forded, owing to the recent heavy rain, and we bivouacked near Mount Carmel Church, crossing the river this morning with 103 men.[3]

Mosby, however, crossed yesterday in a skiff with a few men, swimming their horses, and went on a scout towards Winchester. While riding along the turnpike, a patrol of

---

[2] *Harper's Ferry, May 17, 1864.*

KELLEY to HALLECK : "A company of independent cavalry, raised in Loudoun County, Va., were attacked this A. M. near Waterford, in said county, by a detachment of Mosby's Men, numbering about 100. Our men were driven in here, losing 2 killed and 7 captured."

*Point of Rocks, May 17, 1864.*

DUNCAN to SLOUGH : "Mosby, with his command, is in Loudoun. Had a fight with Captain Keyes yesterday, killing and capturing 8. Three of Mosby's officers will be married in Leesburg to-night. A great frolic. There are about 300 of them. A good chance to catch them."

*Point of Rocks, May 18, 1864.*

WHITE to BURLEIGH : "Up to the present time there has 13 men and 11 horses come in of Captain Keyes' command."

---

[3] HEADQUARTERS, *Harper's Ferry, May 23, 1864.*

BURLEIGH to MAULSBY : "I hear from good authority that 150 of Mosby's men have crossed into Clarke County. Send no trains out unless very well guarded, as they will surely be attacked."

8 men was seen approaching, and, upon being halted, told Mosby to dismount and advance. "No, I will not," said he ; "how do we know who you are?" While the conversation was going on, some of the Rangers manœuvered to get in the front and rear. Mosby then demanded their surrender, and the whole patrol was captured, without firing a shot.

Mosby to-day rejoined the command, which had, in the meantime, moved to a point a few miles from Guard Hill.

At Guard Hill was a picket post of about 75 men. Stopping at a house near by, Mosby questioned a man regarding the position, numbers, etc., of the picket. The man tried to persuade him to give up the idea of attack, saying that the force was too heavy ; that they had been reinforced; that there were 250 cavalry and 50 or 60 infantry at the post, and that the cavalry were well mounted.

"That is so much the better," said Mosby ; "two horses apiece and good ones at that."

The post was in the pines, but we did not know its exact position. Lieutenants Samuel Chapman and Nelson went in to reconnoitre and were twice fired on. Dismounted men were then sent in advance, and moving cautiously in the rear until near enough to charge, the order was given. Firing a volley, we dashed into the camp. The Federals fled on foot, taking refuge in the thick woods. They were heard talking at a short distance, when another volley silenced and scattered them. The horses tied around were driven off, and the men helped themselves to the spoils of the camp. Some horses were left on the road, but 66 horses were brought away,

SERGT. THOMAS BOOKER, CO. E.
From a War-time Photograph.

together with 16 prisoners.   One Federal soldier was killed
and one wounded.   Mosby sustained no loss.[4]

---

[4] In consequence of this capture, the following orders were issued by the
Federal commander :

GENERAL ORDERS }             HDQRS. DEPT. OF WEST VIRGINIA,
     No. 31.     }        *In the Field, near Cedar Creek, May 24, 1864.*

II. Maj. Henry Roessle, Fifteenth New York Cavalry, having grossly neglected his duty while in command of pickets, resulting in the capture of 11 men
and 45 horses, is dishonorably dismissed the service of the United States from
this date, subject to the approval of His Excellency, the President.

III. It has been reported to the Commanding General that Capt. Michael
Auer, Company A, Fifteenth New York Cavalry, dismissed yesterday for the
same offense, behaved bravely when aroused, and exerted himself to rally his
surprised pickets.   Personal bravery is indispensable in a good soldier, but
cannot be urged as an excuse for gross neglect of a vital duty, thus endanger-
ing the lives of thousands of our fellow-soldiers and the welfare of the country.
Picket and outpost duty must be attended to with the greatest strictness.   Careless and inefficient officers must give way to trustworthy privates.

By command of Major-General Hunter.

CHAS. G. HALPINE,
*Assistant Adjutant-General.*

# CHAPTER XI.

The Shenandoah Valley was now the theatre of active and earnest war.  In the early part of May General Sigel was sent with a large force up the Valley, but meeting with defeat at New Market, he was superseded by General Hunter, who undertook an expedition against Lynchburg.  Being compelled to retreat by General Early, who followed up his advantage by invading Maryland and threatening Washington, Hunter was in turn displaced by General Sheridan, to whom was entrusted the command of the Federal forces in the Valley.

*Saturday, May 28.*—The command met at Rectortown, and Mosby with 144 men marched off, passing through Markham and Linden, and bivouacked in a field a short distance from Front Royal.  About midnight a wagon loaded with corn was brought in and the men were roused to feed their horses.  Soon the poor animals were contentedly munching their corn, while their masters lay around on the grass and in the fence corners.

Next morning (29th) we crossed the Shenandoah river and moved on towards Strasburg, halting about a mile or two from the town, where we remained nearly the whole day.  Colonel Mosby and a few men who were watching the road saw a train of wagons passing along, but it was too heavily guarded to be attacked.  Later in the day about 100 cavalry passed by, but as they were supposed to be on their way to escort a train they, too, were suffered to pass unmolested.

In the evening we moved off, keeping a line parallel with, but out of sight of the turnpike leading from Winchester to Strasburg, and halted near Middletown.  At this place the Federals had been butchering cattle, and our noses were greeted with a horrible stench from the heads, feet, paunches and entrails scattered around.

On the morning of the 30th we marched down the Valley turnpike, entering Middletown about daybreak. Few of the inhabitants were then stirring, and quiet reigned in the little town. Occasionally a face would appear at some half-opened

OSCAR DECATUR MILLER, CO. E.

window and then suddenly disappear, after which the door would open and a fair lily-of-the-Valley would be seen coming forward with a supply of bread and milk, which was very acceptable to our hungry men. At one house a door was opened and a man stepped out. He looked as though he had but recently left his bed. Rubbing his eyes, he gazed at us in surprise, as if unwilling to believe his senses, then suddenly exclaimed—"Rebels, by God!" His evident surprise and the earnest manner in which it was expressed were amusing, and caused a ripple of laughter along our line. As we approached Newtown, Mosby and a few men, riding in advance, captured a picket of 3 men.

Between Middletown and Newtown[1] we saw the smoking remains of a train of wagons which had been captured and burned by Major Harry Gilmor during the night. Near by a heavy smoke rolled upward from a barn, the property of a lady. It had been set on fire by the Federals in retaliation for the destruction of the train.[2]

---

[1] Newtown was formerly called Stephensburg, after Peter Stephens, its founder. It is now called Stephens City. It is 8 miles south of Winchester. Middletown is 5 miles south of Newtown.

[2] HEADQUARTERS DEPARTMENT OF WEST VIRGINIA, }
    *In the Field, at Rude's Hill, Va., May 30, 1864.* }

Major T. QUINN, *Commanding First New York Cavalry :*

MAJOR : You will detail from your command 200 men, with the proper complement of commissioned officers, to proceed to Newtown to-morrow morning at 3 o'clock, for the purpose of burning every house, store and outbuilding in

General Hunter, commanding the Federal forces in the Valley, had in the latter part of May issued a proclamation, in which he said:

"For every train fired or soldier *assassinated*, the house and other property of every secession sympathizer residing within a circuit of five miles shall be destroyed by fire; and for all public property taken or destroyed, an assessment of five times the value of such property will be made upon the secession sympathizers residing within a circuit of ten miles around the point at which the offence was committed."

MAJ.-GEN. DAVID HUNTER, U. S. A.

These citizens upon whom Hunter proposed to retaliate were no more responsible for our acts than the most loyal citizen of the North, and they were powerless to prevent them. This brutal edict was in keeping with other acts of Hunter. General Early, in his "Memoirs," enumerates some of the barbarous outrages of Hunter, such as the burning of the Military Institute at Lexington, with its contents, including its library and scientific appara-

that place, except the churches and houses and outbuildings of those who are known to be loyal citizens of the United States. You will also burn the houses, etc., of all rebels between Newtown and Middletown. You will spare the house and premises of Dr. Owens, at Newtown, he having been very kind to our wounded soldiers; and where the burning of the house of a rebel would endanger the property of a loyal citizen, the house or outbuildings of the rebel shall not be burned. You will report back to these headquarters, making a written report of the expedition.

This by command of the major-general commanding.

I am, Major, very obediently, yours,

P. G. BIER, *Assistant Adjutant-General.*

tus; the plundering of Washington College, and the burning and plundering of private houses.  On page 43, he says:

"On this day (July 2d) we passed through Newtown, where several houses, including that of a Methodist minister, had been burned by Hunter's orders, because a part of Mosby's command had attacked a train of supplies for Sigel's forces at this place. The original order was to burn the whole town, but the officer sent to execute it had revolted at the cruel mandate of his superior and another had been sent who but partially executed it, after having forced the people to take an oath of allegiance to the United States to save their houses. Mosby s Battalion, though called 'guerrillas' by the enemy, was a regular organization in the Confederate army, and was merely serving on detached duty under General Lee's orders. The attack on the train was an act of legitimate warfare, and the orders to burn Newtown and the burning of the houses mentioned were most wanton, cruel, unjustifiable and cowardly."[3]

COL. HARRY W. GILMOR, C. S. A.,
Second Maryland Battalion.
From a War-time Photograph.

We were now ordered to leave the pike and go into a piece of woods a short distance off, as a train was observed coming up the turnpike.  Mosby and a few men went out on the pike for the purpose of drawing the cavalry from the train.  Company A was then to charge them in front and Companies B and C to cut them off and attack them in the rear.  Captain Chapman, with 40 men, was in the meantime to charge on the train, drive off the remaining guards and secure the horses, etc.

The cavalry advanced and fired on Mosby, but when

---

[3] A Memoir of the Last Year of the War for Independence in the Confederate States of America.  By Lieutenant-General Jubal A. Early.  New Orleans: Published by Blelock & Co.  1867.

Company A charged we found the Federal cavalry in full retreat.

Captain Richards, with Company B, on emerging from the woods found himself opposed to a force of infantry drawn up in line in a field and along a stone fence on the road side. When he saw the array, he drew off his men, but not before they had received the fire of the infantry, which killed one man, Embrey, of Company B, and wounded another named Hine. Two horses were killed.

Captain Chapman, coming out with his men, found the wagons traveling with all speed back to Winchester with a portion of the infantry, while the rest were going down the turnpike at a double quick. He fired on them, killing 2. Five prisoners, with their horses and equipments, were captured. We then burned 8 wagons which Gilmor had failed to destroy.

Although the train was not captured, these attacks had the effect of compelling Hunter to send heavy guards with all his trains, and at that time, as all his supplies had to be sent by wagons from Martinsburg, a large force was thus kept from the front. (See Mosby's Report, Appendix, IX.)

*Wednesday, June 22.*—A meeting was called at Rectortown. Two hundred men were present. General orders were read, in which bounds were prescribed, within the limits of which the men were to remain when not on duty. They were as follows: From Snickersville, along the Blue Ridge Mountains to Linden; thence to Salem (now called Marshall); to The Plains; thence along the Bull Run Mountains to Aldie, and from thence along the turnpike to the place of beginning, Snickersville. The section thus mapped out was known as "Mosby's Confederacy."

No member was to leave these bounds without permission. Roll was to be called at each meeting, and any man absent from two successive meetings, without satisfactory reason, was to be sent back to regular service.

After all business had been attended to, the command moved on to The Plains and through Thoroughfare Gap, near which we halted for the night.

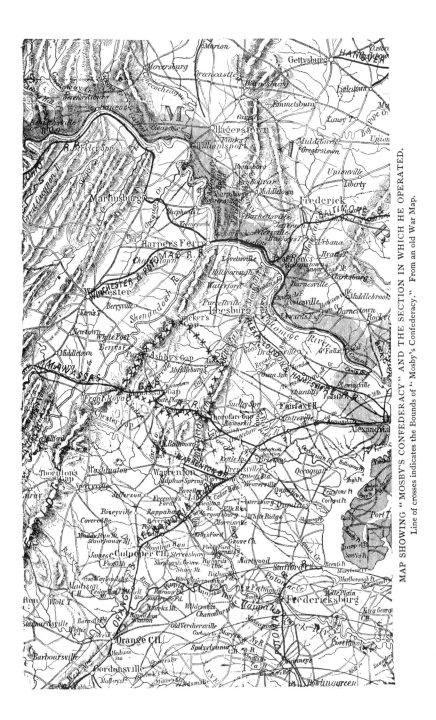

MAP SHOWING "MOSBY'S CONFEDERACY" AND THE SECTION IN WHICH HE OPERATED.
Line of crosses indicates the Bounds of "Mosby's Confederacy." From an old War Map.

The next morning (23d) we saddled up, and after grazing our horses for awhile, started about sunrise in the direction of Fairfax. The roads were dusty and the heat was intense. We passed over the old battlefield of Bull Run, marked on every side by soldiers' graves; the bodies had been but slightly covered, and here and there portions of the skeletons were exposed — some with feet or arms sticking out. One was nearly bare of earth, his belt and cartridge-box still on, but the clothes rotted; on our shaking his belt the bones rattled. Old rusty guns and bayonets, canteens, cartridge and cap boxes, rotten from exposure were lying around. We halted on the field to rest our horses, and then, passing by Manassas Junction, halted about midnight near Union Mills.

On the morning of the 24th, as we neared Centreville, one of our scouts, Walter Whaley, brought us information that a party of 50 or 60 cavalry, a portion of the Sixteenth New York Regiment, was at that place. Company A was sent forward to attack them, but when we arrived at Centreville they had left. Learning that they had gone out on the road leading to Chantilly, we pushed forward with all speed and came out on the Little River turnpike below Chantilly, and advanced to that place to await their arrival, while scouts were sent out to give notice of their approach. Soon a courier came in and said the whole party had been captured.

After the departure of Company A, Companies B, C and D were proceeding slowly along, when some of the men, going to a tree by the roadside to gather some cherries, discovered the Federal cavalry feeding their horses in a field near by. A portion of the command was detached, and charged in among them, killing and wounding 6 and capturing 31 prisoners and 38 horses. Mosby sustained no loss whatever.[4] (See Mosby's Report, Appendix, IX.)

---

[4] *Colonel Lowell's (Federal) Report.*

HEADQUARTERS CAVALRY BRIGADE, }
*Near Fall's Church, Va., June 25, 1864, 11 a. m.* }

LOWELL to TAYLOR: "Major Forbes has just returned from Centreville, and I am able to send a clearer account of Lieutenant Tuck's affair. It seems that Mosby came down on Thursday evening to near Union Mills with about 200

*Tuesday, June 28.*—Command met at Upperville in the evening. Company A being ordered off, crossed the Shenandoah river at Shepherd's Mill, and marched to within about two miles of Charlestown, where we halted for the night. Companies B, C and D, with a howitzer, crossed during the night, and in the morning were in the neighborhood but did not join Company A, which was left at Charlestown to watch the road leading from Harper's Ferry, while the other companies moved on to Duffield Depot on the Baltimore and Ohio Railroad.

Company A, passing through Charlestown, halted a short distance from town on the Harper's Ferry road. While there the ladies brought and sent out bread, meat, pies and an abundance of milk, and for a time we had quite a picnic. William Walston and the writer were placed on picket on a hill near by, but while our eyes were watching the road, our

---

men and an iron gun drawn by 6 horses. Thursday p. m. a small squad of Kincheloe's men took two of Colonel Lazelle's patrol, as reported last night. When Mosby, with a few men, came down to spy out the land, he learned this, and concluded that there would be too much stir for him to carry out his plan, whatever it was. He returned, therefore, to Union Mills Friday morning and marched his column back through Centreville about 10:30 a. m. Half an hour previously Lieutenant Tuck, with his 40 men, had passed through Centreville going toward Little River Pike, and had stopped about one and a half miles north in a field of newly cut hay to feed. Citizens report that the horses were unbitted, some of the men in cherry trees on the other side af the road, some asleep. There was one man on picket sitting on the fence, but in a very poorly chosen position. Mosby, learning about Mr. Tuck in Centreville, sent part of his men rapidly on, who dashed into the field, shooting the man on post and making such a panic that no resistance was attempted. It is said that a couple of men who had gone to a neighboring house for breakfast and saw Mosby's Men going past did the only firing that was done on our part. Three wounded men (2 dangerously) were brought in by Major Forbes, and 5 men are reported to have returned to camp on foot. All the horses and the rest of the men and arms are believed to have been captured. Mosby lost no time, but went right across to the Little River Pike and up toward Aldie. He was on the pike near the double toll-gate at noon.

" The strength of Mosby's column was estimated by Dr. Hart and Mr. Mellen (good Union men), both of whom saw it pass, and another citizen says Lieutenant Frank Fox told him as he passed they had about 200.

" Major Nicholson with his 150 men returned with Major Forbes and reached Centreville yesterday p. m. Got the impression that Mosby was from 400 to 900 strong and remained there, sending party to camp to report what he had learned."

hearts and our thoughts were constantly turning back to
the fair ladies of Charlestown and the rich fare our more
fortunate comrades were enjoying. A cloud of dust rising
on the road leading to Harper's Ferry warned us that the
enemy was approaching, and soon a dark blue line fringed
the edge of the woods.

"They are coming, Walston," said I.

"Yes," said Walston; "you go in and tell Nelson and I
will stay here and watch them."

I galloped in and finding Lieutenant Nelson, reported to
him.

"You get the men in line,
while I go out and see what
force there is," said Nelson.

He rode off, but soon came
back, saying: "Boys, I can
whip them if you will only
stand by me."

"How many are there?"
asked one of the men.

"There are about 60, but we
can whip them, I know. Two
of you men ride out there and
draw them up the pike."

We then formed behind a
little hill, while the two men
went out, and soon we heard
the yells and shouts of the

JAMES J. WILLIAMSON, CO. A.
From a Photograph taken in 1865.

Federals as they came dashing up the pike. Nelson ordered
us to draw our pistols and move off at a walk. We did so,
riding through a narrow strip of woods in a line parallel
with the road and towards the advancing enemy. We
moved off by twos, instead of fours as we usually charged,
so that by lengthening out our line we made our force appear as large as possible. As we commenced moving, the
Federal column appeared, rushing over the hill, and seeing
us then for the first time, they reined up and gazed at us in
amazement. No doubt the small force advancing against
them aroused their suspicions. A number of our men had

gone into Charlestown, and others were scattered among the houses in the neighborhood, so that we had only 23 men then with us. For only a few seconds the enemy hesitated and at the command raised their carbines and fired a volley, doing no other damage than to shower a few leaves on our heads from the trees beside us. Being on the hill and we below them, when they hastily raised their pieces the shots naturally went over our heads.

"Now, boys," said Nelson; "charge them!" and before they could drop their carbines and draw pistols, we dashed with a yell in amongst them, firing in their faces. They turned their horses, and as those in front pressed on the ones behind them, the whole body became panic stricken and retreated in the utmost disorder. Back over the hill they went, and when we reached the top we saw them descending the other side, a struggling mass of men and horses. Those behind the hill seeing the head of our column driving back their comrades, did not wait to ascertain our force, but joined in the headlong flight. We dashed on at their heels, firing into them, and followed them closely to Halltown. The pike was smooth and clear—a good road for a chase—and we gave them no time to rally.

J. W. HAMMOND, CO. B,
(Light Coat),
and
JOHN B. PROUT, CO. A,
(Dark Coat),
From a Photograph taken in March, 1863.

Nelson did not have a man injured, while the Federals lost 3 killed, a number wounded, 25 prisoners and 28 horses.

One Federal soldier who was wounded fell from his horse.

His foot caught in the stirrup and as he fell he grasped at the stirrup leather to release his foot, but fell back. The horse continued galloping on, and at every jump the soldier's head would bounce upon the road and strike against the horse, which would then kick him with its heels. I was not close enough to catch him, but shouted to two Federal soldiers who had halted by the roadside and were awaiting my approach, with their hands thrown up:

"Catch that horse! Don't you see it is killing one of your men?"

"We surrender! We surrender!" was their only reply.

"Throw down your arms and catch that horse!" I yelled; but before they could comprehend what to do, the horse was beyond their reach. It was afterwards secured, but not until the man was dead. In the excitement of a fight we were accustomed to shoot and kill without giving time to reflection, but in this case, to see a fellow creature dragged to his death in what seemed to me an unnatural manner, made me forget for the moment that he was an enemy, and my only thought was to save him.

After we had given up the pursuit and returned to Charlestown with prisoners and captured horses, and were drawn up in line, one of the prisoners, looking at our small force, with evident surprise, said:

"Why, we had men enough to have whipped you fellows!"

A courier now came up and announced that Mosby had captured Duffield Depot with its stores and the force there stationed, and in a short time the companies came in sight, having hurried on to join us, anticipating an attack on our little band from Harper's Ferry.

Mosby waved his hat and slapping Nelson on the shoulder, said:

"Good, Joe! Good for old Company A!"

It was Mosby's intention to capture a train on the Baltimore and Ohio Railroad at Duffield Depot, but the train was behind time, and after waiting some time, Mosby concluded it had passed, so he determined to capture the garrison and destroy the stores.

Sending out parties to cut the telegraph wires, in order to prevent the garrison from communicating with the surrounding forces, he posted his men, placed his gun in position and then sent Captain Richards with a flag of truce to demand the surrender of the post. The force, consisting of 45 infantry, surrendered without firing a shot. Our men took what they wished from the captured stores and then set fire to the camp and store-houses. (See Mosby's Report, Appendix, IX.)

After our forces had united, quite a large body of troops was sent out from Harper's Ferry. They followed us for some distance, and we twice formed in line of battle expect-

JAMES N. MILLER, CO. D.
From a Photograph.

ing an attack, but each time they declined an engagement. Sending the prisoners and horses forward with the other companies, Company A following as a rear guard, we returned unmolested.

Mosby, who with a few men remained behind in the neighborhood of Charlestown, saw a party of 7 Federal cavalry approaching. They charged Mosby, who returned the compliment, severely wounding 2 of them and capturing 4, together with 6 horses. The Federals said they had been sent out on picket, but they were no doubt sent to watch our movements.

Early on the morning of the 30th we returned home by way of Paris. The men had brought a large quantity of dry goods, coffee, etc., from the captured stores at Duffield Depot, and these looked charming to the eyes of the poor people of the "Confederacy," who had not seen the inside of a store for two or three years. The long line of prisoners and captured horses and equipments, and the large United

States flag from the camp at Duffield Depot trailing at the gun, all united to form a picturesque scene.[5]

---

[5] *Report of Brig.-Gen. Max Weber, U. S. A., Commanding at Harper's Ferry.*

HEADQUARTERS, }
*Harper's Ferry, W. Va., June 30, 1864.* }

WEBER to MEYSENBURG : "I have the honor to report that on the morning of the 29th instant I received reliable information to the effect that Mosby with a considerable force was in the vicinity of Charlestown, W. Va., and reported the fact by telegraph to division headquarters at 10.30 a. m.    Between 1 and 2 p. m. the wires between this post and Martinsburg were cut and communication ceased.    About 3 o'clock an attack was made upon my picket-line toward Charlestown, and during the afternoon there was heavy skirmishing along my whole line of pickets on that front.    Later in the day a report was received from the commandant of the forces at Duffield Station that he was attacked by superior numbers of the enemy at that point and calling for reinforcements.    I at once sent 50 cavalry toward Duffield's to feel the enemy and watch their movements, and 300 infantry were ordered to that point.    Subsequently information was received that the enemy had routed our men ; had plundered and burned the camp, stores and storehouses at Duffield's, had retired without doing further damage, and moved in the direction of Key's Ford, intending to cross there. I sent the 300 infantry at once to Key's Ford, where they remained until 7 this a. m., when they returned without seeing anything of the enemy.    Our loss, as nearly as can be now ascertained, is 38 in killed, wounded and missing.    The force of the enemy was not far from 400 men, with two pieces of artillery.    From all the reports received it appears that the force at Duffield's had not even a picket out, were surprised, and consequently retired with hardly a show of resistance.    The matter will be carefully investigated.    Allow me once more to express the opinion that a permanent force of good cavalry are necessary at this point, as the enemy are constantly crossing and recrossing near here, and from Harper's Ferry cavalry can act with promptness and effect."

# CHAPTER XII.

The Fourth of July, 1864, was celebrated by our command at the Point of Rocks on the Potomac. General Early having driven General Hunter out of the Valley, was now preparing to invade Maryland and threaten Washington, and Mosby proceeded to operate on the line of communication between the capital and Harper's Ferry.

The command met at Upperville on Sunday, July 3d; about 250 men present. We started at noon with one 12-pounder Napoleon gun, and the day being very warm, marched leisurely along by way of Bloomfield, camping at night near Wheatland.

Continuing our march on the morning of the 4th, we reached the Potomac, opposite and in view of Berlin. We then moved along the river to a ford about a mile from Point of Rocks. At this place was a force consisting of two companies of cavalry, the Loudoun Rangers, commanded by Captain Keyes, and two companies of infantry. As we approached the ford, the sharpshooters who were concealed in the bushes along the shore, opened fire, and the cavalry drew up in line near the town. Mosby ordered a few men with long-range guns to the river bank, and for some time a brisk fire was kept up, with but little damage to either side—certainly none to us. Lieutenant Chapman now placed his Napoleon in position on a hill opposite the town, supported by Company C, and sent a shell across the river into the bushes. A second shot had the effect of quieting them a little.

Our sharpshooters advanced to a little island in the middle of the river, from which they had dislodged the enemy,

and we were ordered to cross. Captain Richards, with
Company A, then dashed into the river, followed by Companies B and D, carbineers wading on our flanks, the Federals firing on us from the opposite shore. Another shell
went screaming overhead, and away went the Federals
scampering along the tow-path.

Once across the river we pushed ahead on the tow-path,
but when opposite the Point of Rocks were forced to come
to a halt. The Federals, after crossing the bridge over the
canal, had torn up the flooring so that it was impossible to
cross. On a hill near the
camp was a small earthwork
which c o m m a n d e d the
bridge, and from this shelter
the enemy kept up a brisk
fire. Richards immediately
set men at work tearing
boards from an old building
near by, with which to repair
the bridge. In the meantime
Lieut. Harry Hatcher ran
across on the bridge tim-
bers, hauled down the flag
from the flag-staff in the camp
and brought it over in triumph, amid a shower of
balls. Men were then dis-
mounted and, under Capt.
A. E. Richards, crossed the
bridge in like manner and drove the Federals from their
entrenchments.

LIEUT. HARRY HATCHER, CO. A.
From a Photograph taken during the War.

By this time planks had been laid and the command
swept over to the town and set fire to the camp and to a
canal-boat. The Federal forces fled—the cavalry in the direction of Frederick and the infantry concealing themselves
in the mountains, so that but few were captured.

We cut down telegraph poles and cut the wires, breaking
the communication between Harper's Ferry and Washington. A quantity of goods was taken from the stores in the

town, but a great portion of them was returned or sold for the benefit of the owner. Although this was a hazardous enterprise, we sustained no injury.

While we were in possession of the town a train of cars came along the railroad, but the gun was brought into play and the train sent back.

The telegraph operator ran off and hid in the mountains, where he remained until we had all left. He afterwards re-

turned and sent off several despatches. Finding himself unable to give all the details in a telegram, he wound up by saying " the devil was to pay generally." [1]

On the 5th we remained along the river the greater part of the day, making demonstrations as if to cross, and sharp-shooters were kept busy on the river banks. The Federal forces on the Maryland side meanwhile had been reinforced by 230 men of the Eighth Regiment Illinois Cavalry, under Lieut.-Col. Clendenin.

Sergt. Charles L. Hall, with 12 men, crossed over a short distance below, and near Monocacy captured and brought off a few prisoners.

SERGT. CHARLES LANDON
HALL, CO. C.
From a Photograph taken during the
War.

In the evening we moved off in the direction of Leesburg, within a few miles of which place the command halted, and after feeding our horses, unsaddled and prepared to pass the

---

[1] *Monocacy, July 5, 1864.*

TYLER to LAWRENCE : " The Rebel cavalry left Point of Rocks last evening after robbing the people and stores of money and such goods as they wanted to carry into Virginia. They were Mosby's men and were not over 120 strong. Our scouts saw them leaving and could count them. We can get nothing from Harper's Ferry. The Washington troops I sent to Monrovia to be armed and supplied with ammunition there, were in no condition for service on their arrival here."

night. A very short time, however, had elapsed when Lieutenant Hatcher, John Thomas and C. Albert Fox, who had gone to Leesburg, returned with the intelligence that a large force of Federal cavalry was at that place; that they had told some of the citizens that Mosby was in Maryland and they had cut off his retreat—that they had him just where they wanted him.

Orders were given to saddle up, and we moved off, passing around Leesburg and halting near Waterford. Carlisle and Puryear were sent as scouts to Leesburg. On their return they reported the force there to be portions of the Second Massachusetts and Thirteenth New York Cavalry, under Major Forbes—"Colonel Lowell's fighting Major," as he was called—250 in number. We then had only about 175 men, as many had left for home during the day.

On the morning of the 6th we marched to Leesburg. Forbes had left, going towards Oatland. Mosby then pressed on, thinking to cut them off at Ball's Mill, on Goose Creek, but on reaching the ford, found that they had already crossed and gone in the direction of Mount Zion on the Aldie turnpike. Mosby came out on the pike near the toll-gate below Mount Zion. The Federals had been feeding their horses opposite Skinner's house below Mount Zion, but were preparing to move on. Our carbineers, under Lieutenant Hatcher, advanced and opened fire on them from a body of woods, as they came out on the pike. The gun was then brought up and a shell fired, which did no other damage than to give them a fright. They formed in a field near the house and we charged them in front and on their flank. Unable to stand the shock, they broke and ran some distance. but rallied and formed again behind a fence. They rallied and attempted to form three times, but Mosby pressed on and drove them in disorder each time. Some of our men followed the fugitives to Sudley, and two were killed near that place.

Major Forbes, who was in command, fought gallantly, and was always in the thickest of the fight, encouraging and endeavoring to rally his men. Thomas W. T. Richards, brother of Capt. A. E. Richards, at last singled him out, and

a fierce hand-to-hand struggle took place between them
Forbes made a savage cut with his sabre at Richards, inflicting a severe wound on his shoulder, but Richards finally
forced him to surrender.  The Federals were all well armed
and fought desperately.

Mosby had 7 men wounded: Henry Smallwood, mor-
tally; William Davis, Thomas Lake, Hugh T. Waters,
Frank M. Woolf, Thomas W. T. Richards and Robert S.
Walker.

Forbes lost 17 killed, about 40 wounded—12 or 15 mortally, and 57 prisoners.[2]  Over 100 horses were captured.
A number of horses were wounded, and 12 were left dead

FRANK M. WOOLF, CO. A.
Shot through the hand Dec. 22, 1863;
wounded in the knee, July 6, 1864;
shot though the neck, Sept. 4, 1864.

on the field, which presented a
sad sight.    The ground was
strewn with guns, pistols, blankets and equipments of all kinds;
dead and wounded were lying
around; horses, wounded and
maddened with pain and fright,
dashed wildly over the battle-
ground, while others lay trembling, or rearing and falling,
unable to stand.    Skinner's
house was used as a hospital,
and Doctors Dunn and Sowers
were busily engaged in attending to the wounded.  We remained until near midnight,
when we moved off to Middleburg.

Colonel Lowell came up to Mount Zion the day after the
fight with a force and buried the dead Federals and carried
off the wounded.  Four dead soldiers, however, were found

---

    [2] The Massachusetts Official Reports give the following names of the killed
in this fight belonging to the Second Massachusetts Cavalry: Corporal Sam. C.
Hanscom, San Francisco ; Corporal James McDonald, San Francisco ; Privates
Owen Fox, Braintree, Mass.; John Johnson, Spencer; Patrick Riordan, Scitu-
ate; Chas. W. Rollins, Boston; Cornelius Tobin, Marlborough, and Wm. F.
Dumasey, Warwick.

several days after the fight and were buried by the citizens.[3]

*July 9.*—Command met at Upperville, and proceeding down Loudoun, pressed a quantity of corn, which was sent back for the use of the battalion. On the 11th we marched to the Potomac and crossed at Conrad's Ferry into Maryland. We moved on to Poolesville, burning some blockhouses on our way. On the 12th we went to Seneca Mills,

---

[3] *Report of Col. Charles R. Lowell, Jr., Second Mass. Cavalry, Commanding Brigade.*

*Near Falls Church, Va., July 8, 1864.*

COLONEL : I have the honor to report Major Forbes' scout as complete as is yet possible. I have not talked with Lieutenant Kuhls or Captain Stone, who is badly wounded, but send what I learned on the ground.

Major Forbes left here with 150 men (100 Second Massachusetts Cavalry, 50 Thirteenth New York Cavalry) Monday, ρ. m. Tuesday, a. m., went through Aldie, and found all quiet toward the Gaps. Tuesday. p. m., went by Ball's Mill to Leesburg. Heard of Mosby's raid at Point of Rocks, and learned that he had sent four or five wagons of plunder through Leesburg, under a guard of about 60 men, the afternoon before. Heard nothing of any other force this side of the ridge. He returned that night to the south of Goose Creek, as directed, and, on Wednesday, a. m., went again by Ball's Mill to Leesburg. Still heard nothing of Mosby or any force. From what I learn from citizens, I think Mosby passed between Leesburg and the Potomac some time on Tuesday, crossed Goose Creek, and moved westward toward Aldie on Wednesday ; learned of Major Forbes' second visit to Leesburg, and laid in ambush for him at Ball's Mill. Major Forbes returned from Leesburg by Centre's Mill (4 miles above), came down by Aldie, and halted for two or three hours about one and a half miles east, on the Little River Pike ; when Mosby learned this he moved

LIEUT.-COL. DAVID R. CLENDENIN,
Eighth Illinois Cavalry.

south and struck the pike about one and a quarter miles east of the Major's position, being hidden till he had reached about half a mile west on the pike. Major Forbes was duly notified by his advance guard, mounted his men, and moved them from the north to the south of the pike. As the rear was crossing,

thence to Muddy Branch, where we found a deserted camp of the Eighth Illinois Cavalry from which the forces had hurriedly departed, leaving tents standing, with bales of hay, bags of oats, saddles, bridles, and every description of camp equipage lying around. These we burned, together with

---

Mosby fired one shell from his 12-pounder (the only time it was fired), which burst entirely too high. As Major Forbes formed on the south, his advance guard, which had dismounted and fired as Mosby came up, fell back, still keeping a little north of the pike, and took an excellent position somewhat on the flank. Up to this time, I think, all the dispositions were admirable.

CAPT. SAMUEL C. MEANS,
Independent Loudoun (Virginia) Rangers.
(Federal.)

Major Forbes' two squadrons were formed, his third squadron and rear guard not formed but nearly so, and no confusion. Mosby's men, who were not in any order, but were down the road in a "nick," had just reached the fence corner some 225 yards off, and a few had dismounted, under a fire from the advanced guard, to take down the fence. When two panels of fence were down the men trotted through for about 75 yards, and came gradually down to a walk, and almost halted. Major Forbes' first platoon was ordered to fire with carbines. Here was the first mistake. It created confusion among the horses, and the squadron in the rear added to it by firing a few pistol shots. Had the order been given to draw sabres and charge, the rebels would never have got their gun off, but I think Major Forbes, seeing how uneasy his horses were at the firing, must have intended to dismount some of his men. At any rate, he attempted to move the first squadron by the right flank. The rebels saw their chance, gave a yell, and our men, in the confusion of the moment, broke. The two rear squadrons went off in confusion. Attempts were made, with some success, to rally parts of the first squadron in the next field, and again near Little River Church, one mile off.

Captain Stone was wounded here, and I believe all the non-commissioned officers of A and L Companies present wounded or killed. There was little gained. I have only to report a perfect rout and a chase for five to seven miles. We lost Major Forbes, Lieutenant Amory, and Mr. Humphreys (Chaplain), from Second Massachusetts, and Lieutenant Burns, Thirteenth New York Cavalry, prisoners, all unhurt. Captain Stone, Second Massachusetts, and Lieutenant Schuyler, Thirteenth New York, very badly wounded. Lieutenant Kuhls alone came safely to camp. Of men, we lost, killed outright: 7, Second

a large block-house and frame building connected with the camp. We also captured 30 head of fine cattle left behind by the enemy, and then recrossed the river, camping at night near Dranesville. (See Mosby's Report, Appendix, IX.)

---

Massachusetts ; 5, Thirteenth New York. Wounded, we brought in 27 and left 10 too bad to move. I fear of the wounded at least 12 will die. About 40 others have come to camp half mounted, and Mosby was reported to have 44 prisoners ; quite a number, you will see still unaccounted for. Some of them are probably wounded, and some still on their way to camp, and others will be made prisoners.

Mosby went up toward Upperville with his prisoners and his dead and wounded about midnight Wednesday. I reached the ground about 11.30 a. m. and remained in plain sight for about three hours ; then searched through all the woods and moved to Centreville, where I again waited an hour in hopes some stragglers would join us. We only picked up half a dozen, however.

The soldiers and the citizens all speak in high terms of the gallantry of the officers ; Major Forbes especially remained in the first field till every man had left it, emptied his revolver, and, in the second field, where Company A tried to stand, he disabled one man with his sabre, and lunged through Colonel Mosby's coat. His horse was then killed and fell on his leg, pinning him till he was compelled to surrender.

More than 100 horses were taken. Accoutrements, arms, etc., will also be missing. I cannot yet give the precise number.

Mosby's force is variously estimated at from 175 to 250, Mrs. Davis and her daughter putting it at 250 to 300 men. I think he had probably about 200. What his loss was I cannot say, as he picked up all his dead and wounded and took them off in the night. The Union people in Aldie report that he took them in five wagons. A wounded sergeant reports hearing the names of 3 or 4 spoken of as killed ; one mortally wounded man was left on the ground. I think the chance was an excellent one to whip Mosby and take his gun. I have no doubt Major Forbes thought so, too, as the wounded men say there was not enough difference in numbers to talk about. The chance was lost. I have scouting parties out to Centreville to watch Thoroughfare Gap and the country south, but have not at present any party to the north beyond Chantilly and Dranesville. A part of my picket-line had not been relieved for two days. I shall try to see the General this p. m. for a few minutes, if there is nothing new here, and if the orderly brings word that he has returned to the city.

Very respectfully, your obedient servant,

C. R. LOWELL, JR.,
*Col. Second Mass. Cav. Comm'a'g Brigade.*

Lieut.-Col. JOSEPH H. TAYLOR,
*Assistant Adjutant General.*

# CHAPTER XIII.

After invading Maryland and threatening Washington, General Early, on the 14th of July, recrossed the Potomac at White's Ford, and, resting near Leesburg, on the 16th marched to the Shenandoah Valley through Snicker's Gap in the Blue Ridge. General Hunter united with Sigel at Harper's Ferry, and the combined forces, under General Crook, moved into Loudoun, following closely in Early's rear.

General Early presented Mosby with a small rifled cannon, at the same time complimenting him highly on the energy and bravery of his command.

While the Federal forces were passing through "Mosby's Confederacy," in pursuit of Early, detached parties under Mosby, Richards, Chapman, Glasscock and others hovered around, continually harassing them, attacking their outposts and assailing them whenever an opportunity offered. (See Mosby's Report, Appendix, IX.)

On the 18th Averell's troopers endeavored to cross the Shenandoah at Castleman's Ferry in Early's rear, but were driven back with heavy loss, leaving some of their flags floating in the stream. Capt. A. E. Richards with 10 men, being sent to the vicinity in quest of information, came upon a party of Federal cavalry near Snickersville. A sharp skirmish took place, resulting in favor of "Mosby's Men," who killed 5, wounded 2, and captured 4 prisoners and 11 horses with their equipments.

General Duffié, with his whole force of cavalry, with artillery and ambulances, passed through Upperville and Paris and camped on the night of the 18th near the entrance

of Ashby's Gap.   On their march a caisson exploded, killing one and wounding 5 men and 2 horses.

A large tree, known as the "Big Poplar," marks the corner where the three counties of Loudoun, Fauquier and

BREVET MAJ.-GEN. GEORGE CROOK, U. S. A.
From a War-time Photograph.

Clarke unite in the Gap, and at this place the Federals
posted a picket of one squadron from the Twentieth Pennsylvania Calvary.   Capt. Wm. H. Chapman, of Company
C, after reconnoitering the position, divided his command,
and with Lieutenant Fox attacked the post, killing and

wounding several and capturing about 60 men, with horses and equipments.[1] Chapman lost one man, C. Bohrer, of Georgetown, D. C., who was thrown from his horse in the charge, and died from his injuries a few days after.

While the Federal troops were in the vicinity, 5 of our men were captured, and one, Keene, was killed near Upperville. Along the line of march a number of defenseless women were shamefully ill-treated by the Federal soldiers, whose officers did not attempt to restrain them either from pillage or from their disgraceful assaults. At the house of Mrs. O'Rear, above Paris, although she pleaded that she was a widow and alone, they struck her, choked and threatened her; took her provisions, killed her stock, broke up her furniture, and took her bedding and wearing apparel. Her feather beds and pillows they cut open and threw into the filth of the stable. This case was but one of many. Mrs. Doctor Payne, at Paris, and a lady at a mill near Upperville were struck and threatened by them.

Company B was sent down Fairfax, but accomplished little, only capturing 5 prisoners and 7 horses near the Court House.

*Wednesday, July 20.*—Mosby, with Companies A and D, moved down through Loudoun, getting in the rear of the Federal forces. On coming around near Snickersville, a large train was seen in camp with a heavy cavalry guard. Mosby made several ineffectual attempts to draw out a portion of the guard. A few of our men would ride out in full view of the camp and after showing themselves, retreat. Then they would ride closer and fire on the guards. Finding all efforts to entice them away from the train fruitless, Mosby started off, saying he would go back and bring on the remainder of the command, with whom he would meet

[1] General Duffié, in his report, says: "I regret to report that through the shameful mismanagement and neglect of the officer in command—Captain Montgomery, Twentieth Pennsylvania Cavalry—one squadron, which was picketing the rear of the Gap, and within one mile of my command, was captured by Mosby's guerrillas, with all their horses, arms and equipments. The loss by the capture was 2 commissioned officers, 50 enlisted men and about 55 horses. I have recommended the officer commanding this squadron for dismissal."

us about two o'clock next morning, and that he would then push on and attack the train just before daylight.

After dark we moved off, and when near the Leesburg and Snickersville pike the command was halted. Lieutenant Nelson galloped out towards the road, on approaching which he was saluted with three or four shots. He then discovered that a train was passing along the road, but too heavily guarded to be attacked with our small force. Cavalry flankers were out on either side of the road, some of whom passed near enough to Lieut. Samuel Chapman to have touched him, he having crept out to the roadside and concealed himself in a bush to observe the passing train. The infantry were firing into the woods as they passed along, either at imaginary enemies, or to frighten away any real ones who might venture to approach. We moved along and tried to cross the road at another point, but found it blocked with infantry. At several places where we attempted to cross, the road was also filled with troops. Not being able to fathom the mystery surrounding us, it was decided to fall back from the road and wait until daylight, when the meaning of the manœuvre would be revealed.

MAJ.-GEN. HORATIO G. WRIGHT, U. S. A.

We traveled all the rest of the night, crossing Short Hills, and on the morning of the 21st of July halted at the foot of the mountains, where we fed our horses, while scouts were sent out to the turnpike. They soon reported that the Sixth Corps, under General Wright, was marching back to Washington.

Lieut. Harry Hatcher, with 15 men, started off immediately, while the rest of the command were ordered to follow as soon as the horses were given a little rest.

When we came out on the grade we found Hatcher with 83 prisoners that he had picked up on the road. The men with broken down horses were sent back with the prisoners and we moved along the turnpike to Purcellville. The Federals had all passed and the road bore evidence of their passage: fences destroyed; the cavalry had ridden through corn fields, trampling down the corn and feeding their horses on the tops; skins of calves and hogs, with heads and feathers of poultry, etc., were scattered around, with now and then a dead horse. We picked up a few more prisoners, mostly stragglers, and at dark moved on to Union, and thence home.

During the day 104 prisoners, in all, were gathered up by our men and sent South.

THE NIGHT MARCH.

# CHAPTER XIV.

After the battle of Kernstown the Federal forces were driven back to Harper's Ferry, General Early again advanced to the Potomac, and on the 29th of July McCausland crossed above Williamsport and moved on to Chambersburg, in Pennsylvania.

On Thursday, July 28th, at a meeting held at Upperville, Company E was organized. Samuel F. Chapman was elected Captain; Fountain Beattie, First Lieutenant; William Martin, Second Lieutenant, and W. Ben Palmer, Third Lieutenant.

William H. Mosby, brother of Colonel Mosby, was appointed Adjutant of the Battalion, in place of Samuel F. Chapman, now Captain of Company E.

Up to this time Lieutenant Samuel Chapman always had charge of the artillery, but soon after his promotion to the captaincy of Company E an artillery company was regularly organized, with the following officers: Captain, Peter A. Franklin; First Lieutenant, John J. Fray[1]; Second Lieutenant, John P. Page; Third Lieutenant, Frank H. Rahm.

About dusk we moved off with 200 men and 3 small pieces of artillery, halting at Green Garden Mill to feed our horses, and between 8 and 9 o'clock continued our march down Loudoun, camping at night near Purcellville. The 29th was a very warm day and we traveled slowly, halting in the middle of the day and passing the night near Morrisonville.

On the 30th we proceeded to the Potomac river, and at

---

[1] Lieutenant John J. Fray, previous to joining Mosby, commanded a battery of artillery at Yorktown. After the war he removed to Raleigh, N.C., where he established a prosperous school known as the Raleigh Male Academy. He died December 23, 1884.

Cheek's Ford Companies A and D were ordered to cross. Carbineers were dismounted to wade the river on our flanks, and by the time they reached the river bank we heard the sharp crack of carbines. The command "Forward!" was given by Lieutenant Nelson and we dashed into the water; the head of the column was on the towpath before the sharpshooters had crossed. There were but 7 Federal cavalrymen on picket at the Ford—one had gone to the blacksmith's shop to have his horse shod—and the remaining 6 were captured. Along the towpath we went at a gallop, the dust rising in such a cloud that I could not see the man riding in advance of me.

CAPT. SAMUEL F. CHAPMAN, CO. E.
From a Photograph taken during the War.

When we reached Noland's Ferry we saw Company B in the river in the act of crossing. We then moved on to Adamstown, at which place there were a couple of stores, over which Lieutenant Nelson placed a guard and allowed nothing to be disturbed. Telegraph poles were cut down and wires cut. Here we separated. Company B, after moving down towards Monocacy, returned and recrossed the river.

Companies A and D pushed on to within a mile and a half of Barnesville, and by the Sugar Loaf to the Mouth of the Monocacy, where there was a picket post of the Eighth Illinois Cavalry of about 35 men We now learned that the Federal forces were on our trail and would seek to cut us off from the river.

Coming in sight of the picket post, Lieut. Harry Hatcher, with 25 men, was sent around to get in their rear. While Hatcher's party moved off to accomplish the task assigned to them, Lieutenant Nelson with the rest of our men proceeded slowly along to the river, to draw the attention of the enemy.

The picket post was on a high bluff overlooking the road and commanding the ford. As we came in sight the pickets opened fire and we remained for a time in the road, an exposed target, unable to return their fire. They were armed with carbines and from their position were able to fire directly down on our ranks, while, even had we possessed carbines, our shots would have fallen harmless or passed over their heads. One of our men, John H. Alexander, was struck in the side of the head by one of the balls which whistled around our ears, or struck the ground under our horses' feet, knocking up the dust in a lively manner. Being t h u s placed under fire for a good purpose, though an honorable position, was a very uncomfortable one. We soon heard a yell over the hill, and the sharp cracking of pistols, which announced the arrival of Hatcher among them. We could see those who were on the edge of the bluff firing at us, turn in their saddles, fire a few shots and then scamper off. Four or five Federals were killed in the attack and 22 prisoners were brought off. Hatcher had no one hurt, but several horses be-

LIEUT. JOHN J. FRAY,
Artillery Company, 43d Battalion Virginia Cavalry.

longing to his party were shot—one killed. One of our men, Cunningham, fell from his horse; the horse came out, but the rider was left behind. We recrossed the river, bringing 40 horses more than we took over with us.[2]

---

[2] *Poolesville, July 31, 1864.*

WAITE to RAYMOND : "Cheek's Ford, first above Monocacy, where Mosby crossed yesterday, is unguarded, leaving my right exposed. When 18 of my men were fighting Mosby's whole command yesterday, I am informed, Major Thompson was within supporting distance. My loss in that affair—Lieutenant

In a very entertaining sketch of this little raid, written by John H. Alexander, of Company A, and recently published in the Leesburg *Mirror*, he says in conclusion :

We then pushed on up the river to reach the ford at Noland's Ferry before another detachment of Yankees, who

CAPT. PETER A. FRANKLIN,
Artillery Company,
43d Battalion Virginia Cavalry.

were coming down the river, should get there. We barely made it, too. I crossed over with the prisoners among the first. But the enemy came up in time to make it hot for our rear guard. Cab. Maddux, even in those days, made a rather attractive mark, but as the bullets were splashing the water around him, his characteristic solicitude for others was manifested. Seeing a comrade in arms struggling through the waves some distance off and not receiving that attention from the Federal soldiers which he thought due to his rank, Cab. cried out at the top of his voice, " Hurry up, *Major* Hibbs ! Come along, *Major !* " The Yankees at once transferred their shower baths from Cab. to the *Major*, who showed his appreciation of the former's self-sacrifice by spluttering out to him that he was " —— respectful all at once."

As Dr. Sowers was dressing my wound at a farm house on this side of the river (the Virginia side) Harry Hatcher

Delaney wounded, 2 men killed, 3 wounded, 7 or 8 prisoners and about 25 horses and equipments captured."

*Monocacy, July 31, 1864.*

TYLER to WALLACE : " By the disgraceful conduct of Lieutenant Van Ness, of the Third New Jersey Infantry, in charge of the detachment guarding the Potomac from the mouth of Monocacy to the Point of Rocks, one man was killed [and] a lieutenant [and] 15 men of the Eighth Illinois Cavalry captured near Noland's Ferry yesterday by Mosby's thieves. It is reported they captured about 200 horses from citizens on this side. Colonel Clendenin reports the conduct of the lieutenant as cowardly in a superlative degree."

came up and offered this consolation : " Never mind, Johnnie, old boy ; I killed one of them Yankees for that."

When we returned to the Virginia side we found that
Company E had crossed in our absence.  Men came in saying they had been cut off and had lost a great number of
men.  This, however, proved to be an exaggeration.  It appeared that the Federals had been stirred up by Nelson and
Hatcher and wished to cut off their retreat by taking possession of the fords in the neighborhood.  Company E was
proceeding along when they
discovered a force of Federal cavalry immediately in
their front.  Seeing the
force was too strong for
them and advancing rap-
idly, they turned back to
the ford.  They now found
that another detachment
was hurrying on to reach
the ford in advance of them
and cut them off.  Both parties then had a race for the
ford.  Company E had no
time to spare, for as they
were in the river in the act
of crossing, the Federals
were firing at them from
the shore.  One man fell
from his horse and was
drowned.  Several sprang

LIEUT. FRANK H. RAHM,
Artillery Company 43d Battalion Virginia Cavalry.
From a War-time Photograph.

from their horses and swam over, catching their horses as
they came out on the Virginia shore.

When the companies had all united, a report was brought
in that the Federal troops had crossed the river and were
following us.  A halt was ordered and the Battalion drawn
up in line of battle.  It was now about dusk.  The guns
were unlimbered, and one of the howitzers was placed in
the road, the other in a field so as to command the road.
The companies were posted on either side of the road, a

portion of them in a cornfield. After waiting some time expecting an attack, scouts came in and reported that no force had crossed the river. We then quietly resumed our homeward journey. (See Mosby's Report, Appendix, X.)

JOHN C. KANE, CO. D.
(light suit)
JAMES C. KANE, CO. D.
(dark suit)
From a War-time Photograph.

*Sunday, July 31.—* Sent off prisoners, 22 in all, and led horses. Orders were sent for remainder of command to meet at Upperville and join us. At night we camped near Hillsborough, tying our horses to the fences, and lay down to rest. We were now in a land of plenty, with good blue grass and corn for our horses, and bread, meat, cheese, pies and milk for ourselves. So we rested until Monday evening, when we moved off to Snicker's Gap, crossed the Shenandoah at Castleman's Ferry and camped for the night about two miles from the river.

*Tuesday, August 2.—*We went through Kabletown and thence to Charlestown. Mosby with two or three men started off towards General Early's headquarters and we returned home.

# CHAPTER XV.

General Early's retreat ended at Strasburg. Turning upon his pursuers, he drove Crook and Averell down the Valley and soon the Confederate cavalry were crossing the borders and again carrying the War into Pennsylvania.

On the 7th of August, 1864, under orders from the War Department, Washington, General Sheridan assumed command of the Middle Department, with headquarters at Harper's Ferry,[1] and on the same day Grant wrote Sheridan:

" Do not hesitate to give commands to officers in whom you repose confidence, without regard to claims of others on account of rank. If you deem Torbert the best man to command the cavalry, place him in command and give Averell some other command, or relieve him from the expedition, and order him to report to General Hunter. What we want is prompt and active movements after the enemy, in accordance with instructions you already have. I feel every confidence that you will do the very best, and will leave you as far as possible to act on your own judgment, and not embarrass you with orders and instructions."

In accordance with instructions, Sheridan at once moved

---

[1] GENERAL ORDERS, No. 240.      WAR DEPT., ADJT. GENERAL'S OFFICE, *Washington, August 7, 1864.*

1. The Middle Department and the Departments of Washington, of the Susquehanna, and of West Virginia will constitute the Middle Military Division.

2. Maj. Gen. P. H. Sheridan is assigned by the President to the temporary command of the Middle Military Division.

By order of the Secretary of War.

E. D. TOWNSEND,
*Assistant Adjutant General.*

against Early with the entire force which had been concentrated at Harper's Ferry, and the Confederates again fell back up the Valley.

*Saturday, August 6.*—Command met at Upperville, and Mosby, with about 250 men and 4 small pieces of artillery, moved off through the little town of Union and down to the Potomac, halting about midnight. We found the fords along the river all strongly guarded, and large bodies of cavalry moving towards Harper's Ferry on the Maryland side.[2]

We made no attempt to cross the river, and on Sunday, August 7th, the artillery was sent back. Mosby then took Company A for a raid into Fairfax, leaving the remainder of the command to press corn along the river.[3]

Mosby proceeded with Company A down Fairfax, and camped in a piece of woods about three miles below Centreville. Walter Whaley, with 7 men, went on a scout towards Annandale. They returned about 8 o'clock on the morning of Monday, August 8th, bringing in 3 prisoners and 4 horses, captured near Burke's Station. There were 4 men on picket, but one of them, a corporal, had gone to a spring near by to get a drink, and so escaped capture.[4]

---

[2] Major Waite, of the Eighth Illinois Cavalry, was then guarding the river from Point of Rocks to Edward's Ferry, with 600 men.

General Grant, in a despatch to Hunter, dated August 5, 1864, ordering him to concentrate all his available force in the vicinity of Harper's Ferry, says : "The brigade of cavalry now *en route* from Washington, via Rockville, may be taken into account. There are now on the way to join you three other brigades of the best of cavalry, numbering at least 5,000 men and horses."

[3] *Point of Rocks, Md., August 7, 1864.*

COOK to BURLEIGH : "Captain Hewett, provost-marshal, Berlin, reports Mosby, from 400 to 500 strong, in his front. Their pickets extend down to near this point. They are pressing teams and removing forage, probably their only object."

[4] HEADQUARTERS CAVALRY BRIGADE,	⎱
			*Near Falls Church, Va., Aug. 8, 1864.* ⎰

LAZELLE to TAYLOR : "I have the honor to report all quiet in this vicinity. A picket post, supplied from the detachment of the Sixteenth New York Cavalry, at Annandale, consisting of one corporal and three men, stationed on the old Braddock Road, about 3 miles southeast of Annandale, was surrounded and captured by a party of about 15 rebels this morning between 5 and 6 o'clock. Four horses and three of the men were taken by the enemy. The corporal alone escaped to bring the tidings to camp. I have nothing to report from advance scouts.

ATTACK ON SHERIDAN'S SUPPLY TRAIN AT BERRYVILLE.

From a Painting by Philippoteaux.

Lieutenant Nelson, taking 15 or 20 men, started to capture two picket-posts on the old Braddock road. One of these, suspecting an attack, moved off, but the second party was attacked and pursued by Nelson to within 3 miles of Alexandria. Three only, with their horses, were captured.[5]

LIEUT. GEN. JUBAL A. EARLY, C. S. A.

Mosby said the Federals would come out to look after their pickets and then he would attack them.

After Nelson's departure, Mosby moved on with the remainder of the command, 38 men in all. While riding along through the pines, a party of the Thirteenth New York Cavalry, who were in ambush, fired from their place of concealment on our vedettes, Walter Whaley and George M. Slater, wounding Slater in the leg, and his horse in the neck. After firing, the Federals fled in the direction of Fairfax Station, where they united with a company of the Sixteenth New York Cavalry and thus reinforced, they thought themselves more than a match for Mosby.

As Mosby came up with them, he heard the Federal officer give orders to his men to deliver a fire with their carbines and then charge with sabres. Mosby did not

---

[5] *Alexandria August 9, 1864.*

WELLS to TAYLOR: "About 40 guerrillas attacked my pickets near the telegraph road last night at 11 o'clock. Charged on a small reserve and captured 2 horses and 2 men of the Sixteenth New York. They then retreated toward Burke's Station. I am not yet satisfied that the officer in charge of the picket or the men composing the reserve did their duty, but am investigating and shall report to-day."

wait for them, but immediately gave the order to charge, and our men, drawing their pistols, dashed on with a yell. The Federals fired a volley (wounding Frank Turner) and then fled. They were completely routed and lost 6 killed, including Capt. J. H. Flemming, of the Sixteenth New York, who was in command; Captain McMenamin, of the Thirteenth New York, a lieutenant, and a number of privates were wounded. Twenty-seven prisoners were captured, with 37 horses.[6]

GEORGE M. SLATER, CO. E.
From a War-time Photograph.

(See Mosby's Report, Appendix, XI.)

*Friday, August 12.*—Command met at Rectortown, and passing through Snicker's Gap, Mosby crossed the Shenandoah with about 330 men and 2 small howitzers. Scouts brought in the intelligence that a large train with supplies for Sheridan's

---

[6] HEADQUARTERS CAVALRY BRIGADE, }
*Near Falls Church, Va., August 9, 1864.* }

LAZELLE to TAYLOR : " I have the honor to report that two parties sent out from this command, consisting of 30 men each, met yesterday afternoon at Fairfax Station, and that while united and acting together were attacked by a force of rebels, variously estimated at from 40 to 50 men, and were completely dispersed and routed. Citizens report that Mosby himself was in command of the rebels. So far as known our loss is as follows : Capt. J. H. Flemming, Sixteenth New York Cavalry, missing ; 33 men missing ; 39 horses missing. The number of these killed and wounded is not yet known. Captain Flemming, who, at the time of the attack, had command of the party, is reported killed ; no other officers are lost. I have nothing to report except disgraceful mismanagement and consequent complete rout of our men, and a second Aldie disaster. A board of investigation has been called to ascertain who is responsible, and examine into and report upon the facts in the case. It will be forwarded with a complete statement in regard to the affair as soon as possible. A strong party was sent out this morning to the scene of the disaster to pick up stragglers and what wounded men could be found. Nothing has been heard from the force sent above Leesburg. They had orders to communicate any intelligence of importance."

In a later report, dated August 10th, Colonel Lazelle says : " Since last

army, with a heavy guard of cavalry and infantry, was on its way from Harper's Ferry to Winchester.[7]

On the morning of the 13th we moved out in the direction of Berryville, and nearing the pike discovered the long line of wagons moving towards Berryville. A portion of the train had just hauled out of park near a stream, where it had been halted to water the animals. A fog, which the morning sun had not yet dispelled, partially concealed us from the enemy and gave time to bring up our little force.

One of the howitzers was rendered useless by the breaking of a wheel; the other was quietly but quickly placed in position on an eminence in sight of the turnpike, and orders were given for the attack. The First Squadron, under Capt. A. E. Richards, moved out towards Berryville to attack the head of the train, while Capt. Wm. Chapman, with the Second Squadron, was to strike the train from the point he occupied to the right of the artillery. Meanwhile Captain Glasscock, with Company D, was kept behind the hill, out of sight of the pike, to support the gun. The Federals did not at first seem to realize their situation and made no preparations to repel an assault. As the curtain of fog lifted they could plainly see us, being only a little over 200 yards distant, but evidently mistook us for their own men. A shell from our gun struck a forge in the road, and bursting, aroused them and scattered the guard. A second exploded in the midst of their wagons and caused a stampede among the drivers. The third shot was followed by a charge. The cavalry had fled at the first fire, and the infantry now retreated, some taking refuge in the woods,

---

evening's report the following wounded from the disaster at Fairfax Station have been brought in : Thirteenth New York Cavalry, 5 ; Sixteenth New York Cavalry, 3. Five men are known to have been killed, but their regiment cannot be ascertained, as they were buried before our relieving party reached them. Capt. J. H. Flemming, Sixteenth New York Cavalry, in command, was killed. His body was found by the roadside, stripped of much of its clothing, and was brought into camp last evening and buried this morning in the old churchyard at Falls Church. Captain McMenamin, Thirteenth New York Cavalry, had three balls through his clothing and a slight skin wound in the knee."

[7] Original order issued by General Kenly, to be executed in guarding the trains from Halltown to Winchester. (See Appendix, XXVIII.)

and behind stone fences, from which they kept up an incessant fire until dislodged by a charge or a shell. Captain Franklin, with Lieutenants Fray and Rahm and Sergeant Babcock of the artillery, handled the gun well and did good service.

One party sought refuge in a brick church in the suburbs of Berryville, from which they for some time kept up a murderous fire, killing Welby H. Rector, of Middleburg, and wounding Lieutenant Wrenn and killing his horse. Sergeant Edward Rector, of Company A, was also wounded. The howitzer was brought to bear upon the church and the enemy were forced to retire. A body of infantry on the right took up a position behind a stone fence, and in an orchard, and seemed determined to hold their ground, but Captain Chapman charged and drove them out. Lewis Adie, a gallant young soldier, of Leesburg, was killed in the charge, and C. H. Walker, of Company C, severely wounded.

CHAS. H. WALKER, CO. C.
Wounded at Berryville, August 13, 1864.

The head of the train was at Berryville and extended for a long distance along the pike. Mules were taken from the wagons and the wagons then set on fire. The whole line presented a scene of the wildest confusion. The booming of cannon, the bursting shell, the rattling of musketry and the sharp crack of the pistols mingled with the yells and curses of the contending forces ; the braying of mules and the lowing of cattle were heard together with the cries and groans of the wounded. In the road, horses and mules were dashing wildly about like mad ; wagons upset—some blazing or smoking. Teams running off at a furious pace, which it was impossible to check, would attract the notice of some of our men, who, riding alongside, would set fire to the wagon, and as the smoke curled up, the frightened mules rushed frantically along until they fell exhausted or were released by dashing the wagon against a tree or some obstacle in the road.

Over 500 mules, 36 horses, 200 head of fine cattle, 208 prisoners and 4 negroes were captured. A great many Federals were killed and wounded and nearly 100 wagons were destroyed, with their contents.

In one of the wagons was a box which was thrown out on the ground by the roadside with other boxes and trunks containing officers' baggage, and was passed unnoticed among these rich prizes by our men, who afterwards learned to their regret that this box was filled with greenbacks to pay off Sheridan's troops.[8] The Federals, however, came back after our departure and secured the box and contents.

The "Return from the Raid" has already been made the subject of the artist's pencil, but it is impossible to faithfully portray the reality of that scene as it appeared on that summer day. The long line of prisoners, mules, horses and cattle stretched out along the road. Our men, wild with excitement and elated with their success, gave vent to their feelings with shouts and yells and merry songs, the braying mules and lowing cattle joining in the chorus. The bright new captured uniforms of the Federal officers transformed our dusty rebel boys for the time into the holiday soldiers of peaceful days; and the citizens along our route, though well used to raids and the passing of armies through the country, gazed on the scene in mute astonishment, seemingly at a loss whether to stand or run on the approach of the cavalcade.

This was a severe blow to Sheridan, who, crippled by the loss of his supplies and fearful of another attack, fell back to his old position.[9]

---

[8] See Beardsley's Report, Appendix, XXIX.
[9] See Appendix, as follows :
   Mosby's Report, XI.
   Copy of original order issued by Gen. Kenly, XXVIII.
   Report of Major Beardsley, Sixth New York Cavalry, XXIX.
   Report of Capt. E. P. McKinney, Commissary of Subsistence, XXX.
   Testimony of Capt. Mann, Quartermaster First Division, Nineteenth Army Corps, before the Board of Inquiry, XXXI.

Stevenson, in his History of the First New York (Lincoln) Cavalry, referring to this affair, says:

"The watchful Mosby had struck Sheridan's wagon train at Berryville on the 13th of August and captured and destroyed nearly the whole train, carrying off all the baggage of the cavalry corps and causing considerable commotion at headquarters. The train was guarded by Kenly's Maryland Brigade of 100 days men and they offered but feeble resistance.

"General Sheridan was not yet acquainted with Mosby's strength and tactics and deemed it prudent to fall back from his advanced position to avoid a repetition of the raid upon his trains."

BRIG.-GEN. JOHN R. KENLY.
U. S. A.

Encouraged by the success which had crowned his efforts. Mosby determined to continue his assaults on Sheridan's lines and thus cripple his movements. A number of small detachments were sent out by Mosby in various directions, and their vigilance and activity is shown by the tenor of the dispatches taken from the Records of the War Department at Washington.[10]

---

[10] General Max Weber, Harper's Ferry, Aug. 11th, to Captain Parsons, Sheridan's Assistant Adjutant General, says: "Mosby is already between Harper's Ferry and your command, and last night captured and paroled the *Tribune* correspondent."

Lieutenant-Colonel Taylor, Chief of Staff, Washington, Aug. 12th, to Brigadier-General Wilson: "The major general commanding directs that you hold in readiness a good and reliable regiment of your command to escort Colonel Chipman, Aide-de-Camp, bearer of dispatches, to Major-General Sheridan."

Chipman to Secretary Stanton, Aug. 14th, says: "Arrived this a. m., 6 o'clock, having marched 90 miles in 24 hours. Mosby's gang hung on our flank between Goose Creek and Snicker's Gap, firing into our rear at the Gap."

Captain Harrison, at Martinsburg, Aug. 14th, to General Kelley, says: "Several of our scouts here say they cannot get through to Sheridan, Mosby having driven them back."

Major Waite, Eighth Illinois Cavalry, Aug. 14th, writing to Washington says: "A number of squads of rebel cavalry seen on the Virginia side to-day, all along my line, from Monocacy down as far as Great Falls. Think they are watching for stragglers or orderlies with dispatches."

Colonel Chipman, Harper's Ferry, Aug. 16th, to Secretary Stanton: "Guer-

On the 15th of August Capt. A. E. Richards, while scouting with a squad of men on the turnpike between Charlestown and Berryville, fell in with a party of Federal Cavalry, consisting of First Lieutenant J. S. Walker, First U. S. Cavalry brigade commissary, bearer of dispatches, with an escort of 5 men. In the fight which ensued Lieutenant Walker was killed, and First Lieutenant Philip Dwyer, regimental commissary, Fifth U. S. Cavalry, wounded and taken prisoner. Only one of the escort escaped.

*Friday, August 19.*—Scouts having been sent in advance, we crossed the Shenandoah river at Castleman's Ferry.[11]

rillas infest the country between here and Winchester. Trains require strong escorts. A little party, 20 minutes ahead of my escort, was attacked beyond Charlestown. The lieutenant and 2 men killed and 6 captured; 1 escaped."

Colonel Edwards, Aug. 16th, to Major Whittier: "I have the honor to report that 160 to 200 of the enemy, accompanied by Mosby himself, and clothed in the uniform of the U. S. troops, are now a short distance to the left and rear of Middletown. One of the party has been within the limits of our camps today"

Sheridan to Grant, Aug. 17th: "Mosby has annoyed me and captured a few wagons. We hung 1 and shot 6 of his men yesterday."

Averell to Stevenson, Aug. 17th: "General Duffié's Division was at Berryville yesterday evening; 200 of my command have been sent to communicate with him, and to capture, kill or disperse the guerrillas at Charlestown. They should have arrived before this. I have also scouts in that direction. If they do not succeed in clearing out the place, I will send more."

Stevenson to Averell, Aug. 17th: "Mosby with his command is waiting to attack train and will capture it if possible. The supplies are needed at the front and should be put through by all means."

Stevenson to Sheridan, Harper's Ferry, Aug. 17th: "Finding all trains threatened by guerrillas, and that they are in force, largely increased by a concentration of several organizations under Mosby, making the vicinity of Charlestown their theater of operations, I am of opinion that the only safety of our trains and couriers is the posting of a force at Charlestown, with General Duffié at Berryville, and 1,000 of Averell's force at Charlestown, with orders by constant scouting to keep the country clear. I think we can send forward everything without loss. As matters now stand, no small party of trains with small guard is safe."

[11] General Sheridan's position at this time is thus given in his communication to General Augur, dated Charlestown, August 18:

"The position of my troops is as follows: 4 brigades of cavalry in front, at Berryville and well up toward Winchester, at the crossing of the Opequon; 1 division of cavalry at Summit Point; infantry at Clifton, and in rear of Clifton. I am in telegraphic communication with Averell, who is at Martinsburg."

Mosby divided his force as follows: Company B, under Capt. A. E. Richards, moving off in the direction of Charlestown; Companies C, D and E, under Capt. Wm. H. Chapman, to operate in the neighborhood of Berryville; while he (Mosby) proceeded with Company A to the road between Harper's Ferry and Charlestown.

In retaliation for our attacks, the Federal soldiers, acting under orders from their superiors, proceeded to wreak their vengeance on the defenseless citizens, and the burning and destruction, commenced by Hunter, was resumed.

Our scouts, in their search for information last night, captured a picket-post of the Fifth Michigan Cavalry, near Castleman's Ferry. There were but 4 men on post: 1 was killed, 1 wounded and the remaining two captured.

As Captain Chapman moved on with his command, he saw the house of Mr. McCormick in flames, and learned that it had been set on fire in retaliation for the killing of the picket.

A little further on, the Rangers came upon another, the residence of Mr. Sowers. Here the women and poor little children were gathered in a forlorn and

JOHN A. SAUNDERS, CO. D.

weeping group in a corner of the yard, gazing on the blazing pile of what was once their happy home. As our men rode up and looked upon the pale, upturned, pleading faces and met the looks of utter despair there pictured, they felt that it would be mockery to offer sympathy or express regret, and driving their spurs into their horses, they dashed on in pursuit of the destroyers. On they went, like bloodhounds on the trail. Soon they came in sight of the houseburners, who were then in the act of destroying the residence of Colonel

FEDERAL HOUSE-BURNERS ANNIHILATED BY MOSBY'S RANGERS.

Morgan. They had already burned the hay, wheat, barn, etc., and had set fire to the house. Worked up to madness by this scene, as well as what they had just witnessed, the Rangers closed in on the enemy and neither asked nor gave quarter.[12]

(See Mosby's Report, Appendix, XI.)

I received a rough sketch of the following incident connected with this encounter, which the artist has incorporated in the illustration on the opposite page : Three of the Federal cavalry, being hard pressed, left the main body and attempted to make their escape. Two of them jumped a fence on the extreme left and made their way across the field, pursued by Wm. W. Patteson of Company C. Patteson's horse fell in jumping the fence, and before he could get the animal up, the third trooper attacked him with his

---

[12] The New York *Times*, of Aug. 25, 1864, in a letter from its War Correspondent, dated Berryville, Aug. 21, gives the following account of this affair:

" He (General Custer) issued an order directing Colonel Alger, of the Fifth Michigan, to destroy 4 houses belonging to well-known secessionists, in retaliation for the men killed, captured and wounded on Thursday night. This order was promptly carried into effect by a detachment of 50 men, under Captain Drake and Lieutenants Allen, Lounsberry and Bivvins, who were particularly charged to inform all citizens met with the cause for destroying the property. The expedition was accompanied by Dr. Sinclair, and the work was thoroughly and effectually done, but unfortunately not without serious loss of life. Captain Drake, leaving the main part of the command under Lieutenant Allen in line near one house which had been fired, took a few men and proceeded to fire another house about 100 rods distant. While thus engaged 200 rebels suddenly emerged from a ravine and made a furious charge upon the force under Lieutenant Allen before due preparation could be made to receive them. * * * The command was charged while forming to resist an attack. The men, overwhelmed by numbers, broke and fled in confusion. This occurred on the Sheppard's Mill road, not far from the Berryville and Snicker's Gap pike. There are numerous stone fences running at right angles with the road and the way open for retreat was down the road which had been barricaded by our own men, and the only way to get around this was by a narrow passage way through a stone wall, at the side of the road, going around the barricade and through the wall again into the road. As only one horse at a time could go through this narrow passage it was impossible for all the men to escape in that way. The enemy were upon them, and no mercy being shown, a majority of the men ran along a fence running at right angles with the road, hoping to find another passage, but finding none and reaching a corner, surrendered as a last resort. Several squads were cornered in this way, and in every instance the men who surrendered were killed after they had surrendered, or were left for dead.
     *         *         *         *         *

" Casualties in the Fifth Michigan Cavalry in the massacre, August 19, 1864 : Killed—Sergeant E. S. Fields ; Corporals C. C. Craft, Alph. Day; Privates H. Wittington, John G. Lutz, James Kennicut, Oliver Warner, Alfred A. Henry, Clark Osborn, S. R. Epler, Eaton Lewis, Peter Castor, Chas. B. Clyde. Wounded—S. D. Eldred, mortally ; Ab. B. Shaffer, mortally ; John Connell, hand ; Samuel K. Davis, nose; Corporal F. M. Wright, face."

carbine.  The shot tore a hole through Patteson's hat, carrying away one-half of a black plume worn there.  Before the Federal cavalryman could ride over him or get in another shot, Patteson killed him with a shot from his revolver.  The man carried a bundle, tied up in some bedclothes, containing a quantity of silverware and jewelry which he had taken from some of the dwellings burned by this party.

WM. W. PATTESON, CO. C.
From a Photograph taken during the War.

After moving off with Company A, Mosby recrossed the Shenandoah and again crossed at Rock Ford.  Here he divided Company A into three parties, one under Hatcher, another under Wiltshire, and one he reserved for himself. All returned to Fauquier, after operating on the Federal outposts, bringing prisoners and captured horses, without loss or injury to themselves.

# CHAPTER XVI.

*Sunday, August 21, 1864.*—Lieut. William Martin, of Company E, was buried to-day at Upperville. He was accidentally shot by a comrade while riding along the road, the ball passing through his breast, from left to right. He was a brave young soldier—his daring at times seeming reckless. He had many friends, both in the command and among the citizens, and his death was a regret to all.

Channing M. Smith was soon after chosen as Third Lieutenant of Company E, to fill the vacancy occasioned by the death of Lieutenant Martin.

Before joining Mosby's command Channing M. Smith had served in Company H, Fourth Virginia Cavalry. While acting as scout, his gallant conduct had received the recognition and praise of both Generals Lee and Stuart, as will be seen by the following report and endorsement:

HDQRS. CAV. CORPS, ARMY OF NORTHERN VIRGINIA,
*April 20, 1864.*
Lieut.-Col. W. H. TAYLOR, *Assistant Adjutant-General.*

COLONEL: I have the honor to report the following affair (*petite guerre*), which occurred in the operations within the enemy's lines near Catlett's Station on the 16th instant:

Privates Channing M. Smith, Richard Lewis, and Love, of Company H, Fourth Virginia Cavalry, acting as scouts in Fauquier County, met and attacked a party of 5 of the enemy, killing 4, the other escaping. This affair reflects great credit on the valor and skill of the gallant scouts who executed it, and too much praise cannot be awarded them.

Their operations serve to inspire confidence in our cause and keep our enemies in a state of constant and wholesome terror. The attention of the commanding general is called to these young men, who are continually giving evidence of their gallantry and daring by similar exploits.

I have the honor to be, very respectfully, your obedient servant,

J. E. B. STUART, *Major-General.*

[Indorsement.]

HEADQUARTERS, *April 20, 1864.*

Respectfully forwarded for the information of the Department.

I have on several previous occasions called the attention of the Secretary of War to the gallantry of Channing M. Smith and other young scouts of this army.

R. E. LEE, *General.*

*Tuesday, August 23.*—Command met at Rectortown; 300 men reported at roll call. We moved off at noon, with 2 pieces of artillery—one 12-pound rifle and one Napoleon gun; crossed the Bull Run mountains about sunset and pushed on rapidly under cover of night to the Federal camp at Annandale. Reaching the camp, it was discovered that the horses had nearly all been sent off and the garrison was in stockade. Pickets were captured or driven in, the guns were placed in position, and at daylight on the morning of the 24th, Captain Montjoy was sent to demand a surrender, which was refused. A few shells were then fired into camp and a demonstration made, after which Lieut. Harry Hatcher was sent with a flag of truce, again demanding the surrender of the camp. As Hatcher went in, the position of the guns was changed. This the Federals observed, and the officer said to Hatcher:

"I have a mind to burn that rag, and if you send any more, they will not be respected."

"Don't burn that," said Hatcher, "its the only handkerchief I've got!"

When Hatcher returned and reported the result of his mission, the artillery opened fire and the attack was renewed. Out of 15 shells fired, but one fell in the camp. Some went over the stockade and fell near our companies on the opposite side. The camp was strongly fortified and could only have been taken by dismounted men, with a loss which would not have justified the attempt. One point in our mission had been gained : the enemy were well, stirred up and reinforcements for the Valley were not likely to be taken from this part of the line.[1]

---

[1] *Report of Capt. J. Schneider, Sixteenth New York Cavalry.*

HDQRS. DETACH. SIXTEENTH NEW YORK VOL. CAV.,
*Annandale Stockade, Va., Aug. 25, 1864.*

SCHNEIDER to LANSING : " Inclosed I have the honor to forward a report of the repulse of Mosby's forces in an attack on the stockade at Annandale, Va.:

Wednesday morning, at 13 minutes to 5 o'clock the camp was alarmed by 3 shots fired by the picket on the Fairfax Court House road ; immediately after which the rebels who had taken the picket, consisting of 1 sergeant and 3 men, fired about 3 shells into our camp; then a detachment of about 100 men charged up toward our entrance ; being received there by a volley, they swerved to the south, surrounding the south and east side of our camp. A flag of truce was sent, demanding, in Colonel Mosby's name, the surrender of our camp. Under cover of this flag of truce they advanced their 2 pieces (field) to within 300 or 400 yards of our camp—one on the southwest, the other on the northwest corner. The question of surrendering being answered in the negative in the most decisive terms, they commenced to bombard our camp in good earnest, one piece throwing shell, the other one grape. After firing nearly a dozen more shots, they sent another flag of truce on the northwest side, where Captain Mickels had

LOUIS REARDON, CO. E.

charge of the defenses, who told them not to come with any more flags of truce, as he would not respect them, which same answer two bearers of flags of truce received from me on the east side of the camp during a tour of inspection I made around the abatis. Finding their persuasions, both in shelling and negotiating, of no account, they, being probably warned of the approach of re enforcements, after some further demonstrations, sent their field-pieces up the Fairfax Court House road, and then they themselves slowly retired. I had seen about 250 or 300 men and had no means of ascertaining their correct number, and thought it only a feint when they left ; therefore I did not make

The Eighth Illinois was undoubtedly at the time the best cavalry regiment in the Army of the Potomac, and General Sheridan, with the view of driving out Mosby, ordered all

COLONEL WILLIAM GAMBLE and
MAJOR HENRY W. SAWYER.
Eighth Illinois Cavalry.
From a War-time Picture.

any demonstration to pursue them, although Companies B and C had their horses in readiness. The attack lasted nearly one hour and a half, and they fired from thirty to forty cannon shots, besides some small-arm practice. They wounded 2 horses of Company A and deranged some of our quarters and Company C's stable (old barn). The casualties on the rebel side, as far as we can learn, were one man and 3 horses killed and 3 men wounded. We also learned that their force was over 400 men when they passed the Court House. Mrs. Tennison, who lives east of the camp, refused the laundresses to come in her house, and told them 'to get away from here into your camp,' harboring at the same time some of the rebel leaders with whom she was acquainted.

Finally, I have to state, that both officers and men, with but very few exceptions, behaved splendidly.

"N. B.—The re-enforcements arrived too late to be of any service to us, as it was two hours and ten minutes from the first shot to their arrival, under Major Horton, Sixteenth New York Volunteer Cavalry."

*August 24th, —*

LAZELLE to DE RUSSEY: "The attack at Annandale has ceased, and the rebels withdrew, perhaps with the intention of attacking some other part of my picket line. The attacking party is said to have consisted of from less than 200, to 300, even to 500 men, with two pieces of artillery, all under Mosby."

In another despatch, same date, he says: "On learning of the attack every available man was sent out from here to give relief."

LANSING to LYELL, Thirteenth New York Cavalry, at Lewinsville:

"Another attempt will doubtless be made somewhere along our line, either during the day or to-night. The point selected will probably be at your stockade. The colonel commanding directs me to tell you to caution your pickets and your

the cavalry of that regiment to concentrate at Muddy Branch to operate in Loudoun and—as he stated in his orders to General Augur—" exterminate as many of Mosby's gang as they can."

On the 20th of August they left their camp at Muddy Branch and crossed the Potomac with 650 men, the special object of the scout being, as stated in orders to Major Waite, "to break up and exterminate any bands or parties of Mosby's, White's or other guerrillas which may be met." They marched up through Aldie, Middleburg and Upperville to Snicker's Gap, thence to the Potomac, and back to their camp. On their way they picked up and carried off a number of citizens; at Upperville, among others, Rev. Mr. Harris and Rev. Mr. Gallagher and Geo. Brown. This was in accordance with the instructions of General Grant to Sheridan.[2]

men to be on the alert, and assure yourself that they are, especially toward daybreak to-morrow, should an attack not come sooner. Keep 2 horses saddled in the stockade all the day and to-night, and in case of an attack let us know here at once by sending out two in different directions. This will make sure of one of your messengers reaching us. Colonel Lazelle directs you not to surrender your command under any consideration or emergency."

[2] GRANT to SHERIDAN, Aug. 16, 1864: " If you can possibly spare a division of cavalry, send them through Loudoun County to destroy and carry off the crops, animals, negroes and all men under fifty years of age capable of bearing arms. In this way you will get many of Mosby's men. All male citizens under fifty can fairly be held as prisoners of war, and not as citizen prisoners. If not already soldiers, they will be made so the moment the rebel army gets hold of them."

AUGUR to SHERIDAN, August 25th: "Among the persons brought in by Major Waite is one well known to me as a reliable Union man, who has heretofore given me valuable information ; he is from Upperville; says he heard no talk there of the rebel army intending to move this way; says they are conscripting everybody there capable of bearing arms ; those who join Mosby are exempt from joining Lee's army. By this means Mosby can command between 800 and 1,000 men. To get information from Snicker's Gap would require a force able to manage Mosby, whose headquarters are on the route there. Small parties will be picked up. I will send the Eighth Illinois Cavalry again to that vicinity as soon as it can move, and will send with it one of the regiments (very small) from Falls Church. To clean out Loudoun County and destroy the crops there will require a much larger force than I can send ; I will do all I can, however. The horses of the Eighth Illinois have to be shod before they can move ; I will let you know to-morrow when they will move. I have a man at Middleburg who is employed to give me the earliest information of any move of the rebels in this direction ; I trust he will not deceive me."

On the return of the Eighth Illinois to its camp, General
Sheridan, in a communication to General Augur, August
24th, expresses the hope that " the Eighth Illinois has cleaned
out the Loudoun Valley." Yet this fond hope was not realized, and another and more formidable expedition was
planned. The Eighth Illinois was to start from its camp
at Muddy Branch, August 29th, to be joined at Aldie by the
Sixteenth New York Cavalry, from Fairfax, and " move
rapidly on Upperville and Middleburg, surprising any force
of guerrillas lurking in that vicinity." They were to arrest
and bring in all males between the ages of 18 and 50; impress
all wagons and bring them in loaded with forage; destroy
all hay, oats, corn and wheat they could not bring in, and
seize all horses. Attention was also called to " Mosby's
headquarters." [3]

The result, however, was summed up in the following

---

[3] HEADQUARTERS DEPARTMENT OF WASHINGTON,
22D ARMY CORPS.

TAYLOR to WAITE : " The major general commanding directs that you move
August 29th with your regiment, leaving on the left bank of the river only your
camp guard and the detachment protecting the telegraph station at Darnestown.
Your march will be via Aldie, and so timed that you reach that place before
12 m., August 30. At Aldie you will meet the Sixteenth New York Cavalry,
commanded by Major Horton, who will report to you. Assuming command of
the two regiments, you will move rapidly on Upperville and Middleburg, surprising any force of guerrillas lurking in that vicinity. The special object of
your scout is to destroy, as far as practicable, the sources from which Mosby
draws men, horses and support. To this end you will arrest and bring in all
males capable of bearing arms or conveying information, between the ages of
eighteen and fifty, excepting those mentioned in the enclosed list; impress all
wagons and bring them in loaded with forage; destroy all crops of hay, oats,
corn and wheat which you cannot bring in, and seize all horses. When horses
are taken from Union men, make memoranda to that effect, in order that the
horses may be identified or the owners indemnified. Collect all information
within reach of the movements of the enemy and embrace it in your report; any
which you may regard as of great importance should be sent in by a small
party of trusted men. Mosby's headquarters are reported as alternating between
the houses of Mr. Blackwell and Mr. Turner, near Upperville, Middleburg, and
their vicinity. On your return it is desired that you come in by the way of Falls
Church. After the rations you carry for men and animals are exhausted,
live on the country. Inclosed find memorandum for guidance in particular
cases. Report departure and effective strength. The necessary instructions
have been given Major Horton."

brief communication from General Augur to General Sheridan, September 1, 1864:

"Major Waite has returned from Upperville, in the vicinity of Snicker's Gap; reports no rebel forces in that vicinity except Mosby's. He brought in 30 men and 30 horses, and destroyed a good deal of property. No wagons can be found to bring off supplies in any quantity."

*Saturday, September 3.*—Command met at Rectortown. Mosby divided his force, reserving the First Squadron for himself, while the Second Squadron, under Capt. Wm. H. Chapman, moved off through Ashby's Gap and halted for the night near Shepherd's Mill. John Russell was sent on a scout to Berryville, from which place he returned before midnight with the report that a heavy force of Federal cavalry had passed through Berryville, going towards Front Royal. Chapman determined to follow them up, not knowing that the Federals had met with a repulse and that Anderson with Kershaw's division had driven them back.[4]

LIEUT. W. BEN PALMER, CO. E.
From a Painting made during the War.

As Chapman approached the pike a short distance above Berryville, he saw a cavalry skirmish line along the top of a hill in his front. The country was rolling and the main body was completely shut out from view. Captains Wm. H. and Samuel Chapman, with Company C, moved off to the

---

[4] It was decided that Anderson must return to Winchester, and start for the Blue Ridge again by a more southerly road, carrying him past the Union left. Early therefore withdrew his whole army across the Opequon—after a spirited skirmish at Berryville, in which Torbert, returning from the left, was involved—Anderson's trains going first. The Eighth Corps had that morning been ordered to fall back to Clifton; and five days after, with Custer's and Lowell's brigades of Merritt's division, it was sent across to Summit Point, to assure the right flank and the communications with Harper's Ferry. Crook's ambulance train, during these operations, was, in Sheridan's language, "attacked and badly stampeded by six of Mosby's Men."—The Shenandoah Valley in 1864. By George E. Pond. New York: Charles Scribner's Sons, 1883.

right, in order to see what force there was behind the hill, leaving Lieutenant Palmer, with Company E, in a little lane facing the skirmishers. Captain Chapman told Lieutenant Palmer to remain where he was and await orders, whilst he went off some distance, but still keeping in sight. He soon sent back Frank Angelo to Palmer with orders to charge the skirmish line, as well as the regiment on the other side of the hill; that he (Chapman) would charge down the pike at the same time. Palmer quickly led his men through the lane, at the end of which was a closed gate. He ordered Robt. Jarman to get down and open the gate. As Jarman attempted to swing back the gate he was killed by a shot from one of the

skirmishers in front. Palmer then ordered Ben. Iden to dismount and open the gate; he met the same fate as Jarman. A third man was ordered to open the gate, but he hesitated. As there was no time for delay, Palmer sprang from his horse, threw open the gate, and, quickly remounting, led Company E over the hill, driving in the skirmish line and charging the regiment, which proved to be the Sixth New York. Captain Chapman came up at the same time with Company C, and the Federals, who were marching in a column of fours, had no time to reform before they were attacked. Their commander called out to his men:

LIEUT. FRANK FOX, CO. C.
Mortally wounded September 3, 1864, in a fight with the Sixth New York Cavalry.
From a Photograph taken in the early part of the War.

"Fall back to the woods and we will give them hell there!" They retreated toward the woods and attempted to rally, but Chapman and Palmer pushed them so hard that they broke and fled in disorder. They were pursued for a mile, having a number killed and wounded; 30 prisoners and 38 horses, with equipments, were captured. Our loss was Jarman and Iden, killed; Lieut. Frank Fox and Clay Adams, mortally wounded, and several others slightly wounded.

Lieut. Frank Fox, of Fairfax, was wounded in the arm and his horse carried him into the ranks of the enemy, where he was taken prisoner and carried to Harper's Ferry. His arm was amputated, and he died some days after at Sandy Hook.

He was not only a brave officer, but his genial nature had won h i m m a n y friends. His loss was deeply felt by all.

Clay Adams, being deaf, was e x e m p t from military duty, but he entered the service and proved a brave and faithful sol- dier. He was shot through the body and had his lower limbs paralyzed. John Russell and a few c o m p a n i o n s went over the river at night and brought him to the house of

MAJ.-GEN. ALFRED T. A. TORBERT, U. S. A.

his father, at Paris (near Ashby's Gap), where he lingered for some months, when death came to his relief.

General Torbert's cavalry came in sight before the fight was fairly over, but a few shells from Anderson's batteries sent them scampering off in the direction of Charlestown.

We will now return to Mosby. After leaving Rectortown

with the First Squadron, numbering about 90 men, he had proceeded by way of Bloomfield to Snicker's Gap. A heavy rain came up, which lasted all night, and, the road being rough, we traveled slowly and halted on the top of the mountain, where we lay until daylight on the morning of the 4th, and then moved off to Myer's Ford, on the Shenandoah. Mosby, with 15 men, crossed the river on a scout, leaving the squadron, under Lieutenant Nelson, in a piece of woods near the Ford. Captain Richards, taking a few men, also crossed, but learning that a Federal scouting party was on the east side of the river, he recrossed, and, taking Company B, started in pursuit. He followed the trail until it crossed our track of the previous night, when they turned and crossed the river. Thinking the Federals had all returned to the Valley, Richards sent back Company B to Nelson and started off with 5 or 6 men on a scout toward Rippon.

I had been on picket at the Ford, and when relieved rejoined the command in the woods, took off my bridle, loosened the saddle girth, and, haltering my horse to a tree, with a bunch of fodder before him, lay down to sleep beside him. I did not imagine there was an enemy on our side of the river and thought the only danger would be from the other side, at the Ford, where I had been stationed, and of which our pickets could give us ample warning.

I was suddenly awakened by the report of firearms and saw our men rushing to their horses. Looking out into the open ground from the woods, I saw Lieutenant Nelson, of Company A, and Sergeant Horace Johnson,[5] of Company B, rallying the men, while a body of Federal cavalry was charging around the point of woods. For a second I hesitated whether to mount my horse as he was or to put on the bridle, but soon decided. Hastily putting on my bridle, I sprang into the saddle, and as I did so felt a crushing blow in my right side, which for the moment deprived me of breath. The ball was

---

[5] Horace Johnson first served in the Black Horse Cavalry, but afterwards joined Mosby and was made Sergeant of Company B. He died at his residence, near Remington, Virginia, on the 20th of October, 1894, in the 73d year of his age, and his body was borne to its last resting-place by his old comrades of the Black Horse Cavalry.

partly spent, and must have been fired by some one far in
the rear of a party who were then advancing through the
woods.   It passed through my jacket and, striking the ribs,
glanced off.   Wm. Walston, who was beside me, said : " Are
you much hurt ? "   Just at the time I could not speak, but
after catching my breath, said: " I don't think it is much."
Looking around, I saw a body of our men running down hill
towards a gap in the fence,
closely followed by the enemy,
who were firing on them.

WM. R. STONE, CO. A.
Wounded at Myer's Ford, Sept 4, 1864.
From a War-time Photograph.

Seeing our men were com-
pletely demoralized and fleeing in all directions, our only
alternative was to get out as
best we could, so, both being
well mounted, we rode down
with a pack of blue coats at
our heels, and leaping the
fence to the left of the gap,
were soon making our way
across the field, while our pursuers turned and rode through
the gap.   This lengthened the
distance between us, yet they
kept on our track, yelling and
shooting.   The bullets whistled sharply in our ears, but
this only urged our horses
to redoubled speed.   " Hold
on to old Bob," said Walston, "and he will bring you out
all right."   After we had cleared a second fence, our pursuers again turning off to go through an opening, we felt
ourselves comparatively safe.

We afterwards learned the attacking party was Captain
Blazer's Independent Scouts.[6]   He had been informed that
we were at the ford, and came upon us unawares.   Lieutenant Nelson and a few men, who were first in their saddles,

---

[6] See Blazer's Report, Chapter XXI.

met his advance and drove them back; but he renewed his assault, at the same time sending a party of dismounted men through the woods with their seven-shooters to fire on our men exposed in the open field. This, together with the wounding of Lieutenant Nelson, who was in command, threw us in such confusion that it was impossible to rally the men. They gave way and scattered, each one to save himself as best he could. Our loss was: McKim, who broke his neck; —— Mallory, mortally wounded; Lieutenant Nelson, Company A, and Frank M. Woolf, William S. Flynn, W. R. Stone, F. M. Yates, wounded, and 5 captured, among them Geo. Skinner and Richard Moran. Although the affair resulted in favor of Blazer, his loss was, except in prisoners, as heavy as our own.

William R. Stone was struck on the head with a carbine and was left for dead on the field. After recovering consciousness, he went off toward the river to wash the blood from his face. On his way he met Yates, who was wounded and had also been left for dead. As the two reached the river, they found one of our men lying with his head resting on some alders, which kept his face out of water, with his feet on the bank. They pulled him out, and, making a rude litter, carried him to a house near by, where they left him and proceeded to a place of safety. This will probably account for three of our men among the list of killed reported by Blazer.

When Mosby reached the turnpike in Sheridan's rear, he found trains and ambulances moving along with but few men to guard them, and, thinking it a good field to operate in, sent Harry Heaton and Captain Kennon to Myer's Ford to bring up Nelson with his squadron. In the meantime, concealing his men in the woods, Mosby went out on the turnpike with Joseph W. Owen to reconnoiter. On reaching the pike, they saw two cavalrymen riding along toward them, who surrendered on demand. An ambulance was now observed coming down the pike, and Mosby, taking charge of the two prisoners, told Owen to bring in the ambulance. On nearer approach, Owen saw it was filled with infantry, their guns resting between their knees. He rode back to Mosby, saying he thought they were too strong for him. " Try them," said Mosby. Owen again rode out, whistling one of the airs then popular among the soldiers, and as they came up, presented his pistol and called on them to surrender. They appeared astonished and hesitated.

" Talk it out quick," said Owen, " or I will open on you." A voice replied : " I surrender, sir."

" What do you all say in the wagon ? " asked Owen.

" We surrender ; we surrender," came a chorus of voices from the inside.

Owen then told one man to get out, the others to hand their guns out one at a time, and made the man bend them over the stone fence and drop them on the other side, he keeping the party covered with his pistol.

He then made the driver take the ambulance and prisoners to the woods, where he told Mosby to take them quickly ; that he saw another ambulance about half a mile distant. As he had taken the first so easily, it encouraged him to attempt the capture of the second. He rode up laughing, as he called on them to surrender, and they seemed to regard it as a joke, for they, too, laughed as they gave up their arms and joined their fellow prisoners.

There were 14 prisoners in all, among them one gaudily dressed lady, who said she had married General Banks' Corps Commissary, at Baton Rouge, La., six months before. She was much frightened, drew out

JOSEPH W. OWEN, CO. B.
From a Photograph taken when a Member of Mosby's Command.

her purse, and told Owen to take all she had, if he would only release her.

" I do not rob women," said Owen.

There was also a boy riding a cream-colored horse

and carrying the United States mail, accompanying the ambulance.

Mosby sent off his prisoners with the 2 ambulances and 7 captured horses under guard, in charge of Owen. In crossing the mountain, one of the ambulances upset, and one of the prisoners broke his neck; another escaped in the darkness.

Mosby's force was now reduced to 5 or 6 men. While waiting for the squadron to come up, a train of ambulances approached. The temptation was too strong to resist, and Mosby, with his few men, made a dash, which not only threw the train into confusion, but also spread consternation in a large train parked near by. While Mosby's men were industriously unhitching teams, a body of Federal cavalry came up, and Mosby was driven off, after securing 13 horses.[7]

Captain Richards found the road in the neighborhood of Rippon in the same unprotected condition that Mosby discovered lower down, and after capturing a few prisoners and mules, trotted off to Myer's Ford to bring up Companies A and B, but when he reached the Shenandoah and learned of Nelson's surprise, he returned to Fauquier.

---

[7] SHERIDAN to HALLECK, Sept. 8th : "There is no truth in the newspaper report of the loss of Crook's ambulance train. Only one ambulance was lost and some 12 or 13 horses. The train was *attacked and badly stampeded by 6 of Mosby's men.*"

Brigadier-General WILSON to Captain RENO, Chief of Staff, Sept. 5, 1864 : " I have investigated the matter of the stampede in the wagon train yesterday and find the facts to be as follows :

" The train had been parked properly and the guards posted in the most advantageous manner, when doctors, ambulance men and others from General Crooks' ambulance train, then a mile and a half nearer Kabletown, dashed into the park of our train with the report that Mosby had taken their train or attacked it. This spread through our train and before anything could be done the whole thing was in confusion. It was, however, promptly suppressed and without communicating it in any way to the troops. Captain Hull, commanding Second New York, was prompt and vigorous; went to the assistance of General Crooks' train and rescued 5 ambulances. Two wagons and 3 ambulances are there yet deserted. The affair was disgraceful, but not to the troops or officers in charge of the train, they having done all in their power to correct the evil."

# CHAPTER XVII.

September, 1864—Company F Organized—John Russell's Attempt to Capture General Sheridan—Mosby in Fairfax—Enters Camp near Falls Church—Mosby Again Wounded, but Brought Out Safely—Colonel Gansevoort's Report of his Scout in Search of Mosby—General Chapman's Raid—Chapman *vs.* Chapman—Skirmish in Snicker's Gap and Recapture of Prisoners—Captain William Chapman in the Valley—With Lieutenant Fray, Ed. Hurst and a Few Other Bold Rangers Makes a Series of Captures—"Gobbles Up" a Squad of Federal Officers and Gathers in Sutlers.

*Tuesday, September 13.*—Company F organized, at Piedmont, by electing Walter E. Frankland, Captain ; James F. Ames (Big Yankee), First Lieutenant; Walter Bowie, Second Lieutenant; and Frank Turner, Third Lieutenant.

Captain Frankland in his reminiscences of his early days with Mosby in Chapter II., has omitted to mention an incident which occurred about April 5, 1863, when he, with Tom Turner and W. L. Hunter, were surprised at Charles Utterback's, near Warrenton. Turner attempted to fight his way out, but was mortally wounded and carried to Kinloch, the residence of his father, near The Plains, where he died. Hunter and Frankland were captured and carried to General Davis's headquarters at Payne's farm, where Frankland was compelled to " walk a circle " for hours because he refused to betray Mosby. He was exchanged and again captured within a month ; again exchanged and back to his command and on duty—all in less than three months.

In Company C, John S. Russell was elected Third Lieutenant to fill a vacancy.

Lieutenant Russell was not 21 years of age. He joined the command when only 19, but having a thorough knowledge of the Valley section, had acted as guide and scout for Mosby. He was bold and shrewd, and in the performance of his duty had many exciting adventures and narrow escapes.

On one occasion, when General Sheridan was at the house of Haight Willis, in Jefferson County, Russell with 6 men, well mounted, and a spare saddle horse, undertook to capture the General. Sheridan was in the house with two of his officers, having a sentinel at the front gate and another at the rear of the house. Russell's plan was to take the sentinel quietly from his post, and then, while two of his companions covered the two officers with their pistols, three of the Rangers were to take Sheridan out, mount him on the spare horse and ride off as quickly as possible. They crept stealthily out of the thicket, but one of the men, being too hasty, advanced on the soldier when he should have waited until his back was turned, and was challenged. When he attempted to seize the trooper's carbine the man pulled the trigger and the report brought a score of cavalrymen of Sheridan's escort to the scene and Russell and his party scampered off, with bullets whistling around them. They were well acquainted with the country, however, and once under cover had no difficulty in making their escape.

LIEUT. JOHN S. RUSSELL,
CO. C.
From a War-time Photograph.

After the election, several detachments were sent out; one, under Lieutenant Russell, going to the Valley, while Mosby took out a party for a scout in Fairfax. In the neighborhood of Falls Church, Mosby thought to capture a quartermaster's establishment. While reconnoitering the camp with two men, he discovered a butcher sleeping beside a beef he had killed. The man was brought out, with his horse, in spite of his vigorous protest against what he thought was a joke played on him by some of the "funny boys" in camp. The camp being poorly guarded, Mosby sent a party to bring out a number of horses, but before this could be accomplished the camp was alarmed and the attempt was abandoned.[1] Mosby then sent all the

---

[1] LAZELLE to TAYLOR, Sept. 15th : " I omitted to state in last evening's report that a party of 8 guerrillas had found its way night before last into the slaughter yard attached to the brigade commissary department, carrying off with them one man and one horse."

men back to Fauquier, with the exception of Guy Broadwater and Thomas Love.

The Thirteenth New York Cavalry was at this time returning from a scout to Aldie in search of Mosby, and
Colonel Gansevoort learning that Mosby was in the vicinity,
endeavored to intercept him on his way homeward. Mosby
and his two companions came upon five of the men who had
been selected for the duty of taking him. Mosby was recognized by the Federal cavalrymen, being in full uniform,
as he always appeared when on duty, and made a shining
mark. Being within a few yards of each other, all fired at
the same time. One ball shattered the handle of Mosby's
pistol and another entered his groin. He was able to keep
his saddle and ride, with difficulty, until his companions procured a light wagon to carry him off. Two horses belonging to the Federals were killed at the first fire and fell with
their riders under them. The other three Federals fled,
pursued by Love and Broadwater until they were called
back to assist their wounded commander. [2]

Mosby was taken to The Plains, where he was kindly cared
for by the family of Major Foster until he could be removed
to Lynchburg. [3]

---

[2] LAZELLE to TAYLOR, Sept. 22d : "I herewith inclose an extract from the
report of Colonel Gansevoort, Thirteenth New York Cavalry, referring to a fight
between Mosby and a small party detached from his main column on the last
scout of the regiment. Not much confidence was placed in the report at the
time of its receipt, but I now consider it certain that Mosby was really wounded
in this fight in the groin and cheek, and I deem it just that the Thirteenth
Regiment should have the credit attached to the affair. Private Henry Smith,
of Company H, Thirteenth New York Cavalry, is the man who wounded him."

---

[3] HEADQUARTERS THIRTEENTH NEW YORK CAVALRY,
*Near Falls Church, Va., Sept. 15th, 1864.*

GANSEVOORT to LANSING : "I have the honor to report that according to
orders from headquarters cavalry brigade, a portion of the regiment, numbering
210 dismounted and 63 mounted men, including the brigade scouts, moved,
under my command, on scout on the night of the 8th of September, 1864. The
column crossed Fox Ford, on Difficult Run, on the morning of the 9th of September, after a march of 13 miles, in which vicinity it encamped. At nightfall of the 9th of September it moved 12 miles to the vicinity of Coleman's, near
Horse Pen Run, and during the night of the 10th of September bivouacked,
after a march of five miles, on the road to Good Hope Church, near Broad Run,

*Thursday, September 15.*–Gen. Geo. H. Chapman, with about 400 men of the Third Indiana and Eighth New York Cavalry, raided along the Blue Ridge mountains from Snickersville to Paris. On their route they killed sheep, poultry, etc., and carried off a number of men and horses; passing on through to Upperville and back to Snickersville, where the main body halted and a squadron of the Eighth New York Cavalry, numbering about 60 men, was sent on ahead into the Gap with prisoners and captured horses.

---

its farther progress being delayed by a severe storm. On the night of the 11th of September the column encamped beyond Red Hill, after a march of 10 miles, and reached one mile and a half of Aldie, at a covered point at the intersection of the Aldie pike and the Carolina road, on the night of the 12th of September. Here the command was concealed, and at daybreak of the 13th of September the town was entered by the mounted men, the roads in the vicinity having been ambuscaded during a portion of the night. Nothing was, however, accomplished. Information having been gained that Mosby, with a force, had gone down the Aldie pike the night of, but before, the arrival of the column at Aldie, it was deemed best to move after him. The column reached Chantilly after a march of 16 miles, and encamped on the night of the 14th, ambuscading all the roads in the vicinity.

"On the morning of the 15th of September it resumed its march toward Fairfax, all indications and reports of scouts kept on the Centreville road and roads to left of the turnpike tending to show that Mosby, with a large force, but in divided parties, was on the left of the turnpike and between Vienna and Frying Pan. The scouts were driven from Flint Hill, but those at Fairfax reported that Mosby had been seen to pass through the Court House toward Centreville a short time previous, with two men. I dispatched 5 men to the Centreville road, about 3 miles distant, to intercept the party, fearing that more men might fail of an approach. Near Germantown 3 of this number returned and reported a fight with Mosby, in which 2 of the men had lost their horses and had taken to the woods, and that large parties of guerrillas were now on the right. On the return of the other men it was definitely ascertained that Mosby, or a person resembling him, had been wounded and had escaped. Mosby had certainly been in vicinity of Fairfax just previous to the action and had gone towards Centreville. People on the road had seen him, and from the description of his person and recognition of his picture by parties engaged, there seems to be some color for the report that he was in the action and was wounded, as he or the person in question was seen, before riding off, to throw up his hands and give signs of pain. This could be observed, as the action was at very close quarters. I dispatched a squadron to the scene shortly after and moved to Fairfax Court House, sending a party of 30 dismounted men through Vienna to Lewinsville. The regiment reached camp at Falls Church after a march that day of 15 miles from Chantilly.

"During this scout the weather was almost constantly rainy, and violent

Capt. William H. Chapman, collecting about 40 men, reached Upperville some hours after the Federals had left, and cutting across the mountains, attacked the party in the Gap, killing and wounding a number, recapturing all the

BRIG.-GEN. GEORGE H. CHAPMAN AND STAFF.
From a War-time Picture.

prisoners and most of the horses, and also capturing 18 prisoners and 40 horses from the enemy.

When the main body at Snickersville heard the firing, they hurried on to the scene of conflict, and Captain Chapman drew off his men, bringing out all his captures safely.

storms prevented speedy movement which would perhaps have brought the column to Aldie in time for some success, and prevented a movement towards Middleburg and Rector's Cross-Roads, as intended. After the third day the men and horses subsisted on the country, as directed. Twelve horses were taken from suspected rebel citizens, and all suspected houses searched on the line of march."

He lost one man, Joseph Johnson, of Leesburg, killed, and 3 wounded.   He also had 2 horses killed.[4]

---

[4] HEADQUARTERS SECOND BRIGADE, THIRD CAVALRY DIVISION,

*September 17th, 1864.*

CHAPMAN to SIEBERT : " I have the honor to report that with 400 men of this command, I started from this camp on the evening of the 15th instant at 10 o'clock, on an expedition to Ashby's Gap for the purpose of developing what force of the enemy were rendezvoused there or in that vicinity.   Crossing the Shenandoah River at the ford near Snicker's Gap, I there detached 55 men, under Captain Compson, Eighth New York Cavalry, with instructions to proceed up the river on this side the ridge and across the mountain into Ashby's Gap, while with the main body, I crossed through Snicker's Gap and proceeded along the eastern base of the mountain to Paris, which place I reached shortly after sunrise.   Soon after arriving at Paris small parties of the enemy's horsemen began to show themselves on the surrounding heights, but at safe distance, and they continued to watch my movements during the day.   Once they charged upon my rear guard, but were easily driven off.   Returning, I passed through Upperville and reached Snickersville at 2 p. m., where, the men being much fatigued, I ordered an hour's halt, sending forward one squadron of the Eighth New York, Captain Bliss commanding, into the gap. Captain Compson was also in the gap, having crossed from Ashby's to Snicker's Gap by a road on the mountain ridge. About an hour had elapsed and the men had mostly fallen asleep, when they were suddenly charged upon by a force of from 50 to 80 of the enemy, and, being stampeded by the surprise, a number were killed, wounded and captured before I reached the scene of the encounter with the main body.   They had approached the Gap across the mountains and charged down an easy slope, and they retired by the same way, pursued for two miles by my men.   It was near sundown, and in the exhausted state of men and horses I did not deem further pursuit expedient.

ED. HURST, CO. A.
From a Photograph taken in the early part
of the War.

" Captain Compson had captured 12 of the enemy, but they were recaptured. From citizens I ascertained that Mosby was wounded some time ago, and had gone to Richmond.   Judging from indications, I should estimate the force operating under Mosby and his colleague at from 200 to 250.   If they have any encampment it must be in the neighborhood and beyond Upperville."

*Wednesday, September 21.*—Capt. William H. Chapman, with Lieutenant Fray, Ed. Hurst[5] and 5 others, went on a scout to the Shenandoah Valley. On the Harper's Ferry and Winchester road they saw a supply train with a heavy guard, which they followed for some distance, picking up a commissary and 2 cavalrymen. As night came on, they approached a house, around which were a number of horses. Leaving his men, Chapman went forward and inquired if he could get accommodated for the night. He was told the house was full, but that he might go to the stable yard, where he would find an army wagon, and could probably turn in with the driver. Chapman then went back and brought up his men, sending Lieutenant Fray with 2 men to the house, while he went with the others to the stable yard. Lieutenant Fray discovered that the inmates had been alarmed and had all left the house, so he rejoined Chapman. While the mules were being taken from the wagon, a party of Federal officers rode up, one of whom called out:

" Who is that ? "

Chapman answered that one of the Sixth Corps wagons had broken down; and riding in among them with his men, the officers, with one exception, were captured without any resistance. The officers captured were Major Fry, of the Sixteenth Pennsylvania Cavalry; Captain Brown and Lieutenants Stone and Pressy, of the First New Hampshire Cavalry. Lieutenant Gilman, of the First New Hampshire, made his escape in the darkness, and returned to Winchester.[6]

As Chapman was returning with his prisoners and captures, he was halted by a sentinel on the roadside. He discovered that a Federal detachment with 2 sutlers' wagons had camped for the night, and as the sentinel was made prisoner, the rest were "gobbled up" without difficulty. The Federals, supposing that all of Chapman's party, including prisoners, were Confederates, thought themselves

---

[5] Ed. Hurst was wounded seven times ; twice in one fight—at Warrenton Junction, May 3, 1863.

[6] Lieutenant McIntire, reporting this affair to Captain Barney, says : " We reached General Sheridan's headquarters near Strasburg, September 21,

outnumbered and that it was useless to resist; while the prisoners first captured were under the impression that Chapman had carried them into a Confederate camp. Under cover of night, these little delusions were readily encouraged and converted into practical helps by our daring Rangers. Eighteen prisoners, together with 22 horses and 6 mules, were brought out by Chapman and his little party on this occasion.

W. F. LINTZ, CO. C.
From a Photograph taken after the War.

and turned over our command. The Major said to us that an escort was going on to Washington with the captured colors, and we would return to Winchester and there await its coming. Major Fry, Captain Brown, Lieutenants Stone, Gilman, McIntire and Pressey returned to Winchester; I became separated from the party in Winchester, but saw the escort come into town, and reported to the commanding officer. He requested me to look my party up, as he said they were to start in half an hour. I tried to find them, but could not. I find, on getting down to Harper's Ferry, that Major Fry, Captain N. H. Brown, Lieutenants F. P. Stone, A. E. Gilman and Geo. H. Pressey, hearing the escort had passed through Winchester by the Martinsburg road, galloped on (as they supposed) after them, and about 5 miles from Winchester were attacked by Mosby's men, fired upon, and all but Lieutenant Gilman killed or made prisoners; he escaped by returning to Winchester. It was just dark as they started from Winchester. In looking for the party in the morning, not knowing then what had become of them, although I heard a rumor in Winchester that a party of officers were captured by some of Mosby's men the night before, and also 2 sutlers' wagons destroyed, I found myself left by the escort, and came on to Harper's Ferry alone, unmolested, and reported to General Stevenson. From Harper's Ferry I came with my horses to Camp Stoneman ; found Lieutenant Gilman here."

# CHAPTER XVIII.

September, 1864—Capt. Samuel Chapman in the Valley—Fight near Chester Gap—Death of a Brave Federal Officer—Six of "Mosby's Men ' Murdered at Front Royal—" Bob Ridley" and his Dutch Prisoner—Capt. Wm. H. Chapman's Fight with a Detachment of Seventeenth Pennsylvania Cavalry—Raiders at Piedmont—Burning of Joe Blackwell's House, "Mosby's Headquarters"—Examining the Manassas Gap Railroad—Raiding Parties Searching for Mosby—They take a Sick Man Out of Bed, Strip Him and Examine Him for Wounds—"Mosby's Men " in the Valley.

*Thursday, September 22.*—Command met at Piedmont, and Capt. Samuel Chapman with about 120 men proceeded to the Valley with the intention of capturing a picket post of the Sixth New York Cavalry, which was said to be stationed in Chester Gap. Camping for the night a short distance south of Front Royal, he learned that there was no picket at the place named, and was also informed of the repulse of the Federal cavalry by the Confederates.

*Friday, September 23.*—Early in the morning Captain Chapman, with a few men, went out to reconnoitre. Learning ing that an ambulance train, with an escort of about 200 men, was moving down toward Front Royal, he determined to attack it.

Dividing his command, he sent Captain Frankland, with 45 men, to attack the train guard in front, while he with the other portion was to fall upon the rear. From his position, which was nearer than Frankland's to the approaching train, Chapman could see the force following, and noting the heavy body of cavalry advancing (which proved to be the Reserve Brigade of Merritt's Cavalry Division returning from their unsuccessful move on Milford), he ordered Lieutenant Hatcher to fall back with all speed in the direction of Chester Gap, while he went around to Captain Frankland to prevent his making the attack. But before reaching him, Frankland had already charged the escort in front and was driving them back on the ambulances.

"Call off your men; you are attacking a brigade!" said Chapman, as he met Frankland.

"Why, Sam, we've whipped them," returned Frankland, as he reluctantly obeyed orders.

Alternately fighting and retreating, Chapman fell back towards Chester Gap, the heavy mass of cavalry pressing on all sides, as if to overwhelm the little band. A Federal officer, Lieutenant McMaster, of the Second U. S. Cavalry, with a small party, had approached by the Chester Gap road, with the intention of cutting off some of our men who were seeking to escape by crossing Hominy Hollow, and as they made their appearance in our front, Lieutenant McMaster waving his sabre and urging his men to follow, our men naturally supposed the enemy were seeking to throw a force in our front, to cut off all avenues of retreat. As they wildly rushed on, McMaster's horse was killed and he, a brave, dashing fellow, fell riddled with bullets from our rough-riders, who rode over him in their flight. Fifteen or 20, in all, of the Federals were killed and wounded. Two of Chapman's men were wounded, and 6, Thomas E. Anderson, —— Carter, —— Overby, Lucian Love, Lafayette Rhodes and —— Jones, were taken prisoners and afterwards barbarously hung or shot by their captors in retaliation for the death of the Federal officer (McMaster) who, they alleged, was killed after he had surrendered.

THOMAS E. ANDERSON,
CO. D.

One of the six Mosby's Men
Killed at Front Royal by
Custer's Command.

Lieutenant McMaster was killed in the excitement of a fight, by men who were seeking to escape from a superior force, and who were fighting for their lives. It is hardly possible at such a time to say whether he had an opportunity of surrendering, for the affair was only of a few moments duration. The 6 unarmed, defenseless men who were afterwards murdered were put to death in cool, calm moments by men who had time to deliberate, and the act was sanctioned by the Federal officers in command. Three were taken out and shot, while 2, Overby and Love, were hung to a tree in sight of the town of Front Royal, and a paper pinned on the breast of one read : "Such is the fate of all of Mosby's gang."

The sixth and last victim was Lafayette Rhodes, whose home was in Front Royal. He fled up Happy Creek, but was pursued and captured. The townspeople all knew of the executions before he was brought back. As he was carried through the streets his old mother, whose only support he was, rushed out and clasping her arms around his neck, pleaded with all the eloquence of a fond mother's love that the Federals would spare the life of her son. But deaf to all her entreaties, they rudely unclasped her arms, and pushing her roughly to one side, carried their prisoner outside of the village and put him to death.

LAFAYETTE RHODES, CO. D.

One of the six Mosby's Men Killed at Front Royal by Custer's Command.

Our men were much excited when they heard of this outrage, and some of the more impulsive ones proposed retaliating upon some prisoners then in our hands. The prisoners justly fearing an immediate resort to retaliatory measures, entreated to be spared, and said it was very hard to make them suffer for the deeds of others; that they did not kill our men after surrendering and had no such orders. Wiser counsel prevailed, however. The men agreed to wait until Colonel Mosby returned, before acting in the matter, and the prisoners were sent off to Richmond.[1]

---

[1] In a letter written to Capt. Walter E. Frankland, Thomas Moss of Alexandria makes mention of this affair as follows :

"I remember distinctly the charge and driving back the Yankees, and whilst shooting the best I could, I felt a hand on my shoulder and heard these words: 'For God's sake, come out from here !' I can almost feel the touch and hear the words now. On looking around I found it was you. There was not another one of our comrades in view. We passed through a small piece of woods and on coming out to the opening I saw the main column of our boys passing through a gap in the fence. I went to the left and jumped the fence. Harry Hatcher called out to form on the hill. He, with Fount. Beattie, Ab. Minor and myself

Among the "characters" in the Battalion was one Robert W. Eastham, familiarly known as "Bob Ridley." Of a restless, roving disposition, he was never idle. A fight or a foot race, a fox hunt or a raid, were equally gratifying to him. He would often start off with two or three companions, and seldom returned without prisoners and horses.

On the day previous to the fight near Chester Gap he was scouting in Custer's rear with Joseph Foy, John Kirwin, Frank Kennerly and Joseph Griffin. Near Guard Hill they captured 2 couriers with dispatches for General Custer. A little further on, they saw a Federal soldier rid-

---

fell in line. It was then that a regiment of the enemy came in between us and our main body. We passed down the hill and came upon about 20 of the enemy in charge of prisoners. We charged and routed the guards, and I was fortunate in saving Beattie's life by shooting a man who had his pistol within 12 inches of Beattie. I then caught a horse, which I gave to Overby, but before he could mount he was captured. Beattie and I then ran down the road a short distance and turned and went up into a piece of pine woods. While there the enemy sent out a picket of 40 men, who stopped just below where we stood. Beattie told me to remain and watch until he could collect some of our men and capture the picket post before reinforcements could be sent from Front Royal. I remained there nearly all day, until after the enemy had left. I could see there was something going on in Front Royal and heard the shots, but did not learn until afterwards the fate of our comrades."

R. W. EASTHAM, "BOB RIDLEY,"
CO. D.

From a Photograph.

Dr. R. C. Buck, of Orlean, Va., in reply to my letter, wrote :

"I saw this fight, and from a distance saw the killing of Rhodes, who was a friend and playmate of mine. I saw Overby and Carter just before they were hung. They were taken by their captors to Petty's wagon yard, and as I passed by them Gen. Custer and staff rode along the street. The Yankees were taunting the poor fellows, who stood up proud and defiant and apparently unmoved. I recollect the appearance of Overby; he was standing with his hat and coat off, his wavy black hair floating in the breeze. I never saw a finer specimen of manhood."

ing along with half of a sheep before him on his horse. " Bob " suddenly started from behind a bush and presenting his pistol, called on the man to surrender. He was a Dutch-man, and afterwards in relating the story of his capture to one of our men, said :

" You see, der General he kill a sheep unt I put me half on my horse, unt as I vash ride along a man he put a pistol in my face unt he say : ' Surrender, you tam Dutchman ! ' Unt I say ' Yaas.' Unt he make me gif up my gun, unt my pistol, unt my sabre. Den I tells him der gooverment sharge me for dem. But he would take dem. He only laugh at me."

Returning on the Gooney Manor road toward Front Royal, Eastham learned that a party of 37 Federal cavalry had passed but a little while before. As he had been joined by 4 troopers belonging to the Twelfth Virginia cavalry, he left John Kirwin in charge of the 3 prisoners and started in pursuit of the Federal cavalry. As soon as they came in sight Eastham and his little party charged with a yell. In the cloud of dust which enveloped them, the surprised and startled Federals could form no estimate of the number of their assailants, but naturally supposing the force superior to their own, broke and ran at break-neck speed. At a turn in the road one of the enemy's horses fell with its rider, and Eastham being too near to stop, attempted to jump over the prostrate horse and rider. As he did so, the horse started to rise, and threw Eastham's horse down the bank, both horse and rider being lamed in the fall. The pursuit was continued for some distance. Eastham then returned to Front Royal with the prisoners and 17 horses.

*Sunday, September 25.*—Capt. William Chapman, with a small party, returned to-day from a scout in the Valley, bringing 23 prisoners and 27 horses.

They encountered a detachment of the Seventeenth Penn-sylvania Cavalry on the Valley turnpike, and after a sharp little skirmish routed them completely.[2]

---

[2] Colonel Edwards, in his report, dated Sept. 24, says : " A detachment of the Seventeenth Pennsylvania Cavalry were sent out on the Berryville turn-

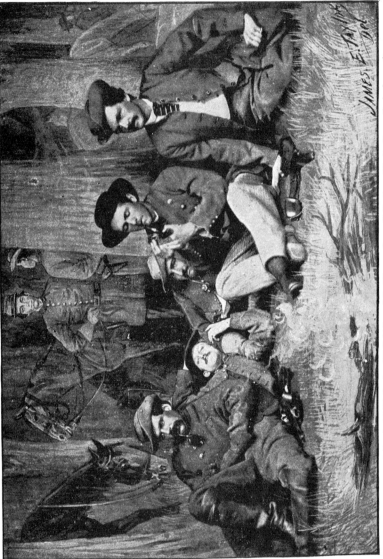

Sergt. A. G. Babcock, W. W. Gosden, W. B. Palmer, John Munson, Sergt. T. Booker ; Charles Paxson (in background).

THE BIVOUAC.

*Monday, September 26.*—A force of about 500 Federal cavalry from Fairfax, came up to-day as far as Piedmont. They burned the house of Joseph Blackwell, near Piedmont, with the barns and outhouses. The Federals had learned that the house was used by Mosby as headquarters. Some ammunition and equipments, including a uniform coat belonging to Colonel Mosby, fell into their hands, and a quantity of arms and ammunition which was concealed in the buildings, and some forage was destroyed.

This body of Federal cavalry came up as an escort to Mr. Bartram, an engineer sent to make an examination of the Manassas Gap railroad.[3]

---

pike half a mile beyond the Opequon to ascertain whether any of our wounded officers and men were, as reported, at that point. This party, consisting of two commissioned officers and 50 men, were attacked by a band of the enemy's guerrillas, numbering 150 or 200, and, although well disposed for a fight, completely routed, but 4 of them having as yet reported. When the news of the disaster reached this post, the entire regiment was at once dispatched to the point where it occurred, the whole country was thoroughly scouted, 2 of our own dead and 1 of the enemy's that fell in the engagement were discovered, but no further information as to the whereabouts of the enemy or the further extent of the loss could be ascertained, except that they saw a squad cutting their way through and moving in the direction of Harper's Ferry. Mosby is hovering around this vicinity with at least 400 men. Two hun..red men of the regiment of cavalry on duty at this post are new recruits, and, I think, with an increase of force he could be probably either captured or used up."

Again, September 26th, he says : "The two commissioned officers who had charge of the detachment of cavalry, reported in my communication of yesterday as having been attacked by the enemy, and 7 enlisted men have returned. They were entirely cut off from their command and pursued as far as Charlestown. There are now but 24 out of the detachment of 46 that are unaccounted for."

[8]HEADQUARTERS THIRTEENTH NEW YORK CAVALRY, }
*Near Falls Church, Va., September 28, 1864.* }

GANSEVOORT to LANSING : "I have the honor to state that the escort of 500 men under my command moved on the evening of the 24th of September through Centreville, and thence through Thoroughfare Gap, striking and following the line of the Manassas Gap Railroad through Rectortown to Piedmont. Near Piedmont the house of Joseph Blackwell was burned, as directed, together with the barns and extensive outhouses. A large quantity of amunition, artillery harness and equipments was destroyed, including a large quantity of pistols and carbines, which were concealed from search in the house and whose destruction was only known by their reports. This evidently was Col. Mosby's arsenal and headquarters, as was shown by some articles of clothing

The news of the wounding of Mosby having by this time reached the Federal lines, raiding parties were sent through the country hoping to capture him.[4]

*Friday, Sept. 30.*—A party of 75 Federal cavalry, supposed to be Blazer's scouts, entered Upperville before sunrise and searched the town for Mosby, whom they understood was lying wounded in that place. They compelled one man, Turner Holmes, who was lying sick in bed, to get up and strip, and examined him for wounds. They carried off 4 horses, but no men, although there were several in town at the time.[5]

---

and equipments. Near this point, having heard the condition of the railroad beyond Piedmont, the engineer, to whose wishes by order I was subordinate, stated that he had sufficient information and desired to return as soon as possible in order to make his report. Having ascertained by moving in close proximity to Manassas Gap that there was no regular force, if any, in the Gap, I pursued the enemy by a detachment a mile beyond Piedmont and returned by the way of Middleburg and Aldie to this camp. The railroad was found to be in good repair, except the growth of grass on track to Piedmont; beyond it was ascertained to be torn up and in need of repair. Nothing of interest occurred *en route* excepting frequent skirmishes with and charges on the enemy. I desire to mention Lieutenant Farrell, Sixteenth New York Cavalry, for his conduct in charge of the rear guard near Rectortown. There are conflicting reports regarding Colonel Mosby—some stating that he is dead; all that he is severely wounded and below Charlottesville, Va."

[4] General Stevenson, in a dispatch to Secretary Stanton, September 28th, says:

" If a cavalry force could be sent from Washington with speed to Upperville, Mosby could be captured. I have information that I consider reliable that he is in a house in Upperville, too badly wounded to be moved; that the report of his being sent to Richmond is false, intended to divert attention. If I had a force of cavalry to use I should send them at once. All my cavalry is compelled to go to front escorting supplies."

[5] The following dispatch from Stevenson to Stanton, dated September 27th, shows how actively our scouting parties were at that time operating in Sheridan's rear:

" Both of my last courier parties were attacked by rebel cavalry; dispersed part of them, capturing the first party at Strasburg, the second at a point between Charlestown and Bunker Hill. Message No. 31 was sent by both parties, and both have failed. I shall try another duplicate to-night. The country between this and Sheridan yesterday and to-day seemed to be alive with parties of rebel guerrillas and cavalry. Last night they attacked ambulances, with escort of 17 men, between this and Charlestown; severely wounded surgeon of Sixth Pennsylvania Cavalry. I doubt if we shall be able to get any dispatches through without sending much larger body of cavalry than I can get hold of. I have but small force for such duty, and it is badly worn down."

# CHAPTER XIX.

Sheridan, in moving up the Valley, felt that it was impossible to keep open his line of communication and maintain his supplies. Writing Grant from near New Market, he says:

" I am now 80 miles from Martinsburg and find it exceedingly difficult to supply this army."

On the 22d of September General Grant wrote to General Halleck:

" Will it not be practicable to open in a short time the railroad from Washington to Strasburg?"

To this General Halleck replied, September 23:

" I now learn that the Manassas Gap Railroad can be put in running order to Piedmont, 16 miles from Front Royal, in 3 days. From there to Front Royal all the iron of the track has been carried away, and it will require about a week to replace it. From Front Royal to Strasburg all the bridges, which are very long, have been destroyed and the rails removed; but it is thought that Front Royal will serve all the purpose for the defense of the Valley that Strasburg would, a pontoon bridge being established across the river at that place. Before any decision is arrived at in regard to the location of a depot, a competent engineer officer should be sent to examine the relative merits of Front Royal and Strasburg."

General Halleck accordingly directed General Augur to furnish

" a sufficient cavalry escort to accompany the engineer officer who has been directed to examine the Manassas Gap Railroad."

Colonel Lazelle says, September 23:

"I have communicated with the engineer sent and have informed him that in my opinion it would be extremely hazardous to send a force of 350 men farther than the vicinity of Piedmont."

General Augur then wrote Lazelle:

"Send the escort, and make it as strong as you deem necessary."

Lazelle thereupon issued orders to Colonel Gansevoort

"to proceed with the escort of 500 men under your command to escort Mr. Bartram, the engineer sent to make an examination of the Manassas Gap Railroad."

General Meigs to General Grant, September 27:

"We wait military protection to open the Manassas Gap Railroad. Reports of time needed—say 3 days to Piedmont, 7 days to Front Royal, 14 days to Strasburg."

Grant to Halleck, October 2:

"Please direct the construction party at work on the railroad to open the road to Front Royal."

Grant to Sheridan, October 3:

"I will direct the railroad to be pushed toward Front Royal, so that you may send your troops back that way."

Troops were then moved forward on the railroad, as will be seen by the following:

General Slough to Taylor, October 3:

"Colonel Gallupe telegraphs me from Manassas this evening that the Fifth Pennsylvania Heavy Artillery is at Gainesville; that he will advance it 17 miles to-morrow, and move the Two Hundred and Second Regiment Pennsylvania Volunteers to Gainesville. Had I not better move to-morrow the 6 companies of the Two Hundred and First Regiment to Manassas Junction?"

General Augur to Colonel Gansevoort, October 3:

"You will prepare one company of your regiment at once for detached service, and send it to Alexandria, to reach that point by 10 a. m. to-morrow. On his arrival there the commanding officer will draw ten days' rations of subsistence and forage for his command, and take the cars to the front, to join the Construction Corps on the Manassas Gap Railroad. This company is to act as couriers between the tele-graph office with the Construction Corps and Major-General Sheridan's headquarters. You will, therefore, select the company whose commanding officer and men are most reli-able, and who are best fitted for this very important duty."

In all this preparation to reconstruct the Manassas Gap Railroad (which had been destroyed by Stonewall Jackson) and thus open communication between the army of Sheridan in the Shenandoah Valley and the Army of the Potomac by way of the Orange and Alexandria Railroad, Mosby was not forgotten. Halleck to Grant, October 4, says:

" In order to keep up com-munication on this line to Manassas Gap and the Shen-andoah Valley it will be necessary to send South all rebel inhabitants between that line and the Potomac, and also to *completely clean out Mosby's gang of robbers who have so long infested that district of country*, and I respectfully suggest that Sheridan's cavalry should be required to accomplish this object before it is sent else-where. *The two small regi-ments under General Augur have been so often cut up by Mosby's band that they are cowed and useless for that pur-pose."*

BRIG.-GEN JOHN D. STEVENSON.
District of Harper's Ferry.

General Stevenson pro-posed using Cole's cavalry for their destruction, and wrote from Harper's Ferry to General Halleck:

" There is a body of about 400 guerrillas (Mosby's and White's bands) infesting the country around Berryville, and between Bunker Hill and Winchester, cutting off small par-ties and threatening our trains. I have here (dismounted) the First Maryland Cavalry. They are about 500 strong. They are good men, and as I have placed their worthless colonel in coventry, I think if they were armed with Spen-cer rifles or carbines, well mounted, and make these guerrillas their specialty, we could effectually destroy them. The men were all raised in this vicinity, are familiar with the country, and are the right troops for such service."

In the latter part of September, Mosby returned to Fauquier, although not entirely recovered from his wounds and still compelled to use crutches. He ordered a meeting of the command at Piedmont, intending to strike Sheridan in the Valley, but on learning of the advance of a body of Federal troops from Fairfax, he sent out scouts and on Monday, October 3, 1864, started from Piedmont with about 300 men and two pieces of artillery, marching by way of Plains to Thoroughfare Gap in the Bull Run Mountains. We passed through Thoroughfare Gap a little after dark. A sharp firing in our front soon warned us of the presence of the enemy. We turned off to the left and moved along, hugging the mountain, until we reached Craven Kings, where we halted for the night. Our scouts reported that they had been fired on near Gainesville by Federal infantry advancing along the railroad towards the Gap.

*Tuesday, October 4.*—Moved off early towards the railroad, where we found a construction train, with infantry and cavalry guard.[1]  The infantry opened fire on us and continued firing on our rear as we fell back, crossing the Bull Run mountains at Hopewell Gap, and camped at Blackwell's, near Piedmont.

*Wednesday, October 5.*—With about 200 men, Mosby advanced on Salem.[2]  Placing his two howitzers in position on Stevenson's Hill, a little south of Salem and overlooking the Federal camp, he opened fire on it, our sharpshooters at

---

[1] General SLOUGH to General AUGUR, Oct. 4 :  " Colonel Gallupe telegraphs me that the train guard has been fired into by about 200 of the enemy about two miles east of Gainesville.  No particulars received.  The cavalry company has arrived, forty strong, in command of First Lieut. H. F. Pugh, Company E, Thirteenth New York Cavalry."

[2] Colonel Gallupe telegraphs General Slough, October 5th :  " The Two hundred and first Pennsylvania is at Manassas Junction and Gainesville, 3 companies at each place ; 2 companies Two hundred and second Pennsylvania at Thoroughfare Gap, 8 companies at Plains ; 1 battalion Fifth Pennsylvania Heavy Artillery at Salem, one between Salem and Rectortown, and one at Rectortown ; the cavalry with the telegraph construction train."

the same time being pushed forward. Our guns no sooner opened fire than the Federals left their camp and fled towards Rectortown, leaving behind their tents and camp equipage. In possession of the camp, our men took what they wished and set fire to and destroyed the remainder. Men were put to work tearing up the railroad and undoing the labors of the construction party.[3]

Our First Squadron, about 80 men, was ordered to follow on after the retreating Federals. Their trail was easily followed, for as they fled they threw away everything likely to inpede their flight—clothing, arms and ammunition, and equipments. In the pursuit 40 prisoners, including 2 lieutenants, were captured. Coming to a turn in the road near Rectortown, we found the infantry drawn up in line. They opened a brisk fire as we dashed forward, but Mosby called out : " Come back, men ; come back ! " Before the order was obeyed we had two men shot, Ed. Anderson and Stinson.

When the Federals found they had checked Mosby's advance, they again started at a double quick and never halted until they joined their forces with those at Rectortown.[4]

At night we bivouacked between Rectortown and Salem. Colonel Mosby ordered Lieutenant Grogan to go to Rectortown to ascertain if the infantry had halted there or had fallen back beyond that point. Grogan approached the rail-

---

[3] *Chaffin's Bluff, Oct. 9, 1864.*

General LEE to Secretary SEDDON : " Colonel Mosby reports that a body of about 1,000 of the enemy advanced up the Manassas road on the 4th with trains of cars loaded with railroad material and occupied Salem and Rectortown. He attacked them at Salem, defeating them, capturing 50 prisoners, all their baggage, camp equipage, stores, etc., and killed and wounded a considerable number. His loss, 2 wounded. Enemy is entrenched at Rectortown with 2 long trains of cars. The railroad is torn up and bridges burned in their rear and all communications cut.

[4] General SLOUGH to Headquarters, Washington, Oct. 6 : " A telegram from Colonel Gallupe, just received, announces an attack of the enemy, with over 400 men and 2 pieces of artillery, near Salem. The account is so confused that it is hard to tell the result. His communication with his command beyond is cut. He has 800 men with him. He asks for artillery and cavalry. I have instructed him to hold his position, if possible ; if not, to fall back in the direction of Manassas Junction. A later dispatch, just received, announces that cannonading is now going on. What shall I do ?"

road station through a tract of woodland, dismounted, tied his horse to a tree, and in advancing on foot up the hill near the station, saw in the darkness (it was raining slightly) shown in relief against the sky to his left, an object so motionless that he thought it was a high-cut stump or a dead tree. Keeping his eyes fixed upon this object, he cautiously advanced, when to his surprise a sentinel stepped from beneath a small tree on his right and approaching, said:

"Is that you, Captain?"

Grogan was startled, but instantly recovering his presence of mind, said:

"Yes. Why are you not walking your beat, sir?"

Drawing his revolver, Grogan thrust it in the face of the

THOROUGHFARE GAP.

astonished sentinel, saying: "One word and you are a dead man. Put down your gun, sir."

Taking the man by the arm, he led him off, telling him Mosby had him. The man was frightened and became so unsteady in his gait that Grogan asked him if he had been drinking. He recovered his speech sufficiently to answer "No." Going to the place where he had left his horse, Grogan took his prisoner to Glen Welby and delivered him to Colonel Mosby, who questioned him and obtained the desired information from him.

As all were weary after the day's work, they slept together in a hay loft. The only order given the prisoner was to go to sleep and not turn over once in the night; that if he did, he would get a ball through him. It is supposed he obeyed this injunction to the letter. If he did not, no one knew it, for all slept soundly, and in the morning the prisoner had to be aroused to take his departure with the rest of the party.

*Thursday, October 6.*—We moved on to Salem. A gun was placed on a hill to command the railroad, and men were set to work destroying the track. A train attempted to come up from the Plains, but was driven back. A second attempt was made, and as the train drew near, the infantry left it and formed along the edge of a body of woods, their glittering bayonets

MAJOR-GENERAL C. C. AUGUR, U. S. VOLS.
Commanding Department of Washington.

glancing in the sun. Our shell falling short, the gun was brought closer and we were formed near the edge of the town to support the gun. The infantry then boarded the train and hurried off.

We now moved off to Rectortown, where the Federals had entrenched themselves, opened fire on their camp with rifle piece and howitzer, and shelled them until evening. We were then dismissed, to meet the next morning at Black-well's, near Piedmont.[5]

*Friday, October 7.*—The command met at Blackwell's and moved off toward Rectortown with 4 guns. We still kept up the work of shelling and driving back trains; tearing up and demolishing the track as fast as it was relaid, and annoying the invading force by every means at our command. The main body of the Federals took up its line of march toward Salem. We followed, harassing them as they marched, until they reached Salem, when they took up a strong position on Stevenson's Hill, from which it was impossible to dislodge them. We had one sharpshooter wounded and the firing was at times quite brisk.

General Augur to-day arrived at the Plains, where he awaited his cavalry.[6]

*Saturday, October 8.*—The infantry here were now rein-

---

[5] *Manassas Junction, Oct 6, 1864.*

McCrickett to McCallum : " Rebel force on the Gap Road at Salem, between us and construction corps. All the material forwarded since yesterday morning is still this side of Plains. Have just returned here from Plains, where I saw Colonel Gallupe with 600 men, who was compelled to fall back from Salem and intrench at Plains. He ordered all trains to be sent this side of Thoroughfare Gap or to Manassas. Four succeeded in reaching here, and one engine and three cars are now on the way between the Gap and Manassas. It is just reported that engine 'Grapeshot' and 12 cars of railroad material are a perfect wreck at Thoroughfare Gap. Report says the track was blown up, but I think the train ran off the switch. The construction corps is out of material. Colonel Gallupe says he will endeavor to advance early in the morning, but he will take the pike road. This course will not assist us much, as the rebel force at Salem is supposed to have destroyed the track. A strong force should advance on the railroad and hold Salem until a connection is made with the construction corps. My first endeavor will be to clear the track at Thoroughfare Gap."

[6] Augur to Waite (Muddy Branch) Oct. 6 : " Collect all your cavalry as soon as possible, leaving only a guard to protect your camp, and proceed with it to Middleburg and thence to Rectortown, on the Manassas Gap Railroad, where I will meet you. It is possible you may have to fight Mosby on the road about Middleburg. Be prepared for him. Be in haste."

Augur (Plains) to Halleck, Oct. 7 : " I arrived here at 7 this morning. The telegraph is just completed to this point. Mosby had possession of Salem for a while, and is said to have destroyed a good deal of the track there. The construction train is now at Rectortown, with the Fifth Pennsylvania Heavy Artillery, well protected. It is said Mosby shelled them a while last night. Nothing is heard of him this morning. I have sent 5 companies

forced by a strong force of cavalry,[7] and Mosby had to operate with more caution. The artillery was concealed in the mountains. Captain Chapman, with a portion of the command, was sent to operate south of the railroad; Capt. A. E. Richards crossed over into the Shenandoah Valley, while Mosby himself, with another portion of the command, kept on the north of the railroad.

*Sunday, October 9.*—As one of our men was riding along the road near Piedmont, he saw a Federal soldier robbing the body of a dead Confederate. Levelling his pistol he fired, mortally wounding the Federal. Then riding up, he discovered the Confederate to be Lieutenant Ames of Company F, familiarly known as "Big Yankee," from his having deserted from the Fifth New York Cavalry. He had long been a brave and faithful follower of Mosby. His death was regretted by all, as he was a universal favorite with the command. He was buried close to the spot where he met his death.

A lieutenant with an escort of 16 men from the Second Ohio Cavalry, carrying dispatches to Winchester, arrived in Upperville this morning. John Thomas, C. A. Fox, John Hern, Jas. Keith and a few others were sent in pursuit and overtook the party in Ashby's Gap near the toll-gate. In the encounter, 9 of the Federals and 16 horses were captured. The remaining 7 fled to the mountains, but before night all

---

from here to Salem, and requested the construction train to return there and repair the road. There is a large and heavy train off the track at Thoroughfare Gap, which will not be cleared away before this afternoon so that trains can pass. As soon as the cavalry arrives, all will be well here."

[7] RAYMOND to AUGUR, Oct. 7: "Major Ludlam reports that at noon to-day he will move with 7 companies of Eighth Illinois Cavalry to Rectortown, via Middleburg."

LAZELLE to TAYLOR, Oct. 7: "Colonel Gansevoort left Alexandria this morning with 625 men, for Rectortown."

McCRICKETT, Superintendant, to General McCALIUM, Oct. 7: "The wreck at Thoroughfare Gap is clear and track repaired, and three trains have arrived at Plains. It is reported that considerable track is destroyed between Salem and Rectortown. Colonel Gallupe, commanding at Plains, has sent word to Mr. Wentz of the condition of the road at Salem. 800 cavalrymen, with horses, etc., have been forwarded from here by train since 9 a. m. I expect to have 1,200 on the way before dark, and one train railroad material."

came into Paris and gave themselves up. The dispatches, which were in cipher, were sent to Richmond.

Lieut. Walter Bowie, of Company F, a Marylander, with Jas. G. Wiltshire, Charles Vest, —— Ratcliffe, George Smith, G. M. O'Bannon, Haney and J. Randolph, made a daring little scout through Maryland. They crossed the Potomac at Matthias' Point, and going to Port Tobacco, captured 17 Federal soldiers and 8 horses. Paroling the prisoners, they took the horses and went to the vicinity of Annapolis, which place Bowie entered and rode through the streets. From thence they went to Sandy Springs, two miles from

LIEUT. WALTER BOWIE,
CO. F.

From a War-time Photograph.

Rockville. While in a thick body of pines feeding their horses, they heard voices outside saying: " They're in here," and found they had been tracked by a citizen, with a party of cavalry. Leaving their horses, they charged out on foot, firing as they came out. The Federals fled. Bowie, mounting his horse, started off in pursuit before the others could get their horses. Two shots were heard and when his comrades got out on the road they saw Bowie lying on the ground, a ball having struck him near the eye, passing out the back

of his head. He was taken to a house near by, where he soon died. His brother, who had joined the party en route, remained with him. After the death of Bowie, his companions crossed the Potomac at Cheek's Ford, and soon were safe in " Mosby's Confederacy."

On the 10th of October, 50 prisoners, chiefly infantry, which had been picked up in small parties along the Manassas Gap Railroad, were sent South.

By this time trains were running to Piedmont, and this was as far as the Federals succeeded in running their trains. At Piedmont the road crosses Goose Creek, which is here quite a stream and required a bridge, which was never built.

Mosby still continued to annoy the Federals along the road. The cars were compelled to run at a very low rate of speed, as it was feared Mosby, by some strategy, would throw them off the track. The trains were sometimes escorted by infantry guards, who walked by the side of the cars. With all of these precautions, mishaps would often occur.

On the morning of October 10th, Lieutenant Glascock, with a few men, displaced a few rails and lay in wait for a train. It came slowly along and was allowed to pass; then a volley was fired into the rear of it. The engineer immediately put on steam, running ahead to escape,

PHILIP B. EASTHAM, CO. B.

when a general smash-up was the consequence. A number of Federal officers were on the train, some of whom were killed. Four Confederate prisoners were on the train and in the confusion escaped, all unhurt except William Fred, who had his arm broken.[8]

---

[8] AUGUR to HALLECK, Oct. 10 : " I have just learned that a rail was taken up about a mile this side of Plains, and a return train from here run off the track, and then fired upon by men concealed in a thicket on the side. I have not learned the amount of damage done. Simply patrolling the track and guarding the bridges is not going to be sufficient on this road ; it must be literally guarded the whole way. I am sending back a battalion of cavalry to remain in the vicinity of Plains and thoroughly search the vicinity of track."

SLOUGH to Headquarters, Washington, Oct. 10 ( " The rebels displaced a rail a short distance beyond White Plains this morning, throwing a train off the track ; they then fired into it. Mr. McCrickett, assistant superintendent of the railroad, and several others, are reported killed."

A party of about 100 Federal cavalry went to the farm of Major Richard H. Carter, " Glen Welby," about 2 miles from Salem, for the purpose of getting hay. As they were leaving, each man mounted with a bundle of hay piled up before him, Lieutenant Grogan with about 20 men suddenly charged them in a narrow lane, killing one and wounding a number, besides capturing 10 horses. The Federals were taken by surprise and burdened with their plunder, fled, scattering their hay as they ran.

On the following day Mosby had a narrow escape. While in the woods near the Plains with Montjoy's company, he rode out with 13 men in sight of a Federal camp. A body of about 50 cavalry started out in pursuit, but instead of charging, they dismounted and took up a position behind a stone fence, to fight at long range. Mosby then sent for Montjoy, and fell back to the woods to draw the enemy out. The Federals followed, thinking he was retreating. Mosby then turned and charged them, when they, no doubt fearing an ambuscade, wheeled and fled. A Federal cavalryman, whom Mosby had passed in the chase, shot his horse and the animal fell, pinning Mosby to the ground in the midst of his enemies. Seeing his situation his men hastened to release him and he came out safely, riding behind one of the men, his only injury being a sprained ankle. Montjoy charged and drove off the Federals, who lost 6 killed and wounded.

# CHAPTER XX.

*Tuesday, October 11, 1864.*—Capt. A. E. Richards, with 32 men, being on a scout in the Valley, espied an ambulance driven by a likely negro boy, with two Federal officers, and escorted by a detachment of the Seventeenth Pennsylvania Cavalry, passing along the Valley turnpike from the direction of Winchester. Near Newtown, Richards suddenly charged upon their rear, and only 2 escaped of the entire party—4 were killed, 6 wounded, and 19 prisoners and 23 horses captured. The ambulance was also brought out, together with a quantity of papers, vouchers and documents, which were forwarded to Richmond.

Among the Federal wounded was Lieut. Col. Cornelius W. Tolles, who had been General Franklin's Chief Quartermaster on the Peninsula, and was at this time serving in the same capacity with General Sheridan; also, Emil Ohlenschlager, Assist. Surgeon and Medical Inspector on Sheridan's staff—both mortally.[1]

---

[1] Gen. W. H. SEWARD to General STEVENSON, Oct. 12 : "Captain Alexander, assistant-quartermaster, General Torbert's staff, just from the front, reports that Lieutenant-Colonel Tolles, chief quartermaster, and Dr. Ohlenschlager, with an escort of 25 men, who started from Winchester for the front yesterday morning, were attacked by a party of guerrillas, variously reported from 50 to 100, three miles this side of Middletown. Colonel Tolles and Dr. Ohlenschlager were both mortally wounded, the former in the head and the latter in the bowels ; last report no hopes of their recovery. Four of the escort were killed and 5 or 6 wounded. Lieutenant-Colonel Tolles and Dr. Ohlenschlager were taken to General Sheridan's headquarters, which are now located one mile this side of Cedar Creek."

The Seventeenth Pennsylvania was reprimanded for the conduct of the escort, which was unjust, as may be seen by reference to the following :

Colonel EDWARDS to Major RUSSELL, Asst. Adjt. Gen., Oct. 14 : "As

*Wednesday, October 12.*—Mosby crossed the Shenandoah just after nightfall, with 84 men, and moved off towards Bunker Hill, in Sheridan's rear. All day on the 13th we lay near the Valley turnpike, picking up an occasional straggler, until near evening, when we saw a detachment of cavalry, dressed in gray, coming from the direction of Winchester. We viewed them with suspicion for some time, and finally Colonel Mosby ordered Lieutenant Grogan to take a few men and meet them. Discovering them to be "Jessie Scouts," Grogan called out to his men:

"Come on, boys; we'll ride over them."

But the "Jessies" did not wait to be ridden over; they broke and ran, with a loss of only 2 of their number—one being killed by Charles Dear and one captured by Jas. G. Wiltshire.[2]

After the return of Grogan and his party, Mosby marched off towards Duffield, on the Baltimore and Ohio Railroad, Harry Heaton, one of our Valley scouts, having reported a good opening in that quarter. We halted about 10 o'clock at night about two miles east of Kearneysville, at a deep cut

---

Major Durland has shown to me your reprimand to his regiment, I feel called upon to state that I have never seen a better disciplined cavalry regiment than the Seventeenth Pennsylvania Cavalry. They have been worked very hard on escort duty, and of all the dispatches carried by them, but one has been lost. The escort in charge of the dispatch I refer to was in charge of a sergeant who cut his way through and arrived at Edenburg safely, where he was furnished an escort from the Fourteenth Pennsylvania Cavalry to proceed to Harrisburg. That escort was captured, together with the sergeant and his dispatches. In every other case they have cut their way through twice their number and safely delivered their dispatches. The escort accompanying Lieutenant Colonel Tolles I think was ready to do all that men could do. I learn that the rear guard gave timely notice of the approach of the guerrillas, that the lieutenant in charge wished to turn and meet them, that Colonel Tolles gave him orders not to do so, but to move on at a steady trot. This enabled the enemy to come close enough to charge, and they being much better mounted were able to charge into the midst of the escort. Perhaps the lieutenant should have commanded his escort in his own way, but I do not consider him much to blame. I have felt called upon to write this in justice to the Seventeenth Pennsylvania Cavalry, and though Major Durland requests to be ordered to the front, I trust he will not be relieved."

[2] SEWARD to STEVENSON, October 14: "So far as I can learn, all small parties on the Winchester pike yesterday were attacked."

in the road near Brown's Crossing, which Nature seemed to have provided for our undertaking. The men were dismounted and Lieut. Harry Hatcher, with a few men, was sent forward to displace a few rails in this cut, where the cars could be thrown from the track with the least injury to the passengers.

It was a clear, starlight night, the air was chilly, and the men hurried through their work and lay down by the roadside. Soon the sound of an approaching train broke on the stillness. Every one was on the alert, but the train rushed by, leaving the astonished Rangers looking after it as it sped onward, as though uncertain whether to mount their horses and start in pursuit, or simply to sit down and "cuss." Only one track had been obstructed, and the east bound train had passed safely on its way. Both tracks were now effectually blocked, by elevating a rail of each track at an angle sufficient to enable the engine of the coming train to turn over gracefully and nestle gently in the cut. Then we again waited, but not long. Between 2 and 3 o'clock in the morning (14th) the west-bound train came rattling along at customary speed, and the engine performed the turn-over trick quite to our most sanguine expectations, only one man, the engineer, being injured.

LIEUT.-COL. CORNELIUS W. TOLLES,

Chief Quartermaster of Sheridan's Army.
Killed near Newtown, in the Shenandoah Valley, October 11, 1864.

As soon as the train came to a halt, James Wiltshire and Charles Dear ran down the bank and boarded the train. They separated, Wiltshire entering the car on his left and Dear the car to his right. As Dear entered, he saw the car was filled with passengers—ladies and gentlemen—and a few soldiers. As he demanded a surrender, a soldier in the far end of the car arose from his seat and drew his pistol.

Dear fired on him and he fell. Noticing a group of five officers around the stove, Dear walked up to them and ordered them to surrender. He attempted to take a satchel from one of the officers, and as the man refused to give it up, his fellow officers told him he had better give it up or they would be killed. The cause of his reluctance to part with the satchel was apparent to Dear when he marched his prisoners from the train and turned them over to Colonel Mosby. To his surprise, he then learned that it was filled with greenbacks; that among his prisoners were Major Moore and Major Ruggles, paymasters, with their funds. The other officers were 2 captains and 1 lieutenant.[3]

Before setting fire to the cars Mosby ordered all the pas-

----

[3] General STEVENSON to STANTON, Oct. 14 : "General Seward reported by telegraph this morning that the express train going west was captured at a point two miles east of Kearneysville by a party of rebel raiders 100 strong. The passengers were robbed and train burned. Major Moore, paymaster, with his funds, was captured. As soon as they destroyed the train, he reports that they moved off in the direction of Winchester. I immediately sent toward Charlestown, to endeavor to intercept them, all the cavalry at this post—about 100, poorly mounted—and have but little hopes of their coming up with the enemy. General Seward also dispatched two detachments in pursuit. I have not heard from any of them up to this hour. Trains have been sent to the point of attack to repair damages, the track being partially destroyed. Will advise you of all particulars as soon as received."

STEVENSON to STANTON, Oct. 14 : "Just heard from captured train. The attacking party was part of Mosby's command. They removed a rail, causing train to be thrown off the track, then robbed passengers and burned the train. The point of attack was about 2 miles east of Kearneysville, about 2.30 a. m. Paymasters Moore and Ruggles, with their funds, were captured and carried off. The whole affair did not last more than one hour, the enemy retiring in great haste in direction of Winchester. General Seward telegraphs that his courier parties were attacked last night twice by Mosby's command, between Bunker Hill and Winchester, and dispersed. Says Mosby with his entire command is between Winchester and Bunker Hill, with view to capture small parties and attack trains. I have no cavalry force here to operate with. Colonel Edwards has a regiment at Winchester, and will doubtless make an effort to disperse them. I shall send orders to him to do so at once. My pursuing party not heard from."

STEVENSON to STANTON, Oct. 14 : "The cavalry sent out in pursuit of Mosby's guerrillas who burned the train have returned. Report that they failed to overtake them. They learned that they moved off in the direction of the Shenandoah, and, having several hours' start, succeeded in getting away with their prisoners and plunder."

sengers out. In one of the cars were a number of emigrants, who could not or would not understand the orders to vacate the premises. There being a quantity of newspapers— weeklies and dailies—in the hands of the newsvender on the train, they were used to make a light blaze and a great smoke in the car. This was a language perfectly intelligible to the unlearned and the unruly, and caused a general stampede from the car.

The cars being emptied of their human freight, Mosby gave orders to burn the train. At the same time he told Grogan to take Dear and Wiltshire, with the greenbacks, and cross the river as speedily as possible. One of the horses stumbled or fell over a stump in the darkness, and the package was broken open in the fall. Relating this circumstance to me afterwards, Grogan said :

" We gathered it up hastily. As to the loss, if any, we knew little and cared less, as a few thousand out of the pile was of small concern to us. We soon crossed over the river and slept the remaining hours of that night in a mountain cabin, quite regardless of newly acquired wealth.

" All met next day at Bloomfield in Loudoun County, examined into the condition of our Sub U. S. Treasury, and finding there a net surplus of $168,000, the same was divided among our stockholders ($2,000 each) and circulated so freely in Loudoun that never afterwards was there a pie or blooded horse sold in that section for Confederate money."

This expedition was always spoken of as the " Greenback Raid."[4]

General Lee reported this affair to Secretary Seddon, as follows :

" On the 14th instant Colonel Mosby struck the Baltimore and Ohio Railroad at Duffield's ; destroyed U. S. military train consisting of locomotive and 10 cars, securing 20 prisoners and 15 horses. Among the prisoners are two paymasters with $168,000 in Government funds."

---

[4] General SEWARD wrote General STEVENSON : " Some of the paymasters are much alarmed, but I guess I can take care of them."

That they were alarmed, is evident from this :

*Martinsburg, Oct. 14, 1864.*

Paymaster LADD to Major BRICE : "I have my funds in the parlor of the United States Hotel here, guarded by a regiment. The express train was

*Friday, October 14.*—Capt. William Chapman, with about 80 men, crossed the Potomac at White's Ford, four miles below the Mouth of Monocacy, and moved up the towpath, burning eight or ten canal boats with their freight, after first securing the horses and mules ; passing through Licksville to Adamstown, cutting the telegraph wires along the route.

Chapman's object was to strike the Baltimore and Ohio Railroad near this point, but learning that, owing to the capture of the train near Duffield by Mosby, no trains would come from Harper's Ferry, he set out to return, as his presence was now known to the Federal troops, which occupied all the principal points along the river, and they would seek to intercept him on his way home. A company of Loudoun Rangers, under Captain Grubb, camped at Adamstown, drew up in line, and as Chapman moved off, followed at a safe distance. Capt. Wm. Chapman said to his brother Samuel, who urged him to start in pursuit of them : " Sam, I

---

burned 8 miles west of Harper's Ferry between 2 and 3 o'clock this a. m. Major Ruggles' clerk escaped, and is now with me. He reports Major Ruggles and money taken. I also have the fact of his and Major Moore's capture from other passengers on the train. Cannot say certainly about Major Moore. It is reported that Major Ruggles is recaptured, and is safe at Harper's Ferry. Was up most of last night. General Seward, who is in command here, says he will use all his efforts to protect us and our money. I shall make no move until I can do so with safety, and in the meantime wait orders from yourself and Major Paulding. Please show this to him."

The moral effect of this capture was not confined to paymasters alone, as will be seen by the following :

WAR DEPARTMENT, ADJUTANT-GENERAL'S OFFICE,
*Washington, Oct. 14, 1864.*

Brigadier-General L. THOMAS,
*Adjutant-General U. S. Army,*
*(with 6 regiments of colored troops en route for Baltimore),*
*Wheeling, W. Va., Balto. and Ohio Depot :*

A part of the Baltimore and Ohio Railroad, between Martinsburg and Harper's Ferry, is broken by Mosby's guerrillas, who may attack other parts of the line. The Secretary thinks it may not be safe for your troops to come over it. He says you are not restricted to that road, and if you send the troops over it, you must be sure proper precautions are taken for their safety. Answer.

E. D. TOWNSEND,
*Assistant Adjutant-General.*

haven't time to stop and go off on a fox-hunt after Grubb," and ordered his men to move off at a trot. Grubb's men, mistaking this for a hasty retreat, came trotting on at a lively pace. When they were within striking distance, Chapman suddenly turned and charged them, killing and wounding 4 or 5, capturing 7, with their horses and equipments, and scattering the rest.

Reaching the canal, Chapman found a detachment of infantry tearing up the bridge and throwing the timber into the canal. He quickly dispersed them, relaid the bridge and crossing the Potomac at Cheek's Ford, reaching the Virginia shore in safety, without having a man injured.[6]

---

[5]Capt. James W. Grubb was born near Lovettsville, in Loudoun County, Va., August 17, 1839; enlisted in Cole's Maryland Cavalry as a private in September, 1861; was commissioned Captain of Company B, Independent Loudoun (Virginia) Rangers, Capt. Samuel C. Means commanding, about November, 1863. Captain Grubb died March 5, 1895, at Bolivar, West Va.

[6] W. P. Smith wrote J. W. Garrett, President of the Baltimore and Ohio R. R., Oct. 15 : "The two affairs (Duffield and Adamstown) have badly deranged the working of the road, and will involve an immense loss to the company in every way."

STEVENSON to STANTON, October 14 : "The force of the enemy that crossed the Potomac to-day were a portion of Mosby's command, about 250 strong. They crossed at White's Ferry, about 5 miles below the mouth

CAPT. JAMES W. GRUBB,[5]
Independent Loudoun (Virginia) Rangers
(Federal.)

of the Monocacy; moved out to Adamstown, at which point they were met by the Loudoun County Rangers, and finally driven back across the river. The loss on our side reported 4 men ; enemy's not known. They burned 5 canal boats and stole a few horses. Their purpose was evidently a raid, including an attack on railroad trains."

BURTNETE (Point of Rocks) to STEVENSON, Oct. 14 : "Two men have this moment come in from Adamstown. Rangers charged and drove enemy, who in turn charged and scattered our force. I have sent to have Grubb rally and keep his men together at all hazards. I have no horse, or I would go. First

While Colonel Mosby was absent with one portion of the command on the " Greenback Raid " in the Valley, Captain Chapman, with another portion, in Maryland and along the Potomac, and other details scouting in Fairfax and in the Valley, Capt. Franklin hid the artillery at Emory's, a secluded spot on the Cobbler Mountain, and Sergeant A. G. Babcock, with a few trusty men, were left as guards. One John H. Lunzeford, who was detailed to act as guide and to assist in concealing the battery, afterwards deserted and piloted Colonel Gansevoort, with the Thirteenth and Sixteenth New York Cavalry and two companies of the Fifth Pennsylvania Artillery, to the place of concealment. The four guns, together with the guard, consisting of Sergeant Babcock, John L. Aylor, E. M. Jones, Nathaniel Pontier, D. L. Smith and A. G. Whar-

COL. HENRY S. GANSEVOORT,
Thirteenth New York Cavalry.

train got through, but the second is just now back. There certainly are from 200 to 300."

BURTNETE to STEVENSON, Oct. 14.—Later: "Captain Grubb, Loudoun Rangers, 100 men, sent back for reinforcements. Reports 250 of the enemy's cavalry between Adamstown and Monocacy River stealing horses. General Tyler, at Monrovia, has been informed; Government wires cut. I have directed Grubb to follow up and pitch into them at the first opportunity; at all events, to hold the enemy and annoy him until further developments. Will wait directions from you. Spence caught the operator, and he will keep him."

STEVENSON to BURTNETE, Oct. 14: "Dispatch received. All right. What force is it? Send word to Grubb to give them no rest. Direct cavalry scout

ton, were all captured and carried off by Colonel Gansevoort. Babcock and his companions were afterwards brought from prison, put into a box-car next to the locomotive, and sent up and down the railroad from Rectortown to Alexandria for five weeks, to deter Mosby from throwing trains off the track.[7]

---

sent down from here to unite with Grubb's command and give all assistance possible. Shall send down to-night additional cavalry."

BURTNETE to STEVENSON: "Captain Grubb returned here half an hour since, and said the enemy were retreating toward the river, but he thought best not to follow. I ordered him immediately back. Since then 2 of his men have come in who followed the enemy and saw about 100 of them cross. Grubb has lost 3 or 4 men ; the enemy's loss is not known. They have all doubtless crossed by this time. Becoming alarmed, Grubb is reprehensible for this retiring, and he met my order on the way coming in. I have sent down the infantry as a precautionary movement. I would not advise the sending of any further force. They are supposed to be 'Mosby's Men.'"

SPENCE to STEVENSON, Oct. 14: "The rebels reported crossing at White's Ferry, and moving toward Frederick, the boatmen say, with a large force. I have sent the Loudoun Rangers to meet them."

STEVENSON to SPENCE: "Move out with all your infantry force to assistance of Captain Grubb. If there are not more than 250 cavalry you ought to whip them easily."

SPENCE to STEVENSON: "I moved down the canal to cut them off."

STEVENSON to Major FRENCH, commanding Remount Camp, Pleasant Valley, Md.: "Move with all your available cavalry at once to Point of Rocks, Md. ; unite your force with the forces in that vicinity, and attack a body of rebel cavalry near Adamstown. The rebel force is reported to be between 200 and 300. If they have moved from that point, follow them up and capture or destroy them."

BURTNETE to STEVENSON, Oct. 14: "All quiet on the Potomac. They have all recrossed. Passenger trains east have gone on. Have directed Grubb to remain at river until further orders. Captain Spence's command are now here, but in readiness. He deserves credit for his promptness in the matter. Will return on next freight train, unless otherwise ordered."

---

[7] *Colonel Gansevoort's Report.*

HEADQUARTERS CAVALRY,
*Near Piedmont, Va., Oct. 15, 1864.*

GANSEVOORT to AUGUR: "I have the honor to state that the portion of the Sixteenth New York under my command, being 2 squadrons, moved, as ordered, at an early hour this morning, by way of Orlean to Plains to report to Colonel Albright. This leaves the entire force under my command, four squadrons of my regiment, Thirteenth New York Cavalry. The movement last night, which resulted in the capture of Colonel Mosby's pieces, was engaged in by my regiment, two squadrons of the Sixteenth New York Cavalry, and two com-

Colonel Mosby sent the following report to General Lee announcing the capture of his artillery:

*Near Upperville, Va., October 23, 1864.*

GENERAL: I desire to make an explanation in reference to the capture of my artillery, which you have probably seen in Secretary Stanton's official bulletin. After the enemy had accumulated such a force on the Manassas road that I could no longer oppose their progress in front, I withdrew my command inside their lines north of the road, in order to be in a position to assail both Sheridan's communications in the Valley and also to strike the road whenever opportunity offered. My artillery was sent out to a place of concealment in Fauquier. Unfortunately, one of my men, deserted and guided the enemy to where it was. They captured no men or horses with it. Since their advance up the railroad, we have killed and captured over 300 of them. My loss so far has been only four wounded and one captured.

---

panies of the Fifth Pennsylvania Artillery. My surmise that this artillery was concealed in the long range of mountains called the Cobblers, was confirmed by a statement drawn from a prisoner, and it was determined to develop the locality. At 9 p. m. 14th instant, the above force was moved over very intricate roads to a point at the base of the mountains, where a sort of bivouac was surprised and 9 members of the battery captured, including Babcock, late captain C S. Army, in charge of the artillery. This determined but little the localities of the pieces, and some time was vainly spent in skirmishing the mountain with my dismounted cavalry and Company E, Fifth Artillery. The localities of the pieces was even a secret not imparted to many of Mosby's men. By intimidation, however, when almost relinquishing the task, a driver of the artillery was forced to discover the trail of the pieces. By deploying skirmishers and moving up the precipitous side of the mountain, covered with heavy undergrowth, for about a mile and a half, and following its summit for some distance, the three-inch ordnance gun, 12-pounder howitzer, and two small mountain howitzers, with limber of caisson, sets of harness, and ammunition, were discovered in a dense thicket. These were drawn down the stony sides of the mountain to the command below, and thence to Piedmont, reaching camp at 6 a. m. to-day. I desire to mention Lieutenant Revell, Thirteenth New York Cavalry, and Captain Anderson, Company E, Fifth Artillery, who rendered valuable assistance. As desired, I have dismounted the pieces with the exception of the small mountain howitzer, weighing only 250 pounds which I have repaired, replenished with ammunition, and would respectfully ask permission to retain with my regiment till it returns to camp. I have it drawn by two horses, and manned by old artillerists. The other three pieces are sent by train as you directed. Prisoners, seven of whom I send, report that a force is expected here from the rebel column in the Valley."

To which General Lee replied:

HEADQUARTERS ARMY OF NORTHERN VIRGINIA, }
                    *October 29, 1864.* }

COLONEL: Your letter of October 23d has been received. I regret the loss of your artillery and will endeavor to have it supplied as soon as practicable; but owing to recent heavy losses of artillery in the Valley, there may be considerable delay. Meantime I hope you may be able to capture some from the enemy. I am sincerely gratified at the energy, boldness, and success with which you have so unceasingly operated. I hope you will continue to damage the enemy on the Manassas railroad as much as possible. As your command increases it will be necessary to be extremely watchful as to the character of the men you enlist. Spare no pains to interrupt the work and use of the railroad.

DR. EMIL OHLENSCHLAGER,
Medical Inspector on General Sherdian's Staff.
Killed near Newtown, October 11, 1864.

The quiet which reigned at Rectortown was so unusual that General Augur communicated the fact to General Halleck, at Washington, in this brief epistle:

*Rectortown, October 15, 1864.*

AUGUR to HALLECK:—"The train from Alexandria arrived and reported on time to-day and without interference from guerrillas. Nothing heard from General Sheridan.

On the day following (16th) he reports the arrival of General Sheridan at Rectortown.

*Sunday, October 16.*—Command met at Bloomfield. Companies C, E and F remained to operate along the railroad, while Mosby, with Companies A, B and D, went down in Fairfax to attack a large wagon train between Burke's Station and Fairfax. We were too late, however, as the wagons had gone into camp, with a heavy infantry guard.[8]

We then moved towards Centreville, built fires in the pines and camped for the night. On the 17th we went to Annandale. Two men were sent to take pickets and draw out the cavalry. One of the pickets was taken and the other escaped to camp. The cavalry came out. We halted and remained in sight for some time, but as they made no demonstration, Companies A and B advanced towards them, when they hurried inside of their fortifications.[9] Companies A and B then proceeded along the Ox Road in the direction of Frying Pan, and thence home.

General Augur had been notified of Mosby's presence in Fairfax, and while Augur's cavalry were being sent to

[8] TAYLOR to SLOUGH, Oct. 15 : "It is reported that a train of quartermasters' wagons (100) between Burk's Station and Fairfax are exposed to surprise from guerrillas. Please take such measures as will insure the safety of the train."

SLOUGH to TAYLOR : "Nothing to report this evening except that 200 men have been sent to guard the quartermaster's train of wagons."

SLOUGH to TAYLOR, Oct. 17 :"Colonel Barnes, at Fairfax Station, has satisfied himself that 200 or 300 rebel cavalry are now south of him near Braddock Road. The telegraph is not working beyond Manassas. Have you any cavalry to send out in direction of Burk's? Anticipating Mosby's next appearance at this end of the line I have strengthened it very much."

[9] TAYLOR to AUGUR, Oct. 17 : "It is reported that Mosby has driven in Lazelle's pickets and is moving on Annandale and Fort Buffalo, camps of the Sixteenth and Thirteenth, with 600 men. The number must be exaggerated. Infantry has already moved from De Russy's line to Buffalo, and I have ordered Slough to send at once the Fifth Wisconsin to Annandale."

TAYLOR to General DE RUSSY, Oct. 17 : "Your dispatch received. I have telegraphed General Slough to send at once 500 infantry to Annandale. A small infantry force at either place, at Annandale or Buffalo, will be sufficient to drive off Mosby, who cannot have 100 men."

LAZELLE to DE RUSSY, Oct. 17 : "In reply to your verbal message by the messenger sent you, I have the honor to inform you that the disposition suggested by you has already been made. I received about half an hour since a message from Captain Schneider, commanding at Annandale, to the effect that a large force of cavalry, estimated at about 400 to 600, had been seen in his vicinity ; his picket posts had been driven in, etc. He says he will do his best to hold his stockade. Mosby was in Fairfax Court House this afternoon, and it is believed had a large force with him. Another messenger just arrived from Annandale. Captain Schneider again has reported that a large force of the enemy's cavalry are about him. I recommend that Annandale be reinforced as soon as possible. I will send half a squadron to Annandale at once from

Fairfax in pursuit, Mosby was quietly marching back to Loudoun.[10]

Montjoy, with Company D, and with Bush. Underwood as guide, moved off towards Falls Church, and at night prepared to attack the camp. The pickets were captured, and some of our men were leading horses out of the stables, when the camp was aroused. The blowing of a horn, which at first was thought by our men to denote the assembling of a party of coon hunters, was discovered to be a signal given by a citizen named Reed to alarm the camp. Reed was shot by one of our men. The enemy, now thoroughly aroused, opened fire, which in the darkness did no damage. Three or four negro infantry were killed ; 6 prisoners and 7 horses were brought out.[11]

---

here. I recommend that a company of infantry be sent here to supply their place. But I can hold this point, I think, against everything that Mosby has. I will have 150 men left here."

[10] AUGUR to TAYLOR, Oct. 18 : "I have sent the Eighth Illinois down through Centreville to find Mosby's force."

TAYLOR to LUDLAM, Oct. 18 : "Mosby passed through Falls Church last evening toward Vienna with perhaps 250 men. The Eighth Illinois Cavalry has been detached from Rectortown in pursuit."

[11] BIRDSALL to TAYLOR, Oct. 19 : "About 2 a. m. on the morning of Oct. 18, a force of Mosby's men, estimated at 75, entered Falls Church village, halted at the church (brigade hospital), and after breaking open the barn of Mr. Sines, a citizen who lives opposite, and taking therefrom 5 valuable horses, passed up the Alexandria and Lewinsville pike toward Vienna. The post at the junction of the Lewinsville road with the pike, consisting of one corporal and three men of the Sixteenth New York Cavalry, was captured, with one horse. A negro named Frank Brooks, belonging to the citizens home guard of the village, was shot dead while attempting to assist the picket in making a defense. Mr. J. B. Reed, a citizen and a member of the same guard, with one of his negro employes, were taken prisoners at the same time. Mr. Reed was afterwards brutally murdered by the party who captured him, in a dense pine wood near Hunter's Mill, and his body has been found and brought into his house. An attempt to kill the negro taken with Mr. Reed was also made, and the rebels, supposing him dead, left him in the woods. He escaped afterwards, however, and has but a slight wound in the head, with the loss of an ear, blown off by a pistol shot. There is no doubt concerning the murder of Mr. Reed, as the surgeon, who has made an examination of the body, states that the skull at the base of the brain is blown to atoms, and the flesh about the wound is filled with powder, as if the pistol had been placed close to the head. The negro who escaped brings information that at or near Vienna, the force which visited Falls Church was joined by a reserve party of 100 or more men."

# CHAPTER XXI.

While the forces of General Augur were in possession of the railroad, but few of our men would sleep in houses, owing to the danger of being surprised. Many of the men put up little shelters, or "shebangs," as they were called, in the woods and in hollows where they could not be seen from the roads. These were made of poles, covered with brush or cornstalks; and when the floor was spread with dry leaves and covered with blankets, afforded a comfortable lodging place. Our horses being haltered to the trees near by, with bunches of hay to munch on during the night, we slept as soundly in our little "shebangs" as in feather beds, except when some careless, sleepy fellow forgot to take off his spurs, and in drawing up or stretching out his feet under the blankets, would rake the shins of his unfortunate neighbor. But these little troubles were soon forgotten. Some few continued to sleep in doors, but nearly all had hiding places, entered by trap doors or secret panels, in which they could find refuge in case the enemy came. Mosby and one or two companions would frequently mount their horses after dark and go to the house of some friend near a Federal camp, and remain there all night, deeming that the safest place for a good night's sleep.

Even citizens or non-combatants, particularly those living in exposed places, were compelled to leave their houses at night and "camp out." The Federal forces on the railroad had carried off a number of citizens, many of them old men,

and kept them running up and down the railroad, in order
to deter Mosby from throwing off the trains.[1]

In a conversation with Colonel Mosby one day, he said:
"The Yankees are worse than Chinese, but no matter
what they do, I will not swerve one inch from my path of
duty. They might as well place women and children in
front of their lines of battle. My mode of warfare is just as
legitimate as that of the army fighting in their front. I am
placed here to annoy them and interrupt their communica-

---

[1] With all the force at his command General Augur found himself unable to
open and guard his road. In a dispatch to Halleck he says : " Simply patrolling
he track and guarding the bridges is not going to be sufficient on this road; it
must be literally guarded the whole way."

AUGUR to HALLECK, Oct. 10: "I shall commence building small stockades,
which will be so near each other as to command the entire track. This will
economize men. If this does not answer I think I shall have to adopt something like Washburn's plan and fit up on each train quarters for prominent
secessionists to accompany it."

HALLECK to AUGUR, Oct. 11: "Your plan of putting prominent citizens on
trains is approved, and you will carry it into effect. They should be so confined as to render escape impossible, and yet be exposed to the fire of the
enemy."

HALLECK to McCALLUM, Oct. 12 : " The Secretary of War directs that in
retaliation for the murderous acts of guerrilla bands, composed of and assisted
by the inhabitants along the Manassas Gap Railroad, and as a measure necessary to keep that road in running order, you proceed to destroy every house
within five miles of the road which is not required for our own purposes, or
which is not occupied by persons known to be friendly. All males suspected of
belonging to, or assisting the robber bands of Mosby will be sent under guard
to the provost-marshal at Washington, to be confined in the Old Capitol Prison.
The women and children will be assisted in going north or south, as they may
select. They will be permitted to carry with them their personal property and
such provisions as they may require for their own use. Forage, animals and
grain will be taken for the use of the United States. All timber and brush within
musketry fire of the road will be cut down and destroyed. Printed notices
will be circulated and posted that any citizens found within five miles of the road
hereafter will be considered as robbers and bushwhackers and be treated accordingly. Copies of these instructions will be sent to General Augur and General
Sheridan with orders to give you all possible military aid for the accomplishment
of these objects. The inhabitants of the country will be notified that for any
further hostilities committed on this road or its employés an additional strip of
ten miles on each side will be laid waste and that section of country entirely
depopulated."

WINSHIP to TAYLOR, Oct. 16: " I have turned over to General Slough 8 guerrillas to be placed on the trains running to the front."

Dickson    Watkins    Montly.    Thomas    Smith    Catlicote    Carden    Myer

GROUP OF MOSBY'S MEN.

tion as much as possible. This I intend doing, and should I again have an opportunity of throwing off a train I will do it, even if I knew my own family were upon it. '

Under the orders received, General Augur arrested a number of prominent citizens, among them Jamieson, Samuel and Albert Ashby, relatives of the renowned Gen. Turner Ashby, and these old men were taken to Rectortown and placed on the cars running up and down the road. While in the hands of the Federals, Mr. Jamieson Ashby was shot in the head by one of the guards on the cars; he was carried to the hospital in Alexandria, where he died.

These and other important matters under consideration at the time, led Colonel Mosby to address the following communication to General Lee. The indorsements and instructions of General Lee and the Secretary of War are sufficient evidence of their approval of Mosby's acts:

Near Middléburg, October 29, 1864.

General R. E. LEE,
  *Commanding Army of Northern Virginia.*

GENERAL: I desire to bring, through you, to the notice of the Government the brutal conduct of the enemy manifested toward citizens of this district since their occupation of the Manassas road. When they first advanced up the road we smashed up one of their trains, killing and wounding a large number. In retaliation they arrested a large number of citizens living along the line, and have been in the habit of sending an installment of them on each train. As my command has done nothing contrary to the usages of war, it seems to me that some attempt at least ought to be made to prevent a repetition of such barbarities.

During my absence from my command, the enemy captured 6 of my men near Front Royal; these were immediately hung by order and in the presence of General Custer. They also hung another in Rappahannock. It is my purpose to hang an equal number of Custer's men whenever I capture

---

NOTE: The names of those shown in the Group of Mosby's Men on the opposite page are the following, counting from left to right:

| | | | |
|---|---|---|---|
| 1 | John T. Dickson. | 5 | —— Smith. |
| 2 | J. R. Watkins. | 6 | D. G. Carlisle. |
| 3 | Col. John S. Mosby. | 7 | Sergt. John W. Corbin. |
| 4 | Daniel L. Thomas. | 8 | Richard McVey. |

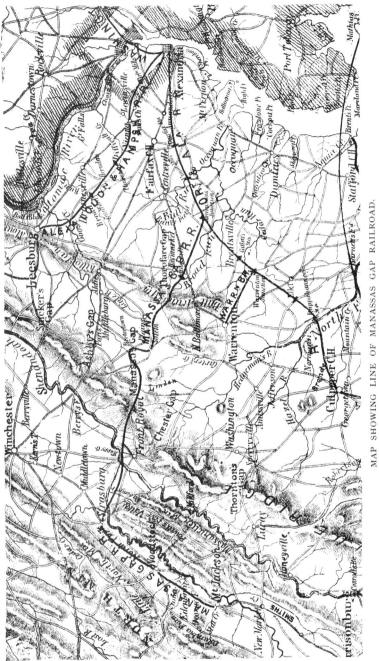

MAP SHOWING LINE OF MANASSAS GAP RAILROAD.

From an old War Map.

them. There was passed by the last U. S. Congress a bill of pains and penalties against guerrillas, and as they profess to consider my men within the definition of the term, I think it would be well to come to some understanding with the enemy in reference to them. The bearer of this, my adjutant, will give all information you desire concerning the enemy in this county. Of course, I did not allow the conduct of the enemy toward citizens to deter me from the use of any legitimate weapon against them, but after throwing off the train they guarded the road so heavily that no opportunities were offered for striking any successful blow, and I thought I would be more usefully employed in annoying Sheridan's communications. I received the list of deserters you sent me. I will do what I can toward arresting them, but none are with my command.

Very respectfully, your obedient servant,
JNO. S. MOSBY, *Lieutenant-Colonel.*

[First Indorsement.]

Respectfully referred to the honorable Secretary of War for his information.

I do not know how we can prevent the cruel conduct of the enemy toward our citizens. I have directed Colonel Mosby, through his adjutant, to hang an equal number of Custer's men in retaliation for those executed by him.

R. E. LEE, *General.*

[Third Indorsement.]

*November 14, 1864.*

General Lee's instructions are cordially approved. In addition, if our citizens are found exposed on any captured train, signal vengeance should be taken on all conductors and officers found on it, and every male passenger of the enemy's country should be treated as prisoners. So instruct.

J. A. S[EDDON], *Secretary.*

*Monday, October 17.*—Towards evening a foraging party of Federal cavalry came out from their camp near Piedmont, and going to the farms around, supplied themselves liberally with food for man and beast. One had the carcass of a calf on his saddle; another a live lamb; chickens and other poultry were plentifully distributed throughout their ranks. As they started to return to camp, each took a bundle of hay in front on his horse. Capt. William Chapman, who had been watching his opportunity, suddenly charged them

in front at Mrs. Fletcher's, on the road leading from Piedmont to Paris, while Capt. Sam. Chapman, with his company, kept on their flank, shooting into their ranks.  En-
cumbered as they were with plunder, they could offer but
poor resistance to the impetuous charge of Mosby's men.
When Chapman first attacked them, they were huddled up
so closely that a great many were killed and wounded by
the close and rapid firing.

JAMES CHANCELLOR, CO. D.
Captured by the Eighth Illinois Cavalry in the
Fight near Upperville.

Twenty prisoners and 30
horses were captured, and
15 or 20 horses which es-
caped in the darkness and
confusion, were picked up
the following day.

General Seward, writing
General Stevenson from
Martinsburg, October
21st, says:

"Mosby, with 75 or 100
men, lay within 300 yards
of the pike when our train
for the front passed yesterday.  The guard being
unusually strong, they
thought best not to attack,
but remained quietly un-
til the train had passed and
then started toward Smithfield.  This was on the
Winchester road, about
half a mile on the other
side of Darkesville.  They
captured a butcher, who was in advance of the train,
and let him go again before dark.  He says that Mosby
questioned him very closely in regard to the number of
troops stationed here, also in regard to our pickets."

When this train left Martinsburg, Frank Leslie's Special
War Artist with Sheridan in the Valley, then on his way to
the front, accompanied it, as a matter of safety, it being very
heavily guarded.  As the hour of noon approached, this
worthy artist, disdaining the humble fare of the poor soldier

(hard tack and bacon), and longing for the dainty food which he knew could be procured at the farm house of one David Stewart, in the hollow on the pike between Bunker Hill and Bucklestown, proposed to a lieutenant of the artillery and three or four cavalrymen that they leave the train and push ahead so as to make sure of some of Mrs. Stewart's famous pies before the train came up.

While our knight of the pencil and brush stood on the porch bargaining with the good lady for a pumpkin pie, he

ARTIST TAYLOR LOSES HIS PIE.

cast his eyes down the hollow to the east and saw several horsemen leaning forward on their horses and scudding along a little lane which led directly to the pike. One glance he gave at the gray uniforms ; then hastily dropping his pie, he called the attention of the lieutenant to the swiftly approaching riders. In an instant Red-straps vaulted the fence and sprang into the saddle, the others following, and up the pike the whole party sped, in the direction of the escort, who were not yet in sight. Our artist being poorly mounted, brought up the rear, but a friendly stone fence between him and the graybacks served as a shield and pre-

vented his being cut off. He has ever since cherished a
more than kindly feeling toward " stone-fences."

"If you fellows had caught me then and killed me, who
would have made your pictures for this book, you 'tarnal
old rebel?" said my friend James E. Taylor, whose name
will be found on these illustrations, and who is the same
worthy artist mentioned above. A drawing made by himself, showing his lucky escape, both for him and me, will be
found on the preceding page.

"Sorry we made you lose your pie that time, old boy,"
said I.

" No, you didn't," replied Taylor; "I went back and got
it after you fellows left."

General Seward's letter, here alluded to, while in the
main correct, is inaccurate in some few details. He says:
" Mosby, with 75 or 100 men, lay within 300 yards of the
pike," etc. While the number is so vastly exaggerated
(which is excusable, as General Seward did not see our
men), Mosby himself was not at that place at the time, although his brother, Adjutant William H. Mosby, was present.
The party was commanded by Capt. A. E. Richards, who
with Adjutant Mosby, Dr. Dunn, George Slater and a small
party, was scouting along the Valley turnpike.[2]

While watching the pike, they captured a newsboy, whom
they held as prisoner for awhile, lest he might give information of their presence. The little fellow watched their operations closely, and appeared to look with eagerness for
the approach of a straggling cavalryman or a few Federal
troopers. When our men started in pursuit, he would view
the chase with great interest; and, when the capture was
made, would clap his hands with delight.

*Monday, Oct. 24.*—Command met at Bloomfield; nearly
400 men reported for duty. Intending to strike another
blow at Sheridan's communications, Mosby crossed the

---

[2] *Harper's Ferry, Oct. 23, 1864.*
       STEVENSON to HALLECK: " Mosby's guerrillas are the only rebels in
force left in this end of the Valley. If I could remount Cole's Cavalry and arm
them with the Spencer carbine, I can safely say that in 60 days I can get rid
of this quasi-military pest."

Shenandoah at Castleman's Ferry about dusk and halted for the night near Summit Point.

We moved off soon after sunrise on the morning of the 25th, halting near the Martinsburg and Winchester turnpike, about 6 miles from the latter place. Leaving the command concealed, Mosby took a few men and went out to reconnoitre the road. He observed a two-horse ambulance with an escort of 12 or 15 cavalrymen coming from the direction of Winchester, and immediately started his men out to bag them. When they saw our men approaching, the driver of the ambulance put on all speed to get away, as did the escort. A long train was seen in the distance, coming from Martinsburg, and their efforts were directed to reach it. Seeing this, and fearing they would escape, Boyd Smith, who with a few others were riding in a field almost abreast of the ambulance, which they were seeking to head off, shot one of the horses. This checked the progress of the wagon, and he and John T. Dickson jumped their horses over the stone fence, into the road, capturing the ambulance and occupants—one General, a Captain, and a civilian, who was driving and also carrying the mail. Three only of the escort were captured. Some of them retreated to the main body of the escort, who, learning of the disaster, betook themselves back to Winchester. The others pushed on to the train.[3] The capture took place within a few hundred yards of the approaching train, and as Boyd Smith and John T. Dickson were hastening

BOYD SMITH, CO. E.
From a War-time Photograph.

---

[3] SEWARD to STEVENSON, Oct. 25: "General Duffié was captured five miles beyond Bunker Hill last evening by Mosby. Colonel Edwards reports that Mosby had from 300 to 400 men, and started in the direction of Smith-

back to the command they met Mosby bringing up his men to attack the train.

"Colonel, here's your General," said Smith, as he saw Mosby advancing.

BRIG.-GEN. ALFRED N. DUFFIÉ,
U. S. A.

field, sending 5 men as a guard to Gen. Duffié. I have notified the troops along the railroad. The express from the east has just arrived all right."

Colonel EDWARDS to FORSYTH, Oct. 25 : "I have the honor to report that at about 9 a. m. the escort that came from Martinsburg last evening with General Neill left this post to return. This escort consisted of 50 men, 30 of whom were from the Twenty - second Pennsylvania Cavalry, under command of Second Lieut. B. F. Hasson, Twenty-second Cavalry. Gen. A. N. Duffié, with his two-horse light spring wagon, and Captain Roome, assistant adjutant general, Second Brigade, First Division, Sixth Corps who was here wounded, with the headquarters light wagon of that brigade, accompanied it on its return. When about 5 miles from this place, General Duffié, with 10 men from the escort, with his light wagon pushed ahead, and when about one mile and a half beyond the main body was attacked by a party from Mosby's or Gilmor's band of guerrillas and captured. The wagon was run off to the side of the road and is supposed to have been taken away. A courier from the escort brought in the news of the disaster, and the other light wagon returned. I immediately sent out the Forty-ninth Pennsylvania Volunteer Infantry and the Seventeenth Pennsylvania Cavalry to hunt up the enemy. The commanding officer of the Seventeenth Pennsylvania Cavalry, having ascertained that the party went off toward Snicker's Ferry, immediately put off in that direction and has not, as yet, returned. The enemy's force is supposed to have been somewhere in the neighborhood of 300 men. Major Durland, commanding Seventeenth Pennsylvania Cavalry, has since returned and reports that he followed this force by a circuitous route as far as Seiver's Ford, on the Opequon, and that they received reliable information from citizens along the route that Gen-

Looking towards the General, Mosby said :

" Who are you?"

" General Duffié," replied that worthy gentleman.

" Take him to the rear," said Mosby as he galloped out to the road.

The train was a large one and had started from Martinsburg early in the morning with a guard composed of Currie's brigade, together with the Fifth Wisconsin Volunteers, the Ninth New York Artillery, and a force of cavalry made up of several detachments, all under command of Colonel Currie.[4]

Not being fully aware of the length or strength of the train and escort, Mosby hurriedly disposed his force for the assault—Chapman and Montjoy, with one squadron to charge in front, while he, with Richard's squadron, were to assail the rear. The cavalry were easily driven back, but the infantry proved too strong, and when the artillery opened fire Mosby drew off his men, hoping the cavalry would follow him up so that he could fall upon them when at a safe distance from the infantry and artillery. But this they would not do. The escort seemed to understand that their duty was to guard the train and they stuck to it.

Poor Duffié was not only a prisoner, but his misfortune drew no word of sympathy from his superior officer. General Sheridan, in his report to General Halleck announcing the fact, says :

" Brigadier-General Duffié was captured between Winchester and Martinsburg. I respectfully request his dismissal from the service. I think him a trifling man and a poor soldier. He was captured by his own stupidity."

---

eral Duffié's spring wagon, with himself and one other officer inside, had passed the vicinity of Brucetown. I will await further orders as when to forward the next."

[4] WATKINS to CURRIE, October 24 : " You will have your brigade in readiness to move at 5:30 a. m. to-morrow, provided with three days' rations. The Fifth Wisconsin Volunteers, Colonel Allen ; Ninth New York Artillery, Captain Lamoreaux, and several detachments of cavalry, will be ordered to report to you at that hour. You will have command of the entire escort for the train, which will be on the Winchester pike, near town, at the hour before mentioned."

Richards, with the First Squadron, was sent back to The Plains in Fauquier, while Mosby, with the remainder of the command, proceeded to the vicinity of Winchester, where he captured a train of 7 wagons—5 with 6 mules and 2 with 4 horses each, together with 54 infantry who were guarding the train.   He then returned, bringing with him 60 prisoners (including one general and one captain), 45 horses and mules, without having a man lost or injured.

LIEUT. ALBERT WRENN, CO. B.
From a War-time Photograph.

Several small scouting parties were scattered through the Valley, all of whom were successful in capturing prisoners and horses.

*Saturday, October 29.*—A strong detachment of the Eighth Illinois Cavalry was sent from Rectortown on a scout towards Upperville. Capt. Walter E. Frankland, with about 100 men, struck their trail and followed, finding them at Hatcher's Mill, dismounted and feeding their horses.  He waited in the woods until they had resumed their march, when he again started on their track.   Meanwhile he had been joined by Colonel Mosby, Harry Hatcher and a number of others who had also been watching the Federal cavalry.  Mosby ordered Frankland to intercept them on their return—to get between them and their camp.

" I want you to make it a second Dranesville," said Mosby. " I will do the scouting and will keep you informed of the enemy's movements."

From Upperville the Eighth Illinois struck across a stretch of level land in the direction of Rectortown.  As they drew near the house of Henry Dulaney, about a mile from Upperville, Frankland determined to attack them in the open field. Dividing his force between Lieut. Albert Wrenn and Lieutenant Grogan, he, with Lieutenant Wrenn and the larger portion, was to attack in front, while Grogan was to march off to the right and strike on their flank.

The Federals formed in three squadrons. Frankland in his charge broke and drove back the first squadron, but the other two remained firm and poured their fire into his party and also into Grogan's men, who now charged on their left. Between Grogan and the Eighth Illinois there was a ditch and also a high rail fence. In the charge he was compelled to take him men through a gate in this fence, which not only delayed but also confused their movements, and in consequence Frankland was beaten off before Grogan could unite with him. The squadron in front of Dulaney's house showed signs of wavering, but the Federals on the right of the gate sat quietly on their horses and poured a steady fire into Grogan's flank.

Though our loss was severe, it is surprising that it was no greater. Had the Federals charged us when crowded in passing through the gate-

J. J. WILLIAMS, SERGEANT CO. F.
Captured near Upperville in the Fight with the Eighth Illinois Cavalry.

way, or cut us off in the inner field, many more would have been lost.

Luther Carrington and George Gulick were killed; John Atkins and Edgar Davis mortally wounded, both dying soon after the fight. Thos. Adams, Geo. Turberville, Maddux and Shaw, wounded. James Chancellor, John Munson, J. J. Williams, C. H. McIntosh and Dennis Darden were taken prisoners.

The Eighth Illinois lost but few, yet they pressed into service a wagon and an ox-cart to carry off their dead and wounded.[5]

John Atkins was an Irish gentleman, who, having heard of Mosby's exploits, left home and country to join his for-

SERGT. EDGAR DAVIS, CO. E.
Mortally wounded in the Fight with the Eighth Illinois Cavalry near Upperville.
From a War-time Photograph.

tune with ours. He was brave, generous, of good education, agreeable in his manner, and had in the short time he was with us made many friends. Poor fellow, he suffered greatly, but when death came it was not that grim monster usually pictured, but a kindly spirit, which transported him in his last moments from scenes of blood and carnage back to home and friends; and as he murmured faintly the words "Oh, my poor mother!" he sank to rest. He was buried in the little cemetery at Paris.

At one time when Atkins was in Richmond on leave of absence, an alarm was sounded that the enemy was about making an attack on the city. Guards were placed on the streets and the provost guard picked up all officers and sol_ diers absent from their commands, sending them out to the trenches to check any advance. Atkins was arrested and taken to the Soldiers' Home and handed a musket. This was too much for his good nature, even. "Let me go back to my command," said he; "when I am at home I have my horse to ride and boots up to my middle, and I am not going out to the trenches to shovel dirt." He was released on

---

[5] AUGUR to HALLECK, October 30: "A portion of the Eighth Illinois had a brush with Mosby yesterday, near Upperville, and whipped him badly, killing 7 or 8, and capturing 9. The track will be taken up half way between this (Salem) and Rectortown to-day. They are getting on very slowly—as fast, however, as they possibly can. I go to Plains this morning,"

the following day, through the good offices of Capt. Ed. Hudson, of General Elzey's staff.

Edgar Davis was thought to be but slightly wounded, but from the first he persisted in saying he would die. He lingered a few days. His horse was shot, as was also the horse of his brother William. Davis was a very quiet, unassuming man and his loss was much regretted.

Lieut. John N. Murphy of Company G was, with a few others, at the house of Captain Richards near Upperville. He had just reached there from the Northern Neck—had not taken off his saddle—when the word came : " There are the Yankees!" He and his companions mounted and quickly rode out to the turnpike just as the fight commenced. Murphy had been a captain in the regular service before joining our command, but this was his first experience in our mode of fighting. Seeing the men scattered over the field in every direction, he was confused. He recognized Lieut. Harry Hatcher dashing across the field at full speed, and being well mounted, on a daughter of the famous old racehorse Bailey Peyton, Murphy spurred on and overtook him.

" Which are our men and which are the Yankees ? " asked Murphy.

Harry's reply was : " Damn the difference! Go right in !" Then, turning with his head toward Murphy, he said : " There's a Yankee, right by you now !" As Murphy turned toward's him, the man wheeled his horse, threw back his hand and fired, the ball from his revolver striking the ground a few feet from Murphy's horse. He then dashed off and rejoined the men of his squadron near Dulaney's house.

NIGHT ON BATTLEFIELD.

# CHAPTER XXII.

*Sunday, November 6, 1864.*—Meeting of the command at
Rectortown. Capt. A. E. Richards returned yesterday from
the Valley, where he had been scouting with a party of 9,
bringing in 14 prisoners, with horses and equipments.
These, with prisoners brought in by others, made up a total
of 27 men,—all belonging to Custer's Cavalry. It was decided that 7 of them should be taken and executed, in retaliation for the 6 men of our command hung or shot at Front
Royal after the fight with Custer's Division, and for another,
A. C. Willis, of Company C, who was hung by Col. William
H. Powell at Gaines' X Roads, on the 13th of October.[1]

The circumstances in this latter case were as follows:
When the Federal raiding parties were passing through our
section, they sent a spy ahead to learn where fine cattle and

---

[1] ADJUTANT AND INSPECTOR GENERAL'S OFFICE,
*Richmond, Va., Nov. 19, 1864.*

General R. E. LEE,
*Commanding Army of Northern Virginia:*

GENERAL: I am directed by the Secretary of War to inform you your instructions to Lieutenant-Colonel Mosby to hang an equal number of Custer's men in
retaliation for those of his command executed by General C. are cordially ap
proved by the Department. He instructs me to say in addition that if our citizens are found exposed upon any captured train signal vengeance should be taken
upon all conductors and officers on it, and every male passenger of the enemy's
country should be treated as a prisoner.

Very respectfully, General, your obedient servant,
H. L. CLAY,
*Assistant Adjutant-General.*

[Indorsement.]

HEADQUARTERS. *Nov. 21, 1864.*
Respectfully referred to Colonel Mosby for his government.
R. E. LEE, *General.*

(See Mosby's letter to Lee, Chapter XXI., with endorsements.)

horses were to be found, and their hiding places when the raiders were about. This man passed himself off on the farmers as a Confederate soldier, who had escaped from Federal prison. Some of our men discovered his true character and making search for him, found him at the residence of Mr. Chancellor. After questioning him and satisfying themselves as to who and what he was, they took him out and shot him. In retaliation for this, General Powell not only burned the house, barn and all outbuildings on Mr. Chancellor's premises, but also hung Willis.[2]

BRIG.-GEN. WILLIAM
H. POWELL.

The 27 prisoners were drawn up in single line. Among them were two officers, one being Captain Brewster, commissary of subsistence, of Custer's command, and the other a lieutenant of artillery. Twenty-seven pieces of paper, seven of which were numbered and the remainder blanks, being put into a hat and the hat shaken up, each prisoner was required to draw. The num-

[2] General Powell, in his report of operations, Oct. 27th, says : " October 13, having learned of the wilful and cold-blooded murder of a U. S. soldier by two men (Chancellor and Myers, members of Mosby's gang of cut-throats and robbers), some two miles from my camp, a few days previous, I ordered the execution of one of Mosby's gang whom I had captured the day previous at Gaines Cross-Roads, and placing the placard on his breast with the following inscription : " A. C. Willis, member of Company C, Mosby's command, hanged by the neck in retaliation for the murder of a U. S. soldier by Messrs. Chancellor and Myers." I also sent a detachment, under command of Captain Howe, First West Virginia Cavalry, with orders to destroy the residence, barn, and all buildings and forage, on the premises of Mr. Chancellor, and to drive off all stock of every description, which orders were promptly carried out."

From a letter to Lieut. W. Ben Palmer of Company E, I take the following :

" Young Willis was captured at Gaines' X Roads on the evening of October 13, 1864, by General Powell's command, then camped on the Marlow farm, in Rappahannock Co., at the foot of the Blue Ridge, on the graded road leading to Chester Gap. On the following morning I was captured by the Federal troops and taken to the Marlow farm. I did not see young Willis, but was within a short distance of him and heard the Federal officers and soldiers talking. They said they had one of Mosby's men at General Powell's head-

bered pieces meant death by hanging, and the blanks
Richmond and Libby prison.

It was a painful scene, and one never to be forgotten.    It
was not merely in a spirit of revenge that these men were
condemned, but it was a measure to which Mosby was
forced to resort, by the brutal acts of Custer and Powell.[3]
One of the captives laid his head on the shoulder of a comrade and wept like a child.    Another prayed earnestly until
it came his turn to draw, which he did with trembling
hand.    Holding up the paper and looking at it, his eyes
brightened as he exclaimed : " Blank, by God !  I knew it
would be so."    One said to a more fortunate companion :

FRED S. HIPKINS, CO. C.

Now Rev. F. S. Hipkins, an Episcopal
Minister.

From a War-time Photograph.

quarters, and did not know whether they
would hang him, shoot him or cut his
throat.  They hung him about 11 o'clock
a. m., on a large poplar tree standing by
the roadside on the Marlow farm, and his
body was taken down by Messrs. John P.
Ricketts, Robert Deatherage and William
Bowling, and carried to the Baptist Church
in the town of Flint Hill ; he was buried
on the following day.  On his breast a card
was found, saying that he was hung in retaliation for a Union soldier said to have
been killed by one of Mosby's command.

"J. D. BAGGASBY.

"To W. BEN PALMER, Richmond, Va."

In conversation with the Rev. Fred. S.
Hipkins, formerly of Company C, Mosby's
Battalion, concerning this affair, he said :

" It was half a mule that saved my neck
that time.  After we had returned from a
raid in the Valley, I was one of the men
detailed to take the prisoners South—a job
I did not like.  When the captures were
divided, there was a horse and half a mule
to each man—that is, a horse to each man
and one mule to each two men.  Half a
mule was of no use to me, and as Willis
thought he could get more work out of a whole mule, he agreed to go out with
the prisoners in my stead if I would give him my half mule ; and by putting
the two halves together he would have a full mule.  It was while taking out
these prisoners that he was captured and hung."

[3] Mosby was compelled to adopt this course, not only on account of

" Tell my mother I died like a man." Some could not overcome their feelings, and begged piteously for their lives.

Among the prisoners captured by Richards in the Valley
were a newsboy and a drummer boy. The newsboy had
been captured by our men on more than one occasion and
had always been released;
claiming his usual privi-
lege, he was allowed to go
free. The drummer boy
was well grown, and but
for a circumstance appar-
ently trivial in itself, might
have passed as a full-
fledged soldier. He was
mounted on a very sorry
horse, which lagged be-
hind in coming off the field,
and Lieutenant Murphy,
who was in the rear in
charge of the prisoners,
rode beside him. The boy
told him an artless story,—
that he was a drummer
boy; and showed a little
silver badge with his drum
and sticks upon it, which
he said his mother had

BVT.-MAJ.-GEN. GEORGE A. CUSTER,
U. S. A.
From a War-time Photograph.

given him. He asked Murphy if he would not be allowed
to keep this token—that we might take everything else.
Murphy told him to hide it in his boot and no one would
see it.

Seeing this boy among the condemned, Murphy immediately went to Richards and told him the story, saying he

these acts of Custer and Powell, but also by the action of the higher
powers.

GRANT to SHERIDAN, Aug. 16, 1864: "Where any of Mosby's men are
caught, hang them without trial."

SHERIDAN to GRANT, Aug. 17: ' Mosby has annoyed me and captured a
few wagons. We hung 1 and shot 6 of his men yesterday."

did not think Mosby wanted to hang a drummer boy, and asked Richards to intercede for him. He did so, and the boy was saved. It may be said that he owed his life really to his poor, old, tired horse.

Mosby said the drummer boy should not have been allowed to draw, and that there must be another drawing to procure a substitute for the boy, who was released.

Again the prisoners were placed in line and compelled to go through the same trying ordeal; this time there being only one number in the hat. Captain Brewster again escaped, but the lieutenant of artillery was not so fortunate—to him the unlucky number fell. His face grew pale and for a moment his voice quivered, as he said: "And must I be hanged?"

The 7 unfortunate prisoners were then sent off under guard, in charge of Lieut. Ed. F. Thomson, with orders to execute them on the Valley turnpike as near General Sheridan's headquarters as possible.

While passing through Ashby's Gap, the party met Captain Montjoy returning from the Shenandoah Valley with some prisoners. Being the ranking officer, he assumed the responsibility of releasing the lieutenant of artillery and one other prisoner and substituted two of the soldiers captured by him.

According to the instructions, the men were to have been executed on the Valley turnpike, near Winchester, but when they reached the turnpike near Berryville, the night being dark and rainy, one of the prisoners had escaped in the darkness; and fearful of meeting with further mishap, it was decided to carry out the sentence there. Five men were executed, and the supply of rope having given out, the executioners determined to shoot the sixth man, when he asked for more time to pray. Lieutenant Thomson ordered the men not to shoot until he gave the word, and then told the man to pray as long as he wished. The prisoner by some means untied his hands and suddenly struck Thomson, who stood in front of him, a blow which knocked him down; then jumping over his prostrate body, he darted off into the wood and was lost to sight. It was an easy matter to escape in the darkness. The man closely hugged a large tree until his pursuers were at a safe distance, when he climbed the tree and quietly waited until they left, and then descended and made his way to Winchester.

A note written by Colonel Mosby and pinned to the clothing of one of the men hung, read:

" These men have been hung in retaliation for an equal number of Colonel Mosby's men hung by order of General Custer at Front Royal. Measure for measure." [4]

---

[1]HEADQUARTERS U. S. FORCES,
*Winchester, Va., November 7, 1864.*

Colonel EDWARDS to KINGSBURY, JR.: "I have the honor to state that G. H. Soule, Company G, Fifth Michigan Cavalry, this day entered our lines from the direction of Perryville and reported as follows: He was taken prisoner by soldiers of Mosby's command on the macadamized road near Newtown, and by them taken to a camp on the Winchester and Berryville turnpike. There he was placed with a squad of Federal prisoners, numbering about 22, and with them compelled to draw lots for the purpose of determining upon a certain number who should be hung. Of the 23 prisoners 7 were to be executed in retaliation for a like number of Mosby's command who were hung by General Custer. Of the 7 upon whom the lot fell, 3 were hung, 2 shot and 2 escaped. The wounded men, one of whom escaped alive by feigning death, are being cared for by Union families in the vicinity of the camp. The men who escaped have reported at this post. The accompanying note was found by a citizen who cut down and buried the bodies, pinned to the clothing of one of the men who were hanged.

LIEUT. ED. F. THOMSON, CO. H.

Captain Brewster, commissary of subsistence of General Custer's command, was among the parties captured. The name of one of the men hanged was ascertained to be George L. Prouty. He was a member Company L, Fifth Michigan Cavalry."

[Inclosure.]

" These men have been hung in retaliation for an equal number of Colonel Mosby's men hung by order of General Custer at Front Royal. Measure for measure.

The place of this hanging was Beemer's Woods, not a hundred yards from the entrance to the grounds of the Shenandoah Driving Park, now a popular racing resort near Berryville.

After the prisoners had been sent off for execution, Colonel Mosby, looking toward Lieutenant Grogan, said ; " Grogan, I want you to take a letter to General Sheridan, notifying him of the hanging of these men."

Grogan regarded it as an extra hazardous enterprise at that time to venture into Sheridan's presence with such a letter, as such an act would probably place the neck of the bearer also within the coils of a halter. Therefore, thinking the Colonel wished to perpetrate a joke at his expense, he quickly answered :

" Oh, no, Colonel ; I don't want to get a rope around my neck yet awhile."

Had Grogan thought for a moment that the Colonel was serious, he never would have made the reply, as he was one who never shirked a duty and whose courage had often been proved.

The Colonel then turned to John Russell, who always took a plain matter-of-fact view of things, and who never stopped to consider the risk when an order was given him. He was entrusted with the delivery of the following letter to General Sheridan :

*November 11, 1864.*

Major-General P. H. Sheridan,
*Commanding U. S. forces in the Valley:*

General : Some time in the month of September, during my absence from my command, six of my men, who had been captured by your forces, were hung and shot in the streets of Front Royal, by the order and in the immediate presence of Brigadier-General Custer. Since then another (captured by a Colonel Powell on a plundering expedition into Rappahannock) shared a similiar fate. A label affixed to the coat of one of the murdered men declared that "this would be the fate of Mosby and all his men."

Since the murder of my men, not less than 700 prisoners, including many officers of high rank, captured from your army by this command, have been forwarded to Richmond, but the execution of my purpose of retaliation was deferred in order, as far as possible, to confine its operation to the men of Custer and Powell. Accordingly, on the 6th instant, seven of your men were by my order executed on the Valley pike, your highway of travel.

Hereafter any prisoners falling into my hands will be treated with the kindness due to their condition, unless some new act of barbarity shall compel me reluctantly to adopt a line of policy repugnant to humanity.

Very respectfully, your obedient servant,

JOHN S. MOSBY, *Lieutenant-Colonel.*

This was not without its good effect, and Mosby was spared the painful duty of resorting to such measures thereafter.

*The Black Flag.*—At one time there was a report widely circulated, both North and South, that Mosby was "fighting under the black flag,"—that he had "hoisted the black flag." Prisoners who were captured expressed surprise that they were taken alive, unless it were our purpose to reserve them for some worse fate than a speedy death. Others, as an apology for resisting capture, said they were told that "Mosby's Men" took no prisoners. Among Southern soldiers the report gained credence, and even among members of our command the matter was often the subject of conversation. Some of the old veterans would regale a new recruit with blood-curdling stories of the men who were fighting under the "black flag," until

MAJ.-GEN. PHILIP H. SHERIDAN, U. S. A.

Commanding Middle Military Division.

From a Photograph taken just before leaving the Shenandoah Valley.

the poor fellow really felt himself already dangling from some forest tree. Others, while not lacking moral or physical courage, could not shake off a little of that natural repugnance to the barbarous and savage cruelties which are sometimes practiced in war by even so-called civilized christian nations—feeling that if the report were accepted as true by our enemies, it would be used as an excuse for the perpetration of atrocious acts under the plea of retaliation.

The whole story, so far as I have been able to trace it, had its origin—its birth, life and death—in the following correspondence, taken from the official records:

ADJUTANT GENERAL'S OFFICE,
*Washington, October 27, 1864.*

Brig.-Gen. E. B. TYLER, *Commanding.*

SIR: It has been stated in the papers that a *black flag, captured between Harper's Ferry and Martinsburg by one of your scouts from some of Mosby's guerrillas,* has been presented by you to the City of Philadelphia. All flags, munitions of war and public property taken from the enemy belong to the United States, and such flags when captured should be forwarded to the Adjutant General.

Please report, for the information of the Secretary of War, whether the statement in the papers is correct; and, if it is, cause the flag to be obtained and forwarded to this office, to be deposited in the archives of the War Department.

I am, sir, etc.,  E. D. TOWNSEND,
*Assistant Adjutant General.*

———

HDQRS. FIRST SEPARATE BRIGADE, EIGHTH ARMY CORPS,
*Relay House, Md., Nov. 9, 1864.*

General E. D. TOWNSEND,
*Assistant Adjutant General, Washington, D. C.*

GENERAL: In compliance with the directions of the Secretary of War, I forward to you the "black flag" captured by Detective C. H. Marsh *from General Early's Command,* Monday night, August 1, 1864, while in their lines near North Mountain. The flag was in charge of two rebels and set up against a tree. One of the rebels went in search of water; Marsh, who had been watching the flag from nightfall, determined to get it, if possible, sprung upon the man left alone, secured him, took the flag from the pole, and brought the flag and prisoner safely through within our lines.

I am, general, very respectfully,
Your obedient servant,
E. B. TYLER, *Brigadier General.*

WAR DEPARTMENT, ADJUTANT GENERAL'S OFFICE,  
*Washington, Nov. 11, 1864.*

Brig.-Gen. E. B. TYLER, *U. S. Volunteers,*  
*Relay House, Md.*

SIR : I acknowledge the receipt of your letter of the 9th instant and the " black flag " accompanying it. The Secretary of War has directed that a medal of honor be given to Detective C. H. Marsh for capturing it. Please give me such description of Marsh as will enable me to have the medal properly engraved. If in service, the company and regiment to which he belongs ; if not, the state that he is from, etc.

I am, sir, etc.,                    E. D. TOWNSEND,  
*Assistant Adjutant General.*

So *we* were not in it, after all !

# CHAPTER XXIII.

The attempt to reconstruct the Manassas Gap Railroad was now being abandoned and the rails were removed to be used in repairing the Winchester and Potomac Road.[1]

General Stevenson, in a dispatch to General Sheridan, November 2, said that a force of 3,000 men would be necessary to protect the road, otherwise portions would be destroyed as fast as constructed. Sheridan then issued an order that if the railroad was interfered with, all male secessionists in Charlestown, Shepherdstown, Smithfield and Berryville, and adjacent country should be arrested and sent to Fort McHenry, their stock driven off and subsistence destroyed.[2]

---

[1] See Mosby to General Lee, Appendix, XIII.

---

[2] GENERAL ORDERS, }      HDQRS. MIL. DIST. OF HARPER'S FERRY,
No 23.     }        *Harper's Ferry, Va., Nov. 17, 1864.*

The general commanding publishes this order for the information of all whom it may concern :

The Government of the United States having rebuilt the railroad from Harper's Ferry to Winchester, Va., to protect the same from molestation from guerrillas and disloyal citizens along the line of the same, the general commanding is instructed by the major-general commanding, in the event that the operations of said railroad are interfered with by guerrillas or disloyal citizens——

To arrest all male secessionists in the towns of Shepherdstown, Charlestown, Smithfield and Berryville, and in the adjacent country, sending them to Fort McHenry, Md., there to be confined during the war ; and also to burn all grain,

On the morning of November 7th General Powell's Division of Cavalry came through Manassas Gap on a raid, passing Markham, Piedmont, Rectortown, Upperville, and Paris. They returned to their camp by way of Ashby's Gap, on the 9th, carrying off all the horses, cattle and stock they could find in the section of country traversed by them.[3]

*Friday, November 11.*—The command was called together at Rectortown for inspection. Five hundred men reported for duty. Captain Meade, of General Early's staff, was the inspector. A number of men had joined the battalion whose names were on the rolls of the regular army. For the purpose of weeding these out, and ridding the command of some unruly and negligent members, Mosby had requested this inspection. As the names were called, these men appeared before Colonel Mosby and the Inspector, their names were stricken from our rolls, they were deprived of their arms and placed under guard, to be turned over to the Provost-Marshal at Gordonsville, Major Boyle. Captain Meade reported ours as the best mounted and equipped body of men he had ever inspected.

*Tuesday, November 15.*—Company D met at Paris, and under command of Captain Montjoy, moved off through Ashby's Gap about noon, crossing the Shenandoah at Island Ford, about a mile from Berry's Ferry. Proceeding cautiously in the direction of Winchester, Montjoy concealed

---

destroy all subsistence, and drive off all stock belonging to such individuals, turning over the stock so seized to the Treasury agent for the benefit of the Government of the United States.

Upon the contingency arising requiring the execution of the instructions herein set forth, the same shall be executed promptly and thoroughly.

By order of Brigadier-General Stevenson :

S. F. ADAMS,
*Acting Assistant Adjutant-General.*

[3] SHERIDAN to HALLECK, Nov. 10 : "I have had a small division of cavalry operating on the east side of the mountains in the vicinity of Upperville, Paris, Bloomfield, and surrounding country. No enemy found there, nor had anything been in that section except Mosby's command. A lot of stock, horses, sheep and cattle were brought in by this force, and the grain, barns, subsistence, etc., so far as practicable, were destroyed. Any reports that you may have heard or received within the last few days of large raiding parties of the enemy, and of a concentration of Mosby near Berryville, are untrue."

his men in a piece of woods until daylight (16th), when he again started. On the road from Winchester to Newtown, a force of Federal cavalry was observed carelessly approaching, apparently unconscious of danger. Montjoy formed his men behind a hill and awaited their coming. When they reached the position occupied by the Rangers, a charge was ordered; the astonished Federals fled in confusion, leaving a number of dead and wounded on the field, and 17 prisoners and horses in the hands of Company D.

When Montjoy reached Berryville, he allowed such of his command as resided in Loudoun to cross the river at Castleman's Ferry, while with about 30 men and the pris-

CAPT. RICHARD BLAZER,
Commanding Independent Scouts.
From a War-time Photograph.

oners, he moved along the river, intending to cross at Berry's Ferry. About two miles trom the Ferry, near the residence of Mr. Frank Whiting, he was attacked by Captain Blazer. At Whiting's house Edward Bredell was killed. He was from St. Louis, Mo., and although he had been a lieutenant in the regular service, he was serving as a private in Company D. Montjoy and Grogan endeavored to rally the men, who were now retreating toward the river, and at the Vineyard, the residence of John Esten Cooke, sought to make a stand; but Blazer had the "bulge" on them, as we termed it, and all efforts to stem the tide were unavailing. William Armstead Braxton, of King William Co., Va., was mortally wounded in the retreat and was taken to the Vineyard, where he died. Some 4 or 5 of Company D were wounded, among them Nottingham, of Maryland. All the prisoners and horses were recaptured. Bredell was buried at midnight in a sand shoal of the Shenandoah, and his remains were afterwards removed to a churchyard near Piedmont.

It was now evident that "Mosby's Men" and "Blazer's Men" could not both occupy the same section of country; one or the other must go, and which one was a question to be settled only by a decisive battle.

Captain Richard Blazer's command was composed of picked men from General Crook's Division and were mostly from Ohio and West Virginia.[4] They were organized to "clean out Mosby's gang." By raiding through the mountains and attacking small scouting parties and detachments, they had captured some of "Mosby's Men" and a number of men belonging to other commands. Capt. Blazer was not only a brave man and a hard fighter, but by his humane and kindly treatment, in striking contrast with the usual conduct of our enemies, he had so disarmed our citizens that instead of fleeing on his approach and notifying all soldiers, thus giving them a chance to escape, but little notice was taken of him. Consequently many of our men were "gobbled up" before they were aware of his presence.[5]

---

[4] SHERIDAN to AUGUR, August 20: "I have 100 men who will take the contract to clean out Mosby's gang. I want 100 Spencer rifles for them. Send them to me if they can be found in Washington."

---

[5] *Captain Blazer's Report.*

HEADQUARTERS INDEPENDENT SCOUTS,
*Middletown, Va. Oct. 24, 1864.*

SIR: I have the honor of submitting the following report of the operations of my command since the 18th of August:

On the 18th, learning that a party of Mosby's guerrillas were in the vicinity of Myerstown, I proceeded to that place and overtook them near the Shenandoah river, and, after a chase of three miles, I drove them across the river, capturing one prisoner. The army having fallen back to Halltown on the 25th, according to your orders, I went into Loudoun County, and after operating for several days I killed five of Mosby's gang and captured three prisoners. The army having again advanced to Berryville, on the night of the 3d of September I learned that Mosby, with a considerable force, was at Snickersville. Early on the morning of the 4th I crossed the river at Backus Ford and moved up the river to where I could get up the mountain through the woods. I struck the pike east of the top of the mountain, and moved on their camp. Finding that he had left during the night in the direction of Charlestown, I determined to follow. I recrossed the mountain through Lewis Gap, and, by a forced march, I overtook them about 2 p.m. at Myer's Ford, and, after a spirited fight for several minutes, I completely routed them, with a loss on his part of 13 killed, 6 wounded, 5 prisoners and 17 horses. My loss was 1 killed and 6 wounded. Since that I have had several small affairs with them, in which I

After the disastrous affair at Myer's Ford, where our First Squadron was so badly used up by Blazer, the men were anxious to wipe out the stain which they felt marred their fair fame. The cutting words used by Mosby when he heard of the defeat of his old Company A, still rang in their ears:

" You let the Yankees whip you ? I'll get hoop skirts for you ! I'll send you into the first Yankee regiment we come across !"

At last the opportunity was given them to win back their lost laurels. On the 17th of November the First Squadron (Companies A and B) under command of Capt. A. E. Richards, met at Bloomfield and started out to hunt up Blazer. One hundred and ten men were present. Scouts were sent out, who reported the enemy at Snickersville, but when we reached there the birds had flown. We then crossed the Shenandoah below Castleman's Ferry and halted for the night in Castleman's Woods. Scouts coming in reported Blazer to have been at Hillsborough, in Loudoun, at 1 p. m., which place he left and crossing the river, reached Kabletown before daylight.

Early on the morning of the 18th, Puryear and McDonough, who were scouting near Kabletown, ran into a party of Blazer's men in the fog and Puryear was captured.

have always defeated them, except twice. On the 20th, Lieutenant Ewing, with five men, was attacked on the Berryville pike, near the Opequon, by a superior force, and all were captured except himself. On the 23d, Sergeant Fuller, of the Fifth Virginia Infantry, with ten men, was attacked near Summit Point by fifty or sixty guerrillas. He fought them until he was overpowered and four of his men were killed, one wounded and the rest all captured but three, who made their escape.

Having learned that a man by the name of Marshall was recruiting a company in the vicinity of Ashby's Gap, and that they were to organize on the 25th, I proceeded to their reported rendezvous, near White Post, and completely surprised them, getting Marshall and four of his men, and capturing all of his papers. In another affair below Front Royal I left eight of his murderers to keep company with some that (were) left by General Custer ; these, with a number of others that I have picked up through the country, make an aggregate, in killed, 44 ; wounded, 12, and prisoners, including two captured in the advance to Cedar Creek the first time, 12.

My entire loss is 5 men killed, 7 wounded and 8 prisoners.

McDonough, who had been placed under the ban by the Federal authorities,[6] refused to allow the strangers to ride up to him, made his escape, and brought in the news of Puryear's capture.

We now moved down the west side of the river. Captain Richards said: " Blazer is now camped near Kabletown; as soon as you come in sight of his pickets, draw your pistols and move off at a gallop, but don't fire a shot or raise a yell until you hear the shooting in front. Don't shoot until you get close to them, among them. They've got Puryear and 4 other prisoners and you may kill some of them."

We moved quietly along and soon came in sight of the blue smoke curling up in the woods near town. When the woods were reached, the command moved on at a gallop and dashed into the camp, but found it deserted. The fires, still burning, a huge pile of corn in the center of the camp, and a bundle of newspapers lying unopened near by, showed that the enemy had left but a short time before. A halt was ordered and scouts were sent out. They soon returned, bringing word that Blazer had passed on but a few moments previous to our coming, and was moving toward the river in search of Richards, who he now knew to be in the neighborhood. A person we met said in reply to a question concerning their number: " There are 105 of them, with 5 prisoners." One of Blazer's men, either a straggler or a scout, came leisurely along, walking his horse, and was made prisoner.

As we moved along the road, a couple of Federal cavalrymen were observed dashing across a field from one piece

[6] STEVENSON to HARDIE, Oct. 22 : " I have this morning received positive information of the fate of Captain Buchanan and his orderly. He was murdered by his captors near Brook's Furnace, on the Shenandoah River, by two men by the name of Charles McDonough and Wirt Ashby, who had captured him. I can recover the bodies at any time. I have the papers found upon the body of Capt. B., fully identifying him."

Indorsement : " Capt. Evan M. Buchanan, commissary of subsistence, Third Division, Sixth Corps, was murdered on the 30th day of September, 1864, by a party under the leadership of Charles McDonough, of Charlestown, Va., a bushwhacker and assassin."

of woods to another, and the whole column soon came in sight, moving slowly along. They also saw us as we marched and followed on, no doubt thinking that Richards wished to avoid a fight.

Turning off from the road near Myerstown through a little skirt of woods, Richards drew up his men in a hollow in the center of an open field facing the woods, which hid them from the view of those in the road. The Federals followed closely after us. Captain Richards and his brother, Thomas Richards, remained in the edge of the woods, watching their movements. Carlisle, who had been imbibing a little, being in a good humor for fighting, amused our boys while we were awaiting the onset, by dashing into the woods and looking at the enemy and then galloping back. He fired a shot at them, and on coming back Lieutenant Hatcher said: "Carlisle, what do you mean by shooting about here?" "I saw Puryear," said Carlisle, "and he told me to shoot. Harry, if you will go with me we can whip them."

SYDNOR G. FERGUSON, CO. B.
From a War Photograph.

Seeing Blazer's men taking down the fence and dismounting, Captain Richards thought their intention was to dismount and fight us at long range, which would give them every advantage, with their guns—they being sheltered by the woods and we being exposed to their fire in the open field.

Richards called out to Lieutenant Hatcher: "Harry, they are dismounting." Hatcher started a few men to pull down a gap in a fence in our rear, and Company A was ordered to move off as if retreating. This ruse had the desired effect, for we had scarcely moved off from the head of our line when Richards again called out: "Harry, they are charging."

Company B was still in line, but as we wheeled we saw them charge up to the woods. Company A, led by Hatcher,

now swept over the intervening space at full speed and
dashed with the fury of a tornado on the flank of the Federal column.  Blazer's men used their carbines at first, until
we got fairly among them, when they drew their revolvers.
They fought desperately, but our men pressed on, broke
them and finally drove them from the field.  The road for a
distance of several miles bore evidence of the deadly conflict, as well as the discomfiture of the Federals.  One tall
fellow, who bore the not uncommon name of Smith, was
pursued by Captain Hamner.  Hamner fired at him repeatedly, especially each time that Smith would turn in his saddle and put up his carbine to get a shot at him.  In lieu of
bullets, Smith sent back volleys of curses at each shot, but
refused to surrender, until a pistol was snapped in his face
and he found escape impossible.

Blazer used every endeavor to rally his flying followers;
but seeing the utter destruction of his command, and being
well mounted, he endeavored to make his escape.  Onward
he dashed, steadily increasing the distance betwen himself
and most of his pursuers, but a young man named Ferguson,[7] mounted on his fleet mare " Fashion," followed close
on Blazer's heels.  After emptying his pistol without being
able to hit or halt the fugitive, he drove spurs into his horse
and urging her alongside the Captain, dealt him a blow with
his pistol which knocked him from his horse and landed
him in a fence corner.

" Boys," said Blazer, when able to speak, " you have
whipped us fairly.  All I ask is that you treat us well."

His wounded head was tied up with a handkerchief, and
he soon appeared somewhat reconciled to his fate.[8]

Twenty-one Federals were killed, a large number wounded—many mortally, and 22 prisoners taken.  Fifty horses,
with their equipments, were captured.

---

[7] Now Rev. Sydnor G. Ferguson, a Methodist Minister of Fredericksburg,
Va.

[8] After his release from prison, Blazer returned to his regiment, the Ninety-
first Ohio.  After the war he lived at Gallipolis, Ohio, until 1878, when he con-
tracted yellow fever from the victims of the ill-fated steamer " John Porter,"
and died.

Richards had one man, Hudgins, from Rappahannock, mortally wounded, and a number of others wounded,—but not seriously—among them Charles McDonough, Richard Farr, William Trammeli, C. Maddux, and Sedgwick, of Norfolk.[9]

In connection with the wounding of McDonough an inci- dent occurred which may be unknown to many of our men. In a hand-to-hand fight with one of Blazer's men, Mc- Donough had fired his last shot, killing his enemy's horse. As he fired he said : " Harrell, you —— ——, I am going to kill you." He then called to one of our men, John Foster, who was passing : " John, lend me a pistol." Knowing that Mc- Donough had sworn never to be taken or to take a prisoner, Foster said, " Go on, and I'll take him." " No," said Mc- Donough ; " the —— —— has shot me." Knowing that some of the Federals in that fight had resumed hostilities after sur- rendering, Foster took it for granted that this one had done the same, and handed McDonough a pistol. McDonough snapped it three times at the man as he lay pinned to the ground by his dead horse. At the third trial the weapon exploded and the ball struck him in the top of the head, the blood spurting up like a fountain. It was afterwards learned that this man, whom McDonough had recognized in

---

[9] HEADQUARTERS MILITARY DISTRICT OF HARPER'S FERRY.

*Harper's Ferry, Nov. 19, 1864.*

STEVENSON to FORSYTH : "Two of Captain Blazer's men came in this morning, privates Harris and Johnson. They report that Mosby, with 300 men, attacked Blazer near Kabletown yesterday about 11 o'clock. They say that the entire command, with the exception of themselves, was either captured or killed.

I have ordered out Major Congdon, with 300 Twelfth Pennsylvania Cav- alry, to Kabletown, to bury dead and take care of wounded, if any, and report all facts he can learn. Shall immediately furnish report as soon as received."

CROWNINSHIELD to DANA, Nov. 20 : " Mosby has not troubled us yet. On the 18th instant Mosby had a fight with a Captain Blazer, who commands an independent company of scouts, and defeated him, taking the captain and most of his men prisoners. Three of Blazer's men came into my camp. I sent them to Harper's Ferry. The fight took place near Kabletown. I suppose Mosby recrossed the river at Smither's Ford. He is reported to have had about 300 men."

the fight, was a deserter from his regiment in the regular service.[10]

The 5 prisoners who had been picked up by Blazer were, of course, released. Puryear was in the rear, under guard, when the charge was made. He had a stout stick in his hand, which he had provided for use, knowing that the party would be attacked, but which he pretended to need to urge his horse forward. As soon as the chase commenced he turned his attention from his horse to his captors, one of whom he belabored to his heart's content, until he procured a pistol, with which he joined in the pursuit.

There have been so many different statements made concerning the killing of Lieutenant Cole that, while not myself a witness to the occurrence, although a participant in the fight, I wish to give what I believe to be the correct version. It was written by one who was an eye-witness, and whom I know to be thoroughly reliable. It is from an account of the fight published in the Richmond *Times*, written by John H. Alexander. I have always felt that the killing of this man, a defenseless prisoner, was unjustifiable and deserving of the severest censure.

Speaking of Puryear's treatment while in the hands of the Federals, he says:

P—— was a brave youth, who bore a heart always ready for a soldier's fate, and he bowed to the inevitable with the best grace he could. But an experience awaited him of which he, poor fellow, little dreamed. When he was carried by his captors back to Lieutenant Cole, the second in command to Blazer, and who had charge of the scouts,

---

[10] McDonough's life had been a desperate one, and his end was tragic. After the surrender, the Federal soldiers were hunting him. One day in the month of June a body of Federal cavalry was seen by McDonough and a companion, coming down the pike in the neighborhood of Middleburg. McDonough galloped up to them by the Plains road, fired several shots at them and then turned to run. After running 200 or 300 yards, his horse ran over a hog in the road and, falling, threw him. He then ran into a grove, pursued by the Federals, one of whom, at the first fire, shot off McDonough's trigger finger. They immediately closed in around him in the grove. Seeing that there was no chance of escape, and having sworn no Federal should ever take him, he took his pistol in his left hand and, placing the muzzle in his mouth, fired, killing himself instantly.

that officer of course questioned him as to the whereabouts
of our command, and equally, of course, he refused to give
any information. Lieutenant Cole should not have expected it from him. But I suppose he was a man who
looked upon war as a barbarous business, anyhow, and considered barbarous means justifiable for the achievement of
a military success. At any rate, he insisted upon P——'s
betraying his comrades, and when threats of instant death
failed to move the loyal-hearted lad, he proceeded apparently to put his threats into execution. A rope was placed
around the prisoner's neck and he was suspended from a
tree until nearly unconscious, and then lowered and again
questioned. Once, even twice, was this repeated. But the
boy still refused to answer, and the brutal torture was
stayed. Possibly the exigencies of the hour were more responsible for it than any spirit of relenting on the part of
Lieutenant Cole.

As to the capture and killing of Cole he says:

As the rout passed Myer's shop I saw a Federal officer
strike out from the main body of flying men, evidently to
seek his own salvation. My horse, which was strong and
fleet, made after him, and in less than a hundred yards' run,
I was alongside of him. On my call to surrender he halted
and raised both hands. I saw that his pistols were in his
holster, and leaned over to unbuckle his belt and secure
them. As I was bent over my attention was attracted by
the sound of horses' feet, and I raised my head to see
P—— rein up behind us. His face was distorted with
anger or excitement, and he was pointing a cocked pistol
at the officer's head.

He was, of course, released from his captivity as soon as
Blazer's column broke. I learned afterwards that he had at
once fell upon his guard and wrested his revolver from him
and fell into the chase. Lieutenant Cole became the single
object of his pursuit, and, his eye once falling upon him, he
had followed him like a Nemesis throughout the whole desperate race until he came up with him in my possession.

I raised my hand and said: "Don't shoot this man: he
has surrendered."

P—— answered, with an oath: "The rascal tried to hang
me this morning." I knew that he had been in the enemy's
hands, and asked the prisoner if what he charged was
true. There was a moment's hesitation, and no response;
then the crack of a pistol, and Lieutenant Cole fell against
my side and rolled to the ground between his horse and

mine. I dismounted and took his belt, with a pair of revolvers, from around him. Let me pay this tribute to his
memory—both pistols were empty. I believe I failed to
state that when I overtook him he was bleeding profusely
from a wound in the breast, which he had received in the
fight. As I moved away he rolled his dying eyes toward
me with a look I shall never forget and I would gladly have
tarried to give him such comfort as I could. But this was
no time for sympathy, and I hurried back to the road.

The prisoners were sent South under guard of 4 men.

Returning from Richmond after delivering our prisoners
at Libby prison, we met near Rapidan Station a party of 19
prisoners and 17 mules, under guard of 5 men, captured

---

PROVOST MARSHAL'S OFFICE, A. N. VA.,

*Nov. 22* 1864.

Pass *Pvt. J. Williamson, guard with*

To *prisoners*

*Richmond & return on 24 Nov.*

By order of Gen. R. E. LEE.

*Cornelius Boyle*

Maj. & P. M., A. N. Va., comd'g at Gordonsville.

---

by Captain Montjoy near Winchester. Farther on, we met
a squad of 8 prisoners captured by Lieutenant Frank Turner
near Summit Point. At Culpeper Court House we fell in
with a guard and 23 prisoners that had been captured by
Captain Chapman in the Valley. From this one can form
some idea of the number of prisoners that, when the armies
were in motion, were captured daily by Mosby's Rangers.

*Sunday, November 20.*—Company F met at Paris. Lieut.
Frank Turner was sent to the Valley with a detachment of
32 men. Within one mile of a brigade camp near Summit
Point he captured 8 men and an equal number of horses and
mules. He sent out his captures under guard and then
moved off toward Winchester.

After marching around through rain, snow and sleet for two days, on the 22d he met Company K (52 men) of the Twelfth New York Cavalry on the turnpike about 2 miles below Charlestown. He routed them, killing and wounding several and capturing 14 prisoners and 12 horses with their equipments. He returned to Fauquier on the 23d, without loss or injury, except one horse wounded.

*Wednesday, November 23.*—About 65 men of Companies C and E met at Paris. Led by Lieut. John Russell, they crossed the Shenandoah at Berry's Ferry towards evening and moving off in the direction of White Post, lay in the woods until midnight, when Mosby and Capt. William Chapman joined them. On the morning of the 24th, while out with a scouting party, Chapman captured 5 prisoners, who were sent off in charge of Frank M. Angelo. Seeing a foraging party with a small train of wagons, Chapman hastened back to the command with this information and Mosby started in pursuit. The wagons were overtaken just as they met another

LIEUT. W. GARLAND SMITH, CO. G.
From a recent Photograph.

train coming from camp. As a charge had been ordered before the approach of the second train had been noticed, the men dashed on and, scattering the guards, drove them into the brigade camp. For a time everything was in confusion, but the Federals rallied and the Rangers were compelled to beat a hasty retreat. Mosby was riding a young horse, which broke its bit and become unmanageble. By the coolness of his men and his own presence of mind he was enabled to escape. Captain Chapman had his horse killed, but John Kirwin, of Company C, dismounted and gave his horse to Chapman, while he jumped up behind a comrade and made his way out.

Frank M. Angelo, while proceeding along with his prisoners, fell in with a party of the Federals who had struck across the country to cut our men off from the river, and was captured. He was taken to Martinsburg and put in jail. On the first night of his imprisonment he opened the jail door and boldly walked out, reaching Fauquier safely on the following day. (See Appendix, XLI.)

*Sunday, November 27.*—Captain Montjoy, with Company D, went down into the lower part of Loudoun, in search of the Loudoun Rangers. Not finding them at Waterford, one of their favorite resorts, he proceeded in the direction of Leesburg. At Goresville he fell in with a detachment under the command of Lieutenant Graham, who had been on a raid to Leesburg, where they had captured Fred. Smith and Cleveland Coleman. As soon as attacked, Keyes' men started on a run, one party, under Graham, making for the Potomac, while the other, under Lieutenant Rhodes, rushed wildly along toward Leesburg. They lost about 20 in all, killed, wounded and captured ; among the prisoners were Lieutenants Graham and Rhodes.[11]

---

[11] BURTNETE to STEVENSON, Nov. 28 : "I have been in Loudoun 4 miles. Mosby is in command. His force is scattered in squads from 25 to 150. About 100 turned off at Hamilton toward Fauquier County ; the balance came this way (Point of Rocks) in detachments. Lieutenant Graham, of Keyes' Cavalry, with 34 men, went out this morning at 6 o'clock beyond Leesburg and captured the assistant adjutant general of General Gordon and one private. Returning he met the enemy at Goresville in force. Graham's command was cut in the center certain, were driven within 2 miles of this place, and Lieutenant Graham captured ; the other made for Leesburg, with Lieutenant Rhodes ; these have not been heard from. But 16 of the command have come in ; what has become of the remainder is unknown. Mosby has returned toward Hamilton, and will in all probability remain there for the night. A force of 200 cavalry from Mouth of Monocacy, 14 miles from Hamilton, and an equal force from Harper's Ferry, 18 miles from there, could use up Mosby's command. I can send Keyes to Monocacy to pilot the 200 stationed there to Hamilton. Captain Keyes has 25 men for duty."

KEYES to ADAMS, Nov. 29 : "I have the honor to report that a detachment of this command of 34 men, under the command of Lieutenant Robt. Graham, left camp on the 28th instant, between 5 and 6 a. m., crossed the river at Cheek's Ford, proceeded toward Leesburg, crossed the Leesburg road at Big

As Captain Montjoy, with Lieutenant Grogan, was leading his men in the pursuit, he was killed by a chance shot
fired by one of the fugitives near the "Burnt Chimney."
One of the Federals, without even looking behind, put his
pistol over his shoulder and fired, the ball striking Montjoy
in the head. He was a
brave, dashing young officer. The following order,
issued by Colonel Mosby,
shows the esteem in which
he was held. He was
buried in the cemetery at
Warrenton.

CAPT. R. P. MONTJOY, CO. D.
Killed near Goresville, Loudoun Co., Va.

"GENERAL ORDERS,
No. —.

"HEADQUARTERS 43D
BATTALION P. R.
*December 3, 1864.*

"The Lieutenant-Colonel
commanding announces to
the Battalion, with emo-
tions of deep sorrow, the
death of Captain R. P.
Montjoy, who fell in action
near Leesburg on the 27th
ultimo, a costly sacrifice to
victory. He died too early
for liberty and his country's cause, but not too early for his
own fame. To his comrades in arms he has bequeathed an
immortal example of daring and valor, and to his country a
name that will brighten the page of her history."

Spring, there struck the Catoctin Mountain, crossed the Winchester pike at
Clark's Gap, then proceeded to Dry Mill, south of Leesburg, there took the road
to Leesburg ; heard that a small force of 15 or 20 rebels were in town ; charged
through the town and captured Captain Smith, adjutant-general on Major-
General Gordon's staff ; also captured one private belonging to the Loudoun
Cavalry. Left Leesburg and took the road leading to Point of Rocks. Met
Mosby's command at Goresville, numbering from 150 to 200 men, where a
small skirmish took place. Lieutenant Graham and Lieutenant Rhodes and 5
or 6 privates are still missing.

"The loss of the enemy was Captain Montjoy killed, who, it was said was in
command ; one lieutenant wounded, and 2 privates killed."

BURTNETE to STEVENSON, Dec. 6 : "Information from various sources,

After Montjoy's death, Lieut. Alfred Glascock was appointed Captain of Company D.

The Artillery Company was disbanded, pursuant to the following order issued by the War department:

SPECIAL ORDERS, }
   No. 261. }

            ADJT. AND INSP. GENERAL'S OFFICE, }
                *Richmond, Nov. 2, 1864.* }

XVII. The company of artillery attached to the command of Lieut. Col. John S. Mosby and organized under the authority of the Secretary of War, is hereby disbanded. The men will be incorporated into the other companies of the command or be forwarded to Camp Lee for general assignment as conscripts.

By order of the Secretary of War.

    JOHN W. RIELY,
   *Assistant Adjutant-General.*

LIEUT. JOHN N. MURPHY, CO. G.
From a Photograph taken when Captain of Co. C, 9th Virginia Cavalry.

On Monday, November 28, the Artillery Company met for reorganization and, as Company G, elected as Captain, Thos. W. T. Richards, brother of Capt. A. E. Richards. The other officers were not elected until some time after, when John N. Murphy was chosen First Lieutenant, W. Garland Smith, Second Lieutenant, and John W. Puryear, Third Lieutenant.

At the breaking out of the war, Capt. T. W. T. Richards left Washington City, where he was a student in Colum-

each not cognizant of the other, satisfies me that Mosby with 300 men, was to-day at Dry Mill, 2½ miles westward from Leesburg. He has Lieutenants Graham and Rhodes, of Keyes' Cavalry, and several prisoners from General Merritt's command. He has informed citizens that he intends to hang Lieu-

bia College, enlisting first in the Eighth Virginia Infantry, and afterwards serving in the Seventh Virginia Cavalry. He joined Mosby, and in the fight on May 3d, 1863, at Warrenton Junction, was wounded and taken prisoner; he returned to his command after an imprisonment of 12 months. The letter here given, from General Lee to Secretary Seddon, is a guarantee of his fitness for the position. He went to the Northern Neck, but did not meet the success anticipated and again returned to his command.

HEADQUARTERS ARMY NORTHERN VIRGINIA, }
*August 9, 1864.* }

Hon. SECRETARY OF WAR, *Richmond.*

SIR: When applied to some time ago to devise some mode to relieve the people of the Northern Neck and the

CAPT. T. W. T. RICHARDS,
CO. G.

From a War-time Photograph.

South side of the Rappahannock from outrages by the enemy, I advised that all citizens capable of bearing arms be organized for the defense of their property and families. At the same time I inquired of Colonel Mosby if he could recommend some one, experienced in the kind of service which the necessities of the exposed districts will require, to aid in organizing the citizens and controlling their operations. He has recently replied to my letter and recommended very highly the bearer of this, Mr. Thomas W. Richards, as a man of approved courage, of good character, and fitted by experience for the duty. I therefore respectfully advise that you send Mr. Richards to the country in question, with a letter to the most prominent citizens, explanatory of his object, and asking their co-operation, at the same time giving him authority to raise a command for local defense in conformity to law, but strictly prohibiting him from receiving any absentees from the army or persons

---

tenant Graham as a deserter from the C. S. Army. Graham's term of service was out before his term of service, one year, had expired. You may rely upon this information as correct. Cannot something be done to take Mosby's command? Corporal Tretapoe, who took French Bill, shot one of Mosby's men yesterday; he died this morning at Lovettsville. He is out again after more."

liable to enrollment in the general service. I think such a command, well managed, will contribute greatly to the security of the people and their property.

Very respectfully, your obedient servant,

R. E. LEE, *General.*

[Indorsement.]

*August 10, 1864.*

Grant such authority as is recommended by General Lee. Let the officer have a certified copy of this letter from General Lee, which will be his best recommendation to the citizens of the Northern Neck. Refer him, too, to General Kemper, to whom he will report for the present, and will co-operate with the reserves.

J. A. S., *Secretary.*

Lieut. John N. Murphy first enlisted in the Ninth Virginia Cavalry, in which regiment he was promoted to the captaincy of Company C. Owing to poor health, he was kept away from his company, and being unwilling to deprive his officers of the promotion they merited by continual service, he resigned. On recovering, a captain's commission was given him to recruit a company in the Northern Neck. He there experienced the same difficulties that Richards did, and joined him in forming Company G.

# CHAPTER XXIV.

On the 28th of November, 1864, while a little party of us were sitting around the fireside after dinner, at the hospitable mansion at Ayreshire, near Upperville, the residence of Mr. George S. Ayre, our host came in and said :

"Boys, I don't know that there is anything wrong, but I think you had better be out and looking around. One of the black boys says he heard a number of shots out toward Upperville, and heard some one calling out ' Halt.' "

We immediately went to the stable and got up our horses. While doing so we heard several shots fired. Soon a boy rode up to the gate, pale with fright, and asked how he could get to the mountains, saying : "The Yankees are in Upperville !"

We soon saw flames bursting out in the direction of town, from burning hay-stacks, barns and stables. Later we learned that two brigades of Federal cavalry, under General Merritt, had crossed the Shenandoah at Berry's Ferry and advanced through Ashby's Gap ; that they had come over for the purpose of laying waste the country. As an excuse for this savage and barbarous proceeding, they claimed to do so with the object of driving Mosby from the country. Mosby, however, remained and was among those least affected by the burning.

At night the Federal forces camped near Upperville, while around them on all sides the dull fires blazed lazily. Ever and anon, as the night wind stirred up the dying embers of the result of some poor farmer's toil, the bright flames would shoot up for a few moments, illuminating the scene and then again relapsing into darkness.

Early on the morning of the 29th we arose, hoping to find the enemy leaving, after their acts of the previous day. But it was a vain hope—we found their work of destruction was only commenced. Another brigade of Federal cavalry crossed the Shenandoah and marched through Snicker's Gap to join the force of military incendiaries. Soon the curling smoke was rising in dense volumes, streaming heavenward, as if appealing to God for mercy, or invoking His vengeance upon the authors of these foul deeds, while around the fires dark forms were flitting, like demons let loose to perform on earth their hellish work. As the fires became more numerous, the heavy mass of smoke spread out and settled over the Valley like a thick fog, obscuring the view so that at one time, while riding along with a few of our men, we could distinctly hear the voices of our enemies in conversation, although we could not see them.

The Federals separated into three parties, one of which went along the Bloomfield road and down Loudoun, in the direction of the Potomac; another passed along the Piedmont pike to Rectortown, Salem and around to Middleburg; while the main body kept along the turnpike to Aldie, where they struck the Snickersville pike. Thus they scoured the country completely from the Blue Ridge to the Bull Run mountains.[1]

---

[1] As all efforts made to drive out or destroy Mosby and his command had so far proved fruitless, Halleck sent the following dispatch to Sheridan:

HALLECK to SHERIDAN, Nov. 26: "It seems to me that before any cavalry is sent away, Mosby's band should be broken up, as he is continually threatening our lines."

"SHERIDAN to HALLECK, Nov. 26: "I will soon commence work on Mosby. Heretofore I have made no attempt to break him up, as I would have employed ten men to his one, and for the reason that I have made a scape-goat of him for the destruction of private rights. Now there is going to be an intense hatred of him in that portion of this Valley, which is nearly a desert. I will soon commence on Loudoun County, and let them know there is a God in Israel. Mosby has annoyed me considerably, but the people are beginning to see that he does not injure me a great deal, but causes a loss to them of all they have spent their lives in accumulating. Those people who live in the vicinity of Harper's Ferry are the most villainous in this Valley, and have not yet been hurt much. If the railroad is interfered with, I will make some of them poor. Those who live at home, in peace and plenty, want the duello part of this war to go on; but when they have to bear their burden by loss of property and comforts, they will cry for peace."

In his determination to rid himself of his troublesome enemy, Sheridan is-

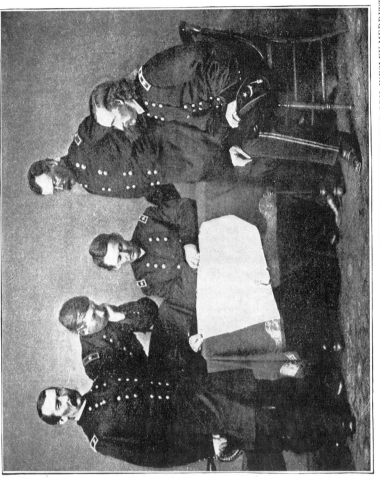

MAJ.-GEN. P. H. SHERIDAN, COL. JAS. W. FORSYTH, CHIEF OF STAFF, BVT. MAJ.-GEN. WESLEY MERRITT, BVT. BRIG.-GEN. THOS. C. DEVIN, BVT. MAJ.-GEN. GEO. A. CUSTER.

From Monday afternoon, November 28th, until Friday morning, December 2d, they ranged through the beautiful Valley of Loudoun and a portion of Fauquier County, burn-

sued these orders to Major-General Merritt, commanding First Cavalry Division, under date of Nov. 27th :

"You are hereby directed to proceed to-morrow morning at 7 o'clock with the two brigades of your Division now in camp to the east side of the Blue Ridge, via Ashby's Gap, and operate against the guerrillas in the district of country bounded on the south by the line of the Manassas Gap Railroad as far east as White Plains, on the east by the Bull Run range, on the west by the Shenandoah River, and on the north by the Potomac. This section has been the hot-bed of lawless bands, who have, from time to time, depredated upon small parties on the line of army communications, on safe-guards left at houses, and on all small parties of our troops. Their real object is plunder and highway robbery. To clear the country of these parties that are bringing destruction upon the innocent as well as their guilty supporters by their cowardly acts, you will consume and destroy all forage and subsistence, burn all barns and mills and their contents, and drive off all stock in the region the boundaries of which are above described. This order must be literally executed, bearing in mind, however, that no dwellings are to be burned and that no personal violence be offered to the citizens. The ultimate results of the guerrilla system of warfare is the total destruction of all private rights in the country occupied by such parties. This destruction may as well commence at once, and the responsibility of it must rest upon the authorities at Richmond, who have acknowledged the legitimacy of guerrilla bands. The injury done this army by them is very slight. The injury they have indirectly inflicted upon the people and upon the rebel army, may be counted by millions. The Reserve Brigade of your division will move to Snickersville on the 29th. Snickersville should be your point of concentration, and the point from which you should operate in destroying toward the Potomac. Four days' subsistence will be taken by the command. Forage can be gathered from the country through which you pass. You will return to your present camp, via Snicker's Gap, on the fifth day."

In addition to Merritt's three brigades, Colonel Stagg was ordered to send out 4 regiments :

Dana to Stagg, Nov. 28 : "You will detail two regiments to march to-morrow morning at daylight, one on the crest of the mountains, the other along the foot, to Paris. These regiments will, when practicable, keep up communication with each other by a line of mounted men, who will pay particular attention to securing the stock which is said to be secreted on the mountains. Both regiments will carry out previous orders in regard to destroying, etc. Send two other regiments at the same time to Millville, and, if possible, to Middleburg, for the purpose of completing unfinished work in that country, as well as to destroy a quantity of rebel government pork said to be secreted at or near Millville. The commanding officers of these regiments will use their best endeavors to discover any work remaining unfinished and give the finishing stroke. All four regiments will concentrate near Philomont in the afternoon, and by patrols and pickets watch the mouth of Loudoun Valley along the pike from this place to Middleburg, securing all stock left behind and any that is being driven away, before the return march of General Devin. They will remain on this duty until the return of General Devin, provided he returns by 4 p. m.; if not, they will march to camp. Let them use every exertion to kill or capture any guerrillas that may be seen, by decoying them into ambush or in some other way."

Stevenson, in order that no loop-hole for escape should be left, and anxious to lend a helping hand, wrote Sheridan, Nov. 28 :

" Mosby is lying with his command to-night in the neighborhood of Hamil--

ing and laying waste.  They robbed the people of everything they could destroy or carry off—horses, cows, cattle, sheep, hogs, etc. ;  killing poultry, insulting women, pillaging houses, and in many cases robbing even the poor negroes.

ton, and between there and Waterford.  If Snicker's Gap could be occupied, I will send Twelfth Pennsylvania Cavalry to Gregory's Gap and Hillsborough crossing, and hold Keyes' Gap with infantry, so that Merritt might use up the concern.  Their only chance of escape would be by Leesburg.  Of course, Merritt should be notified.  If this programme suits you, I will carry it out. My information in regard to Mosby's command is reliable."

SHERIDAN to STEVENSON, in reply :

"Snicker's Gap will be occupied early to-morrow morning, and Merritt will be notified to-night.  Go on with your programme."

Stevenson thereupon issued the following orders to Colonel Pierce of the Twelfth Pennsylvania and Colonel Peale of the Eighteenth Connecticut :

"Colonel Pierce will move promptly at 4 o'clock to-morrow morning with his regiment, every man with 60 rounds of ammunition, two days' rations and forage, so as to occupy Gregory's Gap and the Hillsborough crossing of the Blue Ridge by daylight to-morrow morning.  Send out pickets along the top of the mountain to cover the mountain paths ; cross Shenandoah River at Kabletown. This part of a combined movement must not fail.  Snicker's Gap and Keyes' Gap will be occupied by other troops.  There will be a grand drive for Mosby on east side of ridge, and he must not be permitted to escape by either Gregory's Gap or Hillsborough road crossing.  Connect your command with pickets along the top of the mountain from Gregory's Gap to Hillsborough road. The command will remain at these gaps until Thursday morning unless ordered to return to camp sooner.  A proper camp guard will be left in the camp at Charlestown.

Colonel Peale will move at daylight to-morrow morning promptly, with 350 men of his command, to Harper's Ferry, each man to have 40 rounds of ammunition and two days' rations, leaving the balance of his command as camp guard.  These men are to be used as part of a combined movement to catch Mosby, and therefore there must be no failure to be on prompt time."

This formidable array was still thought insufficient to drive out the little band of " Mosby's Men," and General Augur ordered Colonel Gamble to send 800 cavalry to unite with Merritt :

AUGUR to TAYLOR, Nov. 29 :  " Direct Gamble to send 800 cavalry, under Sweitzer, to report to General Merritt, near Snickersville, with 5 days' rations and as much forage as is necessary.  They must procure corn from the country. They should leave to-morrow morning and by the route indicated in General Sheridan's dispatch."

Yet this "combined movement," powerful as it was, did not drive out Mosby and his men, who continued to occupy the same ground until after the surrender of General Lee.

*Report of Brevet Major-General Wesley Merritt, commanding First Cavalry Division.*

HEADQUARTERS FIRST CAVALRY DIVISION,
*December 6, 1864.*

Major WILLIAM RUSSELL, JR.,
*Asst. Adjt.-Gen., Hdqrs. Cavalry, Middle Military Division.*

MAJOR :  In compliance with instructions received direct from army headquarters, I marched with the division, via Ashby's Gap, to the east of the Blue

They burned all the mills and factories, as well as hay, wheat, corn, straw and every description of forage. Barns and stables, whether full or empty, were burned. At Mrs. Fletcher's (a widow), where the hogs had been killed for her

Ridge, for the purpose of destroying all mills, barns, forage, driving off stock, and capturing and dispersing the guerrilla bands in a district of country described in orders. After passing through Ashby's Gap, two regiments of the Second Brigade were ordered to move to the north, along the foot of the mountains, spreading out well over the country toward Bloomfield, carrying out the orders, while a regiment of the First Brigade, for the same purpose, was sent, via Grigsby's store, to the west of Piedmont. These regiments were ordered to meet the division the same evening near Upperville, where it encamped on the night of the 28th of November.

The following morning the First Brigade was ordered to march to Rectortown, whence it was ordered to send out strong columns to Salem and White Plains, and, marching across the country, collect its strength at Middleburg, the forces from White Plains and Salem to pursue separate routes to that place. From Middleburg the entire force was to move to Philomont, and thence to Snickersville, keeping out strong flanking columns on the right toward Millville and to the left through Bloomfield, to the foot of the mountains. In this manner the country as far north as the Little River turnpike was thoroughly swept over and destroyed by the evening of the second day.

MAJ.-GEN. H. W. HALLECK, U. S. A.

Early on the morning of the third day the Second Brigade was ordered to march via Philomont, Circleville, Hamilton, Waterford, and along the Catoctin Creek to the Potomac, and meeting, at Lovettsville, a force of the Reserve Brigade which was ordered to move east of the Blue Ridge and between the ridge and Short Mountain to the Potomac, both columns to return along the pike from Lovettsville through Hillsborough and Purcellville. Both these commands reached Snickersville on the evening of the fourth day. On the third day a force of the Reserve Brigade was ordered to march down the Shenandoah, between that stream and the Blue Ridge. This force went as far down

winter's supply of meat, the soldiers made a pile of rails upon which the hogs were placed and burned. They even went to the Poor House and burned and destroyed the supplies provided for the helpless and dependent paupers. On various previous occasions, however, the Alms House had been visited by raiding parties, so that at this time there was but little left, but of that little the larger portion was taken.

Colonel Mosby did not call the command together, therefore there was no organized resistance, but Rangers managed to save a great deal of live stock for the farmers by driving it off to places of safety. In many instances, after the first day of the burning, we would run off stock from

---

the river as Rock Ford. The First Brigade marched on the third day, with its collected cattle, to Snickersville, from Philomont sending out parties to complete the work of destruction.

On the morning of the fourth day, four regiments of the First Brigade were detached, two in the direction of Millville and Middleburg, to complete any unfinished work in that country, and the other two to move, one on the crest of the mountains and the other along the foot, keeping up connection, when possible, by a line of mounted men and marching as far as Ashby's Gap. These regiments were ordered to return across the country to the pike near Philomont, and watch the mouth of the valley until the return of the columns from the Potomac, making dispositions to capture or destroy any guerrillas who might be moving in advance of these columns.

In all these movements the orders from army headquarters were most fully carried out ; the country on every side of the general line of march was in every instance swept over by flankers from the columns, and in this way the entire valley was gone over. The guerrillas were exceedingly careful to avoid any encounter with any of the parties, even the smallest, that were out on this duty. Efforts were made to run them down or capture them by stratagem, but these in most instances failed. The sides of the mountain bordering Loudoun Valley are practicable throughout their entire extent for horsemen, and the guerrillas, being few in numbers, mounted on fleet horses and thoroughly conversant with the country, had every advantage of my men.

I transmit herewith reports of brigade commanders, as also tabular statements of the destruction done and cattle driven off. Large numbers of the cattle were destroyed or consumed. Most of the fatted hogs were destroyed on the march to camp. W. MERRITT, *Brevet Maj.-Gen. Comdg.*

---

*Report of Lieut.-Col. Casper Crowninshield, commanding Reserve Brigade.*

Pursuant to instructions received from the brevet major-general commanding the Cavalry Corps to move my brigade to Snickersville and communicate with

the path of the raiders into the limits of the district already burned over, and there it was kept undisturbed or in a situation where it could be more easily driven off and concealed. We also annoyed the raiders considerably by hovering around them in small squads and suddenly dashing in among them, whenever an opportunity offered, shooting on all

Brevet Major-General Merritt, I broke camp at Stephenson's Depot on the 29th of November at 3 a. m. and marched to Snickersville. Leaving the Sixth U. S. Cavalry and 30 men of the Second Massachusetts Cavalry to hold the gap, I marched to Bloomfield, expecting to meet Brevet Major General Merritt near that point. At Bloomfield my advance guard was fired upon by some of Mosby's men, and 2 of the First U. S. Cavalry were slightly wounded. Here I learned that our cavalry had moved toward Union. I followed on to Union, thence to Philomont, and finally joined Brevet Major-General Merritt at Snickersville, where the brigade encamped that night, picketing the gap, the mountain road, the Bloomfield road, and to the left as far as the Snickersville and Aldie pike. 30th, the Second Massachusetts and Second U. S. Cavalry were sent through Wood Grove and Hillsborough to Cave Head, on the Potomac, and thence along

BVT. BRIG.-GEN. THOMAS C. DEVIN, U. S. A.

From a Photograph taken during the War.

the river road to Lovettsville, destroying all grain, forage, mills, distilleries, etc., and driving in all stock in that part of the country; at Lovettsville they joined Brevet Brigadier-General Devin's brigade. The Sixth U. S. Cavalry was sent upon the west side of the Blue Ridge, between the ridge and the river, going as far as Rockford, and returning at night to Snicker's Gap, where they remained. The balance of the brigade remained in camp and guarded the herds which had thus far been driven in.

December 1, the First and Sixth U. S. Cavalry drove the herds across the river and went into camp near the river. The Second U. S. and Second

sides and then scampering off.   In this way quite a number
were killed and wounded.

W elt Hatcher, seeing an officer riding along in the midst
of his men, thought he was General Custer, and riding up,
fired, mortally wounding him.   The officer's men pressed a
carriage into service and took him to the Pot House, where he
died.   After shooting, Hatcher escaped uninjured, although
fired upon from all along the line.

---

Massachusetts returned to Snickersville and went into camp.    2d, the Second
U. S. and Second Massachusetts Cavalry rejoined the brigade.   One regiment of
the brigade assisted in driving the herds and the balance of the brigade
marched in the rear of the division.   The brigade went into camp with the
division near Stone Chapel and picketed the country in its front, connecting
on the left with General Devin's and on the right with Colonel Stagg's pickets.
During the march one of the First U. S. Cavalry, who had straggled from the
column, was killed by a bushwhacker near Berryville.    3d, marched in the
same order as yesterday and went into camp near Kernstown.

# CHAPTER XXV.

For about a week a patrol of from 60 to 100 Federal Cavalry had been coming daily to the river at Berry's Ferry. For the purpose of attacking these, a meet was ordered on Friday, December 16th. Accordingly, Captain Chapman crossed the mountains above Ashby's Gap and bivouacked for the night in a gorge nearly opposite Swift Shoal Mill. Some few of the men from the neighborhood went to their homes, while the others tied their horses and lay down in the snow. Early on the morning of the 17th, Chapman crossed the Shenandoah with about 125 men. As the patrol would sometimes come by way of White Post and return by way of Millwood, and at other times approach from the direction of Millwood and return via White Post, Chapman divided his command so as to strike the party coming either way. Each party put out pickets to give notice of the approach of the enemy.

Just a little before noon the Federals—a detachment of about 100 of the Fourteenth Pennsylvania Cavalry, under command of Capt. William H. Miles—were observed by the party posted nearest Millwood. The Federals were informed of the presence of our men by a negro, but mistook the location. They were advancing cautiously, with flankers thrown out, but on the opposite side of the wooded road from that on which Chapman's men, about 60 in number, were posted. Chapman had been cut off and Lieut. John Russell, being the only commissioned officer present, was in command. He told the men they could not attempt to cross the river without being butchered and must whip the enemy. " Charge them with a yell," said Russell ; " don't fire a shot until you are within 40 paces, and we will whip them." His orders were obeyed to the letter.

To the credit of Captain Miles it should be stated that he made a desperate effort to hold his men, who broke and ran, leaving their brave Captain, with 10 or 12 faithful followers, to stand the brunt of the battle. They, too, were forced to retreat. Miles was mortally wounded by Wiltshire, and the few remaining men were either wounded or escaped through the brush. Miles' horse was a very fine animal. Charles Biedler followed her for some distance, but she escaped in the direction of the Federal camp.

CHARLES E. BIEDLER, CO. C.
From a Photograph taken during the War.

The detachment posted near Swift Shoal Mills came up, but were too late to take a hand in the fight.

Captain Miles was taken to a house near the road, where he died in short time. One lieutenant was killed and another captured. Of the entire patrol but few escaped. About 30 were killed and wounded, and the prisoners, 68 in number, were sent out with a guard of 10 men, Joseph Millan in charge, and turned over to McCausland, at Peola Mills. Over 60 horses were captured, with equipments. None of our men was injured.[1]

---

[1] Gen. TIBBITS to Major RUSSELL: "The party sent to Millwood have just returned, having gone to the river at Berry's Ferry. The patrol under Captain Miles was attacked by about 300 men—2 companies of Mosby's command and a detachment from McCausland's command. Captain Miles was killed, 1 lieutenant wounded, and 1 lieutenant captured. Our loss besides was 10 killed, 17 wounded, with 20 prisoners. The enemy immediately after making the attack, recrossed the river and could not be overtaken. The citizens report that only 20 men were taken across the river as prisoners."

A few days after this, Mosby, who had been on a visit to Richmond, returned to the command, wearing three stars on his collar, showing that he was now a full colonel. Capt. William Chapman was promoted to the rank of Lieutenant-Colonel, and Capt. A. E. Richards to that of Major. This was in accordance with the following recommendation of Colonel Mosby:

*December 6, 1864.*

Hon. JAMES A. SEDDON, *Secretary of War:*

SIR: I beg leave to recommend, in order to secure greater efficiency in my command, that it be divided into two battalions, each to be commanded by a major. The scope of duties devolving upon me being of a much wider extent than on officers of the same rank in the regular service, but small time is allowed me to attend to the details of organization, discipline, etc. I am confident that the arrangement I propose would give me much more time, both for planning and executing enterprises against the enemy. I would recommend Capt. William H. Chapman (commanding Company C, Forty-third Virgina Partizan Rangers Battalion) and Capt. Adolphus E. Richards, commanding Company B, same battalion, for the command of the two battalions proposed. They have both on many occasions been distinguished for valor and skill, to which my reports bear witness, especially so in engagements with the enemy at Dranesville, Aldie, Charlestown and Newtown.

LIEUT.-COL. WILLIAM H. CHAPMAN,
43d Battalion Virginia Cavalry (Mosby's Rangers).
From a War-time Photograph.

Very respectfully, your obedient servant,
JNO. S. MOSBY, *Lieut.-Colonel.*

After the promotion of Richards, Robert S. Walker was selected for the post of Captain in Co. B—a well-merited tribute to his gallant record.

On the 19th of December, Bush. Underwood, while scouting in Fairfax with a detachment of about 20 men, saw an ambulance and two wagons with an escort equal in numbers to his own force, about a mile and a half from Vienna. Underwood instructed O. S. Newcomb to charge the rear of the escort with a portion of the men, while he attacked them in front with the remainder. The men, with the exception of 2 or 3, misunderstanding the order, followed Newcomb, leaving Underwood to fight with his few comrades. Without hesitation Underwood boldly charged, driving back the escort. Before recovering from their surprise they were attacked in the rear by Newcomb and routed. Three men and 7 horses were captured and 3 or 4 of the guards wounded. None of Underwood's party was injured. In the ambulance was Colonel Sweitzer and Captain Gaylord, of the Sixteenth New York Cavalry, both of whom escaped by jumping from the ambulance and running off through the pines, leaving their effects behind.[2]

On the 21st of December, while Col. Mosby was at the house of Joseph Blackwell, in Fauquier, attending the wedding of J. Lavender, our ordnance sergeant, word was brought that a body of Federal cavalry was advancing on the Salem road, a few miles distant. Without interrupting the wed-

[2] Colonel WELLS to TAYLOR, Dec. 19 : " I have just received a telegram from the provost-marshal at Fairfax Court House, stating that 30 rebels attacked an ambulance containing Colonel Sweitzer, Sixteenth New York Cavalry, and Captain Gaylord, same regiment ; wounding 1 man of the escort and capturing 1 wagon and 7 horses. Colonel Sweitzer and Captain Gaylord escaped. The affair occurred 1½ miles from Vienna. Our men are in hot pursuit. Result as yet unknown. The provost-marshal at Vienna reports that it is reported that Colonel Schweitzer has been recaptured."

GAMBLE to RAYMOND, Dec. 20 : " Your telegram received. Colonel Sweitzer is safe. I have just received his report of the affair, which will be forwarded the first opportunity. He had 3 men wounded and 3 horses captured of his escort. His regiment turned out and scoured the country to Aldie. The cavalry ordered from your headquarters last night will leave here in an hour, under Lieutenant-Colonel Clendenin, for the Loudoun Valley."

ding feast, Mosby, with Thomas Love, rode out to reconnoitre. He came up with the Federals on the road to Rectortown, and seeing them building fires, concluded that they
were going into camp. Instead of doing so, they had only
halted to warm themselves and to rest. Sending a man to
notify Chapman and Richards to get their men together so
as to be ready to attack
them in the morning, he
started off with Love to
make arrangements for the
morrow.

As they were passing the
house of Ludwell Lake,
Mosby concluded to stop
and get supper. Leaving
their horses tied at the
front gate, they entered
and were soon seated at
table, enjoying a cup of
coffee and a warm supper.
In the room with Mosby
was Mr. Lake and his
daughter, Mrs. Skinner.

Hearing the tramp of
horses around the house,
Mosby opened the door
leading to the back yard
and saw there a number
of cavalrymen. He hastily
closed the door and turned
to the other door, which

MAJOR A. E. RICHARDS,
43d Battalion Virginia Cavalry (Mosby's
Rangers).
From a War-time Photograph.

then opened and a party of Federal officers and soldiers
entered. Mosby's hat, overcoat and cape were lying in a
corner of the room. As the soldiers entered, he put up his
hands to his coat collar to hide the stars, the emblem of his
rank, as he knew his chances of escape would be better if he
could conceal his identity.

Just then shots were fired from the back yard, and a ball,

passing through the window, struck him in the stomach.
" I am shot!" exclaimed Mosby.  As the firing was continued, the Federal officers and soldiers hurried out of the
room to escape being shot by their own men, leaving Mosby
in the room with Love, Lake and his daughter.  He was
faint, and was bleeding profusely from his wound, but
stepping from the dining room into an adjoining bedroom,
he pulled off his coat with the tell-tale stars, and hiding
it under a bureau, fell on the floor as if dead.

In a few moments the officers returned and struck a light.
They asked Mrs. Skinner who he was.  She replied that he
was a stranger to her.  They then
asked Mosby his name.  He gasped
a few words, saying he was Lieutenant Johnson of the Sixth Virginia.
They opened his pants, pulled up
his shirt, which was saturated with
blood, and the doctor examined the
wound, pronouncing it mortal.  They
then stripped him of his boots and
pants and left the room.

COL. NELSON B. SWEITZER,
16th New York Cavalry.
From a War-time Picture.

When Mosby felt satisfied that
they had all left, he got up and
walked into the room where Lake
and his daughter were sitting by
the fire, to their great astonishment,
for they supposed him dead.  In-
deed Mosby himself at the time thought his wound mortal.
The bullet was in him and he thought his intestines were
cut.

When Mr. Lake regained sufficient composure to realize
the situation, he called a couple of negro boys to get up an
ox-cart and a pair of oxen, to remove Mosby to a place of
safety, in case the enemy should return.  He was rolled up
in blankets and carried to the house of widow Glascock.

A courier was sent to carry the news to the wedding party
at Blackwell's, and soon a number of the men and two doctors
came over.  At Glascock's Mosby found George Slater,

one of our men, and knowing that he was present when
General Stuart was shot, Mosby said: "George, look at
my wound; I think I am shot just like Stuart." Slater
pulled up Mosby's shirt and examined the wound. He said
he thought the ball had passed around from left to right,
which was so. It lodged in the right side, and was extracted
in the morning. Major Richards sent out couriers and ordered the men to meet in the morning at Chappalear's.
Pickets were placed on all the roads, and at the door of
the house where Mosby lay wounded, an ambulance stood,
day and night, with mules harnessed, ready to be driven off
at a moment's warning. In about a week he was removed to
his father's, near Lynchburg.

The cavalrymen Mosby had observed and followed the
night before were detachments of the Thirteenth and Sixteenth New York, under command of Major Frazar.

Adjutant Wm. H. Mosby, with Sergeant H. M. McIlhany, John H. Foster, and four others, learning that the
Federal cavalry were in the neighborhood, started out to
harrass them on their march. They came up with them at
the railroad crossing near Salem, and Adjutant Mosby, seeing the force was so large, gave orders to fall back. In
doing so, Willie Cocke, a youth of about 17, was thrown
from his horse. Thinking the boy would be killed, Sergeant
McIlhany gave him his left arm and stirrup and finally succeeded in getting him up behind him, in the meanwhile firing
on the charging squadron and endeavoring to reach cover
in Bishop's woods. In jumping a fence, his horse fell and
he and Cocke were captured.

When the Federals reached Rectortown, two more of
Mosby's men, Richard Buckner and Robert Parrott, were
added to the number of prisoners. The cavalry then directed their course toward Middleburg, stopping at Lake's,
where Colonel Mosby was wounded, as stated, and Thomas
Love was taken prisoner. At Col. Hamilton Roger's, $2\frac{1}{2}$
miles below Middleburg, they joined the Eighth Illinois
Cavalry, about 11 p. m. Major Frazar and his officers gathered around the prisoners at the camp-fire and exhibited

Colonel Mosby's elegant light colored hat with gilt cord and tassels, with one side turned up and ornamented with a star, together with his overcoat, cape and boots, and tried in vain to have any of the prisoners acknowledge that it belonged to Mosby. The Federals professed great admiration for him, and said if they could be assured he was the wounded man, they would send back their surgeon to attend him. The next morning, when marching down the turnpike, Colonel Clendenin sent for McIlhany and had him ride beside him until they reached Fairfax, questioning him regarding the identity of Mosby and the condition of his command, to all of which McIlhany gave evasive answers.[3] He then tried Love, but with no better success.

At Lake's front gate, hitched to the old-time horse rack, stood Colonel Mosby's fine sorrel, and Love's bay mare. Their equipments were all new and similar to those used by Federal Officers, hence it was supposed that as each man rode off he thought that there were two of his own party

SERGT. H. M. McILHANY, CO. F.
From a War-time Photograph.

[3] McIlhany, giving an account of his treatment, says: "On arriving at Fairfax Court House, the prisoners were placed in the old county jail and the next day sent to the Old Capitol at Washington, where there were about 75 of Mosby's men confined. We were kept there until February 6, 1865, when 86 of Mosby's men were handcuffed in pairs and, under guard of a lieutenant and 28 muskets, marched to the Baltimore and Ohio Depot and taken thence to Fort Warren, Boston Harbor. A more enraged set of men were never seen than these, when standing on Capitol street, handcuffed together. When Clark, the superintendent of the Old Capitol prison was asked for a reason for such treatment, he said it was a shame, but believed the officer was afraid and unwilling to start on the journey unless they were handcuffed. One of the hardships at the Old Capitol was the quality of the food, as well as the quantity. The barrels of beef and mess pork were branded 'I. C.,' which

behind, owners of the horses, for they remained undisturbed after the cavalry had all left.

When the Federals discovered that it was Mosby whom they had let slip through their hands, they made every exertion to discover his whereabouts and capture him, and parties were sent through the country in all directions searching for him.[4]

signified 'Inspected and condemned.' When we arrived at Fort Warren, the officer in command would not receive us until the handcuffs were removed. The treatment and food at Fort Warren were far superior to that at the Old Capitol, though bad enough. We were not released until June 15, 1865."

H. M. McIlhany, formerly of Warrenton, now residing at Staunton, Va., joined Mosby's command in 1864. He had been assistant to Longstreet's chief quartermaster, with the rank of captain, hence the three bars on his collar when this picture was taken. At the organization of Company F he was elected first sergeant, but owing to the death of Lieutenant Bowie while on a raid in Maryland, he usually acted as lieutenant, until his active career was cut short by his capture near Salem.

ADJUTANT WM. H. MOSBY,
43d Battalion Virginia Cavalry, C. S. A.
From a War-time Photograph.

[4] GAMBLE to TAYLOR, December 27th : "I have been collecting from various sources all the information possible in regard to Mosby being wounded. The wounding of the rebel major mentioned in Lieutenant-Colonel Clendenin's report occurred, as I am informed, in this manner : Major Frazar, with a part of the Thirteenth and Sixteenth New York Cavalry, while passing a farmhouse in the vicinity of Middleburg, saw a saddled horse fastened to a fence and went to the house. A rebel officer inside came to the door with his boots off and fired his revolver at our men. The men, of course, returned the fire and the officer was shot in the body. Major Frazar did not search the officer for

The news of the wounding of Colonel Mosby spread rapidly, in spite of the efforts made to keep it secret, and it was

---

papers, nor inquire who he was from the people in the house ; neither did he
search the house ; and, although two ambulances and a medical officer were with
the command, the wounded rebel officer was not examined or brought in ; all
of which, in my opinion, any good, efficient officer should have done. I am
also informed that Major Frazar was too much under the influence of liquor to
perform his duty at that time in a proper manner. Whether the rebel officer
observed to be shot in this house was Mosby, or that Mosby was in the same
room at the time with this officer and wounded by the fire of our men into the
room, I am as yet unable to ascertain with any degree of certainty, because I
have heard so many conflicting accounts in regard to it. Under the circumstances, I have deemed it best to send Major Frazar, with 300 men, to scour
that neighborhood and ascertain if possible something definite about it, he being the officer present at the time the rebel officer was shot in the house where
it is supposed Mosby was wounded. I have considered it my duty to report
all the information I have yet been able to obtain, as stated before, in regard to
the matter."

TAYLOR to GAMBLE, Dec. 27 : "The major of rebels reported wounded
by Colonel Clendenin was Mosby. He is in the vicinity of the place where he
was shot. Let the party now out endeavor to find him. The information is
undoubted."

GAMBLE to TAYLOR, Dec. 27 : "Reports have been received from Fairfax
Station and Vienna. All quiet. No reports from Col. Gansevoort at Prospect
Hill, although I have repeatedly ordered him to send his reports at the proper
time. The scout under Capt. Sargent, Eighth Illinois Cavalry, sent out last
night, has returned. He arrived at Thoroughfare Gap two hours too late, and
only captured two prisoners, who escaped in the darkness by the negligence of
Lieut. Kennedy, Eighth Illinois. I will send out Major Frazar, Thirteenth
New York Cavalry, and 300 men, to-morrow at dark, so as to make a night
march unobserved, to the vicinity of Middleburg, to ascertain about the
wounded rebel officer mentioned in your telegram of to-day."

STEVENSON to SHERIDAN, Dec. 29 : "I have very satisfactory evidence that
Mosby was actually shot in a house near Middleburg. He is not dead, but severely or mortally wounded. He was lying in Middleburg and is either there
yet or at the house of a man by the name of Joe or Jim Blackwell, about 5 miles
from Piedmont, to which my informant thinks he has been removed. The
story of his death is not true, but given out to prevent his capture while
wounded. He stays at Middleburg at the house of a man by the name of
Rogers."

SHERIDAN to STEVENSON, Dec. 29 : "Mosby was shot by a party from
Gen. Augur's command at Rector's Cross-Roads. There were 2 or 3 men in
the party ; they fired at Mosby and some of his men through the windows,
wounding Mosby in the abdomen. He was then moved to the house of Widow
Glascock. Torbert tried to catch him there, but he had been taken away in an
ambulance. Torbert searched the house of Rogers, at Middleburg, but he was

a source of much regret to both citizens and soldiers. His wound, though painful, was not dangerous, although at first it was reported to be mortal.

---

not there. Mosby's wound is mortal. He and his party were eating supper when the attack was made on the house by Augur's men."

SHERIDAN to EMORY, Dec. 31 : "How are you getting along ? This storm is unfortunate. I have no news to-day, except the death of Mosby. He died from his wounds at Charlottesville."

*Fairfax C. H., December 31, 1864.*

Colonel WILLIAM GAMBLE, *Commanding Cavalry Brigade :*

COLONEL : In obedience to your command, I have the honor to report concerning the wounding of Colonel Mosby. He was shot by a man of my advance guard under Captain Brown, in Mr. Lake's house, near the Rector's Cross-roads, on the evening of the 21st instant, about 9 p. m., at which time I was in command of the Sixteenth and Thirteenth New York regiments. Several shots were fired, and I was informed that a rebel lieutenant was wounded. I immediately dismounted and entered the house and found a man lying on the floor, apparently in great agony. I asked him his name—he answered, "Lieutenant Johnson, Sixth Virginia Cavalry." He was in his shirt-sleeves — a light blue cotton shirt—no hat—no boots—no insignia of rank ; nothing to denote in the slightest degree that he was not what he pretended to be. I told him I must see his wounds to see whether to bring him or not. I opened, myself, his pants and found that a pistol bullet had entered the abdomen about two inches below and to the left of the navel ; a wound that I felt assured was mortal. I therefore ordered all from the room, remarking, "He will die in twenty-four hours." Being behind time on account of skirmishing all the afternoon with the enemy, I hurried on to meet Lieutenant Colonel Clendenin at Middleburg, according to orders received. Nearly every officer of

SERGT. ROBERT B. PARROTT, CO. F.
From a War Picture.

my command, if not all, saw this wounded man, and no one had the slightest idea that it was Mosby. Captain Brown and Major Birdsall were both in the room with me when this occurred. After arrival at Middleburg I reported the fact of having wounded a rebel lieutenant to Lieutenant-Colonel Clendenin. As soon

General Torbet had started from Winchester on the 19th of December, with Merritt's and Powell's Divisions of Cavalry, numbering about 5,000 men, and crossed the Blue Ridge at Chester's Gap, with the intention of breaking up the Virginia Central Railroad at Gordonsville. Without effecting his object he was compelled to retreat and fall back to the Valley.

---

as the camp fires were lit so that things could be seen, an orderly brought me Mosby's hat dressed with gold cord and star. I then immediately knew it to be a field officer. I took the hat and went immediately among the prisoners, eight in number, of Mosby's men that I had captured, and told them the man who wore that cap was shot dead, and asked them if it was Mosby or not ; it was no use to conceal it if it was, as he was shot dead. They all said ''no,'' that it was not Mosby, that he never had such a hat, etc., etc. Some of them said it was Major Johnson, Sixth Virginia Cavalry, home on leave. In the morning I reported the facts and showed the cap to Colonel Clendenin and Mr. Davis, the guide ; all this, while I considered, as did all my other officers, that the wound was mortal. From Middleburg I came to camp. On this scout, from which I have just returned to-day, I have the honor to state that the man shot in Lake's house was Colonel Mosby. He was moved half an hour after he was shot to Quilly Glascock's, about a mile and a half distant, where he remained three days and had the ball extracted, it having passed around or through the bowels, coming out behind the right thigh. I conversed with several persons who saw him. He was very low the first two days, the third much better. I tracked him to Piedmont, thence to Salem, and out of Salem toward the Warrenton pike. I met pickets in various parts of the country, and understood that until within the last night or two they had extended as far down as Aldie. Various signalizing was carried on by means of white flags above Piedmont. Several persons who saw him in the ambulance report his spitting blood, and it seems to be the general impression that he cannot live. There is no doubt in my mind but what he is yet in the country, concealed ; seriously, if not mortally wounded. In both expeditions I lost neither man nor horse and captured 9 prisoners.

Very respectfully, your obedient servant,

DOUGLAS FRAZAR, *Major Commanding.*

[Indorsement.]

HEADQUARTERS FIRST SEPARATE BRIGADE,

*Fairfax Court-House, Va., January 1, 1865.*

Respectfully forwarded to department headquarters.

I exceedingly regret that such a blunder was made. I have given directions that all wounded officers and men of the enemy be hereafter brought in, although I thought any officer ought to have brains and common sense enough to do so without an order.

W. GAMBLE, *Colonel, Commanding Brigade.*

On their return march (December 26th and 27th) the two divisions passed through Fauquier County by different routes. Having heard of the wounding of Mosby, they made diligent search for him, some of them even going to the house where he was being cared for. They did not find him, however, as he was placed in the ambulance on their approach and driven into the woods, where he was kept concealed until they left the vicinity.

During the passage of this expedition, a number of horses and cattle were taken from the farmers. Many of the Federal cavalry were killed and wounded in skirmishes with Mosby's men.[5]  Our men not only harrassed them through

FAC-SIMILE OF A CALL FOR MEETING OF COMMAND.

the day while on the march, but at night Lieutenant Beattie, with a few men, hung around their camp, sending up rockets and annoying them, to prevent sleep.

On the 29th of December, a detachment of about 300 Federal cavalry, under Major Frazar, came up from Fairfax in search of Mosby, expecting to find him wounded in some of the farm houses. They scoured the country around in the neighborhood of Middleburg, Piedmont and Salem for two days and returned as they came.

[5] The itinerary of this expedition states that of the Reserve Brigade "some 13 enlisted men were captured and shot by guerrillas."

The year 1864 closed with a gloomy outlook for the Confederacy.  Sherman had reached the coast safely.  The news from Hood was unfavorable, although the Southern newspapers endeavored to make the reverse appear. The winter in Virginia was very severe and the ground was covered with snow and sleet for the greater part of the season.

## CHAPTER XXVI.

Although the war was waged as earnestly, and the Southern people were as true to their cause, as at any time since the commencement, still one could see that there was a longing for peace. Nothing showed this under-current of feeling more plainly than the avidity with which people would grasp and disseminate the peace rumors afloat at this time, no matter how absurd or contradictory they might be.

One report was that the Confederate Peace Commissioners—Stephens, Hunter and Campbell—had been received in Washington with great rejoicing at the prospects of peace. That Colonel Mosby, who was absent in the South, had sent orders to Major Richards that no more raids should be undertaken and that all prisoners on hand (not sent South) should be set free—intimating that an armistice had been agreed upon.

Another was to the effect that France and England had recognized the independence of the Confederacy, and declared war against the United States.

Still another rumor was that Lincoln and the United States Congress had agreed to recognize the independence of the Confederacy, with the understanding that both North and South would unite and join forces against Maximillian in Mexico, and that no foreign power was to be allowed a foothold on this Continent.

*Tuesday, January 3, 1865.*—Companies C, E, F and G met at Salem, and under command of Lieut.-Col. William H. Chapman, started to the Northern Neck of Virginia. It had been determined to winter a portion of the Battalion

there, in order to lighten the burden of the people within
the limits of " Mosby's Confederacy," who, owing to the
scarcity of food and forage after the wanton destruction of
Merritt and Custer, were in many instances barely able to
provide for themselves the necessaries of life. The other
companies remained, and were under the command of
Major Richards, during the absence of Colonel Mosby.

DURAND SHACKLEFORD, CO. E.
From a War-time Photograph.

On the 30th of January Major
Richards started from Bloomfield with 30 men for a raid on
the Baltimore and Ohio Railroad, between Harper's Ferry
and. Winchester. When he
reached the road, about 11
o'clock p. m., he found it heavily
guarded by infantry and pa-
trolled by cavalry, so that he
could accomplish nothing. He
sent a portion of his men back,
but kept with him James and
Charles Wiltshire, Charles Dear,
Joseph Bryan, Edwin Gipson,
Will. Sheppard, Bartlett Bolling, John Hearn, and a few
others, in all about 15 of his
best men, and moved off toward
Charlestown. He endeavored
to cross the railroad, but could
not do so without giving an
alarm. Charles Dear and James Wiltshire were sent to
quietly scout along the road, and soon returned with 2 of the
mounted patrols. Richards questioned them, and then turned
them over to Dear and Wiltshire to get the countersign. The
men were questioned separately, and on finding their answers
the same—the word being " Clear "—Richards sent Charles
Wiltshire and Will Sheppard down the railroad to test the
countersign. They came back with 2 prisoners from the
Twelfth Pennsylvania Cavalry.

Among the prisoners was a very communicative Dutchman. After talking with him a while, Richards determined to pay a visit to Reno Camp of the Twelfth Pennsylvania. Taking the Dutchman for a guide, the entire party moved on toward the camp. On the road they were met and halted by a patrol of 4 men, and in reply to the query as to who they were, Richards answered, "Twelfth Pennsylvania, Captain Cook's Company." "All right," said the patrol, and as they advanced they were captured. Richards sent off his prisoners under guard, but kept the Dutchman with him. His force was now reduced to 10 men, and with these he entered the camp. The camp was laid out with cabins on one side, covered with canvas, and opposite were the stables with the horses. As the party rode along, the sentinels were walking their beats, and a soldier coming out of one of the cabins to replenish the fire was captured by Charles Wiltshire. While some of the men were loosing the horses, Bartlett Bolling rode up to a sentinel a short distance off and demanded his surrender. The sentry replied with a shot, which Bolling returned, bringing the man to the ground. The camp being aroused, Richards

EDWIN GIPSON,[1] CO. D.
From a Photograph.

was compelled to get out in a hurry, firing into the cabins as his party retreated. He brought off 8 horses.

As Richards retreated through Charlestown, the enemy opened quite a brisk fire, but all escaped without injury.

*Sunday, February 5.*—Bush. Underwood returned to-day

---

[1] Edwin Gipson was a promising young lawyer who at the close of the war, having earned the reputation of a good soldier, settled down to the quiet practice of his profession. He was bitten by a snake on his farm in 1876, and died from its effects.

from a scout in Fairfax, bringing in 6 prisoners, with their horses and equipments.

Being in the neighborhood of Vienna, with a few men, he left his companions concealed in the pines, while he and William Trammell rode off to a house at some distance in quest of information. A party of Federal Cavalry, which had been sent out in search of him, dashed up to the house before he was aware of their approach. Underwood and Trammell hastily mounted their horses and rode off, closely pursued by the enemy. Reaching Broad Run at a place where the bank formed a steep bluff, they gave their horses the spurs and took a flying leap, leaving their pursuers hesitating on the brink, uncertain whether to shoot or jump. They fired a few shots after the retreating Rangers, which did no harm. Joining his companions, Underwood returned and attacked the party, capturing 6 cavalrymen with their horses and equipments.

*Sunday, February 19.*—I was aroused from my sleep early in the morning by one of the little black boys clattering up the stairs—his feet being encased in a pair of old shoes many sizes too large for him. At every step he called out at the top of his voice: " Yankees! Yankees! " Jumping out of bed, I soon slipped on my clothes and stepped into the hall, fastening my belt with pistols around my waist as I went out. In the dim light I saw a soldier running up the stairs, clad in a heavy overcoat with cape. My first thought was that the enemy had surrounded and were searching the house, but as he came closer I recognized Captain Walker, of Company B.

" The Yankees have been at Richards' house " (the adjoining farm), " and are now on their way to Upperville," said he. " Go off toward Bloomfield and send all the men you find out on the turnpike, as they will most likely cross the river at Berry's Ferry."

My horse being in the stable, I was soon in the saddle and on my road, stopping at each house to inquire whether any of our men were about, and, if so, directed to hurry them out to the turnpike. At Bloomfield I turned and went back along the Trap road, under cover of the mountain, gathering up all the men on my way and coming out on the pike at the upper end of the town of Upperville. We now found Richards had already passed, on the track of the enemy. Following on, we came up with him as he was about making a charge on the Federal cavalry, which was then entering the Mount Carmel road. A body of 250 Federal cavalry, consisting of detachments of the Fourteenth Pennsylvania and Twenty-first New York Cavalry, guided by a Confederate deserter named Spotts, crossed the Shenandoah river at Shepherd's Mill ford, and, passing through Ashby's Gap, divided at Paris.[2]

---

[2] *Report of Major Thomas Gibson, Fourteenth Pennsylvania Cavalry, commanding Expedition.*

GIBSON to RUMSEY, Feb. 20, 1865 : " I have the honor to report that, agreeable to directions from the Brigadier-General Commanding, I left camp at 6 p. m. for the purpose of crossing the Blue Ridge and making arrests and seizures of certain enemies and public property of the enemy agreeable to information received from two deserters from Mosby's command. I had with me 125 men and 3 officers of the Fourteenth Pennsylvania Cavalry and 100 men of the Twenty-first New York Cavalry, under command of Captain Snow, of the same regiment. There were 150 men detailed from the Fourteenth Pennsylvania Cavalry ; six of the number were not furnished in time, 20 were directed to return to camp by the Assistant Inspector-General of the brigade, because of the non-efficiency of their horses. This reduced the number furnished by that regiment to 124 men, and making the total of the troops engaged 224 enlisted men.

About 11 p. m. I crossed the Shenandoah river at Shepherd's Ford. The expedition was accompanied by Captain Martindale and Lieutenant Baker, both of the staff of the major-general commanding Cavalry Corps. Captain Martindale was accompanied by 6 scouts. Lieutenant Draper, of the Twenty-first New York Cavalry, was detailed to accompany the expedition in charge of all the scouts ; 4 enlisted men of the Twenty-first New York Cavalry were detailed as scouts and ordered to report to Lieutenant Draper.

Before starting from camp, having crossed the Shenandoah river, I ordered that when the command had reached Paris, all the scouts accompanying the command, except 2, should report to Lieutenant Draper ; that Captain Snow, with the Twenty-first New York and one of the deserters from Mosby, should move in the direction of Upperville. Agreeable to the instructions of the brigadier-general commanding, I directed that Captain Snow should give due consideration to all information and suggestions tendered by Lieutenant Draper with regard to roads, etc. ; that Lieutenant Draper should be governed to such an extent as he should deem proper by the information received from

One party of 100 (Twenty-first New York) came to Upperville before daylight, from which place they sent a detachment to the house of Jesse Richards (father of Major
Richards) and surrounded it.   There were in the house at
the time Major Richards, Capt. Robert S. Walker and private John Hipkins.   Hearing a rap at the door, Captain

---

the deserter who accompanied him ; that Lieutenant Draper and Captain
Snow, with that portion of the command, should be at Upperville one hour before daylight on the 19th.

I stated that the Fourteenth Pennsylvania Cavalry would meet them there
and if either regiment should fail to be there at the appointed hour, the one on
the ground should await the arrival of the other until half an hour after daybreak.   If at half an hour after daybreak either portion of the command present, they should move across the Shenandoah and camp.   Before reaching Paris
Captain Martindale expressed himself of
the opinion that Piedmont would be the
better point to meet at.   I accepted Captain Martindale's opinion because I had
always understood that he was well informed regarding the geography of the
country, while I am not.   I sent for Lieutenant Draper, who was near me, in order
to commuicate my change of the place of
rendezvous.   I sent for him and directed
him to communicate my change of orders
to Captain Snow, because the command
was obliged to march by file, and Captain
Snow, who was the rear, would find it
very difficult to pass the column,   We
were near Paris and time was precious.
I told Lieutenant Draper that he would
be held reponsible for the communication
of my orders.   When I reached Paris,
Captain Snow's column took the proper
route ; I think the Fourteenth Pennsylvania Cavalry, 2 scouts and Captain Martin-

BUSHROD UNDERWOOD, CO. A.
Drawn from an old Photograph.

dale and Lieutenant Baker, moved to the
right of Paris.   I proceeded to search such
houses as were pointed out by the deserter
from Mosby, who accompanied me, as the homes of Mosby's men and officers
and the places used for storage of the enemy's supplies.   At the first house I ordered to be searched, Lieutenant Jones, Fourteenth Pennsylvania Cavalry,
whom I had ordered, with 25 men, to search all houses which I thought should
be searched, was left with 2 men.   Before he had finished searching, I moved

Walker got up and was about to open it, when one of the Federal soldiers, growing impatient, thundered away at the door with the butt of his carbine. Walker immediately went back and he and the others hid themselves. Upon forcing open the door, the Federals struck a light and

---

the column, presuming Lieutenant Jones would follow the course the regiment had taken. Lieutenant Jones mistook the route taken by the regiment and failed to overtake it. I moved by way of Markham Station to a point on the road from Upperville to Piedmont, and 2 miles from the latter point. I arrived at this point at 6·30 a. m. I sent a patrol consisting of a sergeant and 10 men from the point to Piedmont. I sent a verbal message by the sergeant to Captain Snow to move immediately to my position, it being on the direct road to Winchester by way of Ashby's Gap. I directed the sergeant to move there and back rapidly. The sergeant having arrived at Piedmont, found that the Twenty first New York Cavalry was not there and had not been there. Thinking Captain Snow might have pursued my first instructions to meet me with his command at Upperville, I expected to find that he had remained there until half an hour after daylight, and consequently he would not be far ahead of me.

On arriving at Upperville, I was astonished to find that Captain Snow had left that place at 5 o'clock that morning, instead of the later hour I had directed. Small parties of the enemy continually harassed our rear, and threatened our front and flanks. On arriving at Paris, they made strong demonstrations, and as we passed through that place the command was harassed by musketry from behind a stone wall. The stone wall was on elevated ground protected by natural obstacles from an attack from cavalry and protected perfectly from our fire. I succeeded in marching the command through the town without sustaining any loss. Up to this time I had captured 18 of the enemy, including Mosby's quartermaster and one lieutenant of the line, together with about 50 horses.

CAPT. ROBERT S. WALKER, CO. B.
From a War-time Photograph.

On arriving at a point on the road from Paris to Berry's Ferry where the road to Shepherd's Ford turns off, it became necessary to march the command by file, owing to a narrow passage through the rocks, of the path known as the road to Shepherd's Ferry. I halted the command to put everything in the best order, lest we should be attacked while in the path.

The following was the disposition of my command at the time : Lieutenant

searched the house, but did not succeed in finding Richards or his companions, though they got most of their clothes. They ransacked every drawer and closet in the house, taking silverware and everything they fancied. The most serious loss to the Major, however, was a handsome new dress uniform and overcoat, which he had just received from Baltimore.

After leaving Richards' house, the detachment of Federal cavalry returned to Upperville to rejoin their companions,

J. L. MOON, CO. D.
From a Photograph taken when a Cadet at the Virginia Military Institute.

Jones was missing from the night before ; Lieutenant Nesmith, Fourteenth Pennsylvania Cavalry, had been seriously wounded the preceding night ; Captain D. K. Duff, Fourteenth Pennsylvania Cavalry, and myself were the only officers present for duty. I placed Captain Duff in charge of the rear guard, which consisted of 40 men. The advance and main portion of the command consisted of 50 men. The prisoners and led horses under guard of 25 men were in the advance of Captain Duff's portion of the command and in the rear of the main body. I made the rear guard so strong, in proportion to the size of my command, owing to the enemy's repeated and vigorous attacks on it. I was at the head of the column. I turned around in order to observe the condition of the column, and looking to the rear, which had not entered the new direction, I observed several men hold up their hands and make gestures which I supposed were intended to inform me that the rear was attacked. I immediately ordered the command "right into line," ordered the prisoners and led horses to be moved forward quickly into the path and to follow the extreme advance, which I did not recall.

No sooner had I issued these commands, than I saw Captain Duff and his

to find them all gloriously drunk—thoroughly saturated with apple-jack. In their search for rebels, they found two barrels of the enemy and in their encounter with old jack they were completely overcome, so that their commander was compelled to withdraw his forces, carrying off his wounded and leaving his dead on the field unburied. Five or six of the New Yorkers were so stupidly drunk that they could not get away. The others were taken across the Shenandoah river and returned to their camp.

party at the rear of the small party who marched in the rear of the led horses. Captain Duff's command was coming at a run. I saw rebels among and in the rear of his party, charging. I ordered the command forward, fired a volley and ordered a charge, which the men did not complete. Captain Duff in the meantime was trying to rally his men in the rear of my line. Before his men had reloaded their pieces, I had fired another volley and ordered a second charge. All the prisoners and led horses had not yet entered the path. The charge was met by one from the enemy and the command was broken. The men had no weapons but their carbines and these were extremely difficult to load, and inefficient in the mêlée that ensued. I made every effort, as did Captain Duff and Captain Martindale and Lieutenant Baker, of the corps staff, to reform the men, but our efforts were fruitless. The rebels had very few sabres, but were well supplied with revolvers, and rode up to our men and shot them down, without meeting more resistance than men could make with carbines. There was a small ridge overlooking both parties, through which the path led. I rode up the side of this and formed the advance guard, which had returned to aid me. The enemy were amidst the men, and both parties were so mixed up that it was impossible to get the men in line. As fast as the men could force their horses into the path, where many of the men were crowded together, they broke for the river. I waited until I was surrounded, and only a half a dozen men left around; the balance had retreated toward the river, or were killed, wounded or captured. Captain Martindale, as he left, said to me: "It is useless to attempt to rally the men here; we'll try it farther on." I tried to ride to the front. The prisoners had placed the horses they were on and leading, across the path, so as to prevent the escape of the men. Men were crowded into the path by twos and threes where there was really only room for one to ride. Men were being thrown and being crushed as they lay on the ground, by others; they were falling from their horses from the enemy's fire in front and rear of me. I rode past about 20 of the men and again tried to rally the men, but all my efforts were fruitless.

I remained at this point until nearly all of our men were past me. I rode ahead of a portion of the command again and begged them to stop, but I couldn't rally them. My right leg was rendered useless by my horse falling over another, and, as he rose, a man riding fell against me, the whole weight of his animal being precipitated against my leg. A couple of rebels were standing fir-

Major Gibson, with his detachment of 150 of the Fourteenth Pennsylvania Cavalry, went along the mountain road to Markham and Piedmont and thence to Upperville, where they expected to join the Twenty-first New York, but not finding them, and seeing little parties of our men watching their movements from the surrounding hills, they became alarmed and pushed on rapidly toward Ashby's Gap.

Sam. Alexander, George Triplett and Clem. Edmonds were sleeping in their little "shebang" when they heard the Fed-

SAM. ALEXANDER, CO. B.

ing at me, and my pistol was unloaded. I turned and passed a number of the men. I again attempted to rally them. I told them that there were only a few following us, and they could be easily taken. My horse had been wounded and my leg was altogether useless. I waited until the last of our men, mixed up with a large number of escaped, led and riderless horses, passed me. I was ordered to surrender, two of the enemy in advance endeavoring to beat me off my horse with their pistols. I succeeded in again passing a number of the men and tried to rally them, but it was impossible ; they were panic-stricken ; one of my own men, as I presented my empty revolver at the head of another, trying to stop him, ran between us and knocked that out of my hand. Again, the rear of the command, now reduced to about 24 men and about 60 horses and mules, passed me, and I was unarmed and alone in the rear. I passed several of the men and endeavored to persuade them of the weakness of the enemy, their unloaded pistols, etc., but it was fruitless ; commands and persuasions were disregarded.

I suffered terribly from physical pain and could do little to stop them by physical force. I reached the river ; my horse fell several times in it, but at last I got across. Captain Martindale forced most of the men across to halt and form here, and cover the crossing of the few who had reached the river. Captain Martindale, myself, 2 scouts and 12 men were saved. We awaited to see if more would come, but none came ; 8 had crossed and arrived at

erals at Mrs. Betsy Edmonds' house. Mounting their horses, they rode out and gave the alarm. At Brown's they found Lieutenant Wrenn, and picking up men as they moved on, followed the Federals, keeping them well closed up, but not yet strong enough to make an attack. At Upperville Wrenn was joined by Major Richards, who had donned a suit of his father's clothes and started in pursuit of the Federals. Richards' force now numbered 43 men, and he decided to attack the Pennsylvanians in the Gap. He overtook them at Mount Carmel, in Ashby's Gap, where the road to Shepherd's Mill leaves the turnpike, and charged them on sight. They attempted to form and delivered a volley with their carbines; but the carbine was no match for the revolver at

---

camp before us. I was placed in a sleigh and arrived at camp at 4.30 p. m. this day.

I ascribe the disaster to, 1st, Captain Snow, commanding Twenty-first New York, failing to go to Piedmont as ordered through Lieutenant Draper, or to Upperville, as I ordered him personally, and to remain at either of the places until half an hour after daybreak. One of Captain Snow's command, who had been drunk and was left by the command, confirmed the information I received from negroes and citizens that Captain Snow left Upperville at 5 a. m. instead of half an hour after daybreak; 2d, to Captain Duff's rear guard being pushed into the rear of the column before I knew he was attacked; 3d, to the paucity of officers detailed with the command, and the large number of men engaged who were new recruits; 4th, to the men having neither sabres nor revolvers and consequently being unable to engage in a mélée successfully with an enemy armed with at least 2 revolvers to the man; also, I didn't know of the attack until I observed the rear guard coming in at full flight, mixed up with and pursued by the enemy. I don't think the enemy's force exceeded between 60 and 75 men.

Lieutenant Jones and 10 men with him have returned to camp safely. The loss is one officer, Lieutenant Nesmith, wounded; Captain Duff, Lieutenant Baker, corps staff, and 78 men missing. I returned to camp by way of Berryville.

I forward, enclosed, the report of Captain Snow, which is incorrect as far as it differs from this. I have not yet received the report of Lieutenant Draper. I feel satisfied that I did all I knew how to make the movement a success, and it having failed and proved a disaster, I earnestly request to be allowed to appear before a court of inquiry to prove that I am not responsible for the failure. A man has just arrived who hid in a thicket and says he saw a party of about 600 of the enemy moving toward Shepherd's Ford.

I have omitted heretofore to state that a party under Lieutenant Baker, of the Corps headquarters, captured a quartermaster's camp of Mosby's com-

close quarters, and our men broke and routed them completely. The road from Mount Carmel to Shepherd's Mill, along which the Federals fled, was very narrow, and on either

side was a thick growth of trees and brush. It was literally strewn with hats, belts, carbines, turkeys and chickens—both living and dead—clothing and plunder of all kinds, which the pillagers in their flight had thrown away. The blood from the wounded men and horses crimsoned the snow along the road.

Thirteen Federals were killed and a great number wounded; 63 prisoners, including several officers, were captured, with 90 horses. Five or six horses were killed. Nineteen prisoners, which the Federals had picked up on their road, were released, and a number of horses were recaptured and restored to their owners.

A. LEE PATTESON, CO. C.
From a War-time Photograph.

mand. There was no property but one wagon and one ambulance, 2 horses and 6 mules in it. We brought the horses and mules along, but they, with the rest, were lost in the fight.

Trusting, general, that you will grant me the court of inquiry at the earliest practicable moment, I remain your obedient servant,

THOS. GIBSON, *Major Commanding Detachment.*

Major WILL RUMSEY, *A. A. G., Second Cav. Division.*

*Report of Capt. Henry E. Snow, Twenty-first N. Y. Cavalry.*

CAMP TWENTY-FIRST N. Y. VOLUNTEER CAVALRY.

*Camp Averell, Va., Feb 18 (19), 1865.*

SIR : I have the honor to report that I was detailed yesterday, the 18th instant, to take command of 100 men of the **Twenty-first** (Griswold's Light)

The only loss on our side was John Iden, of the regular army, who was accidentally killed in the excitement of the chase by one of our own men; and Dr. Sowers, who was slightly wounded.

Efforts were made to capture the deserter, Spotts, but being well mounted, he fled at the first attack and escaped.

In the latter part of the month of February, Colonel Mosby returned from the South to the command.

New York Cavalry, and report to Major Gibson, of the Fourteenth Pennsylvania Cavalry for scout. Left camp at 6. p. m., the 18th instant, crossed the Shenandoah River at Shepherd Mills Ford near Paris, Loudoun County, Virginia ; received orders from Major Gibson to take the road leading to Upperville; and search all houses between Paris and Upperville ; also, to give the latter place a thorough searching. While he would take the road leading to the right to Piedmont, I was to remain at Upperville until one hour before daybreak, where he was to join me. If he did not arrive, on no account was I to remain there longer than half an hour before daybreak, but start with my command to camp. Agreeable to instructions I proceeded to Upperville, and gave the houses there a thorough searching, and in the vicinity, finding 3 Confederate soldiers, one belonging to Mosby's command and two to the Fourth Virginia Cavalry. About 3.30 this a. m. I took 10 men to search Major Richards' house, one mile from Upperville, leaving Lieutenant Meldrum, Twenty-first New York (Griswold's Light) Cavalry, in command until my return, with strict orders to keep the men in column and be in readiness for any emergency. On my return I found about one-third of the men very much under the influence of liquor, they having found two barrels of liquor during my absence. Started for camp and arrived at Paris at daylight, returning by the way of Berry's Bridge. Arrived in camp at 10.30 a. m.

Six of my men were left in Loudoun ; they were so intoxicated that it was impossible to get them along. The horses, arms and accoutrements were brought in by the rear guard.

I have the honor to be, most respectfully, etc.,

HENRY E. SNOW,
*Capt. A. Co., Twenty-first N. Y. Vol. Cav., Commanding Detail.*

To MAJOR GIBSON, *Fourteenth Pennsylvania Cavalry.*

# CHAPTER XXVII.

*Monday, March 6.*—The Battalion assembled at Upperville, and marched down to the lower part of Loudoun, in order to protect the Quartermaster and his details of men, who were gathering up corn and other supplies, and at the same time, by keeping the command there for a short time, relieve that portion of the county, which had been so overrun by Federal raiding parties.[1]

*Sunday, March 12.*—A detachment of between 40 and 50 men, under Captain Glascock, from the command quartered in Loudoun, was sent to Fairfax to attack a cavalry patrol.

Arriving at a point on the road near Lewinsville, where it was expected the patrol would pass (a little hollow in the pines), Captain Glascock, Bush. Underwood and Thomas Moss went to the edge of the pines to watch the road. The patrol, numbering 22 men from the Thirteenth New York Cavalry, soon came along. Moss was sent back with orders to bring forward 10 men, who were put in charge of Bush. Underwood with instructions that, as soon as the enemy

---

[1] STEVENSON (Harper's Ferry) to Brig. Gen. MORGAN, Cumberland, March 8, 1865 : " I have a number of persons from Loudoun County here who came in last night. Mosby, with considerable force, represented to be at least 500 strong, was at Waterford last night. He is conscripting all the inhabitants capable of bearing arms. He is represented to have a light battery of 4 guns (doubtful). I am putting down a pontoon bridge and think a cavalry force should be sent over there sufficiently strong to drive him from the country. I have only the Twelfth Pennsylvania Cavalry ; not reliable."

STEVENSON to SEWARD (Martinsburg), March 8, 1865 : " Mosby crossed the Shenandoah to-day with 300 men, crossing at Snicker's Ferry. Reno thinks he went to White Post. I thought I would advise you to be on the lookout for a raid."

passed, to cross over in their rear, in order to pick up any who might escape Captain Glascock, who would attack in front.

The Federals, seeing us, halted, but mistaking us for some of their own men, again moved on. Glascock, thinking they were about to retreat, ordered a charge, and the fight which ensued being in a narrow road, at close quarters, was very destructive to the enemy, 12 of whom, dead or wounded, lay on the ground at the close, together with 6 horses killed. Nine prisoners were taken. Our loss was one man, Francis Marion Yates, of Rappahannock, who was accidentally killed by our own men in the charge.

THOMAS MOSS, CO. D.
From a Photograph taken during the War.

Ed. O'Brien was wounded in the leg, and Thomas Moss was injured by his horse falling with him. Zach. F. Jones had his horse badly wounded.

John Hipkins was with the party sent to cut off the retreat of the enemy, and his pistol failing to fire, he threw it at one of the Federals across the road and knocked him from his horse.[2]

Ed. Thomson, with 30 picked men, among them Charles Dear, J. Willie Dear, John Newcomb, Crawford, James

---

[2] GAMBLE to TAYLOR, March 12, 1865 : "COLONEL : The patrol—1 officer, sergeant and 20 men, Thirteenth New York Cavalry—was attacked by guerrillas at 1 p. m. about 2 miles beyond Vienna, this side of Peach Grove stockade. Lieutenant Cuyler was with the party and reports by signal from Vienna 2 men killed, 5 wounded, 6 horses killed, and 1 wounded. The balance of the patrol came into Vienna. A detailed report will be sent so soon as received. I have ordered a squadron from Prospect Hill to march through the woods one mile on the flank of the daily patrol until the cavalry now out returns, when the country in front will be swept by the whole cavalry force at night, and every house examined from here to Bull Run Mountains at the same time, where the guerrillas stop at night."

Lowndes, J. S. Mason and L. R. Mason, was sent on a scout from Loudoun. They went through the enemy's lines to Munson's Hill, capturing a patrol of 10 men, whom they met on their route, with their horses and equipments, and afterwards cutting their way through the lines near Springfield Station, returned to the command without loss.[3]

*Wednesday, March 15.*—A detachment of the Eighth Illinois Cavalry, on their return march from a raid into Rappahan-

FRANCIS MARION YATES, CO. D.
Killed March 12, 1865, in skirmish with patrol of 16th N. Y. Cavalry.

nock, passed through Fauquier County. Near The Plains they came upon John T. Waller of Company A and Harry T. Sin-nott of Company B, who being penned up in Fishback's lane, were called upon to surrender. Waller replied by opening fire on the enemy. The Federals returned the fire and Waller was shot through the head and instantly killed. Sinnott jumped the fence and made his escape. One of the Federal officers told George Fishback that Waller was the bravest man he ever saw. He was buried at The Plains, and after the war his remains was removed to Lynchburg.

Lieut. Harry Hatcher, with a few men, followed the Federal cavalry down the turnpike below Aldie, when, thinking they had gone back, he returned to the house and went to bed. In the room with him was a young man who was to be married in a few days.

A party of the cavalry that had been sent back surrounded the house. Hatcher, hearing the bustle outside,

---

[3] TAYLOR to GAMBLE, March 12, 1865: "Guerrillas carried off last night a citizen and 7 horses from the vicinity of Upton's Hill. Your people must be kept on the alert and make continual scouts. Have you heard from the detachment sent to Warrenton and Sperryville?"

put his head out of the window and seeing a number of soldiers around, asked:

"Boys, are the Yankees about?"

"We are Yankees," replied one of them, "come down."

"Wait till I get my clothes on," said Hatcher.

Then turning to the young man, he said in a low voice: "Hide yourself and I will go down. 'Tis better for them to take me than you."

When he opened the door they asked if there were any more rebels about. "No," said Hatcher; and they went on their way, taking him along as a prisoner.[4]

*Monday, March 20.*—A report was brought in by our scouts that a large body of Federal troops had crossed the river at Harper's Ferry and were then camped at Hillsborough. This force we afterwards learned was composed of the Twelfth Pennsylvania Cavalry, Colonel Reno,

HARRY T. SINNOTT, CO. B.[5]
From a War-time Photograph.

and a regiment of infantry under Colonel Bird, and was sent over to drive Mosby's Rangers out of Loudoun County. Colonel Mosby immediately dispatched couriers to order a rendezvous at Hamilton.

*Tuesday, March 21.*—Command met at Hamilton, or as it was more frequently called, Harmony, in the Quaker Settlement. One hundred and twenty-eight men were present

---

[4] Lieut. Harry Hatcher died April 23, 1895, at his residence, about 3 miles from Middleburg, in Fauquier County. He was paralyzed about a year previous to his death. Though a great sufferer, he remained cheerful and enjoyed the society of his friends and old comrades to the last.

[5] Harry T. Sinnott was a member of Company E, Forty-fourth Virginia Infantry. He joined Mosby in June, 1863; was a member of Company A until the organization of Company B, when he was transferred to that company and so remained up to the surrender.

and we moved off to the Quaker church. The Battalion had left but a short time when the Federal forces occupied the town and a portion of their cavalry came in sight of the church, but soon retired. We again moved off, and halted about one mile south of Hamilton on the road to Silcott Springs. Captain Glascock, with Company D and a portion of Company A, was posted in a piece of woods to the left of the road. Six well mounted men were then ordered to ride forward and attack the enemy's advance and then fall back past the woods in which Glascock's men were concealed, in order to draw out the cavalry from the infantry. The ruse succeeded and the whole cavalry force started in pursuit of the 6 men, who fled wildly, as though surprised and terror-stricken. On came the Federal cavalry, shouting and yelling, and their advance swept by before they noticed us. As they approached, orders were given to fall back a little from the road, so as to keep out of sight as much as possible. Some of the men in the rear, not understanding this movement, created some little confusion in the ranks. Noticing this, Captain Glascock said: ' Come, Company D! Come on, Company A!" and dashed on, followed by his men.

Referring to this fight, Lieut. Channing Smith wrote:

" I was sitting on my horse in the edge of the field near Colonel Mosby and saw the whole affair. It was my first experience with the Rangers and I eagerly and excitedly watched the movement. The Captain (Glascock) at the head of his men came trotting out of the woods, and as he struck the open, gave the command to charge and the whole band broke into a gallop and hurled themselves upon the flank and front of the astonished foe. They stood for a short while, but only for a few minutes, then gave way and fled back towards Hamilton pursued by Glascock and his men, who rained bullets among them. Not far from the woods the road entered a narrow lane, with a high, steep bank on each side. Into this lane the panic-stricken men jammed themselves—men and horses pressed so tightly together that some time elapsed before they could get forward. The Colonel sat upon his horse in the field on top of the bank, his eyes flashing, his long black plume tossing in the wind, waving on his men, who with loud cheers followed up the chase. When the retreating Federals reached a piece of woods close to Hamilton, they attempted a rally, and for a few seconds there was a hand to hand fight between us. Here was where we suffered the slight loss of men. But, again breaking, they resumed their flight, and some of them never stopped until safe across the Potomac River, some 25 miles away.

"On the left of the woods, where they made their brief stand, behind an osage orange hedge, was posted the infantry, and but for their fire the pursuit would have been continued, and but few of the cavalry would have escaped. Practically, not more than 60 of our command took part in the fight, as owing to the narrowness of the road the men could not get at them until the fight was over.

"When they made their second stand at the edge of the woods, very few of our men had gotten up, and for a brief space those engaged fought heavy odds. The fight was sharp and desperate so far as we were concerned, but the enemy quickly gave way.

"Having been appointed to the vacancy in Capt. Sam. Chapman's Company (E) in place of Lieutenant Martin, who was killed accidentally by one of his own comrades, and my company not being present, I acted independently in this fight and had good opportunity to see and judge of the fighting qualities of Mosby's men, and came to the conclusion that the conscientious, brave soldier who loved the fierce excitement and danger of battle could be *accommodated* as well with Mosby on the Border as in the ranks of the regulars who followed the lead of Stuart. And the impression then made upon me of the coolness, presence of mind and courage of Colonel Mosby has never been effaced."

When the Federals were crowded in the lane, Lieutenant Smith was near the Colonel on the bank and fired six shots into their ranks. Then, following Mosby, he galloped along their flank up to the woods, and was soon exchanging shots at close range. Spurring his horse out into the road, he was attacked by two of the enemy, one of whom he killed, when the other wheeled and ran off. The fire of the infantry then became so hot that Colonel Mosby ordered the men to fall back. Some, not hearing or heeding the order, went through both cavalry and infantry and back again safely to the command.

Fifteen of the Federals were killed and a number

wounded, some mortally. Thirteen, including one lieutenant, were captured, together with 15 horses.

COLONEL MARCUS A. RENO,
12th Pennsylvania Cavalry.
From a War-time Photograph.

Our loss was 2 killed,
James Keith and Wirt
M. Binford.[6]    John A.
Chew,[7] Ben. Fletcher,
Manning, Shipley and
two or three others
were wounded.

Mosby drew off his
men and halted in a field
in full view of the Fed-
eral cavalry. The men
cheered, waved their
hats, and used every
means to draw the cav-
alry away from the in-
fantry. Some of our
men, venturing too
close to the enemy's
lines, were fired on, and
one, Joseph Griffin was
wounded and his horse
was killed. He attempted to gain the shelter of the woods,
but was pursued and captured.[8]

The Battalion being ordered to meet next morning about
three miles from Hamilton, moved off towards North Fork.
The men scattered about in small squads and remained at
farm houses in the neighborhood. Pickets were placed

---

[6] Wirt M. Binford was a youth but little over 17 years of age. His body
was taken to Richmond after the war and buried in Hollywood Cemetery.

[7] John A. Chew was transferred from Chew's Battery to Mosby's Rangers
in November, 1864. In the fight at Hamilton he was badly wounded and has
never been able to walk since; otherwise he is in good health.

[8] "While engaged in equipping and disciplining this force for active movements, either up the Valley or wherever it might be ordered, I had detachments of
cavalry out daily, scouting the roads south from Winchester; and with the intention of destroying supplies said to be collected at Upperville, I directed
an expedition to that point under Col. M. A. Reno, of the Twelfth Pennsylvania Cavalry, composed of his own regiment and the First Regiment, First

near and around the town to watch the movements of the
enemy, who went into camp.  In the evening a heavy rain-
storm set in and continued all night, accompanied with
thunder and lightning; the wind blew with great force,
throwing down trees and fences.  Shortly before daylight
the storm ceased, and the sun arose in a cloudless sky.

*Wednesday, March 22.*—The command met at Hatcher's,
3 miles from Hamilton, and was joined by the Little Fork
Rangers, Captain Kincheloe, numbering 25 men.  With this
reinforcement Mosby again moved forward to Hamilton,
but the Federals had gone to Snickersville.  On nearing
that place we learned they had marched on to Bloomfield.
Here our scouts came up with the enemy, and for a time
quite a brisk fire was kept up.  They then fell back toward
Snickersville and went into camp.

Mosby halted on a hill overlooking the camp, and again
tried to draw the cavalry away from the infantry.  Failing
to do this, and night coming on, the command was dismissed, with orders to meet in the morning before sunrise at
Eure's Mill, near the turnpike.

At this time Company A was under the command of
Sergeant Corbin, who had but a short time previous been
released from Federal prison.  All the commissioned, as
well as non-commissioned officers of our company, except
Corbin, being either killed, wounded or captured, the
offices were filled, temporarily, by privates.

On the morning of the 23d, the Federals broke camp and
started before sunrise.  Without waiting for all the men to
assemble, Mosby moved on after them with about 50 men.
He was soon joined by others, until his force amounted to
between 150 and 200 men.

At Upperville, where the Federals halted, an attempt was
made to cut off their pickets.  Lieut. Frank Turner was

Corps, under Col. Bird.  Col. Reno crossed the Shenandoah at Harper's Ferry,
and encountered the enemy, about 300 strong, under Mosby at Hillsborough.
According to the reports received by me, Mosby drove the cavalry back in disorder, but hastily retired when he met the infantry skirmishers.  The expedition
returned, having accomplished much less than I had expected it to do."—*General Hancock's Report.*  See also Appendix, XXXIX.

sent with a squad of men for that purpose, but being seen before he was near enough to prevent their reaching the main body, only one was captured, the others all escaping into town.

As the Federals proceeded down the turnpike, we followed close at their heels, to Middleburg. As they would ascend one hill, we would take up a position on the one be_ hind them. On coming to Goose Creek the infantry crossed first, the wagons and cavalry bringing up the rear. After the infantry had crossed, Mosby attempted to attack the cavalry while the wagons were on the narrow bridge, when it would be difficult for the cavalry to get over. But as he moved around and charged on them, the last of the cavalry was seen dashing over the bridge. Finding it impossible to separate the cavalry from the infantry, Mosby thought to charge the former, and, by driving them into the latter, throw both into confusion ; but they, probably divining his intention, took care to keep the infantry at all times between our men and their cavalry.

A continual fire was kept up between the skirmishers on both sides, and a number of Federals were seen to fall from their horses. John H. Foster, of Company A, was wounded near Middleburg. At that place Reno's forces turned off from the turnpike, taking the road to Mountville, where they were joined by a large body of cavalry, which had been sent up from Fairfax. Toward night our command was dismissed, Mosby giving orders that the men should not sleep in houses that night, owing to the risk of being captured by searching parties. The Federals went into camp, and the next day pursued their course homeward.

*Thursday, March 30.*—The command again proceeded to the Quaker settlement in Loudoun, and the business of pressing corn was continued. A detachment of Federal cavalry yesterday crossed the Potomac and picked up 7 of Mosby's men, 3 at Downey's still house and 4 at Waterford, among them our Quartermaster, Wright James. (See Chapter IX).

Among those who had attracted the notice of Colonel Mosby in the fight at Hamilton by their gallant bearing was

Charles B. Wiltshire, a veteran in the regular service. He had been wounded on three occasions : first, at Manassas, then at Kernstown, and again, with General Rosser, in West Virginia. The last was a disabling wound, and he was retired. When he joined Mosby he came with one crutch, which he broke over the head of a Federal cavalryman on the Valley pike while on a scout.

About the latter part of March, Mosby told Wiltshire of his intention to make him a lieutenant in Company H, which he proposed soon to organize, and at the same time ordered him to take a few men for a scout in the Valley, on the Winchester and Potomac Railroad. Wiltshire accordingly started on the 30th of March, with John Orrick, George Murray Gill and

JOHN H. FOSTER, CO. A.

Wounded March 23, 1865, in a skirmish near Middleburg.

From a Photograph taken during the War.

Bartlett Bolling, to fulfil his mission. On the road he met Philip and Robert Eastham ("Bob Ridley") who were on their way with a message to Colonel Mosby, then in Loudoun.

Leaving Philip Eastham to deliver the message, Robert Eastham joined Wiltshire and his little party. They went by way of Berryville, near which place Eastham and Bolling stopped at a house to make some inquiries, while Wiltshire, Gill and Orrick rode on ahead. When Eastham and Bolling reached the top of a hill, in view of the residence of Col. Daniel Bonham, they saw their three companions dashing off at full speed toward the house, while two Federal soldiers, one of whom they afterwards learned was Lieut. Eugene Ferris, of the Thirtieth Massachusetts Infantry, were running from the house to the stable. Spurring their horses, they galloped on, but before they reached the gate which led to the stable they heard a pistol shot and saw Charles Wiltshire fall. He was at the stable door, with his pistol pointed in the door. Then several shots were fired in rapid succession, and as they went through the gate they met Gill and Orrick, both of whom were wounded. Ferris had come out from the stable, and unharmed by the shots of Eastham and Bolling, secured Wiltshire's pistols and mounted Wiltshire's horse, while his orderly, in obedience to his command, mounted, and leading Ferris's horse, the two started for the gate. By this time Bolling also was wounded, but he with Eastham started to follow the retreating Federals. In the road Bolling seized the orderly and pulled him from his horse. Ferris turned on Eastham, who fired, inflicting a slight wound and then raised his pistol to knock him from his horse, but Ferris avoided the blow and set off in the direction of his camp, followed by Orrick and Bolling. Eastham endeavored to cut him off by getting around in his front, but he made his escape. Eastham went back to look after Wiltshire, but was told he was dying, and a young lady handed up his belt and holsters. Just then Orrick and Bolling came riding up, shouting, "Get out quick, Ridley; the Yankees are coming!" "Come on, old 'Steamboat'; we must get out of this," said Eastham as he gave a touch of the spur to his gray horse, to which his comrades had given this title, and the three Rangers started on the home-stretch.

Wiltshire lingered until the 4th of April, when he died.

George Murray Gill was a Baltimorean, who had entered the Confederate army in the early part of the war and had served both in the infantry and cavalry before his transfer to Mosby's command, where he had made many friends. After receiving his wound he endeavored to reach his friends in Fauquier, but was obliged to stop at a house on the road, where he died after a few days.

# CHAPTER XXVIII.

On the 5th of April, at North Fork, in Loudoun County, Company H was organized by electing George Baylor, Captain; Edward F. Thomson, First Lieutenant; James G. Wiltshire, Second Lieutenant, and B. Frank Carter, Jr., Third Lieutenant.

Captain Baylor, though but a youth, had already won distinction in the regular service, first in the Stonewall Brigade and afterwards in the Twelfth Virginia Cavalry in which he had been promoted to a lieutenancy.

Lieutenant Thomson was attached to Capt. M. D. Ball's company when it was captured in Alexandria, May 1, 1861, and after his exchange acted as guide and scout for Gen. J. E. B. Stuart until the Fall of 1862, when he enlisted in the Fifth Virginia Cavalry, commanded by Colonel Rosser. In 1864 the Fifth and Fifteenth regiments were consolidated and Thomson afterwards obtained a transfer to Mosby's command. He had been entrusted with many important missions, all of which he performed in such a creditable manner that he was deemed worthy of the position to which he was now assigned.

Lieutenants Wiltshire and Carter had both established reputations in the command by their gallant conduct, and their promotion was regarded by all as a fitting recognition of their worth.

After the election, Colonel Mosby complimented the men on their choice of officers and told them they could now go and do something to distinguish themselves.

Captain Baylor moved off with his company, numbering 52 men, through Snicker's Gap, thence along the Shenandoah river to Rock Ford, where he crossed, swimming the horses.

Learning that the Loudoun Rangers were camped near Halltown, Baylor was not long in making up his mind to give them attention.

CAPTAIN GEORGE BAYLOR, CO. H.
From a Photograph taken after the War.

Reaching their camp, he led his men to the attack and was soon in possession, capturing 45 prisoners and over 70 horses, together with arms and camp equipage. Baylor had one man wounded— Frank Helm, of Warrenton, while the Federals lost 5 or 6 killed and wounded.[1] (See Colonel Clendenin's Report, Appendix, XXXVIII.)

About this time news was received of the fall of Richmond and the surrender of Lee's army. This cast a gloom over all. Some were hopeful and still looked forward to something, they knew not what, which should bring about a change in the existing state of affairs and lead to a successful result. The rumors of recognition and intervention which had been circulated were now eagerly caught up by

[1] "On the 6th of April a body of Mosby's guerrillas surprised the camp of the Loudoun County Rangers near Charlestown, capturing a number of men and nearly all their horses."—*Report of Major-General W. S. Hancock.*

General MORGAN, *Chief of Staff:*        *Harper's Ferry, Va., April 6, 1865.*

Mosby surprised camp of Loudoun Rangers near Keys' Ford and cleaned

persons who in despair were ready to give credence to anything which might afford the faintest ray of hope. Nearly
all were astounded when they heard of the surrender of
Lee's army, which was looked upon as the shield and armor
of the Confederacy. So often successful and deemed almost
invincible, it was conceded to be a hopeless contest when it
had failed.

The London *Times*, speaking of this army, said :

Not even the Grand Army of Napoleon himself could
count a series of more brilliant victories than the forces
which, raised chiefly from the high spirited population of
Virginia, have defeated so many invasions of that state and
crushed the hopes of so many
National generals. Chiefs and
soldiers have now failed for the
first and last time. They were
victorious until victory was no
longer to be achieved by human
valor, and then they fell with
honor. Theirs has been no gradual
decay in courage or discipline, no
demoralization, the result of successive defeats. What they were
at the Chickahominy and Chancellorsville, they were on the day
when the overpowering forces of
Grant and Sheridan forced them
back from their defenses at Petersburg. If Stonewall Jackson had
been alive to witness the ruin of
the army which he had so often
helped to victory, he would have
no reason to be ashamed of its conduct in its latest
hour.

LIEUT. B. FRANK CARTER, JR.,
CO. H.

From a Photograph taken during the
War.

them out. Made the attack about 10 o'clock. I have sent out some infantry.
When I get a report will send you particulars. Respectfully,

JOHN D. STEVENSON, *Brigadier-General.*

General MORGAN, *Chief of Staff :* *Harper's Ferry, April 6, 1865.*

The force that attacked camp of Loudoun Rangers was a part of Mosby's.
command. They captured 25 men of the Rangers, a small party of the Fifth
New York guarding baggage; also some horses. The number of attacking
force was about 100 men. They crossed at one of the upper fords of the Shenandoah and recrossed at Keys' Ford.

JOHN D. STEVENSON, *Brigadier-General.*

The first news of the surrender of General Lee was accompanied by a report that Gen. Joe Johnson had defeated General Sherman, and was marching on to reinforce General Lee. There being so many conflicting rumors, and being without official information, Colonel Mosby sent Capt. Robert S. Walker with a few men, to Gordonsville to learn the true state of affairs.

*Saturday, April 8.*—Command met at Upperville. Companies D and H were sent off to operate in Fairfax, while Mosby, with Companies A and B, marched through Ashby's Gap and crossed the Shenandoah river at Burrell's Island, swimming our horses, as the river was very high. We halted near Ferguson's, and Colonel Mosby, taking 10 men, went off on a scout. He learned that a division of cavalry was camped below Berryville; that 200 or 300 were at Berryville with a picket of 8 men on the road above the town. Lieut. John Russell, with a few men, approached these and was ordered to halt.

"Oh, pshaw!" said Russell; "what's the matter with you? Don't you know who we are?"

Russell still advancing, the picket again challenged, and the same response was given. By this time Russell was close enough to see the men sitting around, and the man on post cocked his pistol. Our men then rushed forward, firing into the group, 2 of whom were killed, 3 wounded and 3 captured, with 7 horses and equipments. We remained some time within 6 miles of Berryville, expecting a force would be sent out in search of the party who had made the attack, but none came and we moved on.

On the 9th Lieut. Albert Wrenn, Lieut. Frank Turner and Edward Hurst, each with detachments, were sent out, but accomplished nothing of importance, and we all returned to Fauquier. Lieutenant Wrenn's party found itself in close proximity to a Federal camp, from which it was necessary to depart in haste, with a large following. When he crossed the Shenandoah, the Federal cavalry appeared on the opposite shore, but made no attempt to cross.

Companies D and H were less fortunate. Leaving Upperville on the 8th, they marched to The Plains and dispersed, with orders to meet next morning.

On the morning of the 9th (Sunday) they met and remained at The Plains until afternoon, when Captain Baylor gave orders to march, and they set out for Fairfax, intending to capture a train hauling wood to Alexandria. Rain set in about dark and continued all night. On the morning of the 10th, learning that the train would not come out, Baylor started on his return to Fauquier. The Federal commander at Fairfax Station, Colonel Albright, was apprised of their presence, and immediately despatched a f o r c e in pursuit.[2] While partially dismounted at Arundel's, Companies D and H were attacked by a detachment of the Eighth Illinois Cavalry, under Captain Warner.

JOSEPH BRYAN, CO. D.

Lieutenants Thomson and B. Frank Carter, with about 30 men, charged and checked the advance, causing them to waver, but seeing our men in confusion, they rallied and drove us back. In the retreat which followed a few determined men, among them Lieut. B.

---

[2] HEADQUARTERS FIRST SEPARATE BRIGADE,
*Fairfax Court House, April 10, 1865.*
Lieut.-Col. J. H. TAYLOR, *Chief of Staff :*
COLONEL: The detachment of the Eighth Illinois Cavalry which went out this morning, as previously reported, from Fairfax Station, met Mosby's battalion from the Northern Neck, under Captain Baylor, and as usual whipped it like the devil. The Eighth captured a number of horses and some prisoners.

Frank Carter, Lieut. James G. Wiltshire, Sergeant Mohler, Joseph Bryan, Thomas Kidd, B. B. Ransom, H. C. Dear and a

few others, formed a rear guard and saved many from death or capture. This brave little band, for four or five miles of the chase, exposed themselves, with reckless daring, to save their comrades. Mohler's horse becoming exhausted, floundered in the mud near a sharp curve in the road. With the Federal cavalry pressing hard in their rear, and a party seeking to cut them off by crossing the field, so as to come out on the road in their front, they could not get him up behind them, but Wiltshire and Bryan, each taking one of Mohler's hands, carried him along between their horses until they overtook a riderless horse, which they caught and gave to Mohler, and then turned to fire on

H. C. DEAR, CO. D.[3]

Had a few men wounded and half a dozen horses killed.   A detailed report will be made as soon as practicable.                              WM. GAMBLE,
                                                     *Colonel Commanding Brigade.*

*April 10, 1865.*

Colonel GAMBLE :

   I have just come into camp from a fight with a battalion of Mosby's Men under command of Captain Baylor. I whipped him like thunder, captured a number of horses and some provisions. Had a few men wounded and half a dozen horses killed. Will send a full account at an early hour.
                            CHAS. ALBRIGHT, *Colonel.*

   [3] In his letter enclosing pictures of himself and J. W. Dear, Mr. H. C. Dear wrote : " I send you a picture taken in Waterford a few days after the fight at Hamilton. I was with a little scouting party. We entered the town and took turns standing guard while each had his picture taken, and then raced from the town, pursued by Means' Men.
   " My brother J. W. Dear and Tom King were captured by Means' Men

the party seeking to cut them off. After Wiltshire delivered his fire, he saw the horse which they had given to Mohler pass by without a rider, and saw that Mohler was a prisoner, having been captured before he could mount.

The halter strap on Captain Baylor's horse got loose, and as the frightened beast plunged madly on, it was trailing under foot, tripping the animal. Young H. C. Dear, seeing his leader's dilemma, spurred on and secured the strap so that it would not interfere with the horse's movements.

Besides Mohler, the Federals captured Thomas F. Harney, of the Torpedo Bureau, on Special Duty with Mosby, Richard McVey, Edward Hefflebower and Samuel Rogers. McVey was badly wounded.

The Federals continued the pursuit until they reached Wolf Run Shoals; and here ended the last fight of the war in Virginia.[4]

---

near our home in the vicinity of Mt. Gilead, in February, 1865. They were betrayed by a treacherous negro. They had just decked themselves out in their new $200 suits smuggled from Baltimore, to call on some ladies in Leesburg, when the enemy came upon them. They took to the woods, but finding escape impossible, made a stand-up fight before surrendering. Willie had previously been shot in the leg. For their gallant resistance they were sent to Fort McHenry, not to be exchanged during the war.

"I went to Captain Glascock after I saw my brother captured, and asked to be allowed to take his place in Company D. He refused on account of my youth (I was then but a school-boy), but finally gave me permission to go with the Company, which I did, up to the close of the war. Through the kindness of the men I was given a place behind my big cousin, Charlie Dear, which always brought me in the second or third 'fours' in time of danger."

---

[4] *April 10, 1865.—Skirmish near Burke's Station and at Arundel's Farm, Va.—Report of Col. Charles Albright, Two hundred and Second Pennsylvania Infantry, Commanding Post at Fairfax Station.*

*April 10, 1865*

Captain WICKERSHAM :

CAPT : I have the honor to report that this morning I received information through a source I consider reliable, that a force of rebel cavalry was south of this post, moving toward Burke's Station, for the purpose of capturing trains at work there. I immediately ordered out all of the cavalry I have under my command and started in the direction indicated. About 3 miles from here I came upon the trail of the enemy and followed it toward Burke's Station, in the neighborhood of which place some shots were exchanged between the enemy and a detachment of Company K, Eighth Illinois Cavalry. The rebels, upon being discovered, beat back into the woods, and upon my recovering of the

Lieutenant Wiltshire, calling my attention to this circumstance. remarked :

"Has it never struck you as being a notable fact that the
first big fight of the war occurred on Bull Run and the last

trail, again followed, taking with me Lieutenant Hupp's command. At Arundel's
I discovered them formed in line, and behind the house, barn and fences. I

LIEUT. JAMES G. WILTSHIRE,
CO. H.

From a War-time Picture.

ordered my men into line as rapidly as I
could, advanced and opened fire. The
rebels broke and I charged after them.
We drove them to Wolf Run Shoals and saw
their rear cross. I did not deem it prudent
to follow any further, from the fact that our
horses were pretty well exhausted and the
column pretty well scattered along the
road. The enemy's force was a battalion
of Mosby's command, Companies D and
H, Captain Baylor in command—Captain
Briscoe was in command of Company D—
numbering altogether about 150 men.
They started from Upperville Saturday
morning last.

The casualties are as follows : Company
G, 2 men slightly wounded, 3 horses killed
and 3 wounded. Company H, 1 horse
killed. Company K, 1 horse killed and 1
wounded.

List of prisoners and property captured : Richard McVey (wounded severely),
Edward Hefflebower, Thomas F. Harney, Engineer Bureau, Lieutenant Company F, Sixth Missouri—brought ordnance to Colonel Mosby and joined his
command ; First Sergeant David G. Mohler, Company H, Samuel Rogers. Six
horses captured. Six or 8 horses killed ; 7 complete sets of horse equipments.

The road from Mr. Arundel's to Wolf Run Shoals was strewn with blankets,
hats, caps, etc. I have no doubt a number of the enemy were wounded and
probably some killed that were got away through the woods.

I cannot speak too highly of the gallantry of Captain Warner, Lieutenants
Brooks and Hupp, and also of their men. It is also my duty to add that the
information was brought me from Arundel's, a heretofore suspected rebel family. Shall I send the prisoners over ?

I have the honor to be, very truly, your obedient servant,

CHARLES ALBRIGHT,

*Col. 202d Regiment Pennsylvania Vols., Commanding Post.*

[Indorsement.]

HDQRS. SEPARATE BRIGADE,
*Fairfax C. H., April 10, 1865.*

Respectfully forwarded to department headquarters.

Credit is due to Colonel Albright for his energy in obtaining the information

shots of the war in Virginia were fired on the banks of that same stream?"

And it was Wiltshire's lot to shoot the last man who was wounded in this fight.

---

and especially to Captain Warner, who commanded and led the detachment Eighth Illinois Cavalry in his usual way. Captain Warner is and always has been an excellent fighting officer and is eminently worthy of his position and the regiment he belongs to.

W. GAMBLE, *Colonel Commanding Brigade.*

---

*Washington, April 11, 1865.*

General MORGAN, *Chief of Staff :*

A scout just in reports that Mosby with one battalion crossed the Blue Ridge to the Shenandoah Valley April 8th, to prey upon trains. An affair between another portion of Mosby's force and a detachment of Eighth Illinois cavalry occurred April 10th, near Burke's Station. Five of Mosby's men killed. Our loss, 2 slightly wounded. C. C. AUGUR, *Major-General.*

---

*Fairfax Court House, April 11, 1865.*

Major-General AUGUR, *Commanding, etc.:*

GENERAL : The captured prisoners stated that they did not belong to Chapman's command, but were sent by Mosby to capture the quartermaster's animals at Burke's Station, and that Chapman himself is expected in this vicinity every day. From the conflicting accounts that have reached me I am led to believe that Mosby's entire command consists of 2 battalions of 4 companies each, and 2 additional companies, newly organized, 10 companies in all, numbering between 800 and 1,000 men. That 4 companies under Mosby himself crossed the Blue Ridge on Saturday to plunder weak guarded trains south of Winchester. One company sent to Maryland to plunder banks; one company sent to steal horses from my lines, beside the battalion from Northern Neck. W. GAMBLE, *Colonel Commanding Brigade.*

RETURN FROM THE RAID (BERRYVILLE).
From painting by Armand-Dumaresq.

# CHAPTER XXIX.

April, 1865—Companies C, E, F and G Return from Northern Neck—General Hancock Calls on Colonel Mosby to Surrender with his Command—Circular Issued by General Hancock—Colonel Chapman Sent to the Valley with a Flag of Truce—A Truce Between the Federals and "Mosby's Men"—Arranging for Surrender—Correspondence Between Mosby and the Federals—Colonel Mosby Visits Millwood and Confers with the Officers Sent by General Hancock to Meet Him.

The companies which had been sent to the Northern Neck to winter now returned, having done very little except to recruit their horses.[1]

At one time a large force of infantry, with about 250 cavalry, prepared to make an extensive raid through that section of Westmoreland County where Mosby's men were quartered. While on the march, Capt. Samuel Chapman made an attack on their rear and after a sharp engagement, in which a number of the Federals were killed and wounded, they retreated and the force was taken on transports to Point Lookout. Captain Chapman was wounded and John Horseley had his horse shot. At the time of the fight the night was so dark that it was hard to distinguish friend from foe.

---

[1]HEADQUARTERS, *March 27, 1865.*

Col. JOHN S. MOSBY (*Care Major Boyle*) :

Collect your command and watch the country from front of Gordonsville to Blue Ridge, and also Valley. Your command is all now in that section and the General will rely on you to watch and protect the country. If any of your command is in Northern Neck, call it to you.

W. H. TAYLOR, *Assist. Adjt. Gen.*

---

HEADQUARTERS ARMY OF NORTHERN VIRGINIA,
*March 27, 1865.*

Gen. J. A. EARLY :

From reports received Sheridan is now probably on Grant's left. I desire, if possible, to collect cavalry here sufficient to resist his and Gregg's combined forces. I know the need of troops with you, but have thought you might perhaps spare one of Lomax's brigades. If so, send Lomax with it to this point. If one is sent it would be better perhaps to retain Imboden in the Valley where Lomax is. I have ordered Dorsey's (Maryland) cavalry from Gordonsville to Fitz Lee and directed Mosby to collect his command south and protect the country from Gordonsville west.

R. E. LEE, *General.*

Capt. Thomas Richards, of Company G, charged into
Williamsburg one night, driving out the garrison and killing and wounding some 12 or 15 Federals.

Mosby and his command had always been a thorn in their
side and the Federal authorities were in a state of uncertainty regarding them, as will be seen by the correspondence
herewith.[2]

---

[2] WAR DEPARTMENT, *Washington, April 10, 1865.*
Lieut.-Gen. GRANT :

Rosser and the troops operating about Loudoun form part of the Army
of Northern Virginia reporting to Lee.     Are they included in the surrender, or
only those under Lee's immediate personal command ?     The troops in Western
Virginia have also gone as part of the Army of Northern Virginia.

EDWIN M. STANTON, *Secretary of War.*

*Prospect Station, April 10, 1865.*
Hon. E. M. STANTON, *Secretary of War :*

The surrender was only of the men left with the pursued army at the time
of the surrender,  All prisoners captured in battle previous to the surrender
stand same as other prisoners of war, and those who had escaped and were
detached at the time are not included.   I think, however, there will be no
difficulty now in bringing in on the terms voluntarily given to General Lee all
the fragments of the Army of Northern Virginia, and it may be the army under
Johnson also.   I wish Hancock would try it with Mosby.

U. S. GRANT, *Lieut.-General.*

*Richmond, April 10, 1865.*
Lieutenant-General U. S. GRANT :

The people here are anxious that Mosby should be included in Lee's
surrender.   They say he belongs to that army.

G. WEITZEL, *Major-General.*

*Washington, D. C., April 10, 1865.*
Major-General HANCOCK, *Winchester, Va.:*

The Secretary of War directs that you will have printed and circulated the
correspondence between Generals Grant and Lee on the surrender of the Army
of Northern Virginia.   All detachments and stragglers from that army will,
upon complying with the conditions agreed upon, be paroled and permitted to
return to their homes.   Those who do not so surrender will be brought in as
prisoners of war.   The guerrilla chief, Mosby, will not be paroled.

H. W. HALLECK,
*Major-General and Chief of Staff.*

*Winchester, Va., April 12, 1865.*
Major-General H. W. HALLECK, *Chief of Staff :*

In accordance with the instructions of General Grant, I yesterday sent a
communication to Mosby offering to receive the surrender of his command on
the same terms as indicated in General Grant's dispatch to General Lee. I have
as yet no answer.   It is quite as likely that Mosby will disband as that he will

On Wednesday, April 12th, Colonel Mosby received a despatch from General Hancock, commanding the forces in the Valley, calling on him to surrender his command on the

MAJ.-GEN. W. S. HANCOCK AND HIS DIVISION GENERALS.
Gens. Francis C. Barlow, David B. Birney and John Gibbon.

formally surrender, as all his men have fine animals and are generally armed with 2 pistols only. They will not give up these things, I presume, as long as they can escape. I will employ the cavalry force here in hunting them down.

W. S. HANCOCK, *Major-General.*

HDQRS. MIDDLE MILITARY DIVISION,
*April 15, 1865.*

Major T. W. LUSK, *Charlestown, Va.:*

Mosby's Men can surrender on the same terms as Lee's men and go to their homes. It is only necessary that they deliver up their arms and horses and take a parole not to take up arms again unless regularly exchanged.

C. H. MORGAN, *Brevet Brigadier-General.*

same terms which had been accorded General Lee by General Grant. At the same time a circular addressed to the citizens in the vicinity of his lines was sent over:

HEADQ'RS MIDDLE MILITARY DIVISION, }
*Winchester, Va., April 10, 1865.* }

The Major General commanding announces to the citizens in the vicinity of his lines that General Robert E. Lee surrendered with the Army of Northern Virginia yesterday to Lieutenant General Grant near Appomattox Court House.

The arms, artillery, and baggage were delivered up, the Confederate officers being allowed to retain their side-arms and private property. Officers and men were all paroled not to take up arms against the United States until regularly exchanged, and were allowed to return to their homes once more, there to remain without molestation from the authorities of the United States so long as their parole is kept inviolate and they respect the laws in force where they reside.

All detachments and stragglers from the Army of Northern Virginia will, upon complying with the above conditions, be paroled and allowed to go to their homes. Those who do not so surrender will be brought in as prisoners of war. The guerrilla chief Mosby is not included in the parole.

The Major General Commanding trusts that the people to whom this is sent will regard the surrender of General Lee with his army as Lee himself regards it, as the first great step to peace, and will adapt their conduct to the new condition of affairs and make it practicable for him to exhibit towards them every leniency the situation will admit of. Every military restraint shall be removed that is not absolutely essential, and your sons, your husbands, and your brothers shall remain with you unmolested.

It is for you to determine the amount of freedom you are to enjoy. The marauding bands which have so long infested this section, subsisting on the plunder of the defenseless, effecting no great military purpose, and bringing upon you the devastation of your homes, must no longer find shelter and concealment among you. Every outrage committed by them will be followed by the severest infliction, and it is the purpose of the Major General Commanding to destroy utterly the haunts of these bands if their depredations are continued.         W. S. HANCOCK,
*Major-General U. S. Vols.*

Official: GEORGE LEE, *Asst. Adjt. Gen.*

A circular was also received which had been issued by General Augur, declaring Mosby an outlaw; that "the guerrilla chief, Mosby, would not be paroled under any circumstances."

General Hancock sent the following communication to Colonel Mosby:

HEADQUARTERS MIDDLE MILITARY DIVISION,
*April 11, 1865.*

Col. JOHN S. MOSBY, *Commanding Partisans:*

COLONEL: I am directed by Major-General Hancock to inclose to you copies of letters which passed between Generals Grant and Lee on the occasion of the surrender of the Army of Northern Virginia. Major-General Hancock is authorized to receive the surrender of the forces under your command on the same conditions offered to General Lee, and will send an officer of equal rank with yourself to meet you at any point and time you may designate, convenient to the lines, for the purpose of arranging details, should you conclude to be governed by the example of General Lee.

Very respectfully, your obedient servant,
C. H. MORGAN,
*Bvt. Brig.-Gen. and Chief of Staff.*

In reply Colonel Mosby now despatched Lieutenant-Colonel Chapman, Dr. A. Monteiro, Surgeon of our command, Adjutant William H. Mosby and Capt. Walter E. Frankland, under flag of truce, with the following letter:

*April 15, 1865.*

Major-General W. S. HANCOCK, *Commanding, Etc.:*

GENERAL: I am in receipt of a letter from your chief of staff, Brigadier-General Morgan, enclosing copies of correspondence between Generals Grant and Lee, and informing me that you would appoint an officer of equal rank with myself to arrange details for the surrender of the forces under my command. As yet I have no notice, through any other source, of the facts concerning the surrender of the Army of Northern Virginia, nor, in my opinion, has the emergency yet arisen which would justify the surrender of my command. With no disposition, however, to cause the useless effusion of blood, or to inflict on a war-worn population any unnecessary distress, I am ready to agree to a suspension of hostilities for a short time, in order to enable me to communicate with my own authorities, or until I can obtain sufficient intelligence to determine my future action. Should you accede to this proposition, I am ready to meet any person you may designate to arrange the terms of an armistice.[3]

I am, very respectfully, your obedient servant,
JOHN S. MOSBY, *Colonel C. S. A.*

Dr. Monteiro, in his interesting volume of "Reminiscences," gives the following account of the interview with General Hancock:

" We passed into the hall of a large brick house and were informed that the General was in his room, and would soon grant us an audience. We were introduced to his adjutant, whom we found a very agreeable and pleasant fellow. In a few moments' conversation with this polite officer, we were much impressed with his good manners and obliging disposition. He sent a messenger to the General's room to inform him that Lieutenant-Colonel Chapman and Surgeon Monteiro, of Mosby's command, were waiting to see him. We had no well-digested plan of action in the event the General refused our petition, and we were not so sure he would have much regard for our flag of truce. Indeed, we were really at the mercy of our old enemy, and felt no certainty that we would be permitted to return. While conversing pleasantly with Colonel Russell and the adjutant, General Hancock walked into the hall. We were introduced by Colonel Russell. Fourteen eventful years have been gathered to Time's bosom since that interview, yet I have a distinct and vivid mental vision of General Hancock as he approached us and cordially grasped our hands. There was a self-possession, ease and benignant dignity about him that I will never forget. A benevolent expression, illumined by a powerful intellect, spoke volumes of meaning from his bright and handsome face. It may be that an association of

---

[3] *Winchester, Va., April 16, 1865.*

Major-General HALLECK, *Chief of Staff :*

I have this day received a communication from Colonel Mosby and have had an interview with Lieutenant-Colonel Chapman, of his command. I have no doubt but that Mosby will surrender his whole command on the terms given to General Lee. Arrangements have been made for a meeting at Millwood on Tuesday noon, when I expect to receive the surrender. Meanwhile Mosby agrees to refrain from any operations whatever, and I have directed no offensive operations against his command to be made. They are aware of the death of the President.

WINF'D S. HANCOCK,
*Major-Gen. Commanding.*

ideas, caused by receiving kind expressions of sympathy and regard, when I expected a harsh, cruel or haughty reception, impressed me so favorably with this true gentleman and distinguished soldier. Be that as it may, I have never met a man for whom I have a higher regard, or more profound respect than I have, even at this date, for General Hancock. I had never before felt at all ashamed of my old gray uniform, but when this true soldier held my hand and looked kindly and squarely into my face, and said, in a firm and earnest voice, "I sympathize with you in what you be-

DR. A. MONTEIRO,
Surgeon, 43d Battalion Virginia Cavalry, C. S. A.

lieve to be a great misfortune. You have fought bravely and have nothing to be ashamed of. You have, like gallant soldiers, left your cause to the god of battles, and the arbitrament of the sword has decided against you. Let us once more kneel down at the same altar, and be like brothers of the same household," I felt, I suppose, as the Prodigal Son ought to have felt, when he dropped the corn husks and abandoned his riotous living, to return once more to the home of his father. On finding such a man as General Hancock, a great leader, an accomplished officer and a perfect gentleman, against us, I, for the first time, encountered a doubt as to the righteousness of our cause. This noble old hero was so kind, considerate and gentle in his manner to us, when we had so little to expect of him, that he conquered me more effectually by his manly sympathy and noble sentiments than could have been done by brute force and military despotism."

In reply to Colonel Mosby's communication, General Hancock sent the following:

HEADQUARTERS MIDDLE MILITARY DIVISION, }
*Winchester, Va., April 16, 1865.* }

To Colonel JOHN S. MOSBY, *C. S. A.*

COLONEL: Major-General Hancock directs me to acknowledge the receipt of your communication by the hand of Lieutenant-Colonel Chapman, of the 15th instant, in reply to mine of the 11th. The General does not think it necessary to designate an officer to meet you to arrange an armistice, as you suggest.

ROBERT CHEW, CO. D.[4]
From a Photograph taken in April, 1864.

Understanding, however, your motives in hesitating to surrender your command without definite intelligence from your former superiors, the General is very willing to allow a reasonable time for you to acquire the information you desire. It is not practicable for you to communicate with General Lee, as he is no longer in authority. Lieutenant - Colonel Chapman, the bearer of your communication, has been furnished with such evidence as will undoubtedly satisfy you that further resistance on the part of your command can result in no good to the cause in which you have been engaged.

---

[4] Robert Chew enlisted in Company D, Mosby's command, in April, 1864. He was then seventeen years of age. He was badly wounded on Christmas eve, 1864, while scouting with J. West Aldridge near Point of Rocks. He rode 15 miles after being wounded.

In view of these facts, the General will not operate against your command until Tuesday next at 12 m., provided there are no hostilities from your command.  This agreement to be understood to include the Department of Washington and the Potomac River line.  It is possible some difficulty may arise from the operation of guerrilla parties not of your command, but the General hopes you can control the whole matter.  On Tuesday at noon the General will send an officer of equal rank with yourself to Millwood to meet you and ascertain your determination, and if you conclude to surrender your command, to arrange the details.  Lieutenant-Colonel Chapman will be able to give all the information you desire as to the probable terms.

If you consent to the above arrangements, please notify Brigadier-General Chapman, at Berryville, as soon as practicable.[5]

Very respectfully, your obedient servant,
                         C. H. MORGAN,
                *Brevet Brig.-Gen. and Chief of Staff.*

Secretary Stanton could not overcome his dread of these terrible guerrillas and wrote Hancock as follows :

                         WAR DEPARTMENT,
                    *Washington, April 16, 1865.*

Major-General HANCOCK,
         *Winchester, Va. :*

In holding an interview with Mosby, it may be needless to caution an old soldier like you to guard against surprise

---

[5] *Washington, D. C., April 16, 1865.*

Major-General HANCOCK,
         *Winchester, Va.:*

Lieutenant-General Grant authorizes you to give Colonel Mosby and his command the same terms as those agreed upon with General Lee.  It, however, is to be understood that permission to return to their homes does not include former homes in loyal States or the District of Columbia.  Persons from those places must take the oath of allegiance and get special permits from the War Department before they can return.

                         H. W. HALLECK,
                    *Major-General and Chief of Staff.*

HEADQUARTERS MIDDLE MILITARY DIVISION,
                              *April 16, 1865.*

Major-Gen. C. C. AUGUR,
         *Department of Washington :*

General Hancock directs me to inform you that he expects to receive the surrender of Mosby's command about Tuesday next.  Mosby has agreed to suspend all hostile operations whatever as soon as he can communicate with

or danger to yourself; but the recent murders show such astounding wickedness that too much precaution cannot be taken. If Mosby is sincere, he might do much toward detecting and apprehending the murderers of the President.[6]

EDWIN M. STANTON,
*Secretary of War.*

---

his men, and the General requests that you will pursue a defensive course as long as the agreement is respected by Mosby. The agreement includes the whole Military Division.

C. H. MORGAN,
*Brevet Brigadier-General.*

---

*Winchester, Va., April 16, 1865.*

Gen. WILLIAM DWIGHT :

The commanding officers are authorized to parole Confederate soldiers, Mosby's men included, when they come to these lines, on the terms given by General Grant. While the strict ruling required that private horses which have been used for the Government purposes should be delivered up, the General will not require this as a condition to the surrender. It is, however, desirable that all horses that formerly belonged to the United States should be required. After being paroled, the prisoners will be allowed to return to their homes. The arms of the men must be given up, unless they give evidence to show that they have been lost, not secreted. All offensive operations against Mosby's men will cease until further orders, as negotiations are in progress for the surrender of his command. Blank paroles of the prescribed form will be furnished from these headquarters.

C. H. MORGAN,
*Brevet Brigadier-General and Chief of Staff.*

---

[6] *Winchester, Va., April 17, 1865.*

Hon. E. M. STANTON :

Although I have consulted with two of Mosby's officers here, I do not intend to meet him in person at this time. General Chapman is to have an interview with him to-morrow at Millwood. I have reason to believe that Mosby may surrender his forces. His proposition was to suspend hostilities against him until he could hear from the Confederate authorities. I have declined to enter into a suspension of hostilities only until to-morrow. One of his men came in to-day. If Mosby surrenders, I will endeavor to ascertain from or through him something concerning the matter you especially refer to and will probably have an interview with him. I have now a suitable person engaged in seeking information of that kind from Mosby's men. I thank you for your caution to me against surprise.

WINF'D S. HANCOCK, *Major-General.*

The following instructions were given General Torbert:

HEADQUARTERS MIDDLE MILITARY DIVISION,
*April 16, 1865.*

Brevet Major-General TORBERT,

*Chief of Cavalry:*

The Major-General commanding directs me to inform you
that Colonel Mosby, C. S. Army, will be at Millwood, Tuesday next, the 18th
inst., at 12 m., for the
purpose of arranging
the surrender of his
command or defi-
nitely declining; with-
out doubt the former.
The General desires
you to send Briga-
dier - General Chap-
man to meet Colonel
Mosby and conduct
the negotiations with
him. If Mosby is
ready to surrender his
command on Tues-
day, the General
desires General Chap-
man to finish up the
matter. Blank par-
oles will be furnished
him in sufficient num-
ber for that purpose.
The General de-
sires Colonel Mosby
to have a muster roll

CORPL. GEORGE SKINNER, CO. A.

of his command, a duplicate of which is to be retained by
General Chapman. The officers and men are to be paroled
individually, in duplicate, the duplicate forms being forwarded to the Provost-Marshal at these Headquarters. The
enlisted men are to turn in their arms and all Confederate
States' horses or horses formerly belonging to the United
States. The General will not demand the surrender of
their private animals. If Colonel Mosby has any artillery
or public transportation (captured or otherwise) it is to be
included in the surrender. The paroles being given, the
officers and men will be allowed to return to their homes.
The Major-General Commanding wishes General Chapman

to impress very clearly upon Colonel Mosby's mind the great necessity that with this surrender all guerrilla operations should cease. There are known to be some independent parties operating from the vicinity of the Blue Ridge, and it will be for the interest of Mosby's men to hunt them out, as they can only bring further distress upon the people. It would also be well for General Chapman to say that people, refugees from the country he has occupied, must be allowed to return to and remain at their homes unmolested, and that the army will be used effectually, if necessary, to secure this.

C. H. MORGAN,
*Brevet Brigadier-General and Chief of Staff.*

*Monday, April 17.*—The command met to-day at Salem. The men were drawn up in line and Colonel Mosby addressed them. He said they would disperse until further orders ; that there was a truce between us and the Federals, and that for the honor of the command and with due regard for his authority he requested they would respect it. We were then dismissed.

*Tuesday, April 18.*—Colonel Mosby, with a number of his officers and men, met to-day at Paris and proceeded to Millwood to confer with an officer appointed by General Hancock, in accordance with the terms of the truce.[7] He

---

[7] HEADQUARTERS SECOND CAVALRY DIVISION,
MIDDLE MILITARY DIVISION,
*Near Berryville, Va., April 18, 1865.*

Brevet Brigadier-General MORGAN, *Chief of Staff,*
*Winchester, Va.:*

GENERAL : I have the honor to report that agreeable to instructions I met Colonel John S. Mosby, C. S. Army, commanding Forty-third Virginia Battalion, to-day at Millwood, under a flag of truce, to confer with him touching the surrender of his command, and to conclude the details, should he have decided to surrender upon the terms offered him. He declined to surrender at this time, for the reason that his command was not in immediate danger and that he had not such information as yet as would justify him in concluding the " Confederate Cause" altogether hopeless. He expressed himself as anxious to avoid any useless effusion of blood or destruction of property, and desirous therefore of the suspension of hostilities for a short time until he could learn the fate of " Johnson's Army." Should that be defeated or surrender, he said he should regard the " Confederate Cause " as lost and would disband his organization. He does not propose even in that event to surrender them as an

reached Millwood about a half hour before the time appointed for the expiration of the truce, and met General Chapman and Staff, with a number of Federal officers, awaiting his arrival. The interview was conducted with mutual courtesy. Colonel Mosby asked an extension of the time of the truce, to enable him to communicate with the Confederate authorities or learn the exact condition of affairs in the South. General Chapman stated that he had no power to alter the terms fixed by General Hancock, but would assume the responsibility of arranging another truce to expire on the 20th of April at 12 m., and would also submit to General Hancock for approval the following agreement:

---

organization for parole, but to disband the battalion, giving to each individual to choose his own course. He informed me he had already advised his command that those who chose to do so could go and give their parole. For himself, he said, he had no favors to ask, being quite willing to stand by his acts, all of which he believed to be justifiable; and in the course of my conversation with him, he remarked that he did not expect to remain in the country. I made an agreement with him for a suspension of hostilities for forty-eight hours longer, expiring at noon on the 25th, and a conditional agreement for a further suspension for ten days. These agreements are herewith enclosed, and I will inform Colonel Mosby of the action of the General commanding, as soon as advised. I did not give him to hope that this agreement for a ten days' suspension would be concurred in. I regret that I have not the pleasure of communicating the surrender of this force, but trust my action in the premises will meet your approval. The interview throughout was characterized by good feeling. Perhaps I ought, in justice to Colonel Mosby and his officers, to state a universal regret was expressed because of the assassination of the President.

JOHN T. BEAL, CO. D.
From a Photograph taken when a member of
Co. C, 19th Virginia Infantry.

I am very respectfully, your obedient servant,

GEORGE H. CHAPMAN, *Brigadier-General.*

" A cessation of hostilities is hereby agreed upon between the forces of the United States commanded by General Hancock, and the forces of the Confederate States commanded by Colonel John S. Mosby.

" This cessation to be subject to the approval of General Hancock; if approved, to be in force for ten (10) days, commencing on the 20th of April at 12 m. and ending on the 30th at 12 m.

" Colonel Mosby to be notified at Millwood of the approval or disapproval of this agreement, by 12 noon of April 20th.

" Colonel Mosby to use his authority and influence to prevent any acts of hostility being perpetrated or attempted by any bands or organizations of Confederate soldiers operating from Loudoun or Fauquier counties.

" This agreement is made with the understanding that in case, during this interval, the army opposed to the army of General Sherman shall capitulate or be dispersed, Colonel Mosby will disband his organization (the 43d Virginia Battalion).

" GEO. H. CHAPMAN, *Brig.-General, U. S. Vols.*
" JOHN S. MOSBY, *Colonel, C. S. A.*
" *Millwood, April 18th, 1865.*"

General Hancock confirmed the extension of the truce until the 20th, but refused to grant further time, as will appear by the following letter :

HEADQUARTERS MIDDLE MILITARY DIVISION, }
*April 19th, 1865.* }

COLONEL : Major-General Hancock, commanding Middle Military Division, directs me to say that he has confirmed the extension of the cessation of hostilities until noon of the 20th, arranged at Millwood on the 18th, between Brigadier-General Chapman, U. S. Volunteers, and yourself ; but General Hancock can see no sufficient reasons why the cessation of hostilities should be continued. The truce will, therefore, cease at noon on the 20th between the forces commanded by Major-General Hancock and your troops, unless you should decide to surrender at or before that time on the conditions previously offered and explained by Lieutenant-General Grant, which are enclosed.

The officer bearing the flag will wait at Millwood until 12 m. to hear your decision. Unless you then announce your immediate surrender, he will return. In case of your surrender, the arrangements will be immediately perfected at

Millwood. Truce of hostilities in such case will only refer to that point, and be of such duration as only to allow time to prepare and sign the paroles and receive the public property. After the expiration of this truce, General Hancock is commanded not to offer you or your men terms again.[8]

I am, sir, very respectfully, your obedient servant,
W. G. MITCHELL, *Brevet Colonel and A. D. C.*
To Colonel JOHN S. MOSBY, *C. S. A.*,
*Commanding, etc., Millwood, Va.*

---

Maj.-Gen. H. W. HALLECK,
      *Chief of Staff:*

[8] *Winchester, Va., April 19, 1865.*

Colonel Mosby asks for a suspension of hostilities for ten days to learn the fate of Johnson. He says if Johnson surrenders or is beaten he will disperse his command and leave the country. He has already notified his men that they might individually come in and be paroled if they desire. Some of them are coming in. The officers of his command, 15 or 20 in number, yesterday universally expressed regret at the death of the President. The people are all anxious for Mosby to surrender. If the authorities at Washington think it advisable to allow a truce of ten days, I should like to be notified to-day; otherwise the truce will end with him to-morrow at noon.

W. S. HANCOCK,
    *Major-General.*

FRANK M. ANGELO, CO. C.
From a War-time Photograph.

*Washington,*
*April 19, 1865.*
Major-Gen. HANCOCK,
   *Winchester, Va.:*

If Mosby does not avail himself of the present truce, end it and hunt him

On Thusday, April 20th, Colonel Mosby, accompanied by
a number of his officers and men, as before, proceeded to
Millwood.  The officer delegated to confer with him handed
Mosby the following communication from General Hancock:

HEADQUARTERS CAVALRY MIDDLE MILITARY DIVISION,
*April 19th, 1865.*

COLONEL : Major-General Hancock directs me to say to
you that the following instructions have been telegraphed
to him in reference to Confederate officers or soldiers who
surrender :

" *Washington, D. C., April 19, 1865.*

" To Major-General HANCOCK :

" You may receive all rebel officers or soldiers who sur-

---

and his men down.  Guerrillas, after beating the armies of the enemy, will not
be entitled to quarter.

U. S. GRANT, *Lieutenant-General.*

---

*Winchester, April 19, 1865.*

Lieutenant-General GRANT:

GENERAL: I have your dispatch concerning Mosby.  I have already
informed him that there would be no more truce with him after 12 m. to-morrow,
and if he then surrenders there would only be a truce at the point of surrender
sufficiently long to have him sign the parole.

W. S. HANCOCK, *Major-General.*

---

*Winchester, April 20, 1865.*

Major-General AUGUR:

Major-General Hancock directs me to say that the truce with Mosby ended
at noon to-day.  He did not surrender.  I believe his command will disperse,
but it will be well to be on the watch for him.

W. J. MITCHELL,
*Colonel and Aide-de-Camp.*

---

HEADQUARTERS MIDDLE MILITARY DIVISION,
*April 20, 1865.*

Major-General AUGUR,

*Commanding Defenses of Washington :*

GENERAL: Major-General Hancock directs me to say that Colonel Mosby
was met in person at Millwood to-day at 12 m., when the truce ended with him.
He stated, and it appears to be true from the corroboration of Confederate
officers and soldiers who have surrendered, and citizens, that his command has
disbanded, with the exception of a few officers and soldiers.  The Confederate
officers and soldiers and citizens are hostile to him.  General Hancock will hunt
him up if he is in Loudoun Valley.  The worst band of guerrillas in Loudoun
County (Mobberly's) have all been killed or surrendered.

Respectfully,

W. G. MITCHELL,
*Brevet General and Aide-de-Camp.*

render to you on exactly the same terms that were given to General Lee, except have it distinctly understood that all who claim homes in States that never passed Ordinances of Secession have forfeited them, and can only return on compliance with the amnesty proclamation. Maryland, Kentucky, Delaware and Missouri are such States. They may return to West Virginia on their parole.

"U. S. GRANT, *Lieutenant-General.*"

I am, Colonel, very respectfully,
C. McK. GROSER, *A. A. A. G.*

Colonel JOHN S. MOSBY, *C. S. A.*

Dr. Monteiro describes this final interview as follows:

We met at Paris a half hour later than at the previous visit, and consequently arrived at Millwood almost at the exact hour that the second truce expired. We found 15 Federal officers again awaiting us. They were seated in a large room, called a parlor, in the only hotel in the little village of Millwood. Mosby walked in rapidly, followed by 20 of his officers. Taking a seat by one of the Federal officers, whose name I have forgotten, he entered into an earnest conversation with him. The first words were spoken in such low tones that, though sitting near them, I did not hear what they said.

While we were engaged in this interesting interview within doors, some excitement was going on outside The irrepressible Hern had accompanied us, without any special invitation. He was a rough diamond in his own way, and did not recognize the difference between a diplomatic military mission and a regular raid. Hern had formed some acquaintance with the Yankee soldiers immediately on his arrival, and his ruling passion for the turf prompted him at once to propose a horse race with his new made acquaintance. The challenged Yank accepted, and a spirited race was the immediate result. Hern had a vague suspicion that the Yankees had planned this meeting for the purpose of capturing Mosby and his officers. He had never mentioned his suspicions to any one; but in the race with his Yankee competitor an event occurred that ripened his suspicion into a certainty true as "proof of holy writ." Hern and his rival turfman, after testing the speed of their horses nearly a mile, ran into the solid ranks of a Federal brigade. No sooner did this faithful and zealous soldier discover the hostile array of blue uniforms than his suspicion of foul play became a fixed conviction. He abandoned the race and returned, with an earnestness and speed that would have

GROUP OF MOSBY'S MEN.
From a Photograph taken in 1865.

reflected some credit upon the Knight of De La Mancha in his memorable charge upon the insolent wind-mill. Hern was a rough but ready partisan. Like many other people, he was not handsome, neither did he dress well. No careful observer would ever discover any very striking resemblance between Solomon in all his glory and my fellow-soldier Hern. Yet he was faithful, reliable and earnest; determined, daring and brave. When he rode into a strong body of Yankee cavalry just beyond the limits of Millwood he felt sure he had made a far more wonderful and important discovery than Christopher Columbus or Isaac Newton ever did. He came back breathless, excited and alarmed for the safety of his admired and beloved leader. Just as Mosby and the Yankee General had entered upon the most interesting and important phase of their mission, with the strained attention of 30 or 40 officers bearing upon them, eagerly catching every word that escaped their lips; just as the potent and grave representative of Yankee authority announced to Mosby the fiat of his omnipotent judgment; just

Key to group on opposite page :

1. Lee Howison.
2. Lieut. W. Ben. Palmer.
3. Lieut. John W. Puryear.
4. Sergt. Thomas Booker.
5. Sergt. A. G. Babcock
6. N. V. Randolph.
7. Lieut. Frank H. Rahm.
8. Sergt. Robert B. Parrott.
9. Thomas Throop.
10. John W. Munson.
11. Col. John S. Mosby.
12. ———— Noel.
13. Charles Quarles.
14. Walter W. Gosden.
15. Harry T. Sinnott.
16. O. L. Butler.
17. I. A. Gentry.

as he announced the imperative decree (looking the subtle and active guerrilla chief full in the face): " The truce has ended ; we can have no further intercourse under its terms " —at this moment Hern rushed into the room. With frantic gestures and hasty speech he reported the important result of his personal observations. " Colonel, Colonel," he exclaimed; " the infernal devils have sot a trap for you ; I jist now run out about a mile and I found a thousand uv um a hidin' in the bushes ! They're in ambush ! Less fight um, Colonel ; darn um ! It's a trick ; it's a trick to capture us, by God, it is ! "

Taken altogether, the several incidents of this remarkable interview in the parlor at Millwood were well calculated to test the moral courage, determined pluck or military skill of any leader. With the significant voice of the great mouth-piece of Federal power imparting the irritable intelligence that we were no longer protected by the flag of truce, simultaneously with this bad news came the startling apparition of the rough and clumsy Hern, announcing outside perils of our alarming situation. With a look that I shall never forget, Mosby sprang to his feet, instantly grasping one of the murderous weapons in his belt and glaring upon the Yankee officers with an expression that reminded me more of a tiger crouching to spring upon his prey than anything I have ever seen appertaining to the human race, he said in a loud and sharp voice :

" Sir, if we are no longer under the protection of our truce, we are, of course, at the mercy of your men. We shall protect ourselves."

With that inimitable sign and gesture that so often had sent his gallant followers like a thunderbolt into the serried ranks of the foe, he led the way with long·and rapid strides to the door, closely followed by twenty silent but as determined officers as ever bore a military commission. It was a scene difficult to describe, but never to be forgotten. Every partisan was well prepared for instant death and more than ready for a desperate fight. Had a single pistol been discharged by accident, or had Mosby given the word, not one Yankee officer in the room would have lived a minute. With Hern's warning voice ringing in our ears, we mounted our horses in silence and Mosby led the way. His only word of command was "Mount and follow me." We galloped rapidly from Millwood to the Shenandoah River, closely followed by a cloud of Yankee cavalry.

# CHAPTER XXX.

April, 1865—Disbanding of "Mosby's Men"—Mosby's Farewell to his Men—Parting of Old Friends and Comrades—To Winchester to be Paroled—Our Reception by the Federals —Mosby goes South, but Finding the Cause Hopeless, Accepts the Situation and is Paroled.

On Friday, April 21st, the command met at Salem (now called Marshall). The men came in slowly. It had rained in the early part of the morning, and a thick fog hung like a pall over the face of the country. The damp, raw air did not strike the feelings with a more chilling influence than that which was sent to the heart by the gloomy aspect which every object seemed to wear. Not a smile was to be seen on any of the faces around—all looked sad. Mosby was walking up and down the street, occasionally stopping to speak to one or another of the men as they rode in.

About noon the order was given to mount, and the companies formed. The whole command was drawn up in line on the green, north of the town. Well-mounted and equipped, the men presented a magnificent appearance, and as Mosby rode up and down the line he might well feel proud of this gallant band, whose courage and devotion had stood the test on so many occasions. As he glanced from man to man, each familiar face recalled to memory recollections of some deed of daring, some hard fought field, some brilliant victory or some trying hour of defeat.

When all preliminaries were arranged, Mosby's Farewell to his command was read by the commander of each squadron to his men :

*Fauquier, April 21, 1865.*

SOLDIERS :

I have summoned you together for the last time. The visions we have cherished of a free and independent country have vanished, and that country is now the spoil of a conqueror. I disband your organization in preference to surrendering it to our enemies. I am now no longer your

commander.   After an association of more than two eventful years, I part from you with a just pride in the fame of
your achievements, and a grateful recollection of your
generous kindness to myself.   And now, at this moment of
bidding you a final adieu, accept the assurance of my un-
changing confidence and regard.
            Farewell!
                        JOHN SINGLETON MOSBY.

GEN. R. E. LEE, C. S. A.

While the address was being read, a profound silence
reigned ; and when the word " farewell " was uttered, it fell
like a knell upon the ears of the assembled band.   They
gave Mosby three hearty cheers and the order was given to

break ranks. Then ensued a scene trying to all. The men who had fought side by side, who had endured so many hardships and passed through so many dangers together, were now to separate, probably never to meet again. Amid all the surrounding gloom, there was not one cheering thought, save the reflection that they had done their duty. The men pressed forward around their officers to bid them adieu, and soon hardly a dry eye could be seen. Strong men, who had looked unmoved on scenes which would have appalled hearts unused to the painful sights presented on the field of battle, now wept like little children. Mosby stood beside a fence on the main street and took the hands of those who gathered around him. His eyes were red, and he would now and then dash aside the struggling tears which he was unable wholly to suppress. Men would silently grasp each other's hands and then turn their heads aside to hide their tears ; but at last it became so general that no pains were taken to conceal them. It was the most trying ordeal through which we had ever passed. A number of ladies who had assembled to witness the disbanding of the command were apparently as much affected as we were.

On the 22d of April, it being announced that Lieutenant-Colonel Chapman intended going to Winchester to accept the parole, and would meet at Paris such of the men as wished to accompany him, about 200 men assembled, including Captains Frankland, Glascock and Samuel Chapman ; Lieutenants Nelson, Puryear and other officers.[1]

Crossing the Shenandoah at Hilton's Ford, the cavalcade

---

[1] *Winchester, Va., April 22, 1865.*
Hon. E. M. STANTON, *Secretary of War:*
Nearly all Mosby's command has surrendered, including nearly, if not quite, all of the officers, except Mosby himself, who has probably fled. His next in rank, Lieutenant-Colonel Chapman, surrendered with the command. He is as important as Mosby, and, from conversation had with him, I think he will be valuable to the Government hereafter. Some of Mosby's own men are in pursuit of him, for a reward of $2,000, offered by me. · As near as I can tell, about 380 of Mosby's men were paroled. Colonel Reno has paroled about 1,200 or 1,500 men at Newmarket, and has sent down for more blanks. I leave here for Washington city to-morrow morning.
W. S. HANCOCK, *Major-General.*

moved on toward Winchester. At Millwood we were halted
by the Federal picket, but after a little delay passed on.
About 2 miles from Winchester we were again halted by
pickets for about 20 minutes, when we again moved on until
we came in sight of the camps, about a mile outside of town.
Colonel Chapman with some 15 or 20 men then went on to
Winchester, while we remained until the Provost Marshal
came out with our paroles.[2]  By the Federal officers we
were received without any manifestations of exultation;
their manner toward us was gentlemanly and courteous.

Many of the men, thinking their horses would be taken
from them, procured horses for the occasion from the farmers around—some lame, others blind and the majority
afflicted in some way.  After taking a careful survey of a
group of Rosinantes, one of the Federal soldiers remarked:

"These are not the horses you boys have been chasing us
up and down the Valley with?"

Another jestingly inquired of a Ranger, who sat quietly
smoking his pipe:

"Say, Johnny, when were you paid off last?"

"Well," replied he, "not since we ran off that train on

---

[2] "The surrender of General Lee's Army to General Grant, April 9th, 1865,
rendered further preparations for moving unnecessary.  A force was sent up the
Valley to parole such detachments of the enemy as might desire to avail themselves of the terms proposed.  Mosby, the guerrilla chief was at first excepted
from the offer of the parole by instructions from the War Department, but
afterwards, by direction of General Grant, he was tendered the parole by a staff
officer whom I sent to meet him at Millwood, for that purpose, but not receiving
a favorable reply from him, I arranged to move a large force of infantry and
cavalry into Loudoun County, which, co-operating with a force which was to
march from Washington City, would, I had every reason to expect, break up
Mosby's command entirely, as I had accurate information as to their haunts,
habits, places of concealment, etc.  It was my intention, also, at the same
time to have punished severely those of the inhabitants who harbored or
assisted him, but the assassination of President Lincoln occurring on the night
the force from Washington was to have marched (14th of April, 1865), the movement was temporarily postponed, and before preparations to put it into operation had again been completed, the majority of Mosby's forces, commanded by
Lieutenant-Colonel Chapman, came into Winchester and were paroled (April 21,
1865). Mosby, and a few of his followers, refused to surrender and moved off, I
was informed, in the direction of Lynchburg."—*Report of Major-General W. S.
Hancock, U. S. A., Commanding the Middle Military Division Department West
Virginia and the Middle Department.*

the Baltimore and Ohio Railroad"—alluding to the "Greenback Raid" and capture of the two paymasters, with $168,000.

A Federal officer was afterwards sent to Millwood, where a number of the men went and were paroled.

LIEUT.-GEN. U. S. GRANT, U. S. A.

After the disbanding of the command at Salem, Colonel Mosby started South with about 30 or 40 men, with the intention of joining the army under Gen. Joe Johnson, but learning that Johnson's army had surrendered, and that the cause was hopeless, he disbanded the men who accompanied him, near Frederick Hall. They nearly all accepted the parole, and Mosby went to the vicinity of Lynchburg.[3]

Secretary Stanton was unwilling to let Mosby slip through his hands without a squeeze. An attempt to connect him with the assassination of President Lincoln, however, proved a failure, and the matter was dropped with but little comment.[4]

Efforts to capture him being unsuccessful, the following order was issued:

HEADQUARTERS MIDDLE MILITARY DIVISION,
                                *May 3, 1865.*

Brevet Major-General TORBERT,
    *Commanding Army of the Shenandoah,*
                *Winchester, Va.:*

Major-General Hancock directs that you offer a reward of $5,000 for the apprehension and delivery at any military post, of Colonel John S. Mosby, C. S. Army. The money will be paid at once. This to include reward of $2,000 previously offered by the General.

C. H. MORGAN,
    *Brevet Brigadier-General and Chief of Staff.*

Mosby, however, was too wily to be caught, and the silver bullets proved as harmless as the paper pellets hurled after him from the War Department.[5]

---

[3] HEADQUARTERS MIDDLE MILITARY DIVISION,
Brevet Major-General TORBERT,                    *April 28, 1865.*
    *Commanding, Winchester, Va.:*

Major Parsons can return of course, now that Booth has been caught. The General wishes you to try and hunt up Mosby. If more money is needed, it can be had.                    C. H. MORGAN, *Brevet Brigadier-General.*

---

[4] WAR DEPARTMENT,
                    *Washington City, April 19, 1865.*

Major-General HANCOCK, *Winchester:*

There is evidence that Mosby knew Booth's plan and was here in this city with him ; also that some of the gang are endeavoring to escape and by crossing the upper Potomac to get with Mosby or the Secesh there. Atzerodt or "Port Tobacco," as he is called, is known to have gone to Rockville Saturday to escape in that direction.    EDWIN M. STANTON, *Secretary of War.*

---

[5] *Philadelphia, May 4, 1865.*

Major-General HALLECK, *Richmond, Va.:*

I gave General Hancock several days ago, verbal instructions to treat all men in arms in Virginia as you propose to notify them you will do. I wish you

On the thirteenth of June, understanding that he would be paroled if he went in and gave himself up, Mosby went into Lynchburg, and applied for a parole. This was refused him, although he was allowed to leave town without molestation. Afterwards, towards the latter part of June, General Halleck issued an order that, should Colonel Mosby come in, he would be paroled, and Mosby soon after accepted the terms offered.

In Burr and Hinton's Life of General Sheridan, from which I have already quoted, I find the following, with which I close this work:

Here let us pause. The years have passed, summer and winter. Each season in its appointed time has held in its embrace the Northland and the Southland alike. The shell-shattered tree, the cannon-rifted earth, the torn bastions, the fields ploughed by "war's dread enginery," have all changed their rude, sad features. The tender touch of Nature has shrouded in moss, creeper and verdure the riven

---

would have efforts made to arrest Smith, Hunter, Letcher and all other particularly obnoxious political leaders in the State. I would advise offering a reward of $5,000 for Mosby if he is still in the State.

U. S. GRANT, *Lieutenant-General.*

---

*Richmond, May 16, 1865.*

Gen. J. A. RAWLINS, *Chief of Staff:*

Will Mosby be admitted to parole with the other officers of Rosser's command, to which he belongs? The question is asked to determine the action of Mosby and some others who would probably follow him out of the country if he goes. Shall a definite answer be given, or shall it be said that he and others would learn the action of the United States Government after they acknowledge its authority? GEORGE H. SHARPE, *Brevet Brigadier-General.*

---

HEADQUARTERS MILITARY DIVISION OF THE JAMES,

*Richmond, Va., May 18, 1865.*

*Commanding Officer, Charlottesville:*

If John S. Mosby, the Guerrilla Chief, does not surrender himself by the 20th of this month, offer a reward of $5,000 for his capture. Also publish the following reward for the Rebel Governor, William Smith, known as "Extra Billy":

"$25,000 REWARD.

"By direction of the Secretary of War a reward of $25,000 is hereby offered for the arrest and delivery for trial of William Smith, Rebel Governor of Virginia." H. W. HALLECK,

*Major-General Commanding.*

tree. The broken earth has been brought by industry into smiling places of plenty. The wild flowers bloom where the deadly missles hurtled fast and furious. Dear Nature has kissed alike the graves of Union and Confederate, and her robes of verdure or of snow are the proofs of loving impartiality. But memories live. The "boys" came home again—North and South—but, alas! not all of them. As Francis A. Durivage so simply and pathetically sings:

> " There hangs a sabre, and there a rein,
> With rusty buckle and green curb chain;
> A pair of spurs on the old gray wall,
> And a mouldy saddle—well, that is all.

> " Come out to the stable; it is not far,
> The moss-grown door is hanging ajar;
> Look within! There's an empty stall,
> Where once stood a charger—and that is all.

> " The good black steed came riderless home,
> Flecked with the blood-drops, as well as foam.
> Do you see that mound, where the dead leaves fall?
> The good black horse pined to death—that's all.

> " All? O, God! it is all I can speak.
> Question me not—I am old and weak.
> His saddle and sabre hang on the wall,
> And his horse pined to death—I have told you all."

# APPENDIX.

## CONFEDERATE REPORTS, ETC.

### I.

*Report of John S. Mosby, Virginia Cavalry.*

*Fauquier Co., Va., Feb. 4, 1863.*

Major General J. E. B. STUART :

GENERAL: I arrived in this neighborhood about one week ago. Since then I have been, despite the bad weather, quite actively engaged with the enemy. The result, up to this time, has been the capture of 28 Yankee Cavalry, together with all their horses, arms, etc. The evidence of parole I forward with this. I have also paroled a number of deserters. Col. Percy Wyndham, with over 200 cavalry, came up to Middleburg last week to punish me, as he said, for my raids on his picket line. I had a slight skirmish with him, in which my loss was 3 men captured by the falling of their horses; the enemy's loss, 1 man and three horses captured.

He set a very nice trap a few days ago to capture me in. I went into it, but contrary to the Colonel's expectations, brought the trap off with me, killing 1, capturing 12, the balance running. The extent of the annoyance I have been to the Yankees may be judged of by the fact that, baffled in their attempts to capture me, they threaten to retaliate on citizens for my acts.

I forward to you some correspondence I have had on the subject. The most of the infantry have left Fairfax and gone towards Fredericksburg. In Fairfax there are 5 or 6 regiments of cavalry; there are about 300 at Dranesville. They are so isolated from the rest of the command that nothing would be easier than their capture. I have harassed them so much that they do not keep their pickets over half a mile from the camp. There is no artillery there. I start on another trip day after to-morrow.

I am most respectfully yours,

JNO. S. MOSBY.

[Indorsements.]

*Feb. 8, 1863.*

Respectfully forwarded as additional proof of the prowess,

daring, and efficiency of Mosby (without commission) and his band of a dozen chosen spirits.

J. E. B. STUART, *Major-Gen. Comdg.*

*Feb.* 11, 1863.

Respectfully forwarded to the Adjutant and Inspector-General as evidence of the merit of Captain Mosby.

R. E. LEE, *General.*

————

II.

*Report of Capt. John S. Mosby, Virginia Cavalry, including operations, March 16th to April 1, 1863.*

*Fauquier Co., Va., April 7, 1863.*

Gen. J. E. B. STUART:

GENERAL : I have the honor to submit the following report of the operations of the cavalry under my command since rendering my last report :

On Monday, March 16, I proceeded down the Little River pike to capture two outposts of the enemy, each numbering 60 or 70 men. I did not succeed in gaining their rear as I expected, and only captured 4 or 5 vedettes. It being late in the evening and our horses very much jaded, I concluded to return. I had gone on over a mile back when we saw a large body of the enemy's cavalry, which, according to their own reports numbered 200 men, rapidly pursuing. I feigned a retreat, desiring to draw them off from their camps. At a point where the enemy had barricaded the road with fallen trees, I formed to receive them, for with my knowledge of the Yankee character, I knew they would imagine themselves fallen into an ambuscade. When they had come within 100 yards of me I ordered a charge, to which my men responded with a vim that swept everything before them. The Yankees broke when we got within 75 yards of them, and it was more of a chase than a fight for 4 or 5 miles. We killed 5, wounded a considerable number and brought off 1 lieutenant and 35 men prisoners. I didn't have over 50 men with me, some having gone back with the prisoners and others having gone on ahead when we started back, not anticipating any pursuit.

On Monday, March 31, I went down in the direction of Dranesville to capture several strong outposts in the vicinity of this place. On reaching there I discovered that they had fallen back about 10 miles down the Alexandria pike. I then returned 6 or 8 miles back and stopped about 10 o'clock at night at a point about 2 miles from the pike.

Early the next morning one of my men, whom I had left over on the Leesburg pike, came dashing in and announced the rapid approach of the enemy. But he had scarcely given us the information, when the enemy appeared a few hundred yards off, coming up at a gallop. At this time our horses were eating ; all had their bridles off, and some even their saddles ; they were all tied in a barn-yard. Throwing open the gate, I ordered a counter charge, to which the men promptly responded. The Yankees, never dreaming of our assuming the offensive, terrified at the yells of the men as they dashed on, broke and fled in every direction. We drove them in confusion 7 or 8 miles down the pike. We left on the field 9 of them killed, among them a captain and lieutenant, and about 15 too badly wounded for removal ; in this lot, 2 lieutenants. We brought off 82 prisoners, many of these also wounded. I have since visited the scene of the fight. The enemy sent up a flag of truce for their dead and wounded, but many of them being s e v e r e l y wounded, they established a hospital on the ground. The surgeon who attended them informs me that a great number of those who escaped were wounded.

LIEUT. W. BEN PALMER, CO. E,
Drawn from a painting taken during the war.

The force of the enemy was 6 companies of the First Vermont Cavalry, one of their oldest and best regiments, and prisoners informed me that they had every available man with them. There were certainly not less than 200 ; the prisoners say it was more than that. I had about 65 men in this affair. In addition to the prisoners, we took all their arms, and about 100 horses and equipments.

Privates Hart, Hurst, Keys, and Davis were wounded. The latter has since died. Both on this, and several other occasions, they have borne themselves with conspicuous gallantry. In addition to those mentioned above, I desire to place on record the names of several others, whose promptitude and boldness in closing in with the enemy contributed much to the success of the fight ; they are Lieut. (Wm. H.) Chapman (late of Dixie Artillery), Sergeant Hunter, and Privates Wellington, Harry Hatcher, Turner, Wild, Sowers, Ames, and Seibert. There are many others, I have no doubt, deserving of honorable mention, but the above were only those who came under my personal observation.

I confess, that on this occasion, I had not taken sufficient precautions to guard against surprise. It was ten (o'clock) at night when I reached the place where the fight came off, on the succeeding day. We had ridden through snow and mud upwards of 40 miles, and both men and horses were nearly broken down ; besides, the enemy had fallen back a distance of about 18 miles.

I have the honor to be, very respectfully, your obedient servant,

JNO. S. MOSBY, *Capt. Comdg*.

[Indorsements.]

APRIL 11, 1863.

Respectfully forwarded as in perfect keeping with his other brilliant achievements.

Recommended for promotion. J. E. B. STUART.

APRIL 13, 1863.

Respectfully forwarded for the information of the Department. Telegraphic report already sent in.

R. E. LEE, *General*.

APRIL 18, 1863.

Respectfully submitted to the Secretary of War.

H. L. CLAY, *A. A. G*.

Nominated as Major, if it has not been previously done.

J. A. S. (SEDDON), *Secretary*.

III.

*Stuart to Mosby.*

HEADQUARTERS CAMP PELHAM, *April* 26, 1863.

MAJOR: There is now a splendid opportunity to strike the enemy in the rear of Warrenton Junction. The trains are running regularly to that point. (It may be, by the time you get this, the opportunity may have gone.) Capture a train, and interrupt the operation of the railroad. Stoneman's main body of cavalry is located near Warrenton Junction, Bealeton and Warrenton Springs. Keep far enough from a brigade camp to give you time to get off your plunder and prisoners. Information of the movements of large bodies is of the greatest importance to us just now. The marching or transportation of divisions will often indicate the plan of a campaign. Be sure to give dates and numbers and names, as far as possible.

Wishing you all success, I am,

Very truly yours,

J. E. B. STUART. *Major General.*

IV.

*Major John S. Mosby's Report of Operations in Virginia, August* 24 *to September* 30, 1863.

*Fauquier Co., Va., Sept.* 30, 1863.

MOSBY to STUART : I have the honor to submit the following report of the operations of the force under my command from about August 20th to the present time ;

On the morning of August 24, with about 30 men, I reached a point (Annandale) immediately on the enemy's line of communication. Leaving the whole command, except 3 men who accompanied me, in the woods, concealed, I proceeded on a reconnoissance along the railroad to ascertain if there were any bridges unguarded. I discovered there were three. I returned to the command just as a drove of horses with a cavalry escort of about 50 men was passing. These I determined to attack and to await until night to burn the bridges. I ordered Lieutenant Turner to take half of the men and charge them in front, while with the remainder I attacked their rear.

In the meantime the enemy had been joined by another party, making their number about 63. When I overtook them they had dis-

mounted at Gooding's Tavern to water their horses.  My men went at
them with a yell that terrified the Yankees and scattered them in all
directions.  A few taking shelter under cover of the houses, opened
fire upon us.  They were soon silenced, however.  At the very moment when I had succeeded in routing them, I was compelled to retire
from the fight, having been shot through the side and thigh.  My
men, not understanding it, followed me, which gave time to the Yankees
to escape to the woods.  But for this accident, the whole party would
have been captured.  As soon as I perceived this, I ordered the men
to go back, which a portion of them did, just as Lieutenant Turner,
who had met and routed another force above, came gallantly charging up.

Over 100 horses fell into our possession, though a good many were
lost in bringing them out at night ; also 12 prisoners, arms, etc.  I
learn that 6 of the enemy were killed.

Lieutenant Smith, of the Black Horse, then on duty with me, acted,
as he always does, with conspicuous gallantry.  Lieutenant Turner, on
whom the command devolved, showed himself fully competent for
the trust.

In this affair my loss was 2 killed and 3 wounded.  Among the
killed was Norman E. Smith, who, thus early terminating a career of
great usefulness and brilliant promise, has left the memory of a name
that will not be forgotten till honor, virtue, courage, all, shall cease
to claim the homage of the heart.

I afterwards directed Lieutenant Turner to burn the bridges.  He
succeeded in burning one.

During my absence from the command, Lieutenant Turner attacked
an outpost of the enemy near Waterloo, killing 2 and capturing 4 men
and 27 horses.

About September 15 he captured 3 wagons, 20 horses, 7 prisoners
and a large amount of sutlers' goods near Warrenton Junction.

On the 20th and 21st instant, I conducted an expedition along the
enemy's line of communication, in which important information obtained was forwarded to the army headquarters, and I succeeded in
capturing 9 prisoners and 21 fine horses and mules.

On the 27th and 28th instant, I made a reconnoissance in the
vicinity of Alexandria, capturing Colonel Dulany, aide to the bogus
Governor Peirpont, several horses, and burning the railroad bridge
across Cameron's Run, which was immediately under cover of the
guns of two forts.

The military value of the species of warfare I have waged is not
measured by the number of prisoners and material of war captured
from the enemy, but by the heavy detail it has already compelled him
to make, and which I hope to make him increase, in order to guard

his communication and to that extent diminishing his aggressive strength.

Very respectfully, your obedient servant,

JNO. S. MOSBY, *Major.*

[Indorsements.]

HEADQUARTERS CAVALRY CORPS, *October* 5, 1863.

Respectfully forwarded, and recommend that Major Mosby be promoted another grade in recognition of his valuable services. The capture of these prominent Union officials, as well as the destruction of bridges, trains, etc. was the subject of special instructions which he is faithfully carrying out.

J. E. B. STUART, *Major-General.*

HEADQUARTERS, *November* 17, 1863.

Respectfully forwarded.

Major Mosby is entitled to great credit for his boldness and skill in his operations against the enemy. He keeps them in constant apprehension and inflicts repeated injuries. I have hoped that he would have been able to raise his command sufficiently for the command of a Lieutenant-Colonel, and to have it regularly mustered into the service. I am not aware that it numbers over 4 companies.

R. E. LEE, *General.*

----

V.

*Affair near Annandale, Va.—Report of Major John S. Mosby.*

*Loudoun Co., October* 19, 1863.

GENERAL: I did not receive your letter of instructions until late last Tuesday night, on my return from an expedition below.

I collected as many men as I could at so short notice, and on Thursday, 15th, came down into Fairfax, where I have been operating ever since in the enemy's rear.

I have captured over 100 horses and mules, several wagons loaded with valuable stores, and between 75 and 100 prisoners, arms, equipments, etc. Among the prisoners were 5 captains and 1 lieutenant.

I had a sharp skirmish yesterday with double my number of cavalry near Annandale, in which I routed them, capturing the captain commanding and 6 or 7 men and horses. I have so far sustained no loss. It has been my object to detain the troops that are occupying Fairfax, by annoying their communications and preventing them from

CONFEDERATE REPORTS, ETC.

operating in front. Yesterday two divisions left Centreville and went into camp at Fox's Mill. There are 3 regiments of cavalry at Vienna. I contemplate attacking a cavalry camp at Falls Church to-morrow night.

Respectfully, your obedient servant,

JNO. S. MOSBY, *Major.*

[Indorsement.]

Respectfully forwarded.   Major Mosby and command continue to do splendid service.

J. E. B. STUART.

_____

VI.

*Scout about Catlett's Station—Report of John S. Mosby. C. S. A.*

*Fauquier Co.,* Nov. 6, 1863.

General J. E. B. STUART :

GENERAL : I returned yesterday from a scout in the neighborhood of Catlett's. I was accompanied by Captain Smith and 2 men of my command. We killed Kilpatrick's division commissary [1] and captured an adjutant, 4 men, 6 horses, etc. Kilpatrick's Division (now reported unfit for duty) lies around Weaverville. About one brigade of infantry in the vicinity of Catlett's. A good deal of artillery moved forward from Warrenton on the 4th. Sedgwick still remains there. I sent you 4 cavalrymen on Wednesday captured by my scouts.

Respectfully, your obedient servant,

JNO. S. MOSBY, *Major.*

_____

VII.

*Mosby's Operations in Virginia.—Report of Major Mosby, Commanding 43d Virginia Cavalry Battalion.*

HEADQUARTERS 43D VA. CAVALRY BATTALION,

*Nov.* 22, 1863.

GENERAL : Since rendering my report of the 5th inst. we have captured about 75 of the enemy's cavalry, over 100 hundred horses and mules, 6 wagons, a considerable number of arms, equipments, etc.

It would be too tedious to mention in detail the various affairs in

_____

[1] Lieut. Timothy Hedges, Second New York Cavalry, acting commissary of subsistence Kilpatrick's division, was " wounded by guerrillas near Catlett's Station, Nov. 3, 1863."

which these captures have been made, but I would omit the performance of a pleasant duty if I failed to bring to your notice the bold onset of Capt. Smith, when, with only about 40 men, he dashed into the enemy's camp of 150 cavalry near Warrenton, killed some 8 or 10, wounded a number and brought off 9 prisoners, 27 horses, arms, equipments, etc. In various other affairs several of the enemy have been killed and wounded. I have sustained no loss. Capt. Chapman and Lieut. Turner, commanding their respective companies have rendered efficient services.

Gregg's Cavalry division now guards their rear, being distributed along the road leading from Bealeton to Warrenton and thence to the Sulphur Springs. It is very difficult to do any thing on the railroad, as they have sentinels stationed all along in sight of each other, in addition to the guards on each train. Rest assured that if there is any chance of effecting anything there, it will be done.

Respectfully, your obedient servant,

JNO. S. MOSBY, *Major, etc.*

[Indorsement.]

HEADQUARTERS CAVALRY CORPS, ARMY NORTHERN VIRGINIA,

*November* 25, 1863.

Respectfully forwarded.

Major Mosby is very vigilant, very active. The importance of his operations is shown by the heavy guard the enemy is obliged to keep to guard the railroad from his attacks. Particular attention is called to the gallant exploit of Captain Smith, late Second Lieut. Company H, Fourth Virginia Cavalry. This officer promises to distinguish himself highly as a partisan leader.

J. E. B. STUART, *Major General.*

Noted with satisfaction and appreciation of the energy and valor displayed.

J. A. SEDDON, *Secretary.*

## VIII.

*Report of Major John S. Mosby, 43d Virginia Cavalry Battalion, including skirmish, January 10th, at Loudoun Heights.*

*February 1, 1864.*

MAJOR: I have the honor to submit the following report of the operations of this command, since rendering my report of January 4.

On Wednesday, January 6, having previously reconnoitered in person the position of the enemy, I directed Lieutenant Turner, with a detachment of about 30 men, to attack an outpost of the enemy in the vicinity of Warrenton, which he did successfully, routing a superior force of the enemy, killing and wounding several, and capturing 18 prisoners and 45 horses, with arms, equipments, etc.

On Saturday, January 9, having learned through Frank Stringfellow (a scout of Gen. Stuart), that Cole's (Maryland) Cavalry was encamped on Loudoun Heights, with no supports but infantry, which was about one-half mile off, I left Upperville with about 100 men, in hopes of being able to completely surprise his camp by a night attack. By marching my command by file, along a narrow path, I succeeded in gaining a position in the rear of the enemy, between their camp and the Ferry. On searching this point, without creating any alarm, I deemed that the crisis had passed, and the capture of the camp of the enemy a certainty. I had exact information up to dark of that evening of the number of the enemy (which was between 175 and 200), the position of their headquarters, etc. When within 200 yards of the camp, I sent Stringfellow on ahead with about 10 men to capture Major Cole and staff, whose headquarters were in a house about 100 yards from their camp, while I halted to close up my command. The camp was buried in profound sleep; there was not a sentinel awake. All my plans were on the eve of consummation, when suddenly the party sent with Stringfellow came dashing over the hill toward the camp, yelling and shooting. They had made no attempt to secure Cole. Mistaking them for the enemy, I ordered my men to charge.

In the meantime the enemy had taken the alarm, and received us with a volley from their carbines. A severe fight ensued, in which they were driven from their camp, but, taking refuge in the surrounding houses, kept up a desultory firing. Confusion and delay having ensued from the derangement of my plans, consequent on the alarm given to the enemy, rendered it hazardous to continue in my position, as reinforcements were near the enemy. Accordingly, I ordered the men to retire, which was done in good order, bringing off 6 prisoners, and between 50 and 60 horses.

My loss was severe ; more so in the worth than the number of the slain. It was 4 killed, 7 wounded (of whom 4 have since died), and 1 captured. A published list of the enemy's loss gives it at 5 killed and 13 wounded. Among those who fell on this occasion were Capt. William R. Smith and Lieutenant Turner, two of the noblest and bravest officers of this army, who thus sealed a life of devotion and of sacrifice to the cause that they loved.

In numerous other affairs with the enemy, between 75 and 100 horses and mules have been captured, about 40 men killed, wounded and captured. A party of this command also threw one of the enemy's trains off the track, causing a great smash up,

Respectfully, your obedient servant,

JNO. S. MOSBY,
*Major Commanding.*

[Indorsement.]

HEADQUARTERS CAVALRY CORPS,
*February* 9, 1864.

Respectfully forwarded.

The conduct of Major Mosby is warmly commended to the notice of the commanding general. His sleepless vigilance and unceasing activity have done the enemy great damage. He keeps a large force of the enemy's cavalry continually employed in Fairfax in the vain effort to suppress his inroads. His exploits are not surpassed in daring and enterprise by those of *petite guerre* in any age. Unswerving devotion to duty, self-abnegation, and unflinching courage, with a quick perception and appreciation of the opportunity, are the characteristics of this officer. Since I first knew him, in 1861, he has never once alluded to his own rank or promotion ; thus far it has come by the force of his own merit. While self-consciousness of having done his duty well is the patriot soldier's best reward, yet the evidence of the appreciation of his country is a powerful incentive to renewed effort, which should not be undervalued by those who have risen to the highest point of military and civic eminence. That evidence is promotion. If Major Mosby has not won it, no more can daring deeds essay to do it. Capt. W. R. Smith, late lieutenant of Black Horse, has been long distinguished as one of the best cavalry leaders we have. Lieutenant Turner has won an enviable name. Both had inscribed their fame in old Fauquier imperishably, in the blood of her enemies. All honor to the glorious dead.

J. E. B. STUART, *Major-General.*

IX.

*Report of Lieut.-Col. John S. Mosby, 43d Battalion Virginia Cavalry,
including operations to May 1.*

September 11, 1864.

Lieut.-Col. TAYLOR, *Assistant Adjutant General:*

COLONEL: I have the honor to submit, for the information of
the commanding general, the following brief report of the operations
of this command since the first day of March last.

On March 10th (9th) with a detachment of about 40 men, I defeated
a superior force of the enemy's cavalry near Greenwich, severely wounding 3, and capturing 9 prisoners, 10 horses, arms, etc.   On
the same day Lieut. A. E. Richards, with another detachment of
about 30 men, surprised an outpost of the enemy near Charlestown, killed the major commanding and a lieutenant, several privates,
and brought off 21 prisoners with their horses, arms, etc.   In neither
engagement did my command sustain any loss.

During the months of March and April but few opportunities were
offered for making any successful attacks on the enemy, the continual
annoyances to which they had been subjected during the winter
causing them to exert great vigilance in guarding against surprises and interruptions of their communications.   During most of
these months I was myself engaged in scouting in the enemy's rear
for Major-General Stuart and collecting information which was
regularly transmitted to his headquarters, concerning the movements,
numbers and distribution of the enemy's forces both east and west of
the Blue Ridge.   During this time my men were mostly employed in
collecting forage from the country bordering on the Potomac.

About April 15, Captain Richards routed a marauding party of the
enemy's cavalry at Waterford, killing and wounding 5 or 6 and
bringing off 6 or 8 prisoners, 15 horses, arms, etc.

About April 25 I attacked an outpost near Hunter's Mills, in Fairfax, capturing 5 prisoners and 18 horses.   The prisoners and horses
were sent back under charge of Lieutenant Hunter, while I went off
on a scout in another direction.   The enemy pursued and captured
the lieutenant and 6 of the horses.

I have the honor to be, very respectfully, your obedient servant,

JOHN S. MOSBY, *Lieut. Col. Commanding.*

CONFEDERATE REPORTS, ETC.


X.

*Colonel Mosby's Report of his Operations from March* 1.

September 11, 1864.

Lieut.-Col. TAYLOR, *Assistant Adjutant General:*

COLONEL: I have the honor to submit for the information of the commanding general the following brief report of the operations of this command since the first day of March last.[1]

About May 1st, with a party of 10 men, I captured 8 of Sigel's wagons near Bunker Hill, in the valley, but was only able to bring off the horses attached (34 in number) and about 20 prisoners. The horses and prisoners were sent back, while with another detachment of 20 men who had joined me I proceeded to Martinsburg, which place we entered that night, while occupied by several hundred Federal troops, and brought off 15 horses and several prisoners.

Returning to my command, I learned that General Grant had crossed the Rapidan. With about 40 men I moved down the north bank of the Rappahannock to assail his communications wherever opened, and sent two other detachments, under Captain Richards and Chapman, to embarrass Sigel as much as possible. Captain Richards had a skirmish near Winchester (then the enemy's rear) in which several of them were killed and wounded. Captain Chapman attacked a wagon train, which was heavily guarded, near Strasburg, capturing about 30 prisoners with an equal number of horses, &c. Near Belle Plain, in King George, I captured an ambulance train and brought off about 75 horses and mules, and 40 prisoners, etc.

A few days after, I made a second attempt near the same place, but discovered that my late attack had caused them to detach such a heavy force to guard their trains and line of communication that another successful attack on them was impracticable.

About May 10 I attacked a cavalry outpost in the vicinity of Front Royal, capturing 1 captain and 15 men and 75 horses and sustained no loss.

About May 20, with about 150 men, I moved to the vicinity of Strasburg with the view of capturing the wagon trains of General Hunter, who had then moved up the valley. When the train appeared I discovered that it was guarded by about 600 infantry and 100 cavalry. A slight skirmish ensued between their cavalry and a part of my command, in which their cavalry was routed with a loss of 8 prisoners and

[1] For portion here omitted see Appendix, IX.

horses, besides several killed, but falling back on their infantry, my men in turn fell back, with a loss of 1 killed. While we did not capture the train, one great object had been accomplished—the detachment of a heavy force to guard their communications. After the above affair, only one wagon train ever went up to Hunter, which was still more heavily guarded, He then gave up his line of communication.

After the withdrawal of the enemy's forces from Northern Virginia, for several weeks but few opportunities were offered for any successful incursions upon them. Many enterprises on a small scale were, however, undertaken by detachments of the command, of which no note has been taken.

About June 20 I moved into Fairfax and routed a body of cavalry near Centreville, killing and wounding 6 or 8, and capturing 31 prisoners, securing their horses, etc.

A few days afterward we took Duffield's Depot, on the Baltimore and Ohio Railroad; secured about 50 prisoners, including 2 lieutenants and a large amount of stores. The train had passed a few minutes before we reached the place. On my way there I had left Lieutenant Nelson, commanding Company A, at Charlestown, for the purpose of intercepting and notifying me of any approach in my rear from Harper's Ferry. As I had anticipated, a body of cavalry, largely superior in numbers to his force, moved out from that point. Lieutenant Nelson gallantly charged and routed them, killing and wounding several and taking 19 prisoners and 27 horses. We sustained no loss on this expedition,

On July 4, hearing of General Early's movement down the Valley, I moved with my command east of the Blue Ridge for the purpose of co-operating with him, and crossed the Potomac at Point of Rocks, driving out the garrison (250 men, strongly fortified) and securing several prisoners and horses. As I supposed it to be General Early's intention to invest Maryland Heights, I thought the best service I could render would be to sever all communications both by railroad and telegraph between that point and Washington, which I did, keeping it suspended for two days.

As this was the first occasion on which I had used artillery, the magnitude of the invasion was greatly exaggerated by the fears of the enemy, and panic and alarm spread through their territory. I desire especially to bring to the notice of the commanding general the unsurpassed gallantry displayed by Captain Richards, commanding First Squadron. Our crossing was opposed by a body of infantry stationed on the Maryland shore. Dismounting a number of sharpshooters, whom I directed to wade the river above the point held by the enemy, I superintended in person the placing of my piece of artillery in position, at the same time directing Captain Richards whenever the enemy had been dislodged by the sharpshooters and artillery, to charge across the river in order to effect their capture. The enemy were soon routed and Captain Richards charged over, but before he could overtake them they had retreated across the canal, pulling up the bridge in their rear. My order had not, of course, contemplated their pursuit into their fortifications, but the destruction of the bridge was no obstacle to his impetuous valor, and hastily dismounting and throwing down a few planks on the sills, he charged across, under a heavy fire from a redoubt. The enemy fled panic-stricken, leaving in our possession their camp equipage, etc.

Captain Richards has on this, as well as on many other occasions, shown himself worthy to wear the honor bestowed upon him by the Government when, disregarding the rule of seniority, it promoted him for valor and skill to the position whose duties he so ably discharges.

LIEUT. JOSEPH H. NELSON, CO. A.
Drawn from a Photograph taken soon after the War.

On the morning of July 6, while still encamped near the Potomac, information was received that a considerable force of cavalry was at Leesburg. I immediately hastened to meet them. At Leesburg I learned that they had gone toward Aldie, and I accordingly moved on the road to Ball's Mill in order to intercept them returning to their camp in Fairfax, which I succeeding in doing, meeting them at Mount Zion Church, and completely routing them, with a loss of about 80 of their officers and men left dead and severely wounded on the field, besides 57 prisoners. Their loss includes a captain and lieutenant killed and 1 lieutenant severely wounded; the major commanding and 2 lieutenants prisoners. We also secured all their horses, arms, etc.

My loss was 1 killed and 6 wounded—none dangerously.

After this affair the enemy never ventured, in two months after, the experiment of another raid through that portion of our district.

A few days afterward I again crossed the Potomac, in co-operation with General Early, and moved through Poolesville, Md., for the purpose of capturing a body of cavalry encamped near Seneca. They retreated, however, before we reached there, leaving all their camp equipage and a considerable amount of stores. We also captured 30 head of beef cattle.

When General Early fell back from before Washington I recrossed the Potomac, near Seneca, moving thence to the Little River pike in order to protect him from any movement up the south side of the river. The enemy moved through Leesburg in pursuit of General Early and occupied Ashby's and Snicker's Gaps. I distributed my command so as to most effectually protect the country. These detachments—under Captains Richards and Chapman and Lieutenants Glascock, Nelson and Hatcher—while they kept the enemy confined to the main thoroughfares and restrained their ravages, killed and captured about 300, securing their horses, etc. My own attention was principally directed to ascertaining the numbers and movements of the enemy and forwarding the information to General Early, who was then in the valley.

At the time of the second invasion of Maryland by General Early, I moved my command to the Potomac, crossed over 3 companies at Cheek's and Noland's Fords, while the remaining portion was kept in reserve on this side with the artillery, which was posted on the south bank to keep open the fords, keeping one company, (B), under Lieutenant Williams, near the ford on the north bank. Two were sent under Lieutenant Nelson, to Adamstown, on the Baltimore and Ohio Railroad, for the purpose of intercepting the trains from Baltimore, destroying their communications, etc. Apprehending a movement up the river from a considerable body of cavalry which I knew to be stationed below, I remained with a portion of the command guarding the fords.

Lieutenant Nelson reached the road a few minutes too late to capture the train, but destroyed two telegraph lines. On his return he met a force of the enemy's cavalry, near Monocacy, which was charged and routed by the gallant Lieutenant Hatcher, who took about 15 men and horses, besides killing and wounding several.

We recrossed the river in the evening, bringing about 75 horses and between 20 and 30 prisoners.

Our loss, 2 missing.

I have the honor to be, very respectfully, your obedient servant,

JNO. S. MOSBY,
*Lieutenant-Colonel Commanding.*

XI.

*Report of Lieut.-Col. John S. Mosby, Forty-third Virginia Cavalry Battalion.*

HDQRS. 43d VIRGINIA PARTISAN RANGER BATTALION,
*September* 11, 1864.

COLONEL: I have the honor to submit, for the information of the commanding general, the following brief report of the operations of the command since the 1st day of March last.

On August 9, with a detachment of 37 men, I defeated a body of 100 cavalry at Fairfax Station, killing the captain commanding and 6 men, and capturing 21 prisoners and 34 horses. Two detachments sent out at the same time in Fairfax brought in 6 more prisoners and horses; another detachment of 5 sent to Duffield's Depot, brought in 10 prisoners with their horses, etc.

On the morning of August 13 I attacked, near Berryville, the enemy's supply train, which was guarded by some 700 or 800 infantry and cavalry, under command of Brigadier-General Kenly. Completely routed the guard, with a loss of over 200 prisoners, including 3 lieutenants, besides several killed and wounded. Captured and destroyed 75 loaded wagons, and secured over 200 head of beef-cattle, between 500 and 600 horses and mules, and many valuable stores. My loss, 2 killed and 3 wounded. My force numbered something over 300 men, with two mountain howitzers. One howitzer became disabled before being brought into action, by breaking of a wheel; the other after firing a few rounds was rendered useless also, by breaking of the carriage.

Too much praise cannot be awarded to Captains Richards and William Chapman, commanding their respective squadrons, for the bravery with which they scattered largely superior forces of the enemy. The gallant Captain Sam. Chapman, commanding Company E, although burning for the strife, was prudently held in reserve.

A few days after this, Lieutenant Glascock, with 14 men, captured 29 prisoners, including several officers, with their horses, arms, etc., near Kernstown. At the same time Captain Richards, with a small squad, killed a captain and captured 7 or 8 men and horses near Charlestown.

About August 20 I crossed with my command at Snicker's Gap, the enemy being near Berryville, sending the larger portion, under Capt. William Chapman, to operate around Berryville and restrain the enemy from devastating the country. With a small detachment I went to their rear, near Charlestown, and captured 12 prisoners and 10 horses. Captain Chapman, coming upon a portion of the enemy's cavalry

which was engaged in burning houses, attacked and routed them.
Such was the indignation of our men at witnessing some of the finest
residences in that portion of the State enveloped in flames, that no
quarter was shown, and about 25 of them were shot to death for their
villainy. About 30 horses were brought off, but no prisoners.

On Friday, September 3, with a squad of 6 men, I attacked the enemy's outposts in Fairfax, mortally wounding 1 and capturing 6 men
and 11 horses.

On Sunday, September 5, I sent Capt. Sam. Chapman, in command
of Companies C and E, to harass the enemy around Berryville, while I
made a detour to gain their rear near Charlestown. Arriving at the
river, I left the two companies that were with me (A and B), under
Lieutenant Nelson, on the east bank of the river, while, with 6 men, I
went on a reconnoissance across, previous to carrying my whole force
over. Some time after, a force of the enemy's cavalry crossed the mountain in their rear, surprised and stampeded them, killing 1, wounding 3
and capturing 3. One of the enemy's cavalry was killed and 5 wounded.
With the 6 men with me I succeeded in capturing and bringing out
safely about 25 prisoners, 2 ambulances, and 18 horses. Captain
Chapman routed a largely superior force near Berryville, killing and
wounding some 15 or 20, besides securing over 30 prisoners, including
a captain and lieutenant, with their horses, arms, etc.

On September 8, with about 30 men, having gained a position in the
enemy's rear near Charlestown, I divided the command, for greater
safety. One portion, under Captain Richards, captured a captain and
12 men, with their horses, etc.; with mine I captured a lieutenant and 5
men, with their horses, etc.

I have made no attempt, for it would be impossible, to embrace in
this report a full recital of the innumerable affairs with the enemy in
which the heroism of both men and officers of this command has been
illustrated ; yet the fame of their deeds will still live in the grateful
remembrance of those whose homes and whose firesides their valor
has defended.

I have the honor to be, very repectfully, your obedient servant,

JNO. S. MOSBY,
*Lieutenant-Colonel, Commanding.*

Lieutenant-Colonel TAYLOR,
*Assistant Adjutant General.*

[Indorsement.]

HEADQUARTERS ARMY OF NORTHERN VIRGINIA,
*September* 19, 1864.

Respectfully forwarded to the Adjutant and Inspector General, for
the information of the Department.

Attention is invited to the activity and skill of Colonel Mosby, and the intelligence and courage of the officers and men of his command, as displayed in this report. With the loss of little more than 20 men, he has killed, wounded and captured during the period embraced in the report about 1,200 of the enemy and taken more than 1,600 horses and mules, 230 beef-cattle, and 85 wagons and ambulances, without counting many smaller operations. The services rendered by Colonel Mosby and his command in watching and reporting the enemy's movements have also been of great value. His operations have been highly creditable to himself and his command.

R. E. LEE, *General.*

*Report of Gen. R. E. Lee.*

*Chaffin's Bluff, August* 16, 1864.

Colonel Mosby reports that he attacked the enemy's supply train near Berryville on the 13th ; captured and destroyed 75 loaded wagons and secured over 200 prisoners, including several officers, between 500 and 600 horses and mules, upward of 200 beef-cattle, and many valuable stores. Considerable number of the enemy killed and wounded. His loss, 2 killed and 3 wounded.

R. E. LEE.

Hon. J. A. SEDDON, *Secretary of War.*

## XII.

The following letter was published in the Washington *Star*, having been captured by a Federal officer :

*Letter from Lee to Mosby—Lee Approves Guerrilla Warfare.*

HEADQR'S ARMY NORTHERN VIRGINIA, }
19*th September*, 1864. }

Lieut.-Col. JOHN S. MOSBY, *Commanding, etc. :*

COLONEL—Your report of the operations of your command from the 1st March to 11th September, is received.

I am much gratified by the activity and skill you have displayed, and desire to express my thanks to yourself and the brave officers and men of your command for the valuable services to the country.

The smallness of your loss, in comparison with the damage inflicted upon the enemy, is creditable to your own judgment, and to the intel-

ligence and courage of those who executed your orders. I hope you
will continue to harrass the enemy's troops as much as possible, and
restrain his efforts to exercise civil authority in the counties in which
you are operating. I enclose copy of a letter written some time since,
in case the original should not have reached you, and call your attention to the instructions it contains.

Very respectfully, your obedient servant,

R. E. LEE, *General.*

------

## XIII.

*Mosby to General Lee.*

*Near Upperville, Nov. 6, 1864.*

General R. E. LEE,
    *Commanding Army of Northern Virginia :*

GENERAL : The enemy is engaged in removing the rails from the
Manassas road for the purpose of reconstructing the Winchester and
Potomac. The latter is already completed to Charlestown, though it
is considered doubtful whether they will proceed further. On the 4th
instant, Merritt's division of cavalry passed through Charlestown
toward Harper's Ferry. Indications are that the larger portion of
Sheridan's army will be transferred to Grant's. I returned from the
Valley last night, and send out to-day 28 cavalrymen captured there.
I shall send over another detachment to-day, From the time of their
occupation, to the abandonment of the Manassas road, my command
killed and captured about 600 of the enemy, about an equal number of
horses, 10 wagons, etc.; my total loss did not exceed 25. I hope you
will not believe the accounts published in the Northern papers, and
ccpied in ours, of my robbery of passengers on the railroad train I captured. So far from that, I strictly enjoined my officers and men that
nothing of the kind would be permitted. That a great many of the
passengers lost their baggage it is true, because the proximity of a considerable force of the enemy allowed us no time to save it, but I explained to the passengers that persons traveling on a military road
subjected themselves to the incidents of war. I have sent out a party
to plant the torpedoes you sent me.

Very respectfully, your obedient servant,

JOHN S. MOSBY, *Lieut. Colonel.*

FEDERAL REPORTS, ETC.

XIV.

*April 3 to 6, 1863—Scout from Fairfax C. H. to Middleburg.*

*Fairfax C. H., April 11, 1863.*

STAHEL to HEINTZLEMAN : I have the honor to report with regard to the reconnoissance under command of Brigadier-General J. F. Copeland, which left this place on the 3d day of April, and returned here early on the morning of the 6th inst., that it proceeded as far as Middleburg, and searched diligently through that whole section of country without meeting any enemy in force, or ascertaining definitely the whereabouts of Mosby. Small detachments of rebels, however, were occasionally seen, but scattered on the approach of our troops.

On the 4th instant, early in the morning, in front of Middleburg, a collision cccurred between one of his pickets and some of the enemy's, resulting in the death of one and wounding of another on each side. During the expedition, there was captured and arrested 61 prisoners, citizens and soldiers, 53 horses, 2 mules, a quautity of wheat, 3 wagons, saddles, bridles, guns, sabres, etc., all of which were turned over to the provost-marshal of this place, and by him to Col. (Lafayette C.) Baker, Washington, a copy of whose receipt is enclosed within.

XV.

*Washington, August 4, 1863.*

Brigadier-General KING :

The major-general commanding, desires that you send two parties of cavalry, of 60 or 70 men, to scout and beat up thoroughly the county in the vicinity of the Orange and Alexandria Railroad, one party taking the north and the other the south side. The party going south should call upon Stiles, the guide in Alexandria, through Lieutenant-Colonel Wells, provost-marshal-general.

No mercy need be shown to bushwhackers. These guerrillas must be destroyed.

J. H. TAYLOR, *Chief of Staff.*

FEDERAL REPORTS, ETC.

## XVI.

HDQRS. CAVALRY CORPS, ARMY OF THE POTOMAC,
*August* 18, 1863.

Major-General HUMPHREYS, *Chief of Staff:*

GENERAL: General Kilpatrick reports that some of his pickets saw upwards of 2,000 cavalry passing down the right bank of the Rappahannock yesterday at daylight. Had 8 or 10 wagons with them. He has sent a party down the river to watch them. He also sends two letters and a Richmond paper, which are enclosed, that were captured yesterday from a rebel mail carrier. Six rebel soldiers were also captured.

The brigade of General Gregg at Warrenton has 100 men on Watery Mountain, who picket well toward Salem; another force of 100 men at New Baltimore, who picket and patrol toward White Plains; a regiment which pickets and patrols to Waterloo, Orleans, and the mill beyond on Thumb Run. The pickets report but few of the enemy to be seen, and in small parties. Two regiments have also gone direct to Salem, Markham and Manassas Gap, to return by way of Barbee's Cross-roads and Orleans.

General Merritt reports that a rebel patrol had been at Union Mills, in the direction of Dumfries, just before his scouting party arrived there yesterday. All else quiet.

Very respectfully,

A. PLEASONTON, *Major-General Commanding.*

---

## XVII.

HDQRS. ELEVENTH CORPS, ARMY OF THE POTOMAC,
*September* 6, 1863.

Major-General HUMPHREYS, *Chief of Staff:*

Captain Sharra, commanding detachment of First Indiana Cavalry, just returned from the neighborhood of Aldie, captured 3 of Mosby's men near Cool Spring Gap, who will be sent to general headquarters to-morrow. No signs of any raid. Mosby not dead, but wounded at Culpeper. The men think he will be fit for duty in six weeks.

O. O. HOWARD, *Major-General.*

## XVIII.

HEADQUARTERS ELEVENTH CORPS,
*September* 13, 1863.

Major-General SEDGWICK, *Commanding Sixth Corps:*

GENERAL: I send my orderly to you. Will you have the kindness to notify me if you move anywhere, or if the enemy makes any raid toward New Baltimore? I have had sundry intimations, but do not deem them altogether reliable, that the rebels contemplate a raid on some of our depots. The work of to-day may prevent it.

I sent out several scouting parties yesterday. One near White Plains met some of Mosby's men and had a skirmish. One of our party was severely wounded and left at a house at White Plains.

I still have a regiment at Greenwich, a brigade at Bristoe, and two brigades here. My force is very small. I will leave my orderly with you till tomorrow. Please send him with everything important. When it is not smoky, I communicate directly with Watery mountain, and, by telegraph, with headquarters.

Very respectfully,
O. O. HOWARD, *Major-General.*

---

## XIX.

*Manassas Junction, Sept.* 22, 1863.

General KING:

Two officers and 15 men, in pursuit of a lost horse, came upon what they supposed to be a company of cavalry, which they were informed was a part of Mosby's force, near the house of one H. Mathews, on the road from Centreville to Gainesville. They were informed by a man named Settle that there was a regiment of cavalry encamped on the old Bull Run battlefield. My horses becoming unmanageable when the firing commenced, I lost five men with horses and equipments.

My horses are too green to be serviceable as cavalry. I send this information that you may take such action as you deem necessary.

ALFRED GIBBS, *Colonel.*

## XX.

GENERAL ORDERS, }  HEADQUARTERS CAVALRY CORPS,
NO. 42.  }     *November* 5, 1863.

The loss in officers and men sustained in this corps at the hands of guerrillas during the past few days demands the careful attention of all to prevent a recurrence in the future. The command is admonished that we are here in the field for military and not social purposes. Visiting in the families of the country in which our operations are conducted, riding for pleasure, either alone or in small parties, or even any unnecessary exposure when in the line of duty, are directly in violation of every recognized military principle. They will, therefore, be abstained from in future. Every house within or without the lines of the army is a nest of treason, and every grove a lurking place for guerrilla bands. They are on that account, to be watched and avoided.

Division commanders are expressly directed to give to this matter their earnest attention.

In the transmission of orders or the conduct of the public business, care will be taken that individuals or small parties are not unnecessarily exposed and every effort will be made to confine all officers and men to such close attention to their immediate command.

Any infringement of the spirit of this order will be reported to these headquarters, that the appropriate remedy for such neglect of duty may be promptly applied.

By command of Major-General Pleasonton.

    C. C. SUYDAM, *Assistant Adjutant General.*

---

## XXI.

HDQRS. FIRST BRIG., SECOND DIV., CAVALRY CORPS,
*Near Fayetteville, Va., Nov.* 16, 1863.

Capt. H. C. WEIR, *Asst. Adjt. Gen., Second Division:*

SIR : I have the honor to report all quiet along my lines this morning. Night before last, shortly after the line of pickets was established, near Warrenton, 4 men and a corporal were found to be missing; no alarm was given. Last night several shots were fired at the vedettes along the whole front of my lines, but no serious attacks were made.

The guerrillas around Warrenton are very troublesome, always attacking my pickets after nightfall. The citizens do all in their power to help and encourage these people, and I fancy that by putting a section of my battery into position, about $1\frac{1}{2}$ miles this side of the town, with orders to open upon this place in case we are disturbed, no guerrilla raids will hereafter be made upon my lines. We are very short of forage. The missing men belong to First Rhode Island Cavalry.

Very respectfully, your obedient servant,

J. P. TAYLOR,
*Colonel Commanding First Brigade.*

[Indorsement.]

HEADQUARTERS SECOND CAVALRY DIVISION,
*November* 17, 1863.

Respectfully forwarded.

To comply with the instructions to "picket beyond Warrenton," it is found necessary to completely envelop that town, so as to bring it within our lines and cut off communication between its disloyal inhabitants and the guerrillas who infest the country about. These two classes of people, not being permitted to have intercourse, are very angry, and it results from this that the line of pickets is constantly threatened, both in front and rear, and its maintenance will occasion the loss of men, as in this instance.

D. McM. GREGG,
*Brig. Gen. of Vols., Commanding Second Division.*

———

## XXII.

*Cumberland, Md., Dec.* 18, 1863.

Brig.-Gen. G. W. CULLOM, *Chief of Staff:*

General Sullivan reports that a cavalry scout has just returned from Loudoun County, commanded by Captain Keys, of the Twenty-second Pennsylvania. Near Upperville, he captured Colonel Carter, of the First Virginia Cavalry, 5 men and 6 horses. Key's loss, 1 man killed and 2 captured. Enemy's, 1 man and 2 horses killed.

B. F. KELLEY, *Brigadier General.*

FEDERAL REPORTS, ETC.

## XXIII.

HEADQUARTERS ARMY OF THE POTOMAC,
*December* 25, 1863.

Colonel TAYLOR, *Commanding Second Divison Cavalry :*

Dispatch just received states that Mosby has made great preparations to have a frolic, with his principal officers, at the house of Dr. Bispham and Mrs. Murray, in Salem, to-night. Dr. Bispham's is the second house as you go in the village from Warrenton, and Mrs. Murray lives about the middle of the street, in a large white house. The major-general commanding directs that you send a party from the brigade which is at Warrentown, under the command of a smart and competent officer, to capture them.

E. B. PARSONS,
*Captain, Acting Assistant Adjutant General.*

---

## XXIV.

*Skirmish near Aldie, Va.—Reports of Brig. Gen. Robert O. Tyler,*
*U. S. Army.*

HEADQUARTERS DIVISION,
*February* 6, 1864.

Lieut.-Col. TAYLOR, *Chief of Staff :*

I have the honor to report all quiet. The scouting party sent out yesterday returned this afternoon from Aldie and Middleburg. Their rear guard was attacked yesterday noon by 8 of "Mosby's Men;" they were dispersed and the leader, who proved to be William E. Ormsby, who deserted from the Second Massachusetts Cavalry on the night of January 24, was captured, and is now being tried by drum-head court-martial. Two men of the Second Massachusetts Cavalry and 3 rebels were wounded. Five citizens were arrested under suspicious circumstances. No evidence was found of any force being in the vicinity.

R. O. TYLER, *Brigadier-General Commanding.*

---

*Fairfax Court House, February* 7, 1864.

Lieut.-Col. J. H. TAYLOR, *Chief of Staff :*

I have the honor to report all quiet. The deserter [Ormsby] from the Second Massachusetts Cavalry, captured in arms against the United States, was convicted by drum-head court-martial and shot at 12 this noon.

R. O. TYLER,
*Brigadier-General Commanding.*

XXV.

HEADQUARTERS CAVALRY BRIGADE,
*Falls Church, Va., June* 5, 1864.

Lieut.-Col. J. H. TAYLOR,
*Assistant Adjutant-General and Chief of Staff :*

COLONEL: I have the honor to report everything quiet in this vicinity during the last 24 hours. Major Forbes returned with his mounted party from Middleburg and Rector's Cross-Roads last night, bringing 5 rebel hostages (Hamilton Rogers, Dr. Powell, Gurley R. Hatcher, Noland, and Hooper). This party did not see a single guerrilla. The dismounted party which acted with it met a squad of 5 rebels and wounded 2 of them, but they got off. This party has not yet returned ; it was to bring in more hostages from above Dranesville. The regular scouting party which was relieved this p. m. brought in Fenton Beavers and the two Gunnells, of Mosby's command, who have been making themselves very obnoxious recently as horsethieves. Beavers is the same man who feigned desertion from Mosby some two months ago, and, after taking the amnesty oath and spying about Alexandria and Vienna, returned to the enemy. These 3 men, with two Bowies from Maryland and a man named Campbell, are the party which, under orders from Mosby, seized Walters and Dr. Lloyd. I think that these gentlemen will both be back within a day or two.

Very respectfully, your obedient servant,
C. R. LOWELL, JR.,
*Col. Second Massachusetts Cavalry, Comdg. Cav. Brig.*

---

XXVI.

*Report of Federal Scouting Party in the Shenandoah Valley.*

HEADQUARTERS SIXTH WEST VIRGINIA CAVALRY,
*Camp near Bolivar, June* 8, 1864.

Lieut.-Col. F. W. THOMPSON,
*Commanding Sixth West Virginia Cavalry :*

SIR : I have the honor to report that agreeably to orders, I started yesterday at 3 a. m. in command of 83 select men, of whom 38 were from the Sixth West Virginia Cavalry, 25 from the Twelfth Pennsylvania Cavalry, and 20 from First New York Veterans. I adopted the following order of march : First. F. A. Warthen, Company D, of your regiment, dressed in full Confederate uniform, as scout, followed by an advance of 8 men familiar with the country. Second. The detachment in the order in which I have stated them. Third. Rear guard of one corporal and 3 men. I proceeded up the Berryville turnpike road, avoiding Charlestown by passing around to the left, then following the turnpike for about 12 miles. From this place, finding myself ahead of time, I turned my command off the turnpike by a road leading to the Martinsburg turnpike road for about one-half mile, where I rested for about 2 hours. I then resumed the march to the point indicated on the map furnished me by Colonel Pierce, where, turning to the left, I followed a country road, which soon took me to the houses of Mr. Castleman and his neighbor, Mr. DeRue, whose houses I approached unobserved and promptly surrounded at 11 a. m. The information relative to the wedding to come off at Mr. De-Rue's was incorrect. The young lady whom report made the bride of the occasion had gone to the blacksmith's shop at Myerstown, riding, as I was credibly informed, "an old black horse for the purpose of getting him shod to visit this place to-day," and from the uncomely appearance of her parents, the buildings and their surroundings, I think Miss Castleman will never be the bride of a Confederate officer connected with the proud Early family, until their pride shall have been subdued by

NORMAN V. RANDOLPH, CO. E.
From a War-time Photograph.

the whipping which awaits them and all other Southern traitors. Feeling somewhat foiled and desiring to accomplish some good before I returned, I concluded to advance to Snicker's Ferry, 5 miles beyond, where I learned that a small party had crossed the evening before en route for Lee's army. I returned by an obscure road, using all the skill I could command in ferreting out rebel hiding-places, frequently stopping my command to make excursions to the flanks with my scouts and advance party. When within 2 miles of Kabletown, I succeeded in capturing 2 rebel soldiers at the house of Henry Castleman, respectively of the names of William Gibson and G. E. Cordell, Company B, Twelfth Virginia (rebel) Cavalry. I also captured 2 serviceable horses and equipments, which I shall turn over for the use of the cavalry service to some officer competent to receipt for the same.  These young men are intelligent ; were enlisted at Charlestown, and are connected with prominent rebel families of that place.  During the day I made diligent inquiry of the strength and position of Mosby's command.  I was not able to get very definite information, but from all I heard I am disposed to think he is in the vicinity of Berry's Ferry with about 80 men, and would respectfully suggest that by sending a party, say of 100 men, properly officered, directly up the Shenandoah to some point beyond Berry's Ferry, and another similar party to the right of the Winchester railroad, equally as high up the Valley, the two parties, by the use of scouts and conjoint action ought to, as they return, capture Mosby and the greater part of his command.  I fear our scouting parties are too much in the habit of following the public roads and going to villages, instead of selecting the most obscure routes and camping concealed in groves.  I would suggest that scouts be instructed to obtain information from children and servants instead of adult white members of families.

Very respectfully, your obedient servant,

J. H. SHUTTLEWORTH,

*First Lieutenant and Acting Adjutant.*

---

## XXVII.

*Regulations to Guard Against Surprises.*

Circular]                          Headquarters De Russy's Division,
                                    *Arlington, Va., June 9, 1864.*

In view of the possibility of demonstrations on the part of the rebel cavalry, having for their object a diversion in front of the lines defending the Capital, and perhaps contemplating an attack, with the hope of surprise, it becomes the duty of all officers, especially of the post commanders, to resort to unusual vigilance to prevent the success of the enemy in any such endeavor.  The picket will, therefore, be required to perform their duties most strictly.  One company of infantry will bivouac in each of the forts at night, except such as are garrisoned by one company only, and in these the guards will be strengthened.  The gates will habitually be kept closed after retreat and all other precautions taken.  Among these the garrisons will be required to be under arms and in their forts at 3 a. m., the artillery at the guns, and they will so remain until sunrise, when the sentinels on the parapets can overlook and clearly see the country in front of them. In case of an alarm there must be no confusion ; each company, or portions of a company, should have its station designated and understood before nightfall. The limbers of light artillery pieces in the forts will at once be filled, and at least 4 extra rounds of canister per gun for the light guns will be placed on hand. The equipments for the guns will be left with them after retreat until morning. At retreat each night the garrison will be told off into detachments for the guns and will be required to return to these stations in case of alarm at night. The supernumeraries will defend the approaches with musquetry, taking position on the banquettes between the guns.

By command of Brigadier-General De Russy :

THOS. THOMPSON,
*Captain and Assistant Adjutant-General.*

## XXVIII.

*Attack on Sheridan's Supply Train near Berryville, Aug.* 13, 1864.—
*Copy of the Original Order issued by Gen. Kenly, to be executed in guarding trains.*

ORDERS.]                    HEADQUARTERS KENLY'S BRIGADE,
*Halltown, Va., August* 12, 1864.

The brigade will march at once to escort the trains of the army to Winchester, by the Berryville pike. The trains will march in the following order: First, trains of the Sixth Army Corps; second, trains of the Nineteenth Army Corps; third, trains of the army of West Virginia; fourth, trains of the Cavalry Corps; fifth, trains of Kenly's brigade. The troops will march, and be distributed in the following order :

1. Two companies of the Third Maryland Potomac Home Brigade, and the remaining companies of this regiment between every 20 wagons of the train.

2. The One hundred and forty-ninth Regiment Ohio National Guard will be distributed by company between every 30 wagons, next following those guarded by the Third Maryland Regiment.

3. The One hundred and forty-fourth Regiment Ohio National Guard will be distributed in the following manner : Two companies to follow the rearmost wagon as a rear guard, and the remaining companies between every 20 wagons, counting from the rearmost.

Should the battery belonging to General Emory's command report for duty, it will march as follows : One section in rear of the two leading companies ; one section in the center of the train, in rear of a company of infantry, and one section in the rear of the train, in front of the two rear companies of the One hundred and forty-fourth Ohio National Guard. Commanding officers of regiments, and the officer commanding the battery, will personally attend to the posting and distribution of their commands in accordance with these orders, and will give their personal supervision to the safe escort of the train to Winchester. For this purpose they will have entire control of the march of the train under their escort, subject to the orders of the brigadier-general commanding, who will be habitually at the head of the train.

It is of importance that the train should reach Winchester as speedily as possible. Commanding officers will be held responsible that no unnecessary delays occur. Should the train be attacked, or any serious obstacle intervene to its march, regimental commanders will transmit the intelligence promptly to the brigadier-general commanding, and give to each other such support and assistance as may be needed.

By command of Brigadier-General Kenly.

WILL W. PEABODY,
*Captain and Acting (Assistant) Adjutant General.*

---

## XXIX.

*Report of Major William E. Beardsley, Sixth New York Cavalry.*

*Winchester, Va. Aug.* 14, 1864

COLONEL: I have the honor to report the arrival in this place with all of our brigade train, but about 8 or 10 wagons. We were attacked by Mosby at daylight yesterday morning in Berryville (*en route* for Winchester) and a disgraceful panic ensued, resulting in the entire destruction of the Reserve Brigade's train and a portion of ours with battery forges, etc., the running off of nearly all the mules, the capture of a large number of prisoners, killing of 5 men of ours, with many wounded ; among the latter is Captain McKinney, flesh wound in right thigh; he is here and doing well. After emptying my pistol in exchange with an officer, and being hard pressed, without a single man as support,I dashed off and checked the guard (100 days' men), but failed to get them back until, finding Mason and one man of the old Sixth with a carbine, we deployed as skirmishers, and returned to the head of our train, where a party was applying the torch

FEDERAL REPORTS, ETC.

and, by the use of the one carbine, succeeded in driving off the enemy and secured the paymaster's treasure-chest and trunk of pay-rolls, which we carried on our horses to a place of security, when I succeeded in rallying about twelve muskets, under a sergeant, who advanced as skirmishers, when a single volley saved all our train but 8 wagons which were already burned. Lieutenant Allyn had charge of 200 head of cattle ; all missing from the rear of the train. I sent for cavalry, and shortly the First Rhode Island arrived, but about 30 minutes too late, the enemy having disappeared with their booty in the direction of Snicker's Gap, and they did not pursue. I sent to this place for ambulances and have the wounded here. General Kenly, commanding here, sent down his teams, and our brigade train is now here without teams, except 9 wagons, including your wagon and the two regimental ones. Now, what shall we do ? No guard furnished us, neither teams with which to proceed. Major Sawyer is here and anxious to pay. His money, $112,000, is also safe. I have no hesitation in saying that with 50 good men of the Sixth New York I could have repulsed the thieves. Mr. Evarts now informs me that for lack of teams, he was obliged to abandon all the forage and 7 wagons and 3 battery forges, all in good condition, now at Berryville, which, for lack of guards, cannot return for them. The infantry here are only in the way. We shall remain here until we hear from you. I am myself still quite sick.

I have the honor to be, very respectfully, your obedient servant,

W. E. BEARDSLEY,
*Major Sixth New York Cavalry.*

Col. THOMAS C. DEVIN, *Commanding Second Brigade, First Cavalry Division.*

------

## XXX.

*Report of Captain E. P. McKinney.*

*Harper's Ferry, West Va., August 16, 1864.*

Capt. W. H. H. EMMONS,
*Assistant Adjutant General, Reserve Brigade, Calvary Corps.*

SIR : I have the honor to report that on Friday, the 12th instant, I started from this place with 5 days' rations for 2,250 men and extra stores for sales to officers, in wagons. The wagon train of this brigade was composed of a few wagons carrying forage, 10 wagons carrying subsistence stores, and the various regimental and head-quarters wagons, and was in the rear of the entire train, which was commanded by Captain Mann, assistant quartermaster. From one mile this side of Charlestown the train was accompanied by a guard of infantry, said to be a brigade. About 2 a. m. of the 13th instant the rear of the train, *i. e.*, the wagons belonging to the brigade, after much trouble, caused by the inexperience of the drivers and the newness of the mules to harness, went into park with the rest of the train (infantry and cavalry) at the stream this side of Berryville. It was daybreak in the morning before the first part of the train had hauled out of the park, and the wagons of the Second Brigade, which immediately preceded those of this brigade, were beginning to cross the stream when a few shots were fired by light howitzers from, I should think, a quarter of a mile distant into the part of the train which was yet in park, which were almost instantly accompanied by a small number of mounted men, charging as foragers, dressed in gray uniforms and carrying only revolvers, which they used with more noise than precision. The charge and also the howitzer shots came from the side of the road toward Snicker's Gap. The guards who accompanied us, as far as I could see, threw down their arms and ran away without firing a shot. The party that made the attack took away all the mules and fired the wagons which they could not get off, and escaped without any molestation, All the wagons of this brigade were captured or destroyed, as far as I could learn, with the exception of one wagon, carrying officers' baggage of the First U. S. Cavalry. My opinion is that a company of 50 men might have saved the train without loss, if they had made a stand in time. The property lost, for which I am responsible, was 5 days' rations for the brigade, stores destroyed for officers' supplies, all the quartermasters' and commissary property pertaining to the subsistence department of the brigade, and all my papers and vouchers of last month, and this including books, ration returns, invoices and receipts, receipts for payments of commutation of rations, etc. A wound received at the time the train was attacked prevented my making an earlier report.

Very respectfully, sir, your obedient servant,

E. P. McKINNEY,
*Captain and Commissary of Subsistence, Reserve Brigade.*

FEDERAL REPORTS, ETC.

### XXXI.

*Testimony of Capt. J. C. Mann, Quartermaster First Division Nineteenth Army Corps, before the Board of Inquiry.*

On receiving orders from chief quartermaster, I ordered the several trains to hitch up in readiness to move. There were in the neighborhood of 525 wagons in the train to go forward. The advance left Harper's Ferry about 10.30 a. m., August 12, and, from some reason unknown to me, the cavalry trains did not follow promptly. We marched until about 11 p. m. without feeding or watering men or animals, when we arrived at a small creek about one mile this side of Berryville. At that point Captain McGonnigle, acting chief quartermaster Middle Military Division, was present, and ordered the trains to be parked long enough to water the animals, and make coffee for the men. The Sixth Corps train parked on the right side of the road; the Nineteenth on the left; the Army of West Virginia, Eighth Army Corps, on the right of the Sixth Corps, I think; the Cavalry Corps to the rear of the place where the Sixth Corps had parked, and partially on the same ground. The train required about two and a half hours to pass a given point. The Sixth Corps train moved out between 12 and 1 a. m., leaving, consequently, before the cavalry train arrived. They were followed by the Nineteenth Corps in regular order, and this followed by the train of the Army of West Virginia. When the train commenced moving General Kenly gave me the following orders, in presence of Captain McGonnigle, chief quartermaster: " I consider this the most dangerous point in the route. I desire you to remain here, therefore, until every wagon has passed." When the wagons of the Army of West Virginia were moving out, my chief wagon-master reported to me that the cavalry trains were unhooked, and feeding their stock. I immediately went to those trains, roused the officers in charge, ordering them to hook up their teams and start immediately, telling them we were in danger of an attack. Upon passing among the trains, I discovered one

LIEUT.-COL. CASPER
CROWNINSHIELD,
2d Massachusetts Cavalry.
From a Photograph taken
when a Lieutenant.

train that was not being hooked up, and I endeavored to find some officer in charge, but without effect. I then passed through the train again to find a wagon-master, but was unable to do so. It was now nearly daylight, and I dismounted and woke up the drivers myself, one by one, ordering them to immediately hook up their teams. I am under the impression that the animals of this train were unharnessed, but I am not positive. The drivers were so long in getting this train ready, that the sun had fairly risen when the enemy opened fire upon us, throwing 3 shells. Upon the explosion of the second shell, I reported to the lieutenant-colonel commanding the rear guard for instructions. At this time the train was not entirely hooked up, the lead and swing mules being harnessed to their wagons, and the wheel mules in the act of being hooked. Upon the explosion of the first shell, many of the drivers mounted their saddle mule, which was ready saddled, and fled. When I reported to the lieutenant-colonel, he was rallying his men and forming them in line. I should think there were about 75 of them. I reported to the lieutenant-colonel that it was impossible to move the train to corral it, and asked for instructions. He replied he had none to give. I told him the rebel guns held the road, and if he had no instructions for me, I would go around the hill and hurry the balance of the train away. He said, "Very well." By this time the enemy's cavalry, clothed mostly in blue, led by a man in civilian dress, wheeled into line from sets of fours and commenced firing with carbines, and advancing toward the train. At this point I left the train, passed around the hill, and rejoined the balance of the train beyond Berryville. About three miles beyond Berryville, I met 2 squadrons of cavalry going toward Berryville upon a trot. I gave them what information was in my power, and hurried on with the balance of the train, which I reported to General Kenly near Winchester.

I am unable to give an accurate statement of the losses, as I had no report from the officer in command of the train lost, and did not again visit the place of disaster.

---

## XXXII.

HEADQUARTERS CAVALRY BRIGADE,
*Near Fort Buffalo, Va., August* 25, 1864.

Lieut. Col. J. H. TAYLOR,
*Chief of Staff and Assistant Adjutant-General:*

COLONEL: I have the honor to report that the party under Colonel Gansevoort returned early this morning. Colonel Gansevoort ob-

tained positive information that there is no force at either Warrenton or Culpeper; that squads of 50 and 100 men frequently come up on the railroad and pass through Culpeper on their way
to join the main command in the Valley, and that a large force
consisting of over 10,000 infantry and cavalry, passed through
Warrenton about a week since. This is probably the force of which
you have already been informed. The usual small parties of guerrillas
were met with. The party captured and brought in 5 prisoners

J. R. BEAL CO. D

(2 soldiers and 3 citizens), 40 horses, 1 mule,
horse equipments, and harness leather. A number of rebel uniforms were found in a house near
Warrenton and burned. A picket-post, consisting of a corporal and 3 men (near this camp) of
the Sixteenth New York Cavalry, was attacked
at 2 a. m. to-day by a party of mounted rebels; 4
horses and 2 men were taken; 1 man badly
wounded and the corporal escaped. Augustus
Klock, a citizen living near Falls Church, was
arrested by Mosby yesterday near Vienna, and
was released this morning. He states that Mosby
on releasing him told him to inform me that he
(Mosby) had sent Major W. H. Forbes and Captain
Manning, Second Massachusetts Cavalry, to the penitentiary, in retaliation for the confinement of Jack Barnes and Phil Trammell, two of
Mosby's men. Both were tried by a court-martial in Washington and
sentenced to the Albany penitentiary. Barnes, I believe, was tried for
violation of the oath of allegiance and stealing horses; Trammell for
being a guerrilla. It has been ascertained quite positively that the
person alluded to by you in your communication of August 24, as in the
habit of visiting a female in the vicinity of Vienna is not an officer, but
a non-commissioned officer of the Second Massachusetts Cavalry, who
was yesterday relieved and ordered to rejoin his regiment.

Very respectfully, your obedient servant,

H. M. LAZELLE,
*Col. Sixteenth New York Cavalry, Comdg. Cavalry Brigade.*

P. S.—I forgot to state that Colonel Gansevoort brings information
that the rebels obtain their supplies by the way of Thornton's Gap
and Sperryville. The Warrenton route is used but little.

## XXXIII.

### *A Modern Rob Roy.*

[Editorial from the New Yo₁k *Herald*, November 27, 1863.]

In another column will be found a letter which will have a novel interest for our readers, having been penned in the saddle *en route* for Richmond, by one of the *Herald* correspondents recently captured by the guerrilla chief, Major Mosby. It was written by the latter's permission and forwarded to us by his "special express." What that is we are left in ignorance of, but that it does not keep pace with the rapidity of the Major's other movements may be seen by the date, which is November 1. Our correspondent speaks in the highest terms of the treatment which he and his companion received from their captor, who, like his famous Scotch prototype of the Scottish Border, can, it appears, be very much the gentleman when he chooses. He did all he could to make them comfortable, and they seem to have had a capital time with him, all things considered. The only property belonging to them that he appropriated were the animals that they rode—"those gay *Herald* horses"—as he styled them. He promised them others, however, in their stead, which for a guerrilla was, we consider, behaving very handsomely. The Major has evidently a high opinion of our judgment in horseflesh and thinks he is paying us a compliment in adding to his stud these specimens. We trust that his fancy for the *Herald* breed will stop there, as it is rather a heavy item of expenditure to our establishment, these latest captures making nearly a dozen animals that have already been taken from us.

---

### *Our Captured Correspondents.*

---

Letters from them Written en route to Richmond.—Importance of Mosby's Raids to the Rebels.— His Fancy for Horses from the *Herald* Stud, etc.

---

We have received the following from Mr. George H. Hart, one of our correspondents, who was recently captured by the guerrilla chief, Mosby, in Virginia. It was accompanied by a private letter from another of our correspondents, who happened to be with Mr. Hart at the time and who, of course, also fell into the hands of the rebels.[1]

#### HEADQUARTERS IN THE SADDLE,
#### EN ROUTE TO RICHMOND UNDER MOSBY'S ESCORT,
#### *White Plains, Va., Nov.* 1, 1863.

Early in the morning Major Mosby, accompanied by several of his men, suddenly made his appearance at the house of Mr. McCormick,

---

[1] See mention of capture, Chapter V., page 104.

in the town of Auburn. Quietly reposing and totally unconcious of danger, were two of your correspondents in the house alluded to.

One of them was your humble servant, myself, the other name I omit at his request, on his family's account.

The first intimation we received of the presence oft his formidable and almost mythical individual, the mysterious and ubiquitous Mosby, was the scream of the ladies which apprized us of the fact. Shortly after we were summoned to open the door, which we reluctantly obeyed, and found two gentlemen courteonsly tendering us the contents of two revolvers if we did not surrender. To resist was out of the question, the odds being too great, as the house was surrounded and the only weapon in the party being a small pocket pistol. To escape was likewise impracticable, not to speak of the uncertainty of the attempt. So the only remaining alternative was accepted and we surrendered.

The ladies implored and entreated in our behalf, but Mosby was unrelenting, and finding their efforts abortive, the ladies threatened them with General Lee's displeasure, as we acted in the capacity of protectors to the domicile, but all to no avail, and we marched off in triumph—I mean to Mosby's triumph—on our own horses, or I should have said those belonging to the *Herald*, then in our possession. We rode along leisurely, Major Mosby opening the conversation, which soon became highly interesting. We soon discovered that the Major was a very different personage from what he is described.

In his address and demeanor he is a perfect gentleman, and his relations with ourselves was highly courteous. He is about twenty-eight years of age, of prepossessing appearance and certainly the reverse of the picture drawn of him in the newspapers generally. He wears the uniform of a Major in the regular rebel service. By profession he is a lawyer, and with a considerable share of native shrewdness combines the acquired tact of the professional attorney. In his movements he displays great energy and as an evidence of his powers of endurance accompanies his men on all their expeditions. On this occasion the object of his visit to Auburn was to make a reconnoissance, as he frequently does prior to the period he contemplates making a strike. I understand that General Lee was supplied with the information by Major Mosby which induced him to make his last advance, and his movements for acquiring knowledge of the movements of the Union army at any time are perfect.

As an instance :   When the pontoon bridges were in transit to General Meade's army some two or three weeks since, Mosby had conveyed information of the fact to General Stuart before the bridges reached the army.   Hence his services are almost invaluable.

Originally, with a force of sixty or seventy, he has increased it to some two hundred or three hundred men, and with these he annoys our army, which he assails in all positions, and by his frequent captures of valuable and necessary supplies, has rendered himself a person of considerable importance to the rebels. He sent to General Stuart some few days since, one hundred and three mules captured from the Union army, and for which the Quarter-master paid him in rebel funds, $300 per head.

Mosby's men, such as I have seen, are intelligent beyond the average, and seem to revere their leader, who, to use their own words, can wear out any four of them by his labors.

My fellow-prisoner and myself have naught to complain of, save an unceremo-nious disturbance from a sound sleep and a warm bed at a disagreeably early hour in the morning, and a cold ride of some eighteen miles. To counterbalance this, we have the ap-parent prospect of a winter residence at one of the most fash-ionable cities of the South — fair Rich-

JAMES J. WILLIAMSON, CO. A.
From a recent Photograph.

mond—a privilege certainly denied to many eager thousands of the Union army. We are told that the *Hotel de Libby*, in its capacity, number of guests, and extent of reputation, exceeds any hotel in Richmond, and, it is added, that rooms there are prepared for us in ad-vance. What distinguished attention from entire strangers! Who, after this, can doubt Major Mosby's courtesy?

Nothing of interest transpired on the road from Auburn to White Plains, which, to use a bull, was not the road, but the fields and the woods. Arriving at this point, the Major invited us into the residence of a gentleman residing in the vicinity, to whom we were formally in-troduced, and afterwards invited to partake of a warm and bountiful breakfast, which we cordially accepted and did ample justice to. The breakfast was rendered more agreeable by the presence of four very agreeable ladies. After breakfast, we smoked a cigar tendered us by our host and, through the further courtesy of Major Mosby, I now write these particulars and forward them by his special express.

For his very marked attention, if we do not feel grateful, we feel at least complimented, and bid him here accept our thanks for the many kind courtesies which have so far succeeded in their intent as to make us feel his companions, and not as his prisoners.

I am in hopes in my next to be able to despatch you the latest news from Stuart's headquarters, which, if it be not important, will certainly have a claim to one merit—novelty.

## XXXIV.

### A Federal Scouting Party Hunting for Mosby.

Stevenson, in his History of the First New York Cavalry, thus describes the adventures of a Federal scout through "Mosby's Confederacy" hunting for Mosby :

On the 8th of June, Mosby's guerrillas captured our wagon train on its way to Winchester with provisions ; taking 12 mules with the harness and leaving the wagons and their contents in the road untouched. They had evidently been frightened off by the approach of some of our men. The guard, consisting of about 20 infantry, was captured, however, and carried off with their mules.

On the 10th, Captains Boyd and Bailey were ordered out with 100 men to go through "Mosby's Confederacy," on account of the capture of our train. They knew very well that they couldn't capture any of the guerrillas in the daylight, so they made up their minds to try it by night. They crossed the river and the mountains early in the evening and commenced their search for "game" about midnight.

They would noiselessly surround a house, knock at the door, when a female head with nightcap on would peep out to inquire what was wanted. In some cases they had to threaten to break the door or burn the house in order to effect an entrance, while in other cases they were admitted at once. When delayed they always knew there was game inside, but they couldn't always find it, as the "Johnnies" had secret hiding places in the houses which they frequented.

---

[1] "Boots and Saddles." A History of the First Volunteer Cavalry of the War, Known as the First New York (Lincoln) Cavalry, and also as the Sabre Regiment. Its Organization, Campaigns and Battles. By James H. Stevenson, Captain and Brevet Major, U. S. V., A. A. G. Illustrated. Harrisburg, Pa., Patriot Publishing Co., 1879.

They had taken quite a number of prisoners, but had not yet reached Mosby's headquarters, which were said to be in the house of a Mr. Hathaway. Some of the prisoners had escaped in the darkness, and fearing they might carry the alarm to their chief, Bailey set out with a few of the best men and horses in the party to try and effect the capture of so noted a personage. No doubt he was thinking of the flaming newspaper articles in which his name should appear conspicuously as the capturer of Mosby, and it may be that he had one eye upon promotion.

After a short ride of a mile or so, they came upon the house they were seeking and quickly surrounded it. Bailey dismounted, accompanied by one or two of his men, and knocked at the door, but no response. He then struck the door sharply with the butt of his revolver and the window was heard to go up.

" What's the matter? " said a shrill female voice from the window ; evidently very much annoyed at being aroused at such an hour of the night.

" Open this door quickly," said Bailey, " or we'll burst it open."

" Who are you ? " was the reply.

" Never mind who we are, but come down and let us in."

The head was withdrawn, and in a few seconds the door was opened by Mr. Hathaway. On entering, Bailey inquired for Mosby's room and not being answered immediately, he took a light and went to look at it.

The first room he entered was Mosby's but the bird had flown, leaving his mate to keep the nest warm. It was an awkward matter to search the room, but it had to be done, and Mrs. Mosby offered no objections. Nothing could be found except a pair of spurs, giving no clew to Mosby's whereabouts, however, and the party was very much disappointed.

It appears that Mosby had been in the house, but had got out of a window into the branches of a tree, from which he was quietly watching the party, and in the darkness he was not discovered. They got his fine sorrel mare, besides about 25 other very fine horses belonging to his officers and men. I afterwards owned one of these, which had belonged to a Lieutenant Beattie. Sergeant Fokey of Company D owned the Mosby mare, and christened her " Lady Mosby." She was a beauty, and very fast.

## XXXV.

*Poetry of the War.*

The exploits of Mosby and his Men furnished abundant material for the pens of the rustic poets of the time. Two of these ballads I have fortunately preserved, but the names of the authors have been lost.

------

### MOSBY.

There's a rebel guerrilla, one Mosby by name,
To catch U. S. horses his principal aim ;
He proves quite a terror to his keenest foe,
By bagging their pickets, as many do know.

On one occasion brave Wyndham went out,
To catch Mosby's band he took a long scout ;
He marched up to Warrenton, there made a halt ;
He could not find Mosby, but 'twas not his fault.

He opened the stores and every hotel,
And faithfully searched to find the old fel' ;
But much to the Colonel's regret, could not find
The plague and the terror of his picket line.

They made in the town but a short sojourn,
Then, mounting their horses, prepared to return,
Each man was so loaded he could carry no more
With the goods they had honestly found in the store.

As the brave little army marched back down the road,
Their horses exhausted quite by their large load,
Mosby, unthought of, turned up pretty near,
And made the acquaintance of those in the rear.

The Colonel was now so enraged at his fate,
That he swore upon citizens he'd retaliate ;
But this did no good, for Mosby could come
And get their fine horses and carry them home.

There is one other circumstance I will cite—
He went into Fairfax at a late hour of night,
But we who are true to the Union won't laugh,
For he picked up a General and all of his staff.

The General-in-chief said this never would do,
That it must be stopped, and ordered it, too;
He chose a wise course, you'll all say, I'll be bound—
He arrested the farmers for ten miles around.

But I'm afraid, after all, they have not yet found,
The farmers who pilot this Mosby around,
For since they've been arrested, the papers explain,
That Mosby has paid us a visit again.

At Herndon station a few nights ago,
A Major was placing his pickets, when lo !
Mosby came rushing up with a small squad,
And captured the Major and all of his guard.

Now I ask one and all if this is not rough,
It's a disgrace to our army ; it has gone far enough ;
To hang this vile Mosby I think that we ought,
But I believe that the hanging comes after the caught.

————

## MOSBY'S LAST RAID INTO LOUDOUN.

Colonel Mosby's last order I'm glad to relate,
A tenth of the grain from the Quakers to take ;
And for the same purpose his battalion he brought,
And all over Loudoun corn and bacon he sought.

> CHORUS : Oh, Colonel Mosby ; Oh, Colonel Mosby, the
> Quakers' hard fate
> Is pretty hard to relate.

The Yankees they thought to block this bold game,
So the Twelfth Pennsylvania to Harmony came ;
But in spite of the Yankees and all their bombast,
Colonel Mosby will get his provisions at last.

> CHORUS—As above.

The Yankees they thought to draw the Rebs. out,
But in making the effort many went up the spout,—
The infantry ran and the cavalry broke,
And they found fighting Mosby was not all a joke.

> CHORUS—As above.

We followed them next day until the sun set,
And still on the morrow we followed them yet ;
But seeing that fighting 'gainst Mosby was vain,
They all crossed over the river again.

CHORUS—As above.

I'm sorry to say that some ten or fifteen
Of this noble battalion at Pusey's were seen ;
They broke up the dishes and kicked up a fuss,
And got themselves into a terrible muss.

CHORUS : Oh, Mr. Pusey ; Oh, Mr. Pusey, indeed I am
sad
You've been treated so bad.

Some of the party left very soon ;
Some went off later and each brought a spoon ;
And one, not contented with what he had got,
Went back for the urn and a new coffee pot.

CHORUS : Oh, Mr. Pusey, etc.

One of the party to Leesburg then went ;
Two of the battalion to arrest him were sent.
They took him to Harmony, the Colonel to see,
And Mosby decided to let him go free.

CHORUS : Bully for Hipkins ! Bully for Hipkins !
To our great delight
He's found out all right.

Comrades, in future, when to Loudoun you're brought,
You must try and behave yourselves as you ought,
And also in future you must ever beware
Of visiting Pusey and flanking his ware.

CHORUS : Oh, Mr. Pusey, etc.

The following verses were printed in a Southern magazine soon after the war:

## MOSBY AT HAMILTON.

By " Madison Cawein."

Down Loudoun lanes, with swinging reins
   And clash of spur and sabre,
And bugling of battle horn,
Six score and eight we rode at morn,
Six score and eight of Southern born,
   All tried in love and labor.

Full in the sun at Hamilton,
   We met the South's invaders;
Who, over fifteen hundred strong,
'Mid blazing homes had marched along
All night, with Northern shout and song,
   To crush the rebel raiders.

Down Loudoun lanes with streaming manes
   We spurred in wild March weather;
And all along our war-scarred way
The graves of Southern heroes lay,
Our guide posts to revenge that day,
   As we rode grim together.

Old tales still tell some miracle
   Of saints in holy writing—
But who shall say why hundreds fled
Before the few that Mosby led,
Unless the noblest of our dead
   Charged with us then when fighting?

While Yankee cheers still stunned our ears,
   Of troops at Harper's Ferry,
While Sheridan led on his Huns,
And Richmond rocked to roaring guns,
We felt the South still had some sons,
   She would not scorn to bury,

## XXXVI.

*Copy of Letter Inclosing Captain Flint's Picture to James E. Taylor*

*Craftsbury, Vt., Jan.* 15, 1894.

Comrade JAMES E. TAYLOR :

DEAR SIR :

Your communication to Commander of Flint Post was received, requesting a photograph of Captain H. C. Flint. I am Senior Vice in our Post and have a photo. of our Captain, which I will send you, trusting that you will return the same. I was a member of Captain Flint's Company, and was in the First Vermont Cavalry three years. Was not in the fight where our Captain was killed, which we always called the fight at Broad Run. I was with the detachment at Dranesville at that time, but was sent to Washington with a despatch the night before that fight took place.

I know a few things about "Mosby's Men," as I carried despatches from our Brigade Headquarters. I used to be sent up and down the Valley and across the Mountains, through Snicker's, Ashby's and Thoroughfare Gaps, and "Mosby's Men" were our eternal torment.

We have a man in our post who had a bullet put straight through his lung at the Broad Run fight ; he was left to die at Miskell's, but he did not die, but is alive to-day.

I would like to have Mosby or some of his men write up the little engagement near Bealeton Station, where he fired the railroad train, and we chased him into the mountain and captured his little brass gun, and drove them till they did not have two men together.

And another in Throughfare Gap, where they fired on us from the rocks each side of the road.

And another where twenty of us went from Fisher's Hill to Harpers's Ferry, as ambulance guard with a wounded General, and they pitched into us after we had got almost to Bolivar Heights.

Pardon me, but all of these things come to my mind when I think about Mosby.

Our gallant Captain Flint died, as you perhaps know, with six bullets shot through him, which shows that they meant him, anyway.

I am no lover of Colonel Mosby or his way of fighting, and can see but little honor in bushwhacking, but am willing to send you the photo, and our Post will be glad of the design, if you will please send it at your convenience.

Yours in F., C. and Sc.,

A. E. COWLES,

*Flint Post No.* 15, *Craftsbury, Vt.*

## XXXVII.

*April* 8–10, 1865.—*Scout from Vienna into Loudoun County, Va.*—*Report of Col. Nelson B. Sweitzer, Sixteenth N. Y. Cavalry.*

HDQRS. SIXTEENTH NEW YORK VOLUNTEER CAVALRY,
*Vienna, Va., April* 11, 1865.

CAPTAIN : I have the honor to report that agreeable to orders No. 71, headquarters First Separate Brigade, I proceeded with 412 men, by roads on the right of the Little River turnpike, and on reaching Aldie sent a squadron into the town. Here I learned that the Eighth Illinois had passed in the direction of Middleburg. I also learned that Mosby had been quartered near Harmony with his men in the neighborhood, for some time. Crossing the Bull Run mountains about three miles north of Aldie, I proceeded toward Snickersville and turned toward Harmony. I did not see any guerrillas until near Aldie, where several shots were exchanged ; between Aldie and Harmony several charged by my flankers and one rebel shot. Reaching Harmony I found that Mosby had left two days before with all his men quartered in that vicinity, to rendezvous at Upperville, for a raid supposed to be on the Baltimore and Ohio Railroad. I found that the men conscripted lately by Mosby had left, and that his band is becoming very obnoxious to the citizens ; that the recent victories of our armies were creating an active, outspoken Union sentiment. The desire is for peace—with coffee, sugar, etc. Returning by Leesburg, I found the citizens quite sociable—the formerly cold and distant secession element quite anxious that we would accept some token of their hospitality, and the Union men, formerly whispering, now quite independent. I think the political health of this department is rapidly improving.

A great deal of rain having fallen during the scout, I found Goose Creek flooded. I, however, succeeded in crossing the command without loss, though a number were carried past the ford by the current. My men brought me quite a number of prisoners, but I could find nothing to justify me in retaining them—having no arms, and not having been taken in any hostile act. The race of guerrillas is rapidly returning to their former pursuits, the hatred of the Yankee invader not being such now as to incite a population to arms and individual desperation. I had no loss in my command.

Very respectfully,
N. B. SWEITZER,
*Col. Sixteenth N. Y. Vol. Cavalry, Comdg. Regiment.*
Capt. C. I. WICKERSHAM, *A. A. G.*

## XXXVIII.

*April 8–10, 1865.—Scout from Fairfax C. H. into Loudoun County, Va.—
Report of Lieut. Col. David R. Clendenin, Eighth Illinois Cavalry.*

*Fairfax C. H. April 11, 1865.*

SIR: In compliance with instructions from Brevet-Brigadier-General Wm. Gamble, I left this place on the evening of the 8th, with 400 men of the Eighth Illinois Cavalry, for the purpose of scouring Loudoun Valley, south of the Snickersville pike, in search of Mosby's command. Marching at night, I arrived in the Valley about 1 a. m., half my force passing through Cool Spring Gap, and the other half through the gap at Aldie.

Spreading over the country, the houses were searched for concealed soldiers, but not one was found. One half went three miles north of Goose Creek on the Snickersville pike, and the whole force concentrated near Middleburg at daylight. The only intelligence thus far obtained was that Mosby had concentrated his forces at Upperville on the 8th and moved away.

Arriving at Upperville, I learned that Mosby had been there the day previous, as reported, with considerable force, variously estimated, ranging from 400 to 900 men. From the best information I could obtain, one company was sent to Maryland for the purpose of robbing a bank; another company under Bush.Underwood, was sent down to operate on this line; Mosby, with the balance of his command, crossed over into the Shenandoah Valley to operate against Hancock's forces.

On the 6th, 40 Federal prisoners passed through Upperville, having been taken by Mosby's Men, near Harper's Ferry. These prisoners were reported to belong to the Loudoun Rangers.

From Upperville I moved in 3 columns, scouring the country, and encamped between Rectortown and White Plains, from which place I marched to camp yesterday.

During the whole trip not over 15 rebels were seen by the entire command, two of them being captured near Sudley's Mills, and they belonged to White's Battalion; about half a dozen more were seen in that vicinity. I brought in 22 horses, 17 of them U. S. horses; they were found in the woods principally—9 were found in one place, 7 of them being branded. Two were found near Broad Run, with old U. S. saddles on, bridles tied up, etc. They belonged to the two men afterwards captured, who had in the meantime provided other horses.

Twenty-two horses, 4 saddles, 3 revolvers and holsters and 2 belts, comprise the captured property. They are subject to your order.

D. R. CLENDENIN, *Lieut.-Col., Comdg.*

Capt. C. I. WICKERSHAM.

## XXXIX.

*Reports on Affair at Harmony.*

HEADQUARTERS MIDDLE MILITARY DIVISION,
*March* 22, 1865.

Gen. C. C. AUGUR, *Commanding Dept. Washington :*

The regiment of infantry and cavalry under Colonel Reno found Mosby near Harmony, with about 500 men, and had a skirmish, in which we lost about 20. Some of the rebel wounded, including two officers, fell into our hands and Mosby fell back to Upperville, where it is reported he has collected considerable stores.

The river is still high, and Mosby must go down toward White Plains or disperse, as Reno will follow him as far as Ashby's Gap, at least. He has collected quite a large force for a raid, some of our informants putting it as high as 700, including White's battalion, but 500 is thought a large number.

Respectfully,

C. H. MORGAN, *Bvt. Brig.-Gen., etc.*

---

HEADQUARTERS DEPT. WASHINGTON,
TWENTY-SECOND ARMY CORPS,
*Washington, D. C., March* 22, 1865.

Colonel GAMBLE, *Commanding Fairfax Court House :*

The force sent out by General Hancock had a fight yesterday with a party of rebels, about 500 strong. I wish you to send out about 500 men to-morrow to the vicinity of Upperville, where General Hancock's party has gone. Let your party look out for them and not mistake them for rebels or rebels for them. The expedition to Northern Neck is abandoned for the present. Colonel Sweitzer will be out in the morning train.

C. C. AUGUR, *Major-General Commanding.*

---

*Harper's Ferry, W. Va., March* 22, 1865.

Brigadier-General MORGAN, *Chief of Staff :*

Just received the following despatch for the Major-General Commanding, from Colonel Reno :

*Near Harmony, Va., March* 22, 1865.

GENERAL : I have the honor to state that I arrived at this place last evening and had a slight skirmish with the enemy, resulting in the following casualties to them : 2 captains wounded, 2 privates killed, and 2 wounded; all fell into our hands. I have not found many supplies yet, but have burned those I have found. I am informed there are large stores at Middleburg, Upperville and Paris, which places I expect soon to reach.

M. A. RENO, *Colonel Commanding.*

Eleven of our wounded (slight) have arrived; 1 rebel captain wounded; 4 seriously wounded of ours left near the field. We had 1 officer killed. Our total loss reported by wounded officer of Reno's command, 20.

The enemy were commanded by Mosby in person and were about 500 strong. They fell back toward Upperville. This information is derived from our wounded officer.

Respectfully,

J. D. STEVENSON, *Brig.-Gen. Commanding.*

———

*Fairfax Court House, Va., March* 24, 1865.

Lieut.-Col. TAYLOR, *Chief of Staff, etc:*

I have just returned with detachment of the Eighth Illinois Cavalry after a march of 60 miles in two days. I connected with the command of Colonel Reno yesterday at 6 p. m., at Mountville, on the Snickersville Pike. Colonel Reno, with his command, 300 cavalry and 700 infantry, started at 8 a. m., on his return through Snicker's Gap, stating that he had a sufficient force to cope with all that Mosby could bring against him. A detailed report will be forwarded to-morrow.

W. GAMBLE, *Colonel Commanding Brigade.*

———

*Harper's Ferry, Va., March* 25, 1865.

General MORGAN, *Chief of Staff:*

Just received the following from Colonel Reno for you:

*Purcellville, Loudoun County, Va., March* 25, 1865.

GENERAL: I arrived at this point last night and will be in camp with my command to-night or to-morrow. I shall delay here for some time to pick up some wounded men of mine. I have destroyed a good deal of corn and some of Mosby's men. Will report details on my return.

M. A RENO, *Colonel Commanding.*

The Loudoun County Rangers brought in this dispatch. Did the General design this command to report back to me on return of the expedition?

JOHN D. STEVENSON, *Brigadier-General.*

———

*Winchester, Va., March* 22, 1865.

Maj.-Gen. H. W. HALLECK, *Chief of Staff:*

I sent an expedition into Loudoun composed of one regiment of infantry of the First Veteran Corps, and about 500 cavalry, all under Colonel Reno.   Last night, near Harmony, he encountered Mosby, who had about 500 men, and had a slight skirmish, losing about 20 men.   The enemy's dead and wounded fell into our hands and Reno moved on to Upperville and Middleburg, where it is reported considerable stores are collected.

W. S. HANCOCK, *Major-General Commanding.*

HEADQUARTERS,
*Stephenson's Depot, March* 28, 1865.

Brigadier-General MORGAN, *Chief of Staff:*

Captain Inwood, just returned, reports guerrilla band of 26, under a Lieutenant Russell.  Tracked them to Bunker Hill and Smithfield, thence in the direction of Charlestown.   They were recognized by citizens as men from Jefferson County, part of Mosby's original gang but now under command of Ross, who is said to have 500 of these robbers, divided up into small parties.   At Bunker Hill they robbed the post-office, and committed many other robberies along the line of march.

W. H. EMORY, *Bvt. Maj.-Gen. Comdg.*

HDQRS. MIDDLE MILITARY DIVISION,
*March* 28, 1865.

General TORBERT :

A party of guerrillas, estimated at about 50, attacked the wood party near Stephenson's this p. m., wounding several men, but were driven off.   They retreated toward Smithfield.   The general desires an energetic pursuit or attempt to recapture some of them by the party sent out.   Colonel Reno will send out a party from his camp toward Smithfield and Bunker Hill.

C. H. MORGAN, *Bvt. Brig. Gen.*

*Winchester, Va., April* 8, 1865.

Major General H. W. HALLECK, *Chief of Staff:*

I have for some time desired to send a large force of infantry and cavalry through Loudoun and Fauquier Counties with the expectation of putting a stop to Mosby's operations, by going through and over the Blue Ridge so effectually with infantry as to capture most of his band and stock.   He has about 500 men.   This will take several days and I do not feel at liberty to place so large a part of my troops where they would not be immediately available if called on. If I can, at any time hereafter learn that it will be safe to take the time, I will send out the expedition.

W. S. HANCOCK, *Major-General.*

## XL.

*Avenged by General Mosby.*

Retaliation of the Guerrilla for the Hanging of his Men.—Charles Marvin tells His Story.—He was one of the Condemned, but Escaped after he had seen all his Companions Hanged or Shot.—An Untold Chapter of War History.

[From the Washington *Post*, September 6, 1891.]

Chas. E. Marvin was Acting Quartermaster's Sergeant in the Second New York Cavalry, " Harris Light." The following is his story of his capture and escape :

About 5 o'clock on the evening of the 6th of November—while we lay in camp near Cedar Creek, we heard a shot or two, and supposed, as was frequently the case, our pickets had been driven in. A few moments afterwards the bugle sounded " to horse," and supposing we were going to have a skirmish, I mounted my horse and joined the command. Instead of going toward the front, we started to the rear, and when a short distance from Newtown we bivouacked for the night. The weather was very cold and the wind blew hard, still we were compelled to stand in line all night and to build fires out of such boards and rubbish as we could find close at hand. Wood was not to be had, and Colonel Pennington, our commanding officer, being comfortably situated, gave himself no uneasiness.

In the morning we received orders to mount, and proceeded eastward, toward the Shenandoah River. We had gone but a short distance when I spoke to the officer commanding our regiment, and told him my horse had cast a shoe, and as I saw no prospect of there being anything to do but take a long march, with his permission I would return to camp and draw rations. Permission was given me, when one of the men of my old company, named James Bennett, a soldier of ability and as brave a boy as there was in the regiment, seeing me start back, got permission from his captain to accompany me, his horse being also badly used up.

We had passed through Newtown and the infantry pickets just at the outskirts of the town, and had gone but a short distance, when a party of Mosby's Men, wearing our overcoats, black hats and top boots, completely concealing their uniforms, rode up behind us, as if they, too, had just passed the pickets, but there was an elevation between us so that the pickets could not see us.

They said : "Good morning!"

I replied : "Good morning, boys."

They asked : "What regiment do you belong to?"

I replied : "Second New York cavalry, the 'Harris Light.' What regiment is yours?"

They replied : "The Nineteenth Pennsylvania," and with that they had gotten alongside of us, and two of them threw their horses right square across the road in front of us, and put their revolvers, which were lying in front of them on their saddles, in the faces of Bennett and me, at the same time demanding our surrender. There were only two of them. The man who had his revolver pointed at me showed shoot in every wrinkle of his face, and he was too far from me to even make an attempt to strike the pistol from his hand. He was finely mounted, and I discovered at a glance (a man's mind discovers a great deal under such circumstances) that my comrade, Bennett, was in the same position as myself. I simply remarked to my captor that it was a remarkably cool proceeding for even this cool weather, and he replied :

"Give me that revolver, or you will be a good deal cooler in a very short time."

My impulse was to draw my revolver, feeling that could I get it from my holster, which was in the middle of my back, I would, at least so far as shooting was concerned, have an equal chance with him. But he stopped me before my hand could reach the revolver with an admonition not to touch it, but to unbuckle my belt, which I did. He then asked for my carbine, which was a Spencer, loaded with seven balls, and was hanging to my saddle. My impulse at that moment was to raise the muzzle to the proper angle, when all I would have to do was to pull the trigger, and one of us at least would be at liberty for the time being. I had barely placed my hand upon the gun when he discovered my purpose and informed me that if I made another false motion he would empty his revolver into my body.

Having secured my arms—Bennett having given up his in the same manner—we were turned east and rode up on the hill to a piece of woods where Captain Montjoy and his company had been watching the command the night before, and the proceedings of the party that captured us. We were divested of our overcoats, our money, watches and even of our pipes and tobacco.

We were then taken to Captain Montjoy, who wished to know what command we belonged to, and how many there were of us, where we were going, etc. I simply replied to the Captain's question that I was a soldier and didn't know anything. If he wanted information he would have to go to somebody better posted than I was. He passed me by with a smile and questioned my comrade, Bennett, who remarked that he belonged to the same command that I did and knew quite as little. We then started with some other prisoners they had picked up, for Mosby's headquarters at Ashby's Gap, which we reached in the evening about seven o'clock. As nearly as I can remember, we were taken to the home of a man named Williams and were quartered in a cabin formerly used as negro quarters. We had just laid down on the floor, after eating a small piece of corn bread and an apple, the only food we had had for twenty-four hours, as we had nothing since we left camp the night before, when we were aroused by the entrance of two of

Mosby's men, who ordered us to get up. I, being on the right, was the first one questioned as to my command, and replied that I belonged to the Second New York Cavalry, Custer's Division, and he said :

"You are the man we want."

Bennett was then asked the same question, and replied,

"I belong to the same command."

He said: "You are the two men we are after. Come on."

We were taken down the lane to the road, where we found a party of Mosby's men with seven prisoners tied by a rope, one to the other, as convicts are handled, two of whom were released, and Bennett and I were given their places. I asked what it meant, but received no reply except from one of the men tied with the rope, who motioned to me by

LUCIAN LOVE, CO. D.
One of the six Mosby's Men killed at Front
Royal by Custer's command.

drawing his hand across his throat, giving me to understand that we were to be hanged.

I immediately asked to see the commanding officer. He or his representative asked me what I wanted. I demanded the cause for which we were to be executed. He replied that it was in retaliation for seven men executed by Custer, belonging to Mosby's command, some months previous. I told him that at the time that execution took place my regiment was not under General Custer. and that we had nothing whatever to do with it, being in a different part of the country. He said it made no difference ; his orders were imperative. I then demanded to know why it was that a lieutenant of heavy artillery had been released and I substituted, and a private in infantry released and Bennett substituted. He said, " For the reason, I was told that they had taken care of the property of citizens in this part of the country and defended the women from insult or injury." I replied :

" My life is in your hands; if you will take me five miles in any direction from where I now stand, and I cannot find a woman that will say that I have rendered her valuable assistance, I will forfeit my life without a murmur."

He said he had no power to do anything of the kind, and then asked :

" Are you a Mason ? "

I replied, " I am not old enough to be a Mason."

" Is your father a Mason ? "

" My father belonged to nothing but the Abolition party, to my knowledge, but I have a brother-in-law who is one of the highest Masons in our State, and should I live and they will accept me, I expect to some day be a Mason."

He said, " I can do nothing for you but to promise you that if you make an escape you will not be recaptured by me nor by anyone else if I can prevent it."

His talk was during our progress down the mountain to the Shenandoah River at Berry's Ferry, where we crossed, riding horses behind the party who had us in charge.

They had stopped at several houses on the way and taken bedcords off the old-fashioned corded bedsteads with which to hang us.

My name was the first on the death-roll, and had any attention been paid to that, I would have been the first man executed, but in the search for a tree upon which to hang us, the line was placed in such a position that I was the farthest man on it from the tree. The first man was gotten up, his hands tied behind him, a bed-cord doubled and tied around his neck ; he was marched to a large tree beside the road, from which a limb projected. He was lifted in the air, the rope taken by one of the men on horseback and tied to the limb, and there he was left dangling. Two more were treated in the same manner.

It took some considerable time and our executioners were becoming uneasy, not knowing what minute a party of our troops would pass that way, and they decided, as they said, to shoot the balance of us, as " this hanging is too damned slow work." So they immediately ordered us to get up, when to their dismay they discovered there were but three of us, where there should have been four.

It afterwards turned out that one of the men had gotten loose from the line, and as we passed over a ditch in a field had dropped into the ditch and escaped. It was a dark and rainy night.

Our hands were tied behind us with a heavy bedcord. I was completely exhausted, not feeling that it would have been possible for me to have walked a hundred yards farther, but I succeeded in freeing my hands, not because I expected to escape, but having seen men on many battlefields who had evidently used their hands in their dying moments for their comfort or relief, I thought mine might do the same for me.

Having reached the tree where the three men were hanging, three Confederates stepped out in front of us and said to those behind us (we were now standing side by side, the three of us) : "Get away from behind there, boys." When I said, "Is this all the show you are going to give us?" he replied : "It is all you need, you Yankee —— – · — ——," when the three revolvers were placed in our faces.

The revolver on my right went off, the revolver on my left went off, and the revolver that was in my face failed to explode. The click of the hammer on the tube went through me like an electric shock.

I caught my breath, raised onto the balls of my feet, knocked the revolver one side, hit him in the head, jumped over him as he fell into the road, and as they sang out, "There goes the big Yankee —— —— ——," I seemed to find new life, and went at the speed of a streak of lightning down the road about 100 yards, where I entered the same woods they were in and climbed a shellbark hickory tree. Climbing is a feat I had never been able to perform when I was a boy, but I have done a great deal of hunting, and I don't think I ever saw a squirrel go up a tree faster than I went up that one.

Here I remained until I heard them ride away, when I came down and started for Winchester, which I gathered from their conversation was directly west on the road alongside of which they had left my comrades hanging or shot. I avoided the road until it began to get daylight, when feeling that I was as safe in the road as elsewhere, and the walking being much better, I came out into the road proper two miles from the place of the execution, where I discovered the man who had been shot on my left, with a shattered elbow.

On receiving the wound, he had fallen down and they had gone off and left him for dead, after kicking him in the ribs and rolling him over. This man's name was Hoffnagle, of the One Hundred and Fifty-third New York. He was very weak from loss of blood. I walked along slowly with him toward Winchester until it got quite light, when he insisted that I should go and hide myself until night, as a recapture meant certain death for me, and he would make his way to some house to seek assistance. I replied, " I will stay with you until I find you assistance," allowing him to lean upon me.

We approached a large weather-beaten house, at the door of which I knocked and demanded admittance. In answer to a query, evidently from an old woman, as to who was there, I stated that I had a wounded man with me, a Yankee soldier, who needed assistance. The reply came back, "Wait a moment and I will let you in." It was scarcely more than a moment when a very old and poorly-clad woman, with a saucer in which was some grease and a rag, in lieu of a better light, opened the door and admitted us. I told her who we were. She said: "Have no fear; I had three of Custer's men in my house when Mosby's Men were all over it, looking for them; and I had two of Mosby's Men concealed in my house when Custer's men were here looking for them. Any one who comes to me for assistance gets it, if I can give it to them."

At the time of my capture I had in my possession a vest pocket full of revolver caps that had become water-soaked until they had become worthless. When I reluctantly parted with my other assets it was with a twinge of pleasure that I gave up my water-soaked and worthless pistol caps and saw them distributed among the Johnnies who appeared to be greatly in need of such stores. They were greatly in need of caps that would explode, but possibly not the kind I was giving up. I have often thought it was more than possible that my would-be executioner may have received some of these very caps and placed one of them on his revolver, thereby saving my life.

I have told you about the man who was shot on my left, but not about poor Bennett, who stood on my right, and whom I supposed, as did Hoffnagle, had been killed. The shot Bennett received was in the shoulder from a Colt's navy revolver, not more than two feet distant, which he said afterward scarcely moved him, and he exclaimed: "For God's sake kill me if you are going to! Don't torture me to death."

A pistol was then placed close to the left side of his head and fired. The ball entered just at the top of his cheekbone and about half an inch back of his eye, passing entirely through his head and carrying out his right eye. This knocked him over, but did not deprive him of consciousness; so you can guess what kind of stuff he was made of. As soon as his would-be executioners rode away, he got up, crawled to a tree and supporting himself against it until morning, a man passing with a little girl, found him there. The child led him to the house of an ex-Confederate surgeon, who dressed his wounds and took care of him until he had a chance to send him to the hospital at Winchester. He got well—as well as a blind man can get, who has a package of lead in his body for which he has no use. He gets a pension, but his papers were returned three different times, and I swore myself black in the face before he got it. I finally told the examiner to write down what it was necessary for me to swear to in order to get Bennett his pension and I would swear to it without reading the paper. He got it. He is now, or was the last I heard of him, living in Lafayette, Ind.

Mosby's letter to Sheridan shows that it was written before he was aware of all the facts in the case.

The execution did not take place on the Valley pike, as he says, and we know, as told in the foregoing story, that seven men were not executed.

Sheridan, however, informed Mosby in reply that he did not countenance such a mode of warfare.

---

## XLI.

### *Fourteenth Pennsylvania Cavalry.*

The accompanying letters were received by Comrade S. R. Armstrong, of Company E, from one of our old opponents in the Fourteenth Pennsylvania Cavalry, and will be read with interest.

*Clarion, Pa., Dec.* 6, 1894.

S. R. ARMSTRONG :

DEAR SIR : Pardon me for being so tardy in answering your welcome letter, which came to hand Sept. 3d.   Shortly after receiving it, I went to the National Encampment of the Grand Army at Pittsburgh, Pa., Sept. 10th.   I remained there a week with my old comrades and had a very pleasant time.   Then came home and took an active part in the political campaign to Nov. 6, 1894, helping to roll up a big Republican majority in this State, and, by the way, we got it.

I remember distinctly some of the engagements our regiment (the Fourteenth Pennsylvania Cavalry) had with Colonel John S. Mosby's command.   The first engagement you mention in your letter I took part in was near "Camp Russell," Va., about 3 miles south of Winchester, on the road leading from that place to Front Royal, on Thanksgiving Day, November, 1864.   Mosby's command made a dash and captured our wagon train and a small guard protecting it, which was out foraging in the direction of Millwood.   After sending the train and prisoners to the rear, you made another dash at our camp.   We were eating our Thanksgiving dinner when you made the attack. We thought it very ungrateful in you to interrupt us while we were enjoying the good things of the land at our annual feast.

" Boots and Saddles " were sounded and we rushed for the " horse line," saddled and mounted quickly.   Your command was then in line just across a ravine south of our camp, perhaps 300 yards distant. Our batallion was on the right of the regiment and nearest your command.   We commenced firing at you with our carbines from the "horse line."   I had fired but one or two shots when Captain Walker, of Company F, dashed up and gave the command to charge.   We charged, with Walker leading, and drove you back with but little or no resistance, and pursued you sharply to Millwood, some 7 or 8 miles from camp.

In this dash John Feit, of Company K, captured one of your men, a short, thick-set fellow, with plenty of pluck, who had lost his horse and could not keep up with the procession any longer. On his way back to camp with the prisoner, Feit met the Adjutant of the First West Virginia Cavalry, on his way to the front, who said to Feit, " Is that one of Mosby's men?" Feit replied that he was. "You must not take any of them prisoners of war," said the Adjutant, and drawing his revolver, shot the prisoner dead.[1] Feit became infuriated and would have shot the Adjutant if he had had a load in his pistol or any ammunition to put in it. No braver or better soldier ever wore the blue than John Feit, and to this day he feels regret for the killing of that prisoner.

S. R. ARMSTRONG, CO. E.

Captain Duff and Sergeant McLaughlin of our Company still pursued about a mile beyond Millwood and captured a prisoner and returned to camp with him about 6 o'clock that evening. He was a large, fine-looking man, with long, black, wavy hair. He claimed his home was in Richmond, and that his mother was a widow.[2]

The prisoner had not been in camp long till the West Virginia Cavalry found it out and demanded that he be turned over for execution. Captain Duff said, "No, gentlemen; I will turn him over to nobody but General Tibbitts, commander of the brigade." After the prisoner was given his supper he was taken to the General's headquarters under a strong guard, as a prisoner of war.

In the afternoon we retook most of our wagon train which had been captured in the earlier part of the day by your command.

If our command (the Fourteenth Pennsylvania Cavalry) had a brush with Mosby's command at Berryville, I cannot recall it, and I know I was not in it or I would remember something about it.

[1] This young man who was killed was T. A. Carpenter, of Company E, Forty-third Batallion, Virginia Cavalry. He is buried in the Stonewall Cemetery, at Winchester, Va. He was from Madison County, Va.

[2] This captured prisoner was Frank Angelo, of Company C.

There were several engagements which our regiment had with Mosby's command during the rebellion which I have not the time now to tell you the merits or demerits of, as I saw them from our side of the conflict.

Our regimental Reunion will be held next year at Harper's Ferry, some time in the month of October, 1895, and I know our boys will be glad to meet any of the Confederates that can be there. We want to go around and see some of the old battlefields in the Valley. The war is over for nearly thirty years and we are one people.

Yours respectfully,
J. J. FRAZIER.

------

Clarion, Pa., August 12, 1895.

S. R. ARMSTRONG, *Woodville, Va.:*

DEAR SIR: Your kind invitation to the Reunion of Mosby's Men at Marshall, Va., on Wednesday, Aug. 14th, 1895, is at hand.

I can assure you that I am sorry that I cannot be with you on that occasion. Not that I have any sympathy for the cause for which you battled so long and hard more than thirty years ago ; but I would like to look on the faces of those brave and dashing men that our old regiment (the Fourteenth Pennsylvania Cavalry) met in so many well-contested battles, and see what wonderful changes thirty years have made upon them.

My old Captain David K. Duff, Company K, Fourteenth Pennsylvania Cavalry, was personally known to some of your command at least. He was badly wounded and taken prisoner in a fight in February, 1865, near Snicker's Ford, on the Shenandoah,[3] and kept at a little place in the mountains—I think it was called Paris ; we recaptured him there about ten days afterwards, and took him to Winchester, where he partially recovered from his wounds. He died eight years ago at his home at Elderton, Pa. No braver soldier than Duff ever drew a sword.

Our regiment (Fourteenth Pennsylvania Cavalry) expect to hold their reunion this year at Harper's Ferry, some time in October. I will send you the date as soon as I get it. I want to attend that re-union if I possibly can.

My kindest regards to you and all the old boys.

Wishing you all a happy and grand reunion, I remain,

Yours respectfully,
J. J. FRAZIER,
Co. K, 14th Pa. Cavalry.

------

[3] Captain Duff was wounded in the Mt. Carmel fight.

## XLII.

*List of "Mosby's Men" Confined in Room No. 2, Fort Warren, Boston Harbor, Mass., Released June 13, 1865.*

H. G. Harris, of Bluefield, West Va., formerly of Company D, Forty-third Battalion, Virginia Cavalry, wrote as follows :

I send you a list of the boys confined at Fort Warren, Boston Harbor; that is, in my room, No. 2. There were six rooms, in which prisoners were kept, but Mosby's Men were mostly in Rooms Nos. 1, 2 and 3. I think all in my room belonged to our command. You know I was captured the last of October, 1864, and was sent direct to the Old Capitol Prison at Washington, D. C., which was a receiving prison. After a sufficient number were got together they were sent off to other prisons. Mosby's Men were considered too desperate to be treated as ordinary prisoners, so they were held until February 1st, when we were informed that we would be sent to Fort Warren.

There was some talk of

H. G. HARRIS, CO. D.

an attempt to overpower the guards between Washington and Baltimore and make our escape; so the next day when the guard marched up, we saw that each soldier had a pair of handcuffs dangling from his belt, and like a lot of criminals in the prison yard of the Old Capitol we were handcuffed, two and two, and the chains were not taken off until the second day after we were landed in the casemates at Fort Warren. On the cars there was a guard on every other seat, and a squad at each end of the car.

The only escape made while I was in prison was John Munson, from the Old Capitol; and the only death among our boys during the eight

months was that of Aquilla Glascock, at the hospital at Fort Warren.
He and I occupied adjoining bunks.

Aylor, J, L., Slate Mills, Va.
Barr, Charles N., Herndon, Va.
Bencke, John H., Baltimore, Md.
Butler, W. B., Fairfax Station, Va.
Caldwell, C. E., Hillsboro, Va.
Chancellor, J. M., Flint Hill, Va,
Claggett, Johnson, New Baltimore, Va.
Cocke, W. S., Salem, Fauquier Co., Va.
Coons, F. A., Oak Shade, Va.
Cummings, G. W., Oak Vale, Va.
Davis, Americus, Alexandria, Va.
Davis, G. C., Flint Hill, Va.
Davis, L. M., Orlean, Va.
Delaplane, J. H., Buckland, Va,
Farr, Resin S., Buckland, Va.
Fletcher, Benton, Warrenton, Va.
Flynn, Wm. S., Salem, Fauquier Co., Va.
Follin, Ira, Vienna, Va.
Grey, Alfred, Linden, Va.
Griffin, G. C., Abingdon, Va.
Goura, J. A., England.
Harris, H. G., Scottsville, Va.
Hooe, R. M., Hillsboro, Va.
Hopkins, J. E., Bloomfield, Va.
Houdershell, R. A., The Plains, Va.
Hunt, S. W., Vienna, Va.
Hunt, Lewis, Vienna, Va.
Hunton, John W., Buckland, Va.
Hutchinson, J. R., Arcola, Va.
Johnson, James, Markham, Va.
Jones, E. M., Williamsburg, Va.
Kennedy, Thomas, Ireland.
Kephart, J. R., Belmont, Va.
Lake, Thomas W., Warrenton, Va.
Lane, D. F., Arcola, Va.
Love, Thomas R., Fairfax Court-House, Va.
McDonald, James, Scotland.
McIlhany, H. M., Warrenton, Va.
McIntosh, J. T., Leesburg, Va.
Marchant, John A., Charlottesville, Va.
Massie, J. R., Salem, Fauquier Co., Va.
Moran, Richard, Arcola, Va.
Muse, John, Belmont, Va.
Musser, Wm. H., Middlebrook, Montgomery Co., Md.

Nelson, L. M., Culpeper Court-House, Va.
Nicholas, Charles, Va. (Think he was captured before he joined the command.)
Oden, Archibald, Martinsburg, Va.
Orrison, Robert, Pleasant Valley, Va.
Parrott, Robert, Charlottesville, Va.
Pontier, Nathaniel, Baltimore, Md.
Price, C. D., Hillsboro, Va.
Price, Joseph, Harper's Ferry, Va.
Prosser, R. Hylton, Mississippi.
Reed, J. R., Oak Vale, Va.
Richards, Henry, Leesburg, Va.
Russell, T. A., Easton, Md.
Skillman, Samuel, Leesburg, Va.
Skinner, George, Aldie, Va.
Smith, D. L., Fredericksburg, Va.
Thomas, Robert, Oak Vale, Va.
Tongue, T. W., Warrenton, Va.
Wharton, H. A., Richmond, Va.
Williams, John, Upperville, Va.

XLIII.

### LIEUT.-COL. WILLIAM H. CHAPMAN.

*Chapman in the Miskel Fight.*

In the account of the Miskel fight in Chapter III, the name of William H. Chapman is not mentioned. This omission was not noticed until too late for correction. Chapman not only participated in that affair, but fired almost the first shot. He was made prisoner by a party of Federal soldiers that he attempted to capture alone on the north side of the turnpike, and about 2 miles from Miskel's house. He was afterwards recaptured by four of our men, who dashed up just as the party was going into the woods. Chapman snatched a pistol from one of the Federals riding near him and aided in capturing 6 or 7 prisoners.

The St. Louis *Post-Dispatch*, September 22, 1895, contained the following sketch:

*How He Saved Boston Corbett.—Internal Revenue Agent Chapman's Thrilling Experience.*

Mr. Chapman, the United States Internal Revenue Agent for this division, whose mission in life just now is the enforcement of Uncle Sam's tax laws, was not always a Federal official.

One bright day in June, 1863, when he was Colonel Mosby's chief subordinate, Mr. Chapman—then Captain and later Lieutenant-Colonel

—saved the life of "Boston" Corbett, the Union soldier who shot and killed J. Wilkes Booth, the assassin of President Lincoln. The story of that day's scrimmage and its thrilling climax is one of many which Mr. Chapman can tell, and it is deeply interesting.

———

It was in the midst of the great civil strife that the Confederate Congress passed a bill authorizing Captain Mosby to organize a battalion authorized to war on the Union forces between the Potomac and Rappahanock rivers, in Virginia. The troopers were daring raiders.

Mr. Chapman was a junior captain under Mosby when the Corbett episode happened. The command, about sixty strong, was advancing along a highway on the borders of Prince William County, Virginia. Mosby and Captain Chapman were in advance, and they scoured the surrounding county for signs of the enemy. Scouting parties made daily excursions from the camps around Washington, D. C., to watch the enemy. Mosby was looking for a brush with these small bodies, and his sharp eyes were rewarded.

Near an old Southern manor, to the right of the road was a troop of Federal cavalry. The horses were feasting on the new-mown hay which littered the field. The soldiers were lounging about with fatal indifference. Some were in the house, others in the barn, a few were in the hay field and quite a number were up in the cherry trees which flanked the graceful driveway leading to the house.

"Chapman, take the men with you and catch those·fellows," said Mosby to his Lieutenant in a satisfied way. He had no doubt that the Federal troopers could be trapped easily on account of their unsuspecting conduct. Captain Chapman gave the word of command and set out at a terrific pace for the manor gate. They wheeled into the lane and forced their blooded horses at top speed, for they wished to take the enemy completely by surprise and give them not even a moment to form themselves for defense. The ready weapon of Mosby's men, the revolver, was in each trooper's hand. As they advanced the surprised cherry-eaters dropped out of the trees and hid in the grass. Chapman left a few men behind to corral these, and he continued on toward the main body.

He wheeled in front of the house and went to the right of it. He led his men through the barnyard and out into the hayfield. At sight of the enemy in their midst, the Union soldiers became panic-stricken. They lacked organization and few of them had their weapons.

They fled precipitately, and Captain Chapman sent his men after them in squads. They brought back prisoners in bunches and rounded up all the chargers. But a few had scurried from the hay field into a pasture to the left of the house and made for the woods. In the excitement they got beyond the range of the deadly revolvers, and Captain Chapman ordered "Bush." Underwood, one of the best soldiers in the command, to pursue them.

"Bush" was a brave but discrete soldier. He was born and reared in the country where Mosby operated, and he knew every nook and cranny on both sides of the Blue Ridge. Captain Chapman knew the man and had no doubt that he would execute the command to the letter. In a few minutes Underwood returned with several prisoners. "Captain," said he, "there is one fellow over there that gave us some trouble. He is sheltered by a persimmon tree and a small ditch, and he has a seven-shooter repeating rifle."

Captain Chapman listened to this report and directed Underwood to return and get the fellow.

Underwood returned with more prisoners, but the man behind the persimmon tree was still at work with his rifle. Captain Chapman was not pleased when Underwood reported his second failure. He knew the man's courage, however, and told him to go a third time. Captain Chapman went along and took about eight men with him. A body of twenty men swept toward that persimmon tree. The Spencer rifle cracked repeatedly, but did no damage, and in a moment the horsemen were on the brink of the ditch where the Union soldier was concealed.

The first man to dismount was Underwood and he did so in a manner that startled Captain Chapman. The man was wild with rage at his two failures to catch the fellow behind the tree, and he sprang head first out of his saddle and over his horse's head. He did this by bringing his charger to an abrupt stop. Underwood alighted at the feet of the Union soldier, and with a quick movement he knocked the Spencer rifle to the ground. At the same instant he drew his revolver and pointed it at the head of the disarmed prisoner. He would have blown the man's brains out, had not Captain Chapman said in a stern voice :

"Don't shoot that man! He has a right to defend himself to the last!"

Underwood obeyed and lowered his weapon. The prisoner was sent to Richmond and Captain Chapman forgot the incident in the mad rush of war.

———

Two years later Wilkes Booth killed President Lincoln and the assassin fled southward from Washington. He crossed the northern neck of Virginia and when a troop of Federal cavalry pressed him closely, he took refuge in a barn on the south side of the Rappahanock. The soldiers set fire to the barn and one of them shot and killed Booth when he appeared in the midst of the smoke and flames. That soldier was "Boston" Corbett, and he wrote his autobiography after he became famous. In one chapter he told of his escape from death in Prince William County by the intervention of Mosby.

He told of the struggle with "Bush." Underwood as it has been given here, and made the mistake of thinking Chapman was Mosby.

Captain Chapman read the book and recalled the incident. Mosby had not reached his soldiers when the brush with Corbett occurred.

----

## XLIV.

### Mosby's Scouts near Georgetown.

#### By John H. Alexander.

About daybreak one morning in the Summer of 1864, Bush. Underwood aroused me from my slumbers, with an invitation to go with him on a scout about the neighborhood of Georgetown. We had gone into camp near Thoroughfare Gap late the night before, after which I had been on picket for a couple of hours, so I felt very little like facing the hard service which I knew would attend the proposed expedition. But when I learned that the party had been partially made up of such spirits as Charley McDonough, Hugh Waters, Harry Sinnott and Bill Trammell, I recognized the compliment of the invitation and accepted it.

The objects of the expedition were, generally, to gather information, and especially to "confiscate" a certain very fine stallion belonging to a Union man near Lewinsville.

Underwood's description of this horse, together with the very recklessness of venturing so far within the enemy's lines, offered attractions irresistible to a Mosby man. Accordingly, about sunrise a half dozen of us set out across the country in the direction of Georgetown.

By noon we had gotten within the limits of danger, and fearing that our further progress by daylight might bring us in contact with a patrol or scouting party of the enemy, or even a straggling trooper whose discovery of our presence would thwart our expedition, we retired to a body of pines to await nightfall.

After dark set in we resumed our march. Underwood had been raised in that part of Fairfax County, and it was his boast that he knew its every rabbit-path, as well as the political sentiments of all its inhabitants. And his unvarying success in scouting that section seemed to vindicate his claim. He was one of those cold-blooded, clear-headed, nervy fellows who never got "rattled," whatever turned up. Perfectly fearless, he was at the same time cautious and patient, and seemed to have a genius for just this sort of business. Therefore we implicitly followed his lead, though we soon heard on every side the noises from Federal camps and knew that the least accident or inadvertence might at any moment bring hordes of the enemy down upon us.

I suppose it was nearly bed-time, when we approached a house where Bush said that he could get some information that he wanted. While the rest of us remained with his horse under the shadows of the neighboring trees, he cautiously made his way to the rear of the dwelling. He soon returned with some biscuits and sandwiches, which we proceeded "to put where they would do the most good," while he unloaded his budget of news.

He had learned that the prize horse (which, by the way, I believe to this day was a pure myth, conjured up by him to allure us) had been sent to Washington that afternoon. But he had ascertained the location of the various camps in the neighborhood, with the names and numbers of the different regiments composing them. This was invaluable knowledge to us.

Furthermore, he informed us that there was a certain house near the Big Falls of the Potomac which a number of Yankee officers from a neighboring camp were in the habit of visiting, the attraction being some very fascinating girls.

There was some debate among us as to whether it was exactly the fair thing to break up so interesting a party. But the chance of carrying back with us some Yankee shoulder-straps, and possibly stars, not to speak of fine horses, overcame our scruples, and we determined to put in an appearance there during the evening, even at the risk of being regarded as intruders.

This house, however, was several miles away, and the road to it not altogether as safe and open to travelers as it is

THORNTON V. LEACH, CO. F

to-day. Nor did we go very far before our adventures began. It was now considerably past midnight, and, from the fact that we had been riding for some time within sound of the roar of the Big Falls I judged that we were nearing our destination.

We had been following our leader in perfect silence, and I confess that my meditations were not altogether cheerful. Here we were, a half dozen foolish boys, forty miles from our comrades, surrounded on all sides by enemies—military and non-combatant—and liable at any moment to stir up a hornet's nest. Should our leader and guide fall in a night skirmish, or by any chance become separated from us, the brightest prospect that awaited us would be to ride humbly into the nearest camp, and take our chances at being received and treated as prisoners of war.

It turned out that I was not the only one in the party whose resolution was being "sicklied o'er by the pale cast of thought." Presently Hugh Waters, who was riding by my side, leaned toward me and said, in tones of becoming seriousness:

"Johnny, I have got a presentiment. I feel that I am going to be killed to-night."

The fact is, I felt very much that way myself—and possibly I would have said it, if he had waited a little while. But he spoke first, and gave me the start on him. As much to hide my own weakness as to banter him, I answered:

"Oh, pshaw, that's all stuff. We'll be talking to pretty girls directly."

"Now Johnnie, don't laugh at me. You know I am not afraid" (I wasn't so sure of that—judging him by myself). "But I am serious; I know that I am not going to get home, and there are some things I want you to attend to for me."

Then he proceeded to make his will and appointed me his Executor. He divided out his few assets—"the spoils of many a chase"—among his relatives and friends, no doubt very judiciously. Finally he came to the mare he was riding. She was a superb animal, handsome as a picture and distinguished among the boys for her speed and endurance.

"And Bess," he continued, patting her upon the neck, "I want you to try and carry her out with you and give her to Mollie L."

This last request aroused my interest.

"To Mollie L.?" I asked; "why, what's your reason for that?"

"Well, I suppose I'll have to tell you, as it won't make much difference now." And his voice became a shade more doleful. "Well, the truth is, I am in love with her—and—she's my sweetheart!"

"The mischief you say! You are not engaged to her?"

"Yes, I am, Johnnie, old fellow. You see I had to tell you, although I promised her not to."

"By George! I am engaged to her myself!" I answered, an incipient feeling of rivalry imparting some warmth to my tones, perhaps, in spite of the solemn business we had in hand.

Just at this interesting point our conversation was interrupted by a pistol shot, and Underwood, who had paced some distance ahead of us up the hill which we were ascending, came dashing back, lying flat on his horse. As we wheeled around, our movements were expedited by some shots from a party of men who now appeared on the brow of the hill. They did not follow us very promptly, however, and after running a few hundred yards we pulled off into an old field and huddled behind a clump of bushes to await developments.

In a short while the squad of Federals, who, we supposed, were a patrol upon their rounds, passed leisurely along the road in front of us, and we picked up such scraps as these from their conversation :

" Where the devil did those fellows go ? " " They couldn't have been any of Mosby's men, away down here." " No, I guess they are a a lot of Eighth Illinois boys out on a lark." " Well, we turned the joke upon them, anyhow.''

It was no little relief to us that they took this view of the matter. Nevertheless, the questions submitted to the council of war which we held after they had gone, were still very serious ones.

It would not be very late in the next day when they would find out their mistake, and we might expect the country to be scoured by scouting parties. Especially would the situation be aggravated if we persisted in our project of raiding the house on the river. Had ordinary discretion presided at our council, doubtless we would have set out for home and safety, forthwith. But the very foolhardiness of the venture prevented any one of us from proposing a backdown, lest he be suspected of weakness—and we continued on our fatuous course.

Finally we reached the house we were seeking. Fortunately there were no dogs about the premises and we dismounted and surrounded the dwelling without being discovered. Our knocking at the front door brought a head out of an upper window, and a female voice inquired who we were and what was our business.

" If there are any officers here, they are wanted at camp immediately," Bush. replied.

" There are none here—nor soldiers either," was the answer. " But you can't come that over me, Bush. Underwood. What in the world are you doing here ? "

" Hello ! that's Nannie Bell ! What luck ! Some of us boys are here, hungry as wolves. Come down and let us in."

Sure enough, she was an old acquaintance. But as we heard her steps descending the stairs, we took the precaution to cock our revolvers—for even ladies are not always to be trusted when there may be a sweetheart lost or saved. But she was " true blue "—or gray, rather—and, with the other ladies who soon joined us, gave us such comfort as the unseasonable hour of our call enabled them to offer. But they could not console us for the officers whom we failed to catch, and we soon rode away, decidedly crestfallen.

We were now unanimously of opinion to strike for Loudoun forth-with, content if we should reach there with whole hides and our stock of adventures—still further to be added to—instead of the booty we had hoped for.

We soon reached the shelter of the Big Pine Forest; and for hours threaded its obscure and devious bridle paths in single file, turning and twisting and doubling, it seemed to me, long after all idea of dis-tance or direction had been lost.

About noon next day we came to a clearing in which stood the humble abode of one of Bush's friends. They were but poor folk, at best; and I doubt not that, what with the precarious means of tilling their sterile soil and the frequent harrassments and depreda-tions to which they were subjected, Hard Times kept up a pretty constant " knocking at their cottage door." But they gave us a hearty welcome and we had no reason to suspect that the larder was low. Often have I recalled with gratitude and something of regret the sweetly cooked and daintily served ham and eggs and richly browned corn-bread which that day greeted our keen appetites.

One of the sons of the family stood watch for us on a neighboring hill, and we ate and baited our horses and rested in peace. After the refreshment, we took up our march toward the Dranesville pike, which we approached through the woods, and very cautiously, for we were still within the Federal lines, and liable to run against a patrol or scout-ing party. Besides, we were not without hopes of picking up some unwary passenger along that highway.

We reached the pike safely, and tying our horses back in the pines a short distance, "laid for our luck" along the wayside.

One squad of cavalry did indeed pass along within ten feet of us, but their numbers secured them undisturbed right of way. A few moments after, a solitary straggler came jauntily along, sitting cross-legged on his horse and inquiring at the top of his voice, " Who will care for mother now ? "

Charley McDonough stepped out from behind a bush and informed him that, if he had no objections, we would take care of *him ;* and he might reasonably commit the old lady to a kind Providence—or words to that effect.

This matter-of-fact, not to say rude response to his sentimental in-quiry, evidently shocked his sensibilities; and before he recovered himself he had been fully introduced to our party. We found him not unworthy game. His money, jewelry, and arms were divided out among the rest of us ; while his horse was assigned to Charley and Bush, in joint ownership. Neither one of them, however, cared to have the trouble and responsibility of getting the other one's half back to Loudoun; so while the others of us kept watch, they produced the inevitable " deck " and sat down there by the road side and played out a game of " seven-up " to determine which should own the whole of the nag. Charley won, a result which some of us had reason to regret before we reached home.

By dark we had gotten well beyond the picket lines and into a section of country with which we all were more or less familiar. Here the prisoner was paroled and turned loose, and McDonough took possession of his hard earned asset. Here, too, Underwood and Trammell went off on some affair of their own, leaving the rest of us to make our way home.

We came out upon the Little River turnpike about five miles below Aldie ; and as our horses' feet struck the paved road we felt that we were indeed "almost home." But when we stopped at a house on the roadside to get a drink of water, we noticed considerable restraint, to say the least, in the manner of the good lady, who was generally rejoiced to see Mosby's Men. A few inquiries developed the fact that she mistook us

JOHN H. ALEXANDER AND HUGH T. WATERS, CO. A.
From a Photograph taken during the War.[1]

for Yankees, a large body of whom, she informed us, had gone up the road that afternoon.

This news brought a change over our spirits and put us again on the *qui vive*. The night was very dark and a high win was blowing. This made marching on a road upon which we were liable at any time to meet the enemy returning, decidedly dangerous, but we were dead homesick and determined to risk it.

Sinnott and I rode about a hundred yards in advance of Charley and Hugh with the led horse ; and in order that they might have a

---

[1] " What seems to be an exuberance of stomach in this picture is an inordinate wealth of uniform—blockade goods purchased with some of the proceeds of the Greenback Raid. You may also recognize the tobacco pouches (gifts of our sweethearts), which we usually carried slung to a buttonhole in front."—*J. H. A.*

better chance to escape in case of trouble, we carried our revolvers in our hands, ready cocked, and it was understood that we should fire incontinently into anything we met.

We had ridden in this order more than a mile, and Sinnott and myself, riding closely side by side, had descended into a little vale, where the darkness could almost be felt. Suddenly our horses stopped. Straining our looks forward, we distinguished the forms of men and horses, just in front of us. Our horses and theirs had been stopped by touching noses.

Like a flash it came to me that they might be some of our own men, scouting; and instinctively I hailed them. But Sinnott, more obedient to instructions, fired; and the response to my challenge was a groan, as the man opposite him fell to the ground. It was no time now for the amenities of war; the echo to the groan was the report of my pistol, and down went my *vis-a-vis*.

As we turned our horses, Pandemonium broke loose. The flashings of pistols threw a weird light on the scene, while the sounds of the arms and the shouts of the men and the clattering of horses' hoofs, "made night hideous." I fired back once or twice as I ran, but found that my shots only be-

SERGEANT-MAJOR GUY BROADWATER.

trayed my whereabouts, and drew the enemy's fire upon me. So I addressed all my energies to getting away from there.

When I came up to Charley he was dismounted in the road; and my horse striking Hugh's just as he was turning, laid him and his rider sprawling by the wayside. That was the last I saw of any of my companions that night. As I subsequently learned, their experiences were as follows:

McDonough had been riding the captured horse, to rest his own, and when the firing commenced he jumped down to change to his more reliable nag. Before he could mount, the enemy was upon him.

He had been outlawed by the Federal authorities for some desperate deed, and to him, capture meant certain death. But with wonderful presence of mind he lay flat in the road, with pistol cocked and hand on trigger, ready to deliver that last shot which he always reserved for his own heart as the final alternative to capture. Poor fellow! before many months the awful emergency came, and he unfalteringly fired that fatal shot.

But that night he was spared, by the narrowest shave. The Yankees rode past him—one of them whose horse stumbled over him remarking that "there was one damned rebel they had killed." At the first opportunity he rolled out of their way and hied off into the darkness.

When Waters was dismounted in my unfortunate collision with him, he, too, crept out of the road, as the Federals came charging up, and lay quietly in the fence corner until they had gone by. Then he arose and made for the Bull Run Mountains.

JOHN A. LLEWELLYN, CO. D.

Their horses followed Sinnott down the pike and found a safe harbor in some citizen's close, until they were reclaimed.

I turned off the pike, and, coming to some convenient thickets, spent the residue of the night there. With morning light I made my way back to Mosby's Confederacy.

In the course of the afternoon I cleaned up, donned my "best blockade goods" and rode over to Mollie L.'s to seek in her gracious presence refreshment from my hardships.

Imagine my surprise at finding Hugh Waters already there, ensconced in the best arm chair, playing invalid over some bruises and scratches which he had incurred in his fall of the night before. But so far from their being a source of discomfort to him, the scamp was supremely blest in the gentle ministration which they were evoking from " Our Mutual Sweetheart."

He was evidently master of the situation; and "the subsequent proceedings interested me no more."

MAP OF FAUQUIER COUNTY, VIRGINIA.

# ROSTER

OF THE

## FORTY-THIRD BATTALION VIRGINIA CAVALRY,

### ARMY OF NORTHERN VIRGINIA,

### Confederate States of America.

---

Colonel, JOHN S. MOSBY.

Lieutenant Colonel, WILLIAM H. CHAPMAN.

Major, ADOLPHUS E. RICHARDS.

Adjutant, WILLIAM H. MOSBY.

Quartermaster, J. WRIGHT JAMES.

Surgeon, DR. A. MONTEIRO.

Assistant Surgeon, DR. W. L. DUNN.

Sergeant-Major, GUY BROADWATER.

## COMPANY A.

*From Roll furnished by Lieut. Joseph H. Nelson; amended by John H. Foster.*

Captain, James Wm. Foster.
First Lieutenant, Thomas Turner (killed).
"       "    Wm. L. Hunter.
Second Lieutenant, Joseph H. Nelson.
Third Lieutenant, George H. Whitescarver (killed).
Third Lieutenant, Harry Hatcher.
First Sergeant, John W. Corbin.

Second Sergeant, W. Ben Palmer (promoted).
Third Sergeant, John E. Rowzee.
Fourth Sergeant, John Thomas.
Fifth Sergeant, Edward Rector.
First Corporal, Chas. Davis.
Second Corporal, John T. Gulick.
Third Corporal, Geo. Skinner.
Fourth Corporal, Walter Whaley.

### PRIVATES.

Adams, Thomas W.,
Alexander, David,
Alexander, John H.,
Ames, James F. ("Big Yankee," promoted, killed),
Anderson, Wm. A.,
Ayre, Geo. H.,
Bailey, John T.,
Ballard, John N.,
Barnes, John H.,
Barr, Charles N.,
Barton Benj. (killed),
Beavers, Fenton,
Berryman, Frank C.,
Betts, Edward R.,
Bishop, George,
Bonnell, Dallas,
Bowie, John W.,
Boyd, Henry C.,
Brawner, H. N.,
Brawner, Wm. A.,

Brent, James R.,
Brethod, Isaac,
Brewer, Charles W.,
Broadwater, Guy (promoted),
Broadwater, Richard F.,
Burke, Thomas T.,
Campbell, John W.,
Carlisle, D. Grafton,
Castleman, John R.,
Cocke, Wm. F.,
Cockrill, John H.,
Coiner, John E.,
Coiner, John W.,
Craig, F. T.,
Creel, Eppa H ,
Cromwell, Wm.,
Crosen, Samuel E.,
Crowley, Barney,
Cummings, James H.,
Darden, Francis M.,
Davis, John B ,

Davis, Thomas F.,
DeButts, John P.,
DeButts, Richard E.,
Donohoe, Charles,
Dowell, Peter G.,
Dulany, Daniel F. (killed),
Eliason, Thomas,
Ellis, James W.,
Elzey, Wm.,
Flannery, M. W. (killed),
Flynn, Wm. S.,
Foster, John H.,
Fox, A. G.,
Fox, C. A.,
Furr, Dallas,
Furr, Thompson,
Gaines, David,
Gessell, Adolphus,
Gibson, Howard,
Glascock, Aquilla,
Green, John W.,
Green, T. Nelson,
Gulick, George M.,
Hatcher, R. Welt,
Hawling, Charles T.,
Heflin, John W.,
Heflin, Wm. A.,
Herrington, Geo. W.,
Hibbs, Henry C.,
Hibbs, William ("Major"),
Hooe, Robert M.,
Hutchinson, Lycurgus E.,
Jackson, Edgar M.,
Knapp, Ludwell,
Lake, James Robert,
Lake, Ludwell,
Lake, Thomas W.,
Lane, Frank,
Law, David,
Lynn, John T.,
Lyons, James,
McDaniel, Mahlon T.,
McDonough, Charles,
McLane, Thomas,
Maddux, H. C. ("Cab"),
Martin, T.,
Mattocks, Robert,
Miller, Thomas F.,
Minor, Albert G.,
Moffet, Daniel J.,
Mohler, Theodore,
Moore, S. H.,
Moran, Richard,
Mosby, William H. (promoted),
Nelson, Lucian N.,
Newland, Bushrod,
Oden, Archibald,
Page, John P. (promoted),
Page, Mortimer M.,

Phillips, Wm. A.,
Pool, Joshua,
Presgraves, Richard,
Priest, John H.,
Prout, John B.,
Puryear, John W. (promoted),
Rector, Thomas B.,
Rector, Welby H. (killed),
Reed, John R.,
Richards, Dulany,
Rixey, James M.,
Robey, Francis E.,
Robinson, John D.,
Rogers, Samuel E.,
Rosson, John A.,
Rowzee, Geo. A.,
Rudd, Royal S.,
Rutter, John W.,
Shaw, Christopher C.,
Sherman, R. F.,
Silcott, Braden T.,
Simpson, Benjamin ("Tobe"),
Sinclair, James W.,
Sinclair, John,
Skeldon, Nicholas B. (Buckholtz),
Smallwood, Henry (killed),
Smallwood, John L.,
Spindle, Benjamin,
Spitzer, Charles H.,
Stone, William R.,
Strother, Francis A.,
Strother, James M.,
Summers, Geo. W.,
Symons, John W.,
Thompson, Edward,
Thompson, Wm. B.,
Trammell, Wm.,
Trammell, B. L.,
Trundle, Wm. H. (promoted, killed),
Turberville, Geo. R. L.,
Turley, Richard,
Underwood, Bushrod,
Underwood, Samuel,
Vandeventer, J. H.,
Waggaman, Samuel,
Walker, George C.,
Waller, John T. (killed),
Walls, Wm. A.,
Walston, Wm. B.,
Waters, Hugh T.,
Wilbourne, Henry A.,
Wild, John (killed),
Williams, Sewell,
Williamson, James J.,
Wilson, J. T.,
Wilson, Stephen H.,
Woolf, Francis M.,
Yellott, George.

## COMPANY B.

*Have been unable to find any roll of this Company; the names here given are with the assistance of Mr. John H. Foster.*

Captain, William R. Smith (killed).
" Adolphus E. Richards (promoted).
" Robert S. Walker.
First Lieutenant, Franklin Williams.
Second Lieutenant, Albert Wrenn.

Third Lieutenant, Robert Gray.
First Sergeant, Horace Johnson.
Second Sergeant, James W. Wrenn.
Third Sergeant, Dorsey Warfield.

### PRIVATES.

Adrian, J. M ,
Alexander, Doctor,
Alexander, John,
Alexander, Samuel,
Anderson. Ed.,
Ashby, Henry S.,
Barber, Slice,
Belvin, W. D.,
Bowen, A. J.,
Bowen, Fred F.,
Bowen, James,
Brown, L.,
Browning, Lafayette,
Browning, Thomas E.,
Buckner, Richard P.,
Chappalear, J. Pendleton (killed).
Chew, John A.,
Colston, William E. (killed),
Crawford, J. Marshall,
Crawford, Robert,
Darden, Dennis,
Downing, J. A.,
Embrey, —— (killed),
Eastham, Philip B.,
Edmonds, Clem.,
Edmonds, John C.,
Edmunds, Henry,
Farr, Resin S.,
Farr, Richard,
Ferguson, Sydnor G.,
Fitzhugh, Champ,
Fristoe, French,
Gillespie, John,
Gray, Charles Henry,
Gray, James A.,
Hammond, J. W.,
Hamner, "Captain,"
Harrover, Robert M.,
Hudgins, —— (killed),
Hurst, Edward.
Johnson, Frank ("Zoo"),

Johnson, James M.,
Kennon, "Captain" George S.,
Lambert, Charles,
Lavender, J.,
Lee, Philip,
McKay, Thomas B.,
McKim, —— (killed),
Mallory, —— (killed),
Mason, Charles (killed),
Milholland, A. V.,
Munson, John W.,
Northcraft, —— (from Balto.),
Ogg, Thomas J.,
Orrick, John C.,
Owen, Joseph W.,
Pitts, J. Emery,
Renner, J. S.,
Renner, J. W.,
Robinson, "Captain,"
Seay, Thomas R.,
Sedgwick, —— (from Norfolk)
Settle, Albert,
Shaw, Harry,
Shriver, Chas. Eltinge (killed),
Sinnott, Harry T.,
Smith, Edward (killed),
Spindle, Robert,
Spinkx, ——,
Stinson, ——,
Stratton. Dr. Ed.,
Strother, Alfred,
Sweeting, B. H. (Harry),
Triplett, Geo. W.,
Triplett, Richard,
Tyler, Charles,
Walter, Henry S.,
White, Hugh W ,
Wilson, J. D.,
Withers, Henry M.,
Withers, John.

## COMPANY C.

*Roll furnished by John S. Russell, Lieutenant commanding.*

Captain, William H. Chapman (promoted).
First Lieutenant, A. E. Richards (promoted).
Second Lieutenant, Frank Fox (killed).
Third Lieutenant, Frank W. Yager.
Lieutenant Commanding, John S. Russell.
First Sergeant, C. Bohrer (killed).
"       "    Charles Landon Hall.
Second Sergeant, Charles Whiting.

Third Sergeant, L. A. Corbin.
Fourth Sergeant, B. Grove.
"       "   W. T. Biedler.
Fifth Sergeant, C. C. Horseford.
First Corporal, Wm. Jackson.
Second Corporal, P. A. Davis.
Third Corporal, S. B. Triplett.
Fourth Corporal, A. J. Hobson.

### PRIVATES.

Adams, H. C.,
Anderson, Peyton,
Anderson, G. W.,
Angelo, Frank M.,
Atwell, Ewell B.,
Atwell, W. H.,
Ayler, F. F.,
Ayler, J. M.,
Ball, B. F.,
Balthrope, G. R.,
Bartenstein, A. R.,
Baylor, R. W.,
Bear, Charles A.,
Beckham, John G.,
Bickers, J. M.,
Biedler, A. J.,
Biedler, Charles E.,
Botts, John F.,
Bowen, C. O.,
Boxley, E. S.,
Boyd, H.,
Bramham, N.,
Brumback, E. T.,
Burnley, J. N.,
Calvert, J. C.,
Carr, Richard,
Carver, Joseph M.,
Chelf, C. F.,
Chuning, B. F.,
Chuning, W. S.,
Coiner, Cornelius J.,
Compton, J. C.,
Conrad, G. W.,
Conrad, M. O.,
Crable, M. O.,
Crigler, W. G.,
Cunningham, G.,
Davis, Frank C.,
Dearmont, Washington,
Dent, George,
Divine, William,
Douglas, L. P.,
Elzey, Robert,

Finley, George,
Fish, C. W.,
Fletcher, Benton,
Fletcher, R. V. W.,
Fletcher, W. H.,
Fleury, Wm.,
Flint, James A.,
Ford, John, Jr.,
Ford, John, Sr.,
Forrer, E. F.,
Forrer, Judah,
Garrison, W. H.,
Garth, James H.
Garth, John W.,
Gibson, John T.,
Gray, Thaddeus,
Gunnell, George W.,
Guthrie, Samuel,
Hansford, C. C.,
Harden, F. M.,
Harn, C. T.,
Harrell, J. C.,
Harrell, M. D.,
Hays, T. M.,
Hearn, John,
Heflebower, John N.,
Heflin, Robert,
Herning, C. M.,
Henry W.,
Henson, S. P.,
Hickes, S. P.,
Hipkins, Fred. S.,
Hiter, P. M.,
Hutchinson, Lewis,
Iden, Ben.,
Jackson, R. A.,
Johnson, Wm.,
Jones, C. S.,
Judd, James,
Kinsey, G. T.,
Kinsey, G. W.,
Kirby, J. R.,
Kirwin, John,

Kite, Charles,
Kite, Martin,
Laws, J. L.,
Legg, James E.,
Leonard, D. E.,
Lewis, J. B.,
Lintz, W. F.,
Lofland, G. S.,
Luckett, S. T.,
McCue, John B.,
McKim, Allan,
Macoy, B. C.,
Marcellus, J. H.,
Marshall, G. R.,
Marshall, J. R.,
Massie, G. W.,
Massie, H. I.,
Miller, J. M.,
Morecock, W. H. E.,
Nunn, John W.,
Orrick, John C.,
Overfield, Marshall,
Patteson, A. Lee,
Patteson, Wm. W.,
Pearson, Craven,
Pearson, H. C.,
Pearson, John,
Pearson, Taylor,
Pendleton, C. H.,
Perry, J. Taylor,
Phillips, John,
Printz, Isabeus,
Redwin, John,
Rice, Thomas,
Richards, A. J.,
Richards, Henry,
Richardson, J. R.,
Richardson, M. L.,
Richeson, A. J.,
Ritter, David H.,
Robertson, W. H.,

Robinson, Monroe,
Russell, John W.,
Russell, H. C.,
Sanford, E. L.,
Shacklett, Edward,
Shaw, Jackson,
Sinclair, J. M.,
Smith, J. M.,
Smith, J. P.,
Smith, R. C.,
Spencer, J. M.,
Starke, James,
Starke, J. T.,
Storke, J. E.,
Taylor, George,
Thompson, Thomas J.,
Throop, Thomas,
Trenairy, J. S.,
Triplett, B. Addison,
Triplett, L. B.,
Vest, C. B.,
Vest, Thomas,
Vorus, Jacob,
Walker, C. H.,
Walker, C. S.,
Walker, J. M.,
Ward, Jerry,
Wayman, E. F.,
Wayman, J. M.,
Welch, W. R.,
Whitescarver, B. ٭.,
Whitlow, A. J.,
Willis, A. C.,
Wilson, A. S.,
Wines, A. L.,
Wines, G. S.,
Wines, T. S.,
Woodward, W.,
Yager, Charles M.,
Yowell, James.

## COMPANY D.

*The greater part of this list was furnished by Charles H. Dear, John H. Foster, Zach. F. Jones, J. S. Mason and John A. Saunders.*

Captain, R. P. Montjoy (killed).
"      Alfred Glascock.
First Lieutenant, Charles E. Grogan.
Second Lieutenant, —— Magner.

Third Lieutenant, Wm. H. Trundle (killed).
"      "      David S. Briscoe.
(Commanding at close of War).

### PRIVATES.

Adie, Lewis (killed),
Aldridge, J. West,
Anderson, Boswell P.,
Anderson, Thomas E. (killed),
Atkins, John (killed),
Baker, T. R.,
Beal, John T.,
Beal, Joseph R ,
Best, Richard,
Binford, Ballard W.,
Binford, Wirt M. (killed),
Bispham. S. B.
Blanchard, ——,
Bolling, Bartlett,
Bolling, John,
Brander, William,
Braxton, Wm. Armstead (killed),
Bredell, Edward (killed),
Brock, George Wallen,
Brock, Harry,
Brooke, William T.,
Brown —— (of Maryland),
Bryan, Joseph,
Burk —— (killed),
Campbell, Joseph,
Carr, Upshur,
Carrington, Luther (killed),
Carter, Thomas,
Chamblin, H. Clay,
Chancellor, James M.,
Cheatwood, ——,
Chew, John A.,
Chew, Robert.
Chilton, James V ,
Christian, E. W ,
Coakley, James,
Cochran, —— (Delaware),
Copley, James,
Core, John H.,
Darneille, Philip A.,
Dear, Charles H.,
Dear, H. Clay,
Dear, J. Wm.,
Delaplane, J.,
Dorsey, Charles,
Dorsey, Harry,

Dorsey, Pugh,
Dorsey, Reuben,
Dunnington, Charles A.,
Eastham, Robert W. (" Bob Ridley "),
Flack, —— (killed),
Foy, Joseph,
Frere, George,
Gibbs, Willie A. (killed),
Gibson, Henry C.,
Gill, George Murray,
Gill. John,
Gipson, Edwin,
Goldsborough, Charles,
Gray, John,
Grayson, Robert,
Griffin, Joseph,
Harris, H. G.,
Heaton, Henry,
Heaton, Tiny,
Heiskell, J. Monroe,
Horner, Gus B.,
Hoyle, George,
Huff, Gresham,
Hunton, Ernest,
Hunton, John W.,
Jarboe, William,
Jarman, Henry,
Jarvis, B. F.,
Johnson, Edward,
Jones, Philip,
Jones, Zach. F.,
Jordan, H. C.,
Kane, James C.,
Kane, John C.,
Keith, James (killed),
Kennerley, Frank,
Keblinger, C.,
Keblinger, Wilber,
Lambert, M. W.,
Larrabee, Harrison C.,
Llewellyn, John A.,
Love, Lucian (killed),
Love, Thomas R.,
Lowndes, James,
McBlair, ——,
McCobb, —— (killed),

McIntosh, C.,
Mackall, R. M.,
Manning (" Captain "),
Mason, J. S.,
Mason, Landon R.,
Massie, J. R.,
Mercer, Corbin W.,
Millan, Joseph C.,
Miller, James N.,
Mitchell, —— ,
Moon, Jacob L.,
Moon, James M.
Moss, Thomas,
Neal, D.,
Nott, Andrew H.,
Nott, Roger,
Nottingham, John J.,
Nottingham, Tobe,
O'Brien, E. H.,
Overby, —— (killed),
Pattie, H. W.,
Randolph, John,
Ratcliffe, —— ,
Read, J. W.,
Riggs, Joshua,

Riley, P. O.,
Robertson, —— ,
Robinson, Claiborne,
Rogers, S. E.,
Saunders, John A.,
Saunders, Thomas,
Saunders, William E.,
Sealock, Thomas,
Shields, —— (killed),
Slater, Henry,
Smith, Henry,
Smith, Philip,
Sowers, Dr. J. R.,
Staton, W. W.,
Steele, Billings,
Thomas, W. P.,
Tongue, Wm.,
Vandeventer, William,
Ware, Felix H.,
Weir, W. B.,
White, John W.,
Williams, J. F.,
Wooden, Peter,
Woodhouse, W. W.
Yates, Francis Marion (killed).

---

## COMPANY E.

*Copy of original Muster Roll furnished by Lieutenant W. Ben Palmer.*

Muster Roll of Captain Samuel F. Chapman, Company E, of the 43d Battalion Virginia Cavalry, Army of the Confederate States of America, Lieutenant Colonel John S. Mosby, from the 28th day of July, 1864, when last mustered, to the 31st day of August, 1864.

Captain, Samuel F. Chapman.
First Lieutenant, Fountain Beattie.
Second Lieutenant, W. Ben Palmer.
Third Lieutenant, William Martin (killed).
"            "        Channing M. Smith.
First Sergeant, Boyd M. Smith.
Second Sergeant, T. Benton Shipley.

Third Sergeant, Edgar Davis (killed).
Fourth Sergeant, Thomas Booker.
First Corporal, George L. Revercomb.
Second Corporal, Wm. Davis.
Third Corporal, Henry R. Moore.
Fourth Corporal, Daniel N. Mason.

### PRIVATES.

Armstrong, S. R.,
Ashby, John,
Ball, A. P.,
Bayne, Richard B.,
Bell, J. W.,
Bolling, Samuel,
Bolling, W. A.,
Brown, L. B.,
Brown, R.,

Burgess, Moses,
Burke, John C.,
Butler, J. F.,
Butler, O. L.,
Carey, Alex.,
Carpenter, T. A.,
Coleman, C.,
Colvin, J. B.,
Coons, F. A.,

Coons, J. W.,
Copenhaver, G. W.,
Cox, J. E.,
Davis, Americus,
Davis, L. Morgan,
Dennis, C. H.,
Dennis, W. F.,
Detherage, R.,
Dickson, John T.,
Downing, W. H.,
Edwards, Wm. H.,
Faulkner, J. F.,
Faulkner, W. W.,
Flinn, J. N.,
Flinn, R. R.,
Flippo, A. C.,
Floweree, S. C.,
Flynn, Wm.,
Flynn, J. F.,
Foreman, P. G.,
Forrest, J. J.,
Gentry, I. A.,
Gibson, S.,
Greg, H. W.,
Hall, S.,
Hazlett, M.,
Heflin, H. W.,
Howison, Lee,
Inloes, A.,
Jarman, Robert,
Jones, F. J.,
Kirkpatrick, E.,
Latham, Thomas R.,
Lawrence, J. M.,
Lyttleton, J.,
McCourt, C. A.,
McIntosh, J. P.,
McLane, T.,
Maclay, Thomas,
Majors, J. B.,
Majors, L. C.,
Mason, D. N.,
Metcalfe, S. G.,
Miller, T. A.,
Milton, J.,

Monroe, S. L.,
Myers, J. J.,
Nalls, Benoni F.,
Nalls, E.,
Nalls, J. P.,
Newcomb, O. S.,
O'Bannon, G. M.,
Pendleton, C. H.,
Picket, George K.,
Picket, James E.,
Poston, H. A.,
Ramey, J. M.,
Ramey, L. W.,
Randolph, Norman V.,
Reardon, Louis,
Reardon, P. J.,
Reavercomb, P. N.,
Redd, P. D.,
Robinson, D. F.,
Robinson, W. H.,
Robson, O.,
Rutter, H.,
Seaton, J. J.,
Shackleford, Durand,
Shackleford, Elzey D.,
Sheafer, George,
Sheppard, J. W.
Simpson, J.,
Slater, George M.,
Smith, J. B.,
Smith, R. T.,
Stanley, Howard,
Sutton, Wm.,
Terry, R. Stockton,
Utz, John C.,
Vaughn, F. D.,
Walker, J.,
Walker, J. P.,
Walker, L. F.,
Watkins, J. R.,
Weaver, James W.,
Welch, Wm.,
Wood, H. K.,
Woodward, L. E.

## COMPANY F.

*Muster Roll Company F, 43d Battalion Virginia Cavalry, C. S. A., or Mosby's Battalion, 1864-65. Furnished by Capt. Walter E. Frankland.*

Captain, Walter E. Frankland.
First Lieutenant, Walter Bowie (killed).
Second Lieutenant, James F. Ames (killed).
Third Lieutenant, J. Frank Turner.
First Sergeant, H. M. McIlhany.
Second Sergeant, Robert B. Parrott.
Third Sergeant, Thomas A. Russell.

Fourth Sergeant, John J. Williams.
Fifth Sergeant, James P. Triplett.
First Corporal, Charles W. Harris.
Second Corporal, James E. Haney.
Third Corporal, Benj. R. Cowherd.
Fourth Corporal, John L. Schackleford.

PRIVATES.

Alexander, B. R.,
Austin, George B.,
Baggasby, J.,
Bankhead, Charles L.,
Barker, John E.,
Barker, L. A.,
Bayne, John C.,
Bayne, Washington,
Broadus, Wm. S.,
Brooks, Charles,
Brown, Joseph D.,
Brown, Thomas R.,
Burgess, Alex.,
Burke, Arthur,
Burton, H.,
Cahill, John J.,
Carter, Isaiah,
Chandler, Henry H.,
Chase, Irvin K.,
Clarke, John J.,
Cockrell, Wm.,
Conner, F. M.,
Coode, Demetrius,
Cooksey, Morgan,
Corder, Butler,
Crawford, George Wm.,
Crow, T. W.,
Crook, Robert N.,
Crum, C. A.,
Crutchfield, Edgar M.,
Culbreth, John,
Daniel, Peter M.,
Danne, Charles,
Davis, Alexander,
Dawson, Reuben,
Deems, ——,
Dunnaway, Roger W.,
Dunton, King Agrippa,
Eastham, Bird,
Eubank, Frederick D.,
Flynn, Robert N.,
Franklin, Benjamin,
Gaskins, Hezekiah,

Gayle, J. P.,
Gayle, Mordecai J.,
Gayle, Thomas B.,
Goddin, I. H.,
Gooch, James J.,
Goodall, Abner,
Gooding, Lewis E.,
Gore, Jesse P.,
Gresham, James R.,
Griffith, John B.,
Hill, Francis L.,
Hockman, Noah,
Hopkins, H. H.,
Howard, Reuben F.,
Hunton, Isaiah,
Imboden, Jacob,
Jennings, Matthew,
Johnson, C. W.,
Jones, A. H.,
Jones, Montgomery A.,
Kelley, John C.,
Keyseear, Hugh P.,
Kite, James P.,
Kite, Thomas O.,
Knott, Richard,
Lacy, M. P.,
Landrum, Willis J.,
Leach, Thornton V.,
Leavell, Edmund G.,
Lee, Clifton,
Limbrick, J. W.,
Lowe, Daniel W.,
Lucas, Fielding,
McKenney, John,
Manley, Wm. L.,
Melton, J. M.,
Meredith, S. E.,
Miller, Oscar D.,
Myers, Eleamander,
Norris, Williamson,
Parr, Thomas,
Payne, John R.,
Peebles, James A.,

Porter, John J.,
Powell, H. F.,
Powell, Rupert R.,
Priest, George H.,
Prince, John W.,
Pritchard, John T.,
Reeves, David,
Reiley, Thomas H.,
Ricketts, John E.,
Ridgeley, T. R.,
Rollins, Sanders B.,
Rosan, ——,
Royston, John W.,
Scott, Robert,
Scurry, Matthew V.,
Silman, James A.,
Silman, John A.,
Sinclair, John C.,

Smith, Edward T.,
Smoot, J. G.,
Sours, W. S,
Spottswood, F.,
Strother, James W.,
Swan, Baynard,
Taylor, William,
Thomas, Daniel L.,
Thompson, Alfred,
Towles, E. M.,
Travis, Alonzo,
Viers, Charles O.,
Walker, Chas. P.,
Wayman, N. B.,
Weems, G. W.,
Wheatley, John W.,
Winzelle, A. F.,
Yerby, Wm. M.

## COMPANY G.

*Names chiefly furnished by John H. Foster, H. G. Harris and Lieutenant John N. Murphy.*

Captain, Thomas W. T. Richards.
First Lieutenant, John N. Murphy.

Second Lieutenant, W. Garland Smith.
Third Lieutenant, John W. Puryear.

PRIVATES.

Anderson, Wm. C.,
Armstrong, J. A.,
Bainbridge, A. R.,
Barr, H.,
Bayne, H. T.,
Bencke, John H.,
Birney, ——,
Bradshaw, ——,
Brown, F. S.,
Burgess, M. M.,
Caldwell, C. E.,
Carr, Lawrence,
Carroll, ——,
Claggett, Johnson,
Clark, Joseph B.,
Claybrook, F. W.,
Cloyd, ——,
Crabbe, George,
Crews, ——,
Cross, Charles,
Cummings, G. W.,
Dealman, ——,
Dickell, C.,
Dishman, S.,

Dorrity, J. W.,
Follin, Ira,
Garnett, ——,
Golding, T. R.,
Golding, W.,
Grey, Alfred,
Griffin, G. C.,
Hackley, George,
Hardwick, G. B
Hogg, ——,
Hopkins, J. E.,
Horner, R. C ,
Hornes, Thomas,
Houdershell, Rufus A.,
Hughes, -——,
Hume (Lieut.),
Huntt, Lewis,
Huntt, G. W.,
Hutchinson, J. R.,
Jackson, W. E.,
Jett, Lucius Leland,
Jett, William,
Johnson, James,
Kennedy, Thomas,

Kennedy, W. H.,
Kephart, J. R.,
Kerrick, John R.,
King, Thomas,
Legg, James L.,
McDonald, James,
Marchant, John A.,
Marmaduke, M. W.
Menefee, H. S.,
Mitchell, ——,
Moyo, Wm.,
Murphy, R. W.,
Muse, John,
Musser, Wm. H.,
Newbil, ——,
Newell, ——,
Norfolk, George,
O'Brien, John,
O'Neil, John,
Orrison, Robert,
Parker, J. H.,
Parrow, ——,
Perron, ——, Lieut.,

Perron, S.,
Price, C. D.,
Prosser, R. Hylton,
Reamy, Ashton,
Reamy, Robert,
Renwick, J.,
Riddick, C.,
Ridgeway, ——,
Rixey, R.,
Shumate, B. J.,
Sidnor, G.,
Skillman, ——,
Smoot, W. F.,
Talliaferro, L.,
Thomas, Robert,
Thompson, Gilbert,
Turner, John W.,
Washington, G.,
Wheelwright, ——,
White, John W.,
Wiltshire, Charles,
Winder, ——,
Yerby, Albert.

## COMPANY H.

*This list is very imperfect, as the Company was organized but a few days before the surren-*
*der. Many of the names are no doubt included in the rolls of the other companies. Most*
*of Capt. J. C. Kincheloe's men (Capt. Brawner's old company) were transferred to*
*Company H, and Mr. W. S. Kincheloe furnished a list of these.*

Captain, George Baylor.  
First Lieutenant, Edward F. Thomson.  
Second Lieutenant, James G. Wiltshire.

Third Lieutenant, B. Frank Carter.  
First Sergeant, David G. Mohler.

### PRIVATES.

Bell, ——,  
Brawner, Richard,  
Butler, Charles,  
Butler, W. B.,  
Cole, E. D.,  
Cornwell, George,  
Cornwell, J. L.,  
Cornwell, R. H.,  
Davis, George,  
Davis, H. E.,  
Davis, J. P.,  
Davis, W. D.,  
Dowell, Thaddeus,  
Fairfax, Thomas,  
Fairfax, Wellington,  
Gosden, Walter W.,  
Helm, Frank,  
Hipkins, John,  
Jones, H. C.,  
Kerfoot, Howard,

Kincheloe, J. C.,  
Kincheloe, Redmond,  
Kincheloe, W. S.,  
Kincheloe, W. W.,  
Lynn, Albert,  
Lynn, Benjamin,  
Lynn, Shirley,  
Maddox, L.,  
Owen, M. B.,  
Raney, Wm.,  
Richardson, G. H.,  
Stone, J. E.,  
Spittle, Lewis,  
Spittle, W. Randolph,  
Tansill, W. W.,  
Tillett, John R.,  
Utterback, B. D.,  
Vandevender, ——,  
Young, Lewis.

## ARTILLERY COMPANY.

Captain, Peter A. Franklin.  
First Lieutenant, John J. Fray.  
Second Lieutenant, John P. Page.  
Third Lieutenant, Frank H. Rahm.  
First Sergeant, A. G. Babcock.

### PRIVATES.

Aylor, John L.,  
Hitt, E. W.,  
Jones, E. M.,  
Pontier, Nathaniel,

Smith, D. L.,  
Snead, Edwin,  
Wharton, A. G.

*Present Whereabouts and Occupation of Surviving Members of Forty-third Battalion Virginia Cavalry (Mosby's Rangers), Army of Northern Virginia, Confederate States of America.*

Colonel John S. Mosby, lawyer, San Francisco, Cal. Was U. S. Consul at Hong Kong, China, during the terms of President U. S. Grant.

Lieutenant-Colonel William H. Chapman, U. S. Revenue Service, St. Louis, Mo.

Major Adolphus E. Richards, lawyer, (Richards, Weissinger & Baskin), Louisville, Ky.

Adjutant William H. Mosby, postmaster at Bedford City, Va.

Surgeon A. Monteiro, physician and surgeon, Richmond, Va.

Assistant Surgeon William L. Dunn, physician and surgeon, Glade Spring, Va.

Adrian, J. M., Brick Haven, Va,

Aldridge, J. West, Waterford, Va.

Alexander, J. (Co. B), Warren, Albemarle Co., Va.

Alexander, John H. (Co. A), lawyer (Alexander & Hughes), San Diego, Cal.

Anderson, Boswell P., resident physician, Colorado Springs, Col.

Anderson, W. A., Alexandria, Va.

Anderson, W. C., Markham, Va.

Angelo, Frank M., Alexandria, Va.

Armstrong, S. R., Woodville, Va.

Ashby, Henry S., Delaplane, Va.

Atwell, Ewell B., Leesburg, Va.

Aylor, John L., Marshall, Va.

Ayre, George H., Upperville, Va.

Baker, T. R., Washington, D. C.

Ball, A. P., The Plains, Va.

Ballard, John N., Commissioner of Revenue, Pender P. O., Fairfax Co., Va.

Barnes, John H., U. S. Revenue Service, Fairfax C. H., Va.

Bartenstein, A. R., Warrenton, Va.

Baylor, Capt. George, lawyer, Charlestown, West Va. Counsel Baltimore & Ohio R. R. Co.

Beal, J. R., general store, Roanoke, Va.

Beattie, Lieut. Fountain, Alexandria, Va.

Beckham, John G., general commission merchant, Alexandria, Va. Was mayor of the city of Alexandria.

Bell, J. W., Gainesville, Va,

Belvin, W. D., Theological Seminary, Va.

Berryman, Frank C,, Alexandria, Va.

Biedler, Charles E. (Biedler Bros.), wholesale boots and shoes, Baltimore, Md.

Biedler, William T. (Wm. T. Biedler & Co.), importers and jobbers dry goods and notions, Baltimore, Md.

Binford, B. W., Verdon, Va.

Bispham, Stacy B. (Russell & Erwin Mfg. Co.), New York City.

Bolling, Bartlett, Keswick, Va.

Bolling, Samuel, Bedford City, Va.

Booker, Sergt. Thomas, Richmond, Va.

Bowen, A. J., Success, Warren Co., Va.

Bowen, Fred F., lawyer, Danville, Va.

Bowen, James, Remington, Va.

Brawner, H. N., Broad Run, Va.

Brent, James R., Silver City, New Mexico.

Briscoe, Lieut. David S., attorney-at-law, Baltimore, Md.

Broadwater, Richard F., Fairfax Court House, Va.

Brock, Harry, commercial agency, New York City.

Brooke, Wm. T., Norfolk, Va.

Brown, L., Alexandria, Va.

Browning, Lafayette, Amissville, Va.

Brumback, E. T., Luray, Va.

Bryan, Joseph, president (Richmond *Times*), Richmond, Va.

Buckner, R. P., Falls Church, Va.

Burke, John C., Alexandria, Va.

Burke, Thomas T., Washington, D. C.

Carlisle, D. Grafton, Baltimore, Md.

Carter, Lieut. B. Frank, Middleburg, Va.

Cary, Alexander, Flint Hill, Va.

Castleman, John R., Gaylord, Va.

Chamblin, H. Clay, Richmond, Va.

Chancellor, James M., Roanoke, Va.

Chapman, Capt. Samuel F., Baptist minister, Covington, Va.

Chew, John A., Charlestown, West Va.

Chew, Robert, Charlestown, West Va.

Chilton, James V., stationery, Warrenton, Va.

Christian, E. W., Mobile, Ala.

Claybrook, Rev. F. W., Baptist minister, Northern Neck, Va.

Coiner, Cornelius J., Swope, Va.

Coons, G. W., Culpeper, Va.

Corbin, Sergt. John W. (Co. A.), Harborton, Va.

Corbin, Sergt. L. A. (Co. C.), Ryland, Va.

Core, John H. (John H. Core & Co., importers', manufacturers' and packers' agents), Norfolk, Va.

Cowherd, B. R., Columbia, Va.

Craig, F. T., Landmark, Va.

Crook, Robert N., Alexandria, Va.

Crosen, Samuel E., Hillsborough, Va.

Danne, C., Trevillian, Va.

Darden, Frank M., Washington, D. C.

Darnielle, Philip A., Washington, D. C.

Davis, Americus, Washington, D. C.

Davis, Corpl. Charles, Middleburg, Va.

Davis, J. Peter, Farr, Va.

Davis, L. Morgan, Alexandria, Va.

Dear, Charles H., Internal Revenue Service, Washington, Rappahannock Co., Va.

Dear, H. Clay, West Superior, Wis.

DeButts, John P., Welbourne, Loudoun Co., Va.

Dickson, John T., New York City.

Dowell, Peter G., The Plains, Va.

Dowell, Thaddeus, Lynchburg, Va.

Downing, J. A., Hitch P. O., Va.

Eastham, Phil. B., Flint Hill, Va.

Eastham, Robert W. (" Bob Ridley"), Davis, West Virginia.

Edmonds, John C., Sherman, Texas.

Faulkner, J. F., Winchester, Va.

Faulkner, W. W., Newport News, Va.

Ferguson, Rev. Sydnor G., minister, Fredericksburg, Va.

Fletcher, Benton, Warrenton, Va.

Floweree, S. C., Marshall, Va.

Flynn, Robert N., Middleburg, Va.

Flynn, William (Co. E.), Swamp, Fauquier Co., Va.

Flynn, William S. (Co. A.), Washington, D. C.

Foster, Capt. James William, Schuyler, Va.

Foster, John H., merchant, Marshall, Va.

Fox, Dr. C. A. (surgeon Balto. and Ohio R.R. Co.), Beltsville, Md.

Frankland, Capt. Walter E., postmaster, Stephens City, Va.

Franklin, Captain Peter A. (with H. B. Claflin Co.), New York City.

Furr, Dallas, Aldie, Va.

Furr, Thompson, Bloomfield, Va.

Garrison, W. H., Marshall, Va.

Gibson, Henry C., Waterford, Va.

Gill, John (Gill & Fisher, grain shippers), Baltimore, Md.

Goldsborough, Charles (The Uhlman-Goldsborough Co.), Baltimore, Md.

Gosden, Walter W. (Planters' National Bank), Richmond, Va.

Green, John W., Delaplane, Va.

Gresham, James R., Lancaster Co., Va.

Griffin, Joseph, Charlottesville, Va.

Gunnell, George W., Vienna, Va.

Hammond, J. W. (J. W. Hammond & Sons, ice dealers), Alexandria, Va.

Harris, H. G., Bluefield, West Va.

Harrover, Robert M., ranges, stoves and kitchen requisites, Washington, D. C.

Hawling, C. T., Oatland, Va.

Heiskell, J. Monroe, U. S. Revenue Service.

Hipkins, Rev. Fred. S., Episcopal minister.

Hitt, E. W., Norman, Culpeper Co., Va.

Hobson, Corpl. Andrew J., Berryville, Va.

Hunter, Lieut. Wm L., Independence, Inyo Co., Cal.

Hutchinson, Lycurgus E., Herndon, Va.

Jarvis, B. F., Scottsville, Va.

Johnson, Frank ("Zoo"), Gainesville, Va.

Johnson, James M., New Baltimore, Va.

Jones, H. C., Dutch Mills, Arkansas.

Jones, Zach. F., traveling salesman, Scottsville, Va.

Jordan, H. C., Richmond, Va.

Kane, James C. (Pacific Gas Improvement Co.), San Francisco, Cal.

Kane, John C., vice-president Silverton Deep Mining and Tunnel Co., Silverton, Colorado.

Keblinger, Wilber, Charlottesville. Va.

Kennon, Capt. George S., Loudoun Co., Va.

Kerfoot, Howard, professor Southern Baptist Theological Seminary, Louisville, Ky.

Kerrick, John R., Slate Mills, Va.

Kincheloe, W. S., Clifton Station, Va.

Kirkpatrick, W. Smith, Warrenton, Va.

Lake, Ludwell, Homeland, Culpeper Co., Va.

Lake, Thomas W., Philomont, Va.

Lane, Frank, Weihle, Fairfax Co., Va.

Larrabee, Harrison C., Baltimore, Md.

Leach, Thornton V., agricultural implements, etc., Fort Royal, Va.

Lee, Philip, Centerville, Fairfax Co., Va.

Lintz, William F. (W. F. Lintz & Co., watchmakers and jewelers), Norfolk, Va.

Lofland, George S., Earleysville, Va.

McCourt, C. A., Norfolk, Va.

McCue, John B., Norwood, Va.

McIlhany, Hugh M. (McIlhany & Hilleary), real estate and insurance, Staunton, Va.

McIntosh, Charles, Warrenton, Va.

McKim, Allan, Luray, Va.

Mackall, Robert M., Olney, Montgomery Co., Md.

Macoy, B. C., Culpeper, Va.

Maddux, H. Cabell, Marshall, Va.

Marmaduke, M. W., Washington, D. C.

Mason, J. S., Marshall, Va.

Mason, Rev. Landon R., minister, Richmond, Va.

Massie, George W., Louisa Court House, Va.

Mercer, Corbin W., Richmond, Va.

Miller, James N., Slate Mills, Va.

Miller, Oscar Decatur, Slate Mills, Va.

Mohler, Sergt. David G. (Lyell & Mohler), The Capital Mill and Elevator, flour and feed, Washington, D. C.

Moon, Jacob L., Scottsville, Va.

Moon, James M., Scottsville, Va.

Moon, John B., Scottsville, Va.

Moore, Corpl. Henry R. (Co. E.), Hillsborough, Va.

Moss, Thomas (Southern Railway Co.), Alexandria, Va.

Munson, John W. (Munson Stencil Machine Co.), St. Louis, Mo.

Murphy, Lieut. John N., attorney-at-law, Machodoc, Va.

Nalls, Benoni F., Culpeper, Va.

Nelson, Lieut. Joseph H., Washington, D. C.

Nunn, John W., Louisa Court House, Va.

O'Brien, E. H., Alexandria, Va.

Ogg, Thomas J., Catletts, Va.

Orrison, Robert, Herndon, Va.

Owen, Joseph W., Bristol, Va.

Owen, M. B., Soldiers' Home, Richmond, Va.

Palmer, Lieut. W. Ben (W. B. Palmer & Co., commission merchants), Richmond, Va.

Parrot, Sergt. Robert B., manager Texas, Arkansas and Pacific Slope Provident Savings Life Assurance Society, Waco, Texas.

Patteson, Dr. A. Lee, physician, Pond Gap, Va.

Patteson, Wm. W., Staunton, Va.

Pearson, H. C., Delaplane, Va.

Perry, J. Taylor, Culpeper, Va.

Pickett, Geo. K., Fairfax Co., Va.

Pickett, James E., Haymarket, Va.

Pitts, J. Emory, Philadelphia, Pa.

Powell, Rupert R., Belmont, Spottsylvania Co., Va.

Priest, John H., Middleburg, Va.

Pritchard, J. T., Staunton, Va.

Prout, John B., staple and fancy grocer, Washington, D. C.

Rahm, Lieut. Frank H., traveling salesman, Richmond, Va.

Ramey, J. M., Marshall, Va.

Randolph, Norman V., president Randolph Paper Box Co., Richmond, Va.

Reardon, Louis, Baltimore, Md.

Rector, Thomas B., Landmark, Va.
Renner, J. N., Wheatland, West Va.
Renner, J. S., Alexandria, Va.
Ricketts, John E., Flint Hill, Va.
Richards, Capt. T. W. T., real estate and broker, Los Angeles, Cal.
Riggs, Joshua, Baltimore, Md.
Rixey, J. M., Alexandria, Va.
Robey, Francis E., Philomont, Va.
Rogers, Samuel E., Hamilton, Va.
Rowzee, G. A., general store, Dranesville, Va.
Russell, Lieut. John S., Berryville, Va.
Russell, Sergt. Thomas A., Orlean, Va.
Saunders, William E., Bryan, Texas.
Scott, Robert, Vernon Mills, Va.
Sealock, Thomas ("Roderick Dhu"), Linden, Va.
Shackleford, Durand, president U. S. Bureau of Correspondence and
    Advertising Agency, Washington, D. C.
Shackleford, Elzey D., Broad Run, Va.
Simpson, Benjamin, Fairfax Court House, Va.
Sinclair, James W., Pleasant Valley, Va.
Sinnott, Harry T., contracting agent and bridge engineer, Youngs-
    town Bridge Co., Nashville, Tenn.
Skinner, George (G. Skinner & Co., wholesale liquors), Baltimore, Md.
Slater, George M., Paris, Va.
Smith, Boyd, mining engineer, Washington, D. C.
Smith, Lieut. Channing M., clerk Marshall School Board, Dela-
    plane, Va.
Smith, David L., Soldiers' Home, Richmond, Va.
Smith, G. W., Lynchburg, Va.
Smith, J. P., Waterford, Va.
Smith, Lieut. W. Garland, physician, Saluda, Va.
Sowers, Dr. J. R., physician, Warrenton, Va.
Spindle, Robert, Centreville, Va.
Spittle, Wm. R., Alexandria, Va.
Staton, W. W., Pocahontas, Va,
Steele, Billings, Annapolis, Md.
Stone, Wm. R., druggist, Washington, D. C.
Strother, Alfred M., Paris, Va.
Strother, Francis A., Stephens City, Va.
Terry, R. Stockton (Dingee, Weinman & Co., barytes), Lynchburg, Va.
Thomas, Daniel L. (Robert Poole & Son Co.), Baltimore, Md.
Thomas W. P., Aldie, Va.
Thompson, Thomas J., Washington, D. C.
Thomson, Lieut. Ed. F., Washington, D. C.
Tillett, John R., Manassas, Va.

Tongue, William, Baltimore, Md.

Triplett, B. Addison, Rectortown, Va.

Triplett, George W., Franconia, Va.

Triplett, Richard, Franconia, Va.

Turberville, George R. L., Government Printing Office, Washington, D. C.

Turner, John W., Alexandria, Va.

Underwood, Bushrod, Washington, D. C.

Underwood, Samuel, Sterling, Va.

Utterback, B. D., Centreville, Va.

Utz, John C., Madison Court House, Va., member State Legislature.

Vandeventer, T. H., Waterford, Va.

Vest, C. B , Green Spring, Va.

Waggaman, Dr. Samuel, physician, Washington, D. C.

Walker, Charles H., general store, Rectortown, Va.

Walker, Lewis F., Marshall, Va.

Walker, Capt. Robert S., principal Woodberry Forest High School, Orange, Va.

Ware, Felix H., Huntington, West Va.

Waters, Hugh T., Washington, D. C.

Watkins, J. R., Baltimore, Md.

Wayman, E. F., Staunton, Va.

Wayman, N. B., Waterloo, Va.

White, Hugh W., Broad Run, Va.

White, John M. (Judge of Albemarle Co.), Charlottesville, Va.

White, John W., Chicago, Ills.

Wilbourne, Henry A., Farmville, Va.

Williams, Lieut. Franklin, hotel, Vienna, Va.

Williams, Rev. J. F., minister, Falls Church, Va.

Williams, Dr. J. J., physician, Baltimore, Md.

Williamson, J. J., Tribune Building, New York City.

Wilson, S. H., Washington, D. C.

Wiltshire, Lieut. James G., physician, Baltimore, Md.

Withers, Henry, Galveston, Texas.

Woodhouse, W. W., Norfolk, Va.

Woolf, Frank M., Rectortown, Va.

Wrenn, Lieut. Albert (Great Atlantic and Pacific Tea Co.), Washington, D. C.

Wrenn, Sergt. James W., Washington, D. C.

Young, Lewis, Alexandria, Va.

---

NOTE.—John H. Foster, Charles H. Dear and Zach. F. Jones have rendered valuable assistance in making up this list.

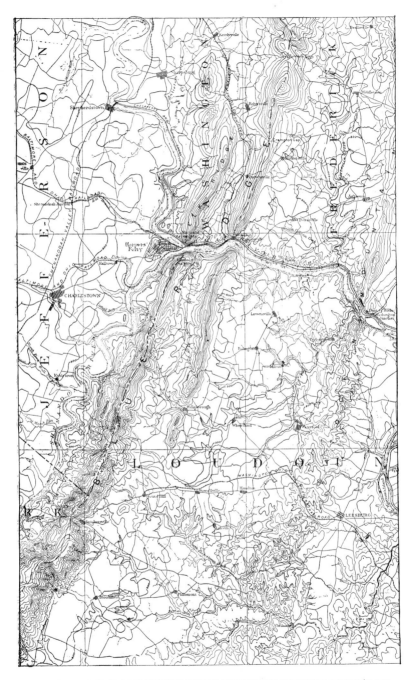

MAP OF VICINITY OF HARPER'S FERRY, INCLUDING GREATER PORTION OF
LOUDOUN COUNTY.

## REUNIONS

*Of the Forty-third Battalion Virginia Cavalry.*

Nearly thirty years after the disbanding of the Forty-third Bat-talion Virginia Cavalry at Old Salem, the happy thought occurred to a few of the old members to have a reunion of the surviving remnant of the old command. After arranging some of the preliminaries the following circular was sent out:

*Leesburg, Va., Dec.* 22, 1894.

DEAR SIR: There will be a Reunion of "MOSBY'S COMMAND" at Alexandria, Va., on Wednesday, January 16th, 1895. COLONEL MOSBY and other officers will be present, and we have assurances of a large attendance of our old companions in arms. I ask that you will indicate to me promptly your determination to attend.

It is proposed to celebrate the occasion with a *Banquet* at 6 p. m., and exercises that shall make it thoroughly enjoyable. The expense of this is estimated to be about $3.00 per capita; but as it is probable that some will wish to be present who will not be able to contribute to the expenses, you are at liberty to increase your contribution as you see proper. We insist, however, that you will not let your inability to contribute at all, deprive us of the pleasure of your presence there.

Remittances may be sent to me or to Mr. John G. Beckham, Alexandria, Va.

Yours truly,

JNO. H. ALEXANDER.

In response to this call there was a gathering of the old veterans at Odd Fellows Hall, Columbus street, Alexandria, Va., on the 16th of January, 1895. Despite the inclement weather, there were present about 150 old comrades, among them many of the former officers of the Battalion.

At a meeting held in the afternoon it was decided to form a permanent organization to be known as the "John S. Mosby Camp, Confederate Veterans," and the following officers were selected:

Commander, JOHN S. MOSBY.

First Lieutenant-Commander, JOHN H. ALEXANDER.

Second Lieutenant-Commander. JAMES WM. FOSTER.

Third Lieutenant-Commander. FOUNTAIN BEATTIE.

Adjutant, WILLIAM H. MOSBY.

Sergeant-Major and Treasurer, JOHN G. BECKHAM.

Chaplain, SAMUEL F. CHAPMAN.

Surgeon, Dr. W. L. DUNN.

Quartermaster, GEO. R. L. TURBERVILLE.

Executive Committee: J. W. HAMMOND, B. FRANK CARTER, JR., J. F. FAULKNER and GEO. D. HUNT.

The first regular meeting was arranged to be held on the second

Wednesday in August, 1895, at Marshall, Fauquier Co., Va. (Old Salem), the place where Mosby disbanded his command after the surrender of General Lee.

The time up to the hour set for the banquet was spent in friendly greetings. Old songs were sung and little groups of attentive listeners were entertained with recitals of stories of the old war times, which drew forth rounds of applause or provoked loud bursts of laughter.

At the banquet in the evening Major A. E. Richards acted as toastmaster and introduced the speakers. To the first toast, "The Forty-third Battalion Virginia Cavalry," Colonel Mosby responded as follows:

COMRADES: When, on April 21, 1865, I told you that I was no longer your commander, and bade you what we then considered a long and and perhaps an eternal farewell, the most hopeful among us could not reasonably have expected ever to witness a scene like this. Nearly thirty years have passed away, and we meet once more on the banks of the Potomac and in sight of the Capitol, not in hostile array, but as citizens of a great and united country. Gun-boats no longer patrol the river—there are no picket guards on its banks to challenge our crossing. Your presence here this evening recalls our last parting. I see the line drawn up to hear read the last order I ever gave you. I see the moistened eyes and quivering lips. I hear the command to break ranks. I feel the grasp of the hand and see the tears on the cheeks of men who had dared death so long that it had lost its terror. And I know now, as I knew then, that each heart suffered with mine the agony of the Titan in his resignation to fate:

"The rock, the vulture and the chain—
All that the proud can feel of pain."

I miss among you the faces of some who were present that day, but have since passed over the great river, and memory brings back the image of many of that glorious band who then slept in the red burial of war.

Modern skepticism has destroyed one of the most beautiful creations of the Epic ages—the belief that the spirits of dead warriors meet daily in the halls of Valhalla, and there around the festive board recount the deeds they did in the other world. For this evening, at least, let us adopt the ancient superstition, if superstition it be. It may seem presumption in me, but a man who belonged to my command may be forgiven for thinking that in that assembly of heroes—when the feast of the wild boar is spread—Smith and Turner, Montjoy and Glascock, Fox and Whitescarver and their companions will not be unnoted in the mighty throng. I shall make no particular allusion to the part you played in the great tragedy of war. Our personal associations were so intimate, it would not become me to do so. But, standing here as I do amid the wreck of perished hopes, this much at least I can say, that in all the vicissitudes of fortune and in all the trials of life I have never ceased to feel, as I told you when parting, a just pride in the fame of your achievements and grateful recollections of your generous kindness to myself.

I remember—and may my right arm wither if I ever forget—how, when the mournful tidings came from Appomattox that " Young

Harry Percy's spur is cold," you stood with unshaken fidelity to the last, and never quit my side until I told you to go.

A great poet of antiquity said, as descriptive of the Romans, that they changed their sky but not their hearts when they crossed over the sea. As long as I lived in far Cathay my heart, untraveled, dwelt among the people in whose defense I had shed my blood and given the best years of my life. In the solitude of exile it was a solace to hear that my name was sometimes mentioned by them with expressions of good will. Nothing that concerns the honor and welfare of Virginia can ever be indifferent to me. I wish that life's descending shadows had fallen upon me in the midst of the friends and the scenes I love best. But destiny—not my will—compels me to abide far away on the shore of that sea, where

" The god of gladness sheds his parting smile."

I must soon say to you again *farewell*, a word that must be and hath been. I shall carry back to my home by the Golden Gate proud recollections of this evening. And I shall still feel, as I have always felt, that life cannot offer a more bitter cup than the one I drained when we parted at Salem, nor any higher reward to ambition than that I received as commander of the Forty-third Virginia Battalion of Cavalry.

Gen. John B. Gordon answered to " The Army of Northern Virginia."

Senator John W. Daniel to " Gen. Robert E. Lee."

Major R. W. Hunter, " The Ladies of the South, who cheered us in our victories, and wept with us in our defeat."

Mr. Joseph Bryan, "The last days of the Confederacy."

Gen. Marcus J. Wright delivered an address on the history of Mosby and his Men.

Speeches were also made by Senator Eppa Hunton, Lieut.-Colonel Wm. H. Chapman, Gen. W. H. Payne, of the famous Black Horse Cavalry and Dr. A. Monteiro.

The happy strains of "Dixie," " Hail Columbia," and other airs enlivened the company, and when the soul-stirring music of the "Star Spangled Banner" fell upon their ears, there was present Billings Steele (a grandson of Francis S. Key, the author of that immortal ode), who had followed the banner of the Confederacy and Mosby through his eventful career.

Toastmaster Major Richards announced the close of the entertainment in a brief but eloquent address, and Mosby's Men dispersed, carrying with them an addition to their store of pleasant reminiscences from this peaceful raid on Alexandria.

*Reunion at Marshall (old Salem).*

The following circular was sent out by the Committee of Arrangement :

## REUNION OF MOSBY'S MEN.

There will be a reunion of the surviving members of the 43d Battalion of Virginia Cavalry, better known as " Mosby's Men," at Marshall, Fauquier County, Va. (formerly called "Salem"), on Wednesday, August 14th, 1895.

Every member is invited and expected to be present without further notice, and, as there are numbers of them whose post-office addresses are unknown to the committee, it is earnestly requested that every effort be made to give the greatest possible publicity to the notice.

Therefore, all who receive a copy of this circular are urged to mail it AT ONCE to some other friend or acquaintance, who was a Mosbyite, with the request that HE IN TURN, SHALL "PASS THE WORD ALONG," as we used to do in the old time, in order that we may have a full turn-out and a royal good time.

All are invited, the only qualification being that they shall have been members of Mosby's command, and they will be welcome and well cared for.

Those who expect to attend will please signify the same by dropping a line to one of the undersigned.

J. H. FOSTER, Marshall, Va.
J. M. RAMEY, Marshall, Va.
C. H. WALKER, Rectortown, Va.
H. S. ASHBY, Delaplane, Va.
GEO. M. SLATER, Paris, Va.

Of Committee.

Marshall, Va., August 1st, 1895.

P. S. Every Mosby Man into whose hands this circular may fall, whether he attends this meeting or not, is requested to send his name, and the company he belonged to and his present post-office address at once, so he may be registered on a permanent list I wish to make up. Don't fail to do this.

J. H. FOSTER, Marshall, Va.

This reunion took place in a pretty little grove near the town of Marshall, Virginia (formerly called "Salem"), in the rear of the field where Mosby's Men were disbanded on the 21st of April, 1865.

There were present 130 of " Mosby's Rangers " and about 3,000 spectators.

The meeting was opened by prayer by the Rev. Sydnor G. Ferguson, the " fighting parson." Speeches were made by Capt. James William Foster, J. S. Mason and Joseph Bryan.

The regret felt for the absence of Colonel Mosby was partly made up by the presence of his four daughters, Mrs. R. R. Campbell, Mrs. W. E. Coleman, Miss Pauline Mosby, Miss Ada Mosby, and Mosby's two grandsons.

A resolution was passed to start a subscription fund to erect a monument to those of Mosby's Men who were murdered by Custer's command at Front Royal.

Another resolution was passed, that as Miss Winnie Davis was known as "the Daughter of the Confederacy," Miss Pauline Mosby be chosen by the Camp as "the Daughter of Mosby's Confederacy."

It was decided to hold the next reunion at Richmond, Va.

The Committee in charge, above-named, left nothing undone which could contribute to the comfort and enjoyment of those present. The generous people of the community had prepared a bountiful repast, which furnished an abundance for all.

Mosby and his men are dear to the people of Fauquier, and on this occasion they gave evidence of the sincerity of their affection for them in the warm greeting extended to the survivors of that gallant band.

There were no formal ceremonies, but all were left free to enjoy the event in a manner most pleasing to themselves and the day was indeed a happy reunion.

GROUP TAKEN AT SECOND REUNION AT MARSHALL, VA.

REUNION GROUP.

Key to Group at the Second Reunion of the 43d Battalion, Virginia Cavalry (Mosby's Rangers) at Marshall (old Salem), August 14, 1875.
Copied from Photograph taken by L. C. Handy, Photographer, Washington, D. C.

1. Thomas B. Rector,
2. Lieut. Channing M. Smith.
3. J. Bowen,
4. Samuel Waggaman,
5. J. M. Johnson,
6. Benton Fletcher,
7. R. F. Heflin,
8. S. E. Rogers,
9. John W. Green,
10. J. M. Rixey,
11. J. A. Silman,
12. Frank Johnson ("Zoo"),
13. James J. Williamson,
14. John H. Foster,
15. T. A. Russell,
16. C. H. Walker,
17. John R. Kerrick,
18. W. P. Fuggitt,
19. Luther Hurst,
20. Frank M. Woolf,
21. James I. Seaton,
22. L. M. Davis,
23. F. T. Craig.
24. John H. Elkins,
25. J. V. Kerns,
26. J. P. Smith,
27. Wm. H. Garrison,
28. S. R. Armstrong,
29. J. M. Ramey,
30. J. C. Burke,
31. C. T. Hawling,
32. W. P. Thomas,
33. Shelton Lunzeford,
34. F. E. Robey,
35. Thomas R. O'Meara,
36. J. M. Strother,
37. Rev. Sydnor G. Ferguson,
38. E. S. Hurst,
39. Capt. James Wm. Foster,
40. Wm. H. Lake,
41. George S. Ayre,
42. J. H. Lunzeford,
43. W. B. Weir,
44. John M. Lawrence,
45. R. N. Flynn,
46. Lieut. W. Ben Palmer,
47. Charles E. Biedler,
48. L. E. Woodward,
49. J. E. Legg,
50. R. M. Mackall,
51. George R. L. Turberville,
52. Miss Ada Mosby,
53. Mrs. R. R. Campbell,
54. Mrs. W. E. Coleman,
55. Miss Pauline Mosby,
A. Spottswood Campbell,
B. Mosby Campbell,
56. Capt. Walter E. Frankland,
57. C. J. Coiner,
58. W. G. Pearson,
59. W. C. Anderson,
60. F. D. Vaughan,
61. James A. Gray,
62. Robert M. Harrover,
63. Ludwell Lake,
65. W. Cockerill,
66. Capt. Peter A. Franklin,
67. Denoni F. Nalls,
68. L. F. Walker,
69. H. C. Pearson,
70. Wm. A. Anderson,
71. J. W. Hammond,
72. Benjamin Simpson,
73. John C. Utz,
74. John N. Ballard,
75. John R. Castleman,
76. Lieut. Joseph H. Nelson,
77. Thomas W. Lake,
78. Claude (son of Lieut. Harry Hatcher),
79. L. E. Hutchinson,
80. Harry T. Sinnott,
81. Henry S. Ashby,
82. Dr. J. J. Williams,
83. H. M. McIlhany,
84. J. E. Pickett,
85. S. C. Floweree,
86. J. S. Mason,
87. J. P. Walker,
88. J. W. Bell,
89. F. G. Hatcher (son of R. Welt. Hatcher),
90. Charles H. Gray,
91. Lieut. B. Frank Carter,
92. Charles E. Davis,
93. H. N. Brawner,
94. D. J. Moffett,
95. B. Addison Triplett.

# INDEX.

# INDEX TO APPENDIX.

Library of Congress Cataloguing in Publication Data

Williamson, James Joseph, 1834-1915.
Mosby's Rangers.
(Collector's library of the Civil War)
Reprint. Originally published: New York: R. B. Kenyon, 1896.
1. Williamson, James Joseph, 1834-1915.
2. Confederate States of America. Army.
Virginia Cavalry Battalion, Forty-third—Biography.
3. United States—History—Civil War, 1861-1865—
Regimental histories—Confederate States of America—
Virginia Cavalry Battalion—43rd.
4. United States—History—Civil War, 1861-1865—
Personal narratives—Confederate side.
I. Title.   II. Series.
E581.6 43rd.W54 1982    973.7'455    82-668 AACR2
ISBN 0-8094-4227-2
ISBN 0-8094-4226-4 (library)
ISBN 0-8094-4225-6 (retail)


Printed in the United States of America

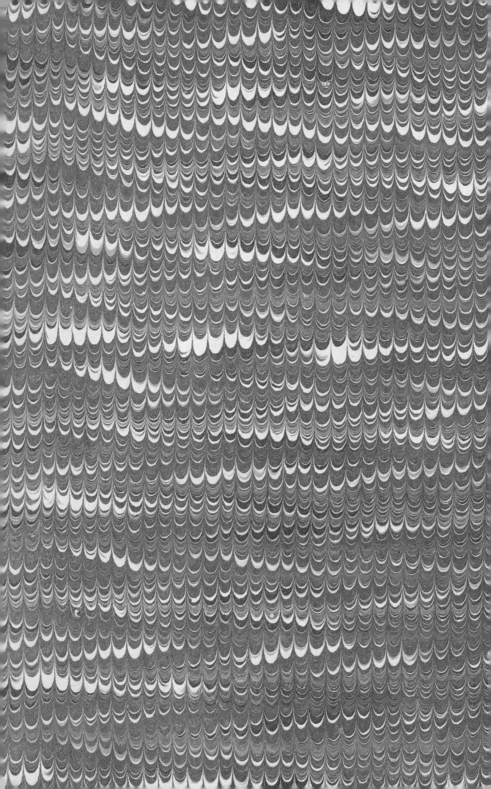